Ad Serving Technology

Understand the marketing revelation that commercialized the Internet

Gregory Cristal

Cover Design by Andreas Brooks

ISBN: 1484867572
ISBN-13: 978-1484867570

CONTENTS

PURPOSE

Why write a book about third party ad serving?

Working in online media or digital advertising, there are certain levels of technical expertise which exist across any connected organisations in the space. From a distance it would be easy to assume that everyone has the same level of training but when it comes to using the technical tools which enable to work that we do, the space is complex and the idea of learning everything is daunting. Some of us that work in Online believe we do not need to learn everything, that the task is too great and the necessity, trivial. The truth is that the knowledge in any online advertising organisation is unfairly balanced between those that take the time to learn as much as they can and those that rely on the learned. Learning the role of the Media Agency planner, The Advertiser marketer, The Creative Agency developer or the trafficker only lifts the lid on a corner of the complex technical workflow of which we are all mandatory parts.

I wrote a book about ad serving for one reason: there are not enough educational resources about Digital Marketing, Online Advertising and third party ad serving to satisfy any of its stakeholders.

When a topic this complex comes along and the work requires an academic background which does not exist, the number of experts in the field shrinks and the circulation of verifiable knowledge becomes thin. The knock on effect is a culture of assumptions, a culture of the fear to ask too many technical questions of the few that have the knowledge and an environment which is risky to conduct business within.

This book provides in academia, a record of the technology as it stands today. I have grown up with technology that is growing at the same pace, and I am sharing what I know. I have tried my very best to not make any assumptions about how this technology works but despite asking many sources, the sources are too few to be completely verifiable across the board and for this reason I apologise for any incorrect assumptions I may have made about how this technology works. My aim is to keep the information up to date by offering revised editions and maintaining an internet presence; I am open to technical questions you may have regarding this material.

I currently work for a well-known third party ad server but I have tried my best not to be bias towards its technology. Indeed there are some features mentioned in this book that the technology provider I work for does not offer today but that exist elsewhere in the industry.

I really hope you get enjoyment and value from this book and that it helps your personal and professional understanding of these technologies. I put a lot of effort into bringing the parts together in a digestible way (which given the matrix-nature of the subject matter, is not easy). I welcome with open arms any feedback you may have regarding the content and any opinions I may have expressed within (my contributing editors have helped me to keep these to a minimum).

Thanks for buying and happy reading!

Part A

Setting the Stage

Part A
Setting the Stage

- The flow of this book
- What is third party ad serving?
- Getting some perspective
    - Users
    - Publisher
    - Agencies
    - The Advertiser
- Definitions and Methodology

The flow of this book

The interconnected nature of Online Advertising technologies reminds me of neurons in the brain. Their connected nature could be drawn two dimensionally and the resulting image would be a weave of connections. But the truth is that almost all nodes of this image would communicate with each other in some way, spanning distances that would make a visual connection in three dimensional space, too painful on the eyes to observe and too detailed for the brain to absorb. I was asked by colleagues and my network contacts as I was planning this book as to how I would lay it out given this almost quantum nature of the technology landscape. I decided to focus on the campaign management workflow and build concepts up from there.

In this sense the book starts with some background for the reader (Part A), relating each of the concepts back to third party ad serving, such as the base technologies on a user's machine and in "the Cloud" (Chapter 1) and the industry players or stakeholders that assemble and pay each other to bring an online ad campaign to life (Chapter 2). In Part B we look at campaign management broken down by the various channels available today (Chapter 3) before looking at the concept of conversion tracking (attributing a sale online as a result of an ad campaign). Part C then focusses on understanding the analytic and reporting capabilities of an ad server (Chapter 5) before looking at strategies to act on that data such as Optimization (Chapter 6) Retargeting (Chapter 7) and Programmatic buying (Chapter 8).

This book also contains a whole heap of words and phrases that have been more or less adopted across the industry. Due to the infancy of the digital advertising industry the meanings of some of these words are not wholly universal or understood therefore there is a convenient glossary located at the end of this book for your reference. Words which appear in quotation marks can be referenced in the glossary at the back.

There are also some technology and company names that will appear in *italics*. These names are used as examples of technologies that may not be available in every market around the world but are growing or well adopted technologies used by big Agencies and Advertisers in Europe and the US. To provide the most balanced understanding of the technology landscape I have tried to offer the names of as many technology providers as possible although a large number of technology companies such as *Google* now offer many of the discussed features as part of their core *DoubleClick* marketing suite. The names featured are suggested examples. It is recommended that if you choose to utilise these technologies for digital marketing activity that you test their products first, preferably against a control group where a technology is not in use and also against a competitor tool which claims to offer the same results. This on-going experimentation will ensure that you are using the best tools available in the market today.

As the flow of the various chapters suggests, the campaign management workflow is cyclical; the setup of all the ads can be changed at any point during a campaign based on trends in the analytics data which is accessible just by logging into the ad serving interface. In this way the ad serving interface is made up of two core areas: campaign management and reporting.

Perhaps most importantly let's address the elephant in the room:

What is third party ad serving?
A third party ad server is a business to business machine or system that does a specific service. This machine lives in various locations around the world to complete the tasks of the service; it lives in "the Cloud". As with other services that live in the Cloud it is possible to access them only via a web browser. Third party ad serving core "customers" are Media Agencies and Advertisers. These customers pay to have access to be able to log into the third party ad serving interface. Once inside the interface, the tasks are broken down into two separate areas: campaign management and reporting.

Customers choose to use a third party ad server for these main reasons:

1. Accredited Independent third party
2. Consistent Counting Methodology
3. Reliability to serve and Server uptime
4. Format Support and Publisher certification
5. Single location Reporting
6. De-Duplicated Reporting
7. Campaign Specific Needs and Features

Customers of third party ad servers pay initially for the ad space and then pay a tiny fee on top for each advert to benefit from the above. The third party ad serving space, as a section of the advertising technology industry has matured, the third party ad servers available to potential customers today is rather small. In fact there are only really two truly global third party ad servers left choose from: *DoubleClick* and *DG/Mediamind*. The others have seen diminishing growth or have never seen adoption beyond a handful of countries and a global ad server is important so that global Advertisers are seeing the above benefits in all markets. These more local third party ad servers include *Adform, Mediaplex, AdRiver, Atlas, Flashtalking* and *Weborama*. Thankfully there is uniformity among these technologies - they all work in basically the same way so all the concepts in this book are valid across the board although one or two features may not be available in some ad servers.

Getting Some Perspective
Now with the global third party ad server humming away in the cloud, its tasks permeate out across the web affecting various groups of people. Let's now look in detail at who these people are:

Users
Everyone is a user, we all "use" the internet. Anyone accessing the internet or browsing the web is considered a user. This concept seems simple but if you work in online advertising you are a user but you also fall into another of the categories that follow. When talking to other media professionals about technology it always helps to declare your position: "In this problem that I am seeing with this ad; I am taking on the role of the user". Users will interact with the third party ad server when loading pretty much every web page and the total number of users in the world is around a couple of billion.

Publishers
Own a website with ads on it? Then you are a Publisher (your website is your publication). If you own or represent lots of websites you are a Publisher network. Publishers tend to see the world from their own perspective; they do not look beyond their own networks and use every tactic possible to drive "media

spend" (advertising dollars) into their own pocket. Advertisers and Agencies have tough jobs to do to spread that spend around effectively and this is where ad serving comes into its own. Publishers interacting with the third party ad server by receiving code from it show the third party ads on its pages and will have to work with its reporting systems. How many Publishers are there in the world: upwards of hundreds of thousands of big sites but in actual fact hundreds of millions due to the number of web sites on the internet.

Agencies

Agencies fit into two buckets. First there is the Creative Agency; who undertake the work of creating and building the ad (and do not need to trouble themselves too much with the world of third party ad serving). And secondly there is the Media Agency - a middleman in the advertising campaign workflow, managing and optimizing to make sure advertising dollars are spent effectively. The Media Agency has a tough job swimming through a minefield of technologies to achieve this. Any single piece of kit that can track all the ad serving data, automate planning and buying, costing and reporting are the magic bullet for a successful agency. How do Agencies use third party ad servers? The Creative Agency builds ads for the ad server and uploads them onto the system. The Media Agency will do the campaign management and reporting.

The Advertiser

The Advertiser is any company with products or services to sell that has enough money for a marketing budget for advertising. References in this book to the Advertiser are references to the marketing team working for that Advertiser. To afford to utilise enterprise level technology like an ad server there have to be a fair few media dollars in the bank for the marketer to use, yet well over ten thousand Advertisers globally utilise these crucial technologies. Few Advertisers choose to stand alone without a Media Agency and given the complex nature of the digital environment it is no surprise. How does the Advertiser use a third party ad server? For Campaign management and reporting.

Selecting the right ad server is a tricky business, there are so many features to consider and yet the differences between them are very small. This is all thanks to industry standardisation which has been crucial to allowing Agencies and Advertisers to switch from one Ad server to another. It all begins with definitions and methodology.

Definitions and Methodology

The *Internet Advertising Bureau* (*IAB*); arguably the most widely recognised regularity body globally for digital marketing activity, has been instrumental in the shaping of digital advertising. Standardisation of words and phrases is probably the most important and fundamental concept in digital advertising. And although the *IAB* has done a lot of work to reduce miscommunication, there are still occurrences of the same concepts being given different names. For example *DoubleClick* have a "Floodlight tag", Atlas have a "Universal Action Tag", Mediamind has a "Container tag" (all are the same thing). The methodology that underpins what is meant by a "click" or an "impression" still causes headaches industry wide despite clear guidelines being set down. In online tracking it always comes back to methodology.

In my first job in the industry my line manager sat me down to read through thoroughly the methodologies of the big research companies; *Neilsen* and *ComScore*. These respected platforms were revealed to me as building their datasets on a sample of people from a panel. This meant that the reported figures in these systems were not accurate when low numbers were listed as they represented only one or two people and were not an absolutely accurate representation when scaled up (despite the growth of these panels in recent years, there is still some truth to these statements). Collecting information based on a panel of users as opposed to measuring the behaviour of all users helps to demonstrate the importance of methodology; two datasets could differ wildly if one comes from a sample and the other comes from a full audience measurement. The methodology provides an indispensable context.

The lesson is that the devil is in the detail and technology companies are not always wholly transparent in their methodologies so it is vital to ask questions about any data. Sometimes two systems measuring the same things at the same time will not report exactly the same figures. The *IAB* has done its best to close the gap (such as allowing for a maximum of a ten per cent discrepancy between technologies measuring the same thing) but at the core these technologies are designed differently and might use different methods to "ping" servers at slightly different times, resulting in mismatched figures. This universal acknowledgment (like the unstable world of measurement in quantum mechanics) does not mean that all systems are flawed, but that using a single system to track all advertising activity reduces confusion and discrepancy because all things are measured under the same methodology. This requirement led to the advent of the tools we call third party ad servers (one counting tool used to measure all activity). Without getting too complex, it can also be argued that using multiple tools to measure the same things and then taking an average is the most accurate way to capture data. In an ideal world many Agencies would choose to use multiple third party ad servers for a single campaign but the costs often do not justify the rewards gained from a more accurate measurement.

Now that we have set the stage and given a very high level view of who uses third party ad servers and why they are used, we will now move to look at the neighbouring technologies on the web page and on the user's machine. These have an impact on how ad serving works and what the limitations are in data collection.

Chapter 1

Local vs. Remote Technologies

Chapter 1 - Section 1
Browsers and Devices

- The role of the browser in Digital advertising
    - *Figure 1.1*
    - *Figure 1.2*
- Tracking across multiple browsers
- first party Vs. third Party Cookies
    - *Figure 1.3*
- Cookie Deletion
- Distinction between Devices and Computers
- Ad blocking Tools
- Why is there advertising on the Internet?

Third party ad servers do not work isolation. Many technologies work hand in hand to form websites and web channels that create a user's internet experience (such web channels include "Search Marketing" and "Rich Media"). The ways these channels operate and grow affect the usability of the internet such as through web page loading speed and the pace of innovations in web technology development. This section looks at the tools and technologies that we come into contact everyday as internet users, (whether we are aware of them or not) and looks and how they each relate to the world of Advertising and tracking. The bottom-up approach to considering the capabilities of underlying tracking technologies (learning how core code like HTML and JavaScript relate to the capabilities of the browser) will provide a solid framework of understanding which can be applied to complex problem solving in ad campaign setup and optimization (e.g. if you understand how JavaScript works you can understand how to use it to adapt ad technology to fit unique problems and situations which will arise every day). Perhaps more importantly, this introduction provides a stable grounding from which to understand more about the web channels themselves.

Despite being such a ubiquitous technology the concept of the "Internet" is commonly misunderstood as just meaning the World Wide Web (the bit of internet that loads into the browser window). The Internet is in fact a far bigger entity and "the internet" in the context of online advertising means; the visual web, its applications and access points. Where information can be shared across the world automatically, this is the internet we speak of. It is important to be clear on this so that all industry stakeholders have a common understanding. When work with new clients, Advertisers and Publishers, the syntax and definition of such principles is best bedded in early on bearing in mind that the media industry attracts folk from all walks of life.

So as not to get our heads too far into the cloud (pardon the pun) let's just think simply about the browser to start off with:

The role of the browser in Digital advertising
Despite its paramount importance to the world of Digital Advertising, the browser-owning technology companies almost never engage in an active dialogue with any of the other Digital Stakeholders (Publishers, Advertisers and Agencies).The work of updating a browser and releasing a new version (however wild the impact may be on the design of Websites and Ads) has virtually no consideration or input from the vast Advertising community that it supports. This statement is therefore true:

> Browsers were not built to support the creative range of designs available for online ads and websites. Truly creative websites and ads have been predominantly born out of the skill and vision of artists and creative designers, who take the foundation of a new browser release and learn how to build the best user experience on top of it. The browser release will clearly provide new avenues to take code and design but the browser does not arrive with a flurry of supported ad and website designs.

The key takeaway here is not to ever expect support for any campaign from the browser themselves no matter how large the campaign may be. In my experience finding a technical contact working browser-side (even if you work somewhere like *Microsoft* and you are absolutely desperate to see if your campaign can utilise some kind of exception) is a goose chase not worth taking up and it's safe to assume you'll never be able to point out the *Mozilla* team in a crowd and buy these guys a drink. The browser remains an unknowable force working by its own rules, which the whole industry has learned to adapt to over time.

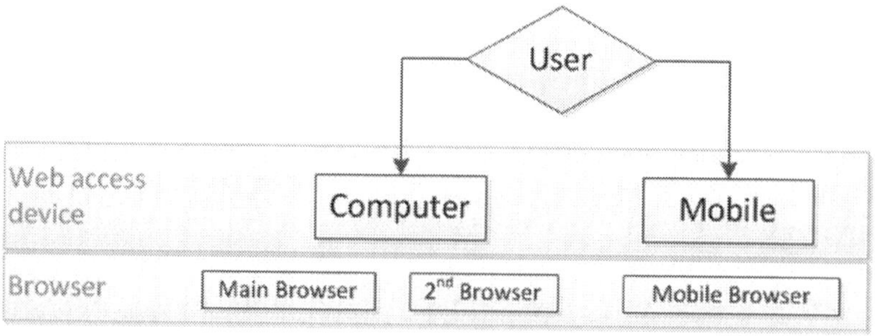

Figure 1.1: *Users access the web through an internet enabled device (Computer or Mobile) and then navigate web pages from within the browser.*

User opinion is divided on the best browsers to use to surf the web and the battle for the top browser is set to continue for many years to come. Firefox, Internet Explorer, Chrome and Safari dominate the browser space. But what relevance does the browser have to third party ad serving? (And does it make any difference which browser the user uses?).

The browser is very important to online Advertising because the user experience with the vast majority of the adverts on the internet is had inside the browser environment. Ideally the user would be sitting at the same computer while using the web all of the time, as they surf the web and encounter relevant, innovative ads. In fact to store and track the most accurate data in the third party ad server, a single user would need to browse the web on a single device (using the same browser all the time). In this single browser the user would rarely delete their browser cookies and this browser would have acted as the single conduit for the full record of that user's fully web journey, engaging with ads and using the internet. The user's web activities are occurring in just one place (one browser and one device).

We are now going to start referencing "cookies". In simplified terms, a cookie can be thought of as a document. On this document is written a unique number which identifies the user called a cookieID. Now, if each user had only one cookieID and the cookie that it belonged to was never deleted, every user would have just one unique number. If you were to count all the total unique cookieIDs in existence, you would have an accurate reading of the total number of users on the Internet. As you may have gathered, things are not quite as simple as this.

First if all, cookies are not stored on a computer or device in a folder called "cookies". Each browser has its own "cookie-vault" which does not let other browsers in. So if one did want to compare and contrast users between browsers, the process required to do it is somewhat complex.

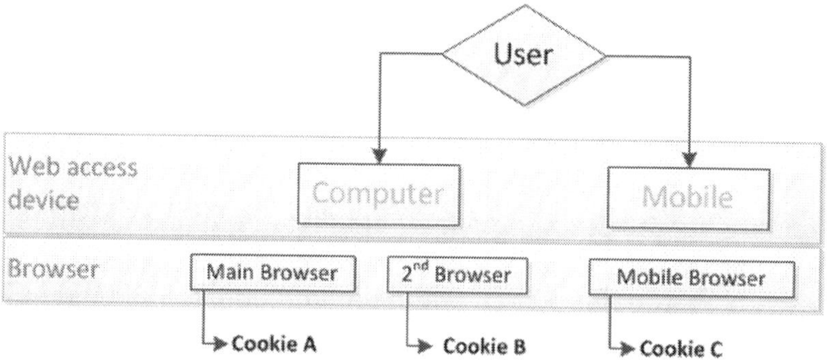

Figure 1.2: *Each browser has the facility to store cookies. Although a cookie is meant to represent a single User, the use of multiple browsers creates multiple cookies - a known industry problem.*

Tracking across multiple browsers

The second and perhaps more obvious problem is that users very rarely use a single access point or single browser to use the internet. Instead users come on from different devices and browsers, sometimes using more than one device at the same time. This is a pain for online advertising for the simple reason that multiple cookies look like multiple individuals in the data that comes out of the ad server after it has completed tracking and processing its gargantuan datasets.

Users who use multiple browsers frequently are harder to track as activity is recorded against two separate cookieID's which are never matched and technically speaking the ad server sees two separate individuals.

This is a danger for the marketer and the Agency because the true number of users seeing adverts is skewed. If there was just a single browser in existence then online ad measurement would be far more reliable. In the reporting chapter later on in this book we will see that ad server reporting still does not offer a solution to rooting out the uniqueness of all cookies when faced with the problem of users that use multiple browsers. Bearing this in mind when conducting analysis of the ad serving data may help in providing a clearer picture of the total number of users interacting with ads in the campaign. Let's look at cookies in more detail.

First party vs. third Party Cookies

There are two main types of cookie. The "first party cookie" is placed on the user's computer or 'dropped' by the website the user is visiting. By dropping, we mean that a remote machine or server sends a tiny file to user's computer or device, whereby the file is delivered and remains until it is deleted or removed. This file is a cookie and usually contains the cookieID, the timestamp of when the cookie was dropped and the filename for the file will reference the domain it came from. If a website drops a cookie file onto your computer from its own domain, it is a first party cookie (The web address of the website is part of the websites "domain" so in http://autos.msn.com "msn.com" is the domain and "autos." is the subdomain). If a website drops a cookie on your machine from another domain (such as the domain belonging to a third party ad server) this is called a "third party cookie".

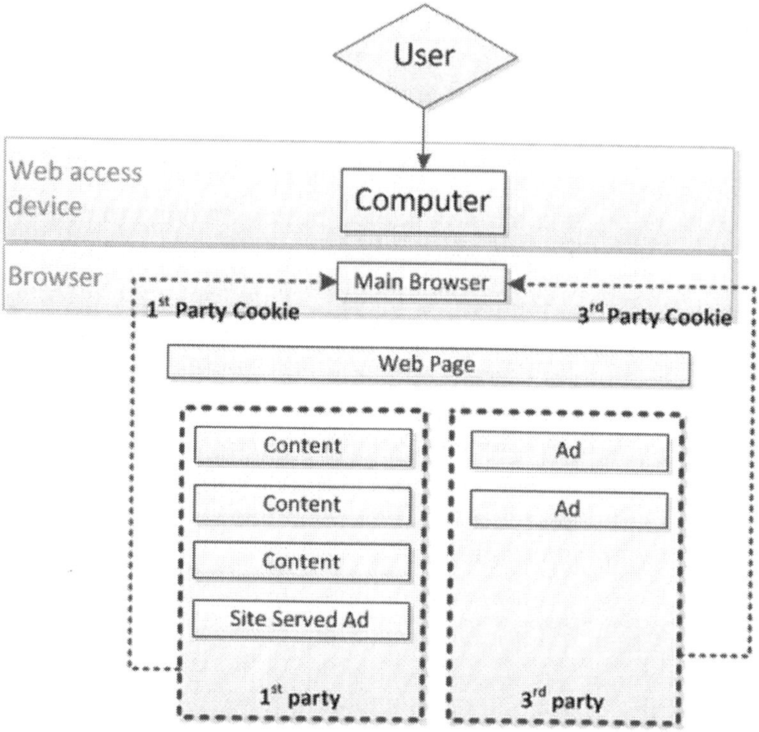

Figure 1.3: *Where a user uses a single browser, browsing to web pages triggers the downloading of content and ads. The native identifiers for the user belonging to the content and then ads are first and then third party cookies.*

Cookies are a website's way of remembering some information about you as a user because once they have been dropped they remain on the machine until they are removed. Since the cookie is residing on the user's machine it is said to 'live' on the "client side" and the cookie remains as a signpost or unique reference point, for a website to lookup that unique number against its own database (where there may be more information about each cookie stored on the databases our its own machines; this is called the "server side")

This lookup or matching process allows a website to 'remember' things like some settings or changes the user may have made to a website. Most commonly the first party cookie can be used to remember the information the user put into forms on a website, (so that when they visit that site again, they save time by not having to re-input this information). This is very useful when you, as a user, have to login to a website each time and it remembers your username for instance.

Third party cookies such as those belonging to the third party ad server have a record of the user's activity matched alongside engagement with an ad campaign. The ad server can report on whether the user saw an ad, clicked on an ad, or went on to buy a product after seeing or clicking an ad online. To be clear, it is not the actual user's name that the server is remembering, but the unique reference number stored in that user's cookie. The server stores no personally identifiable information and so never knows that you are you; it just knows that your cookie allows the server to remember behavioural information about that cookieID. Those readers who live and breathe *Excel* and databases can begin to picture a master table sitting in the deep backend of the ad server, where every ad engagement can be tied back to a cookieID (see Chapter 5 - Cookie Level Data)

Cookie Deletion

A new consideration if you were just beginning to get comfortable with cookies and cookieID's:

1. Cookies do not live forever.
2. The more time passes the higher the likelihood of a user deleting a cookie.

Cookie Deletion affects third party ad serving because each new cookie is treated as a new user. Users that delete their cookies frequently skew the data available in the ad server since there is no way to tie a deleted cookie from a user machine to the new cookie dropped by the server to replace it. As we will see later this affects a lot of different reports including Unique Reach and Frequency and Performance reports (see Chapter 5).

There is lots of research posted around the internet regarding cookie deletion. Some technologies claim to be able to forecast and predict cookie deletion in different counties. Some ad servers offer alternative reporting methods that can account for cookie deletion (See Chapter 5 - Reporting - Adjusted Unique reporting).

It is in the best interest of Advertisers, Agencies and Publishers to prevent cookies from being deleted, the benefits of their use are hotly debated in the forum of rights protection organisations in the field of personal privacy and it is here that the Digital Advertising stakeholders defend the use of cookies where information that is held about users does not lead to a direct identification of that user. In this legal minefield the debate continues globally as to the acceptance and regulation of cookie-use, where the user is given the option to opt-in or out of the automatic action of cookie dropping (see Chapter 7 - Retargeting).

Distinction between Devices and Computers

The web browser on a user's phone or tablet offers a different experience than the one on a desktop computer. Examples include the screen size and mouse-free navigation. Considerations should be made for these differences when planning an ad campaign, from the building of the ads to the design of the website that the user should end up on when clicking on the ad. In some cases, Advertisers will pay a Creative Agency to produce different types of ads and design different websites for users using different browsers.

This variety increases the cost of running an ad campaign, and in some instances is used to preserve the same user experience across devices and in others offers a creative diversity. Ad serving technology allows for browser-specific targeting (see Chapter 2 - Publishers - Publisher Ad Servers) to enable different ads to be displayed on different devices.

Technically speaking "mobile" browsers are just different versions of the same pc and mac based browsers that users the world over are now used to using. As with desktop device browsers, the differences between the versions can affect the way that ads and pages appear or are rendered. This presents a real problem for consistent ad delivery, especially for more complex formats like Rich Media (for definition see Chapter 3 - Rich Media). The Advertiser or Agency may plan with the intent of offering the same user experience to all users across all devices but to do so means testing ads on all such devices before a campaign begins. The same is true in the world of Publishing where all web pages must be checked in all new devices and browsers too. Some Agencies have opted to fill vast rooms with all of the available consumer internet-enabled devices for the purposes of such testing. Others will try to emulate the multitude of available browsers using software found online.

HTML5 may finally be a light at the end of a long awaited tunnel, as it is a leap forward in standardisation for both page and ad rendering. HTML5 has been devised to try and eradicate the need for device by device testing, which has extended the testing time required before a campaign launches, creating industry-wide inefficiency.

HTML5 is one of the most important things to happen to advertising in recent memory since the timelines of an ad campaign will affect all parties; and the improvement in the flexibility in the coding of an ad can mean the difference between a frustrating internet experience and a fully-fledged engagement between user and ad. HTML5 is not really a component of the browser itself but a mark-up language, something we will look at in more detail in the next section. Beyond HTML support, browsers bring plug-in technologies to consideration and these are controlled by the user. One plug-in type in particular has historically caused a stir in the birth and growth of Online Advertising and these are Ad blocking plugins.

Ad blocking tools in the browser

Some users install software or browser extensions (also called "plugins") to "block" ads from appearing on their machine. These tools disrupt the delivery of the image of the ad or in fact any information from the Publisher-side ad server (See Chapter 2 - Publishers) to the user's browser. Ad blocking was more functional in the days of dial-up when bandwidth was precious and loading an ad meant an extra ten minutes of page load time. Today bandwidth is so quick that ad blocking would serve very little purpose in speeding up page load times (ads usually make up a tiny percentage of the "weight" of the whole page as the files are downloaded from the server). Instead these ad blocking tools are used to provide an ad-free internet experience. All stakeholders operating in Online Advertising need to be able to respond to questions about Ad Blocking but since the mechanism is so simple it is the wider impact of these tools that requires focus as an Ad-Free internet experience is a threat to the whole medium of the web. This in turn concludes our summary of the relevant features of the browser in Online Advertising.

Why is there advertising on the Internet?

With such far reaching potential, the web comes with its own politics and the politics frame the development and demands for further supporting technologies. The web is predominantly used, by its users to source and digest written and (more recently) video content. Content takes time to produce. I once set about building a content heavy website: it took hours, days and weeks of time to compile. Apart from learning obtaining new skills and having the warming experience of contributing to a giant database of useful information about the world, I was only compelled to continue adding such content by receiving money in return.

The two most compelling options for a website owner to produce quality content are to charge a subscription fee for the service (plaguing the user with a cost out of their own wallet) or to seem to offer the content for free to the user, at the cost to the Advertiser (who are really just paying for the attention span of a "targeted" user).

Ad blocking is not an undetectable weapon on consumer combat; the failed attempt by the server to deliver ads is detected each time it occurs. As this failure rate grows, there is an inverse decline in the size of the audience for the website/Publisher to offer to their Advertiser base. A decline in the audience size means a decline in revenue, which ultimately leads to a decline in both the amount (and more importantly) the quality of the content because less money is available to help produce it.

Content is king online. The best content draws the most attention and although the growth of user generated content (UGC) has been rapid and far reaching; the quality user "traffic" remains with big Publishers where it always has done (and more niche "long tail" audiences hop to more obscure websites with lower levers of traffic). Thankfully technologies like Advertising Exchanges are making some ground in balancing the books, but this is a topic for Chapter 8.

Let's move on from the browser to the content of the web; the websites and the ads themselves and the base technologies on which they are constructed.

Chapter 1 - Section 2
The Anatomy of Sites and Ads

- What the user sees
    - *Figure 1.4*
- HTML
    - *Figure 1.5*
- JavaScript
- Images
- Text Links
    - *Figure 1.6*
- Flash
- The advent of HTML5

What the user sees

Take a magnifying glass and peer into the source code of any web page (or just use the browser buttons to load up the page source) and inside you will find a rather difficult to read set of instructions and code. The educated eye can pick out commands in the code that help identify how the web page has been constructed. This includes information about where the ads come from as well. Both HTML and JavaScript are the most common languages to find inside this source code. They load the content in the browser window, rendering as a website constructed by a set of common elements or entities. Text, Images and Flash make up the vast majority of the web today (soon to be overtaken by an explosion in video). Without these components the web could not support advertising as it exists today. Understanding more about them personifies their importance, highlighting technical encounters on all sides of the Advertising ecosystem.

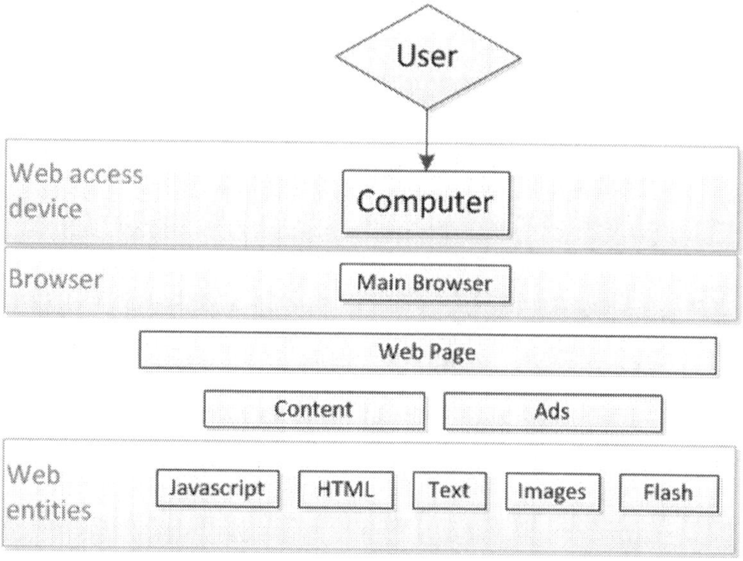

Figure 1.4: *Navigating to the Web Page via the main browser, the user encounters Content and Ads. These are made up of what can be classed as entities: technologies and code that form the very foundations of the familiar web.*

HTML

"HTML" (Hyper-Text Mark-up Language) is the core 'code' of the web based browsing experience. It literally is the code that describes to the browser what the content of each web page should be and the browser renders this code to give the effect of a page of information. HTML is the language of "tags" and when we refer to "tags" in third party ad serving, we are talking about a few lines of HTML code. This code can be embedded directly onto a web page by a web development team working on the website and when a page is loaded up in a browser by a user the code 'executes', and an ad or more content is displayed. (To see an HTML ad tag, skip to Chapter 3 - Display Ad serving Operations - Ad Tags).

HTML is how almost all of the ads served today are requested from the ad server. If the environment in which an ad needs to be served does not support HTML, then other code can be used to make that request (such as in a computer gaming environment). In fact in most instances, the HTML is used to house a more complex request which occurs in JavaScript. JavaScript does the fetching, carrying and calculating of the content. HTML is simply a way of carrying the required ad code that the Publisher can quite easily slip onto their websites.

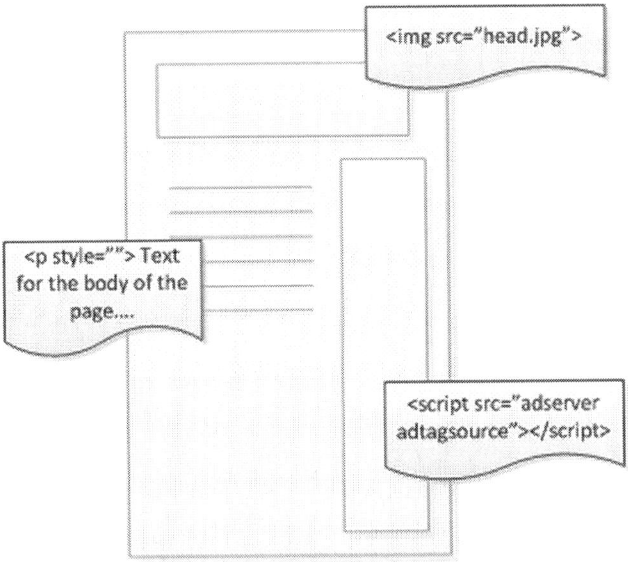

Figure 1.5: *Behind the scenes a standard web page is made up of a series of HTML tags. An Ad tag is no different, which can sit on any web page to display an ad to the user. In this instance (bottom right) the HTML tag contains a reference to JavaScript.*

JavaScript

JavaScript is called a client-side language. It runs or "executes" in the user's browser and allows for a whole host of important web page tricks such as popup windows and browser manipulation (like a command to print something on the page). JavaScript can gather and send a user's information and to a remote server so that the server is capable of responding by sending out a new piece of information (like making a previously hidden part of the website, suddenly appear).

JavaScript is the most common method of ad delivery that third party ad servers use. The flexibility of the JavaScript code allows the ad to be pulled directly into a Publisher's web page from the third party ad server and make decisions about what ad to display in real time. JavaScript can do interesting things like work out what time it is, or find out what browser the user is using: information like this can be passed back into the ad server when the ad loads allowing for some impressive customisation inside the ad itself. It is not common for an Advertiser to want to get this technical when running a campaign but every now and then JavaScript does come to the rescue when an ad campaign just wants to be a little cleverer or more innovative.

To understand how JavaScript is essential in the technical process of ad request and delivery we will look in more detail at the relationship between Ad Serving and JavaScript in Chapter 1 - Basics on Server hardware. For the time being it is sufficient to say that JavaScript returns one of four remote entities from the ad server and pulls them into the web page as the page loads. These four entities are Image files, Flash files, text links and video files. Video files are a little more complex to explain so this is explained after providing a more thorough technical introduction - details for video can be found in Chapter 3 - Instream Video).

Images

Images transformed the early web from a completely text-based environment to something that could be digested as an entertainment form by the masses and advertising was one of the first places to utilise the ability of early browsers to load images. The GIF type of image was more favoured by the advertising space because GIFs can contain more than one image at a time and so a very rudimentary form of frame by frame animation was possible. The trouble with GIFs is that they are very restricting in terms of creativity. They are not interactive and images look poor next to Flash. Today, GIFs are still used in online advertising as a "fall-back option" in case the user's browser cannot support Flash (after all, a grainy image of a company logo is better than completely wasted and white ad space). The traditional *.gif file extension is also no longer mandatory and better image compression methods such as in the *.png format or *.jpeg formats are commonly utilised. The legacy of the ad as an image remains with ad serving technology today where all standard display ads are comprised of an image portion of the HTML code as well as a click or text link portion. The two sections which make up this HTML ad tag allow all display ads to report back to the ad server; counting the loading of the image as an "impression" metric and the user action of the "click" as a click metric (more detail on this in Chapter 5 - Reporting).

Text-Links

Since HTML code allows any piece of text, object or image to be clickable by the user via the use of the "Anchor tag", a simple text link can be issued by the Ad Server as the most basic type of Ad. These text-link ads are extremely common all over the web and are mostly utilised by ads that exist in Search engines. By issuing an image and text link together, the image is clickable but the two parts of the code can be separated out so that the image can simply be programmed to appear without the ability to click, or the text link can be implemented without any image present.

1. <!-- Begin Ad Tag code -->
2. <a href="URL">
1. Starts here
4. <img src="">
5. </a>
6. <!--End Ad tag code -->

Figure 1.6: *A sample of a very basic non-JavaScript ad tag. The numbered rows are for reference purposes: Row 2 describes the opening of the anchor tag: the URL described is the clickthrough URL. The code in rows 3 and 4 is surrounded by the anchor tag which acts as the click redirect portion of the ad tag. Row 4 can contain a 1x1 otherwise known as a tracking pixel.*

The text in **figure 1.6** (row 3) is clickable inside the web page that the user can see. This is the "text-link". Text-links are the most basic building block of an online ad; their use and behaviour are described in a series of widely recognised phrases. As many of these sound similar it is important to clarify this with participating parties when setting up and running an ad campaign.

- The action of a user clicking and being directed to an Advertiser site is called a "**click through**".
- The process of a user completing the clickthrough successfully is called a "**click-to-land**".
- The destination address is called a "**click through URL**"
- The portion of the ad tag which declares the click through URL as part of any ad or text link is called a "**click redirect**".
- A click redirect may also be referred to as a "**click tracker**"
- The equivalent for measuring the loading of the ad (even as a text link) is called a "**tracking pixel**". (Covered off in more detail in Chapter 3 - Display Ad serving).

So far we have described the two elements of an ad tag as being the image portion and the click portion. However it is not common for a "static image" (i.e. a still picture) to be used as the visual ad; rather the image displays as a Flash animation.

Flash

Having a familiarity with Flash is essential to working in the Display and Rich Media channels in Digital Advertising. "Flash" are the animated and interactive panels dotted around the internet that can house video, get bigger, or show multiple images in an impactful delivery.

Flash is nascent to the web browsing experience and Flash files or ads themselves are created in *Adobe's* Flash authoring environment (more on this in Chapter 2 - Creative Agencies). Flash is so widely used and adopted across the web because of its ease to create animations and its flexibility to be creative with the code and the development environment. In Chapter 2 we will look in much more granular detail to understand more about Flash and its capabilities. Flash is so popular that it seems that it will be in use across the internet forever but new technologies are emerging that will replace it. HTML5 is the favourite.

The Advent of HTML5

HTML5 is created to amalgamate all the capabilities of both Flash and HTML in an experience which provides a consistent user experience on the web. Flash was popular for so long because of a similar consistent usability but the flaw in Flash is the need for users to have installed the Flash player plugin. With more devices and browsers available to users, supporting the plugin has become difficult for *Adobe* and since using the Flash authoring tool comes at a cost to the creative developer, but the development of HTML5 is free, HTML wins as the standard for the future. With HTML5 there is no need for Flash, as video and animation become part of HTML. The vector animations and functions that Flash built fame for facilitating are now supported in HTML5 and the community of supporters for this new standard are stronger where the updates and maintenance of the authoring environment of HTML5 will become increasingly faster and stronger than Flash.

So far we covered off internet technologies to give context to online advertising. The next section moves focus from the local user computer to the servers.

Chapter 1 - Section 3
Ad Serving

- What does the ad server do?
    - *Figure 1.7*
    - Table of Definitions
    - *Figure 1.8*
- The role of the CDN
- Waiting around for Ad Delivery - the user experience
    - Pre-ad display
    - During ad display
    - On ad close

This section will touch lightly on the relationship between the user's computer and the technologies sending packets of information to that user's machine. This is useful to explain what is really going on beyond the familiar glare of your own PC and browser. The words and phrases contained in this section are commonly thrown around in technical conversations where an Advertising technology is involved.

What does the ad server do?
Many other available texts describe how user's machines and servers exchange information to load the various pages of the web. The focus for this section is to explain the exchanges that occur between machines to distribute, load and count ads right across the web. As a reminder the Third Party Ad Server has two core functions:

1. The function to serve or deliver the ads to the users machine
2. To count and track the delivery and performance of these ads

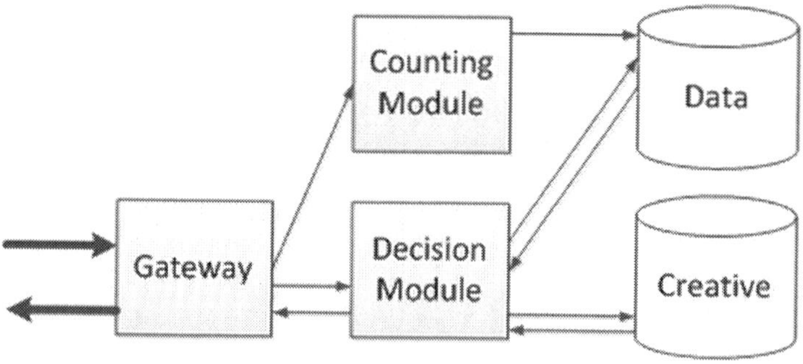

Figure 1.7: *Data in and out on-site at the ad server. This highly generalised diagram shows how the user request into the ad server gateway gets split for the two functions. First the ad server counts using a counting module and in parallel makes a decision to serve the correct asset back to the user.*

Figure 1.7 shows the fast function of the ad server to count and deliver an ad but the bold arrows on the left only show data coming into and going out of the ad server. The internet infrastructure that will carry this data to this point undergoes a longer journey. Before we undertake this journey we need to make sure we are using the right language to describe the various ports of call and processes that the data undergoes.

	Definition
Local Machine	The user's computer or device to access the web
Remote Machine	The server that the user's computer is exchanging data with
Host Server	Another name for remote machine, the server is "hosting" the users request for content or ads
Packet	Data is transmitted between machines in

	packets. Utilizing the best server route between the local and remote machine. Sometimes packets get lost and this can have a minor impact on the counting of ads served.
Router	To connect to the ISP the user's machine must utilize a local switch or router. Again, all data comes through here.
ISP	Internet Service Provider; the user's access point to the web, all data packets come and go through the ISP
CDN	Content Delivery Network; a large network of geographically located content servers allowing users to download content from a regional source. Ad servers themselves do not distribute replicas of the files all over the world. They work with CDNs to achieve this.
Data Center	Data Centers are the physical buildings that house ad servers and servers of the CDN. As the user's browser makes a call directly to the ad server to request an ad, the ad server must deliver the information back and count the request as soon as possible. Having strategically located buildings in global hubs and highly populated cities ensures a faster delivery.
Server Farm	A non-technical term to describe a data center or group of data centers
Ad Request	The initial loading of the ad tag on a Publisher page sends an HTTP request for to display the correct ad to the ad server. This

	is called an Ad Request.
JavaScript Response	The ad server responds to the ad request with a response; this is response predominantly occurs in JavaScript.
Impression Tracker	All ads contain Impression Tracker code which sends data as an "ad request" to the counting module or "ad counter" at the ad server
Impression	When an ad counter receives and responds to an HTTP request for a tracking asset from a client (*IAB.net* Guidelines)
Click Tracker	When the user initiates a click, this code routes data to the "ad counter" at the ad server to count a "click"
Ad Call	Another name for Ad Request
Ad Play	An industry wide disputed meaning, not backed by the IAB.
Ad Close	When a JavaScript served ad is closed or the browser leaves the page, the Ad can make a final request to the server

Before we look at the bigger picture it is important to note that the technical delivery of the ad is not the same as an industry agreed count of the impression metric (which can be found here: http://www.iab.net/media/file/Global_meas_guidelines.pdf). However as this definition has certified industry adoption, it is taken as to the true measure of delivered ads across all ad counting systems.

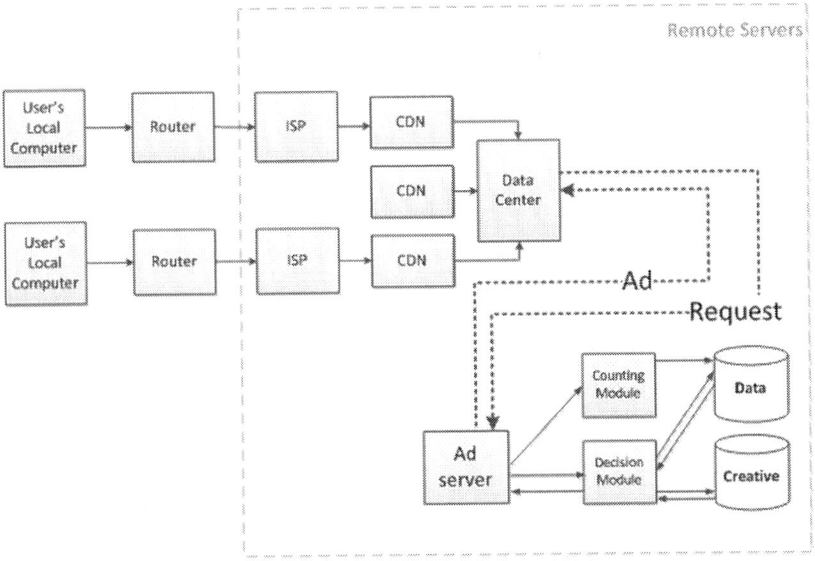

Figure 1.8: *User requests channel up to the ad server's data center where counting and ad serving decisions are made. As multiple requests are being made by multiple users for the same assets, the ad server decision module does not need to distribute the same ad every time but rather lets the CDN distribute the ad.*

The role of the CDN

The Content Delivery Network traces all the flight paths in the world, joining up the dots between the cities and the ISPs (Internet Service Providers) around the world and routing replicated information onto users' devices where-ever they may be. Ads stored in the ad server need to be replicated in the ad server data centres, prepared for the most strategic delivery of the assets (a delay called "ad replication") and a process that occurs when the campaign is being "trafficked" (more on trafficking in Chapter 3). When an ad call is received the ad server transmits the ads to the CDN's. *Akamai*, described by some as the internet's backbone, is one of the largest CDN's and ad servers utilise its services consistently. Larger Publishers like *MSN*, rely on *Microsoft's* own technology rather than outsource to systems like *Akamai*. The *MSN* CDN has the capacity to allow other internet technologies requiring CDN distribution to utilise it for such needs.

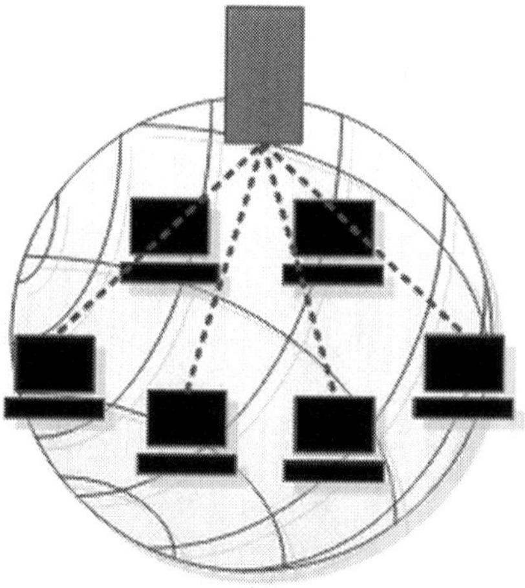

Figure 1.9: *CDN content delivery is most frequently represented in common conversation by reference to "The cloud". By offering servers in local proximity to user devices internet access speeds are greatly increased and files can easily be replicated across the world, this includes both site content and ads.*

Waiting around for ad Delivery - the user experience
So what is the effect on the user? Is it glaringly obvious that the most miniscule of delays actually has a shed-load of processes behind it? For the most part the answer is no, but with so many processes in place, once in a blue moon, the user will be stuck on a page where an ad fails to load. The purpose of the ad servers reporting capability is to quantify the investment clients make in online advertising, including demonstrating consistent ad delivery and performance which the Agency or Advertiser will reference frequently to ensure their messaging is reaching its audience, if not only to check that there is nothing clogging up the pipes (more details in Chapter 5 - Reporting). Providing there are no problems the optimum user experience will look like this:

Pre-ad display

1. User arrives at Publisher page
2. Ad request is sent to Publisher ad server, while the request for the content goes to the Publisher CMS
3. The Publisher content loads
4. The Publisher ad server calls the third party ad server
5. The ad request arrives at the local data center depending on the users location
6. The counting module counts an impression
7. The decision module selects the most suitable ad
8. The ad server sends a JavaScript to initiate the loading of the ad
9. The JavaScript loads on the Publisher page and loads in makes calls to all the necessary assets
10. The assets are pulled in from the CDN which in turn pulls in data from the ad server creative database
11. An Image or Flash execution appears in the user's browser window

During ad display

12. The ad server counts an "Ad Play" - which is an Instream Video metric (See Chapter 3 - Instream) or delivered impression metric
13. Piggybacked third party impression trackers load (See Chapter 3 - Standard Display)
14. Viewability begins counting (See Chapter 5 - Ad Verification)
15. Rich Media constantly reports "interactions" to the counting module (See Chapter 3 - Rich Media).

On ad close

16. Viewability ends counting and sends data to the ad server counting module (See Chapter 5 - Ad Verification)
17. Rich Media interactions that utilise a timer are reported to the ad server counting module (See Chapter 3 - Rich Media)

This exposes the mini cosmos of work that the ad server is doing. It is clear why the work is all done by machines in faraway places. The next section turns attention back to the online advertising industry to look at who the players in this space, and how many people and hands it takes to launch an online advertising campaign and make the most of ad serving technology.

Chapter 2

The Industry Players

Chapter 2
The Industry Players

- The agency holding groups
- Who are the big Agencies?
- Running a Media Agency
- Creative Agencies
    - *Figure 2.1*
- Publishers

To frame the context of advertising technology the books includes information about the various industry players. Given the nature of the advertising industry to shift clients and accounts, this section may well fall out of date quite quickly; however this is an attempt to represent it at a high level.

The agency holding groups

The largest and most powerful advertising Agencies sit under holding groups which themselves are home to a multiverse of Creative Agencies, PR Agencies and Media Agencies. With so many Agencies under a single umbrella, careful precautions are taken to ensure that Agencies can take on the work and business of many competing Advertisers without allowing sensitive information to spread to those competitors or separated divisions. Since a holding group may house ten or more Media Agencies which themselves may house ten or more Advertisers and somewhere down the line two Advertisers are bound to fall into the same vertical. In some instances Media Agencies and holding groups have been known to build out whole new Agencies just to ensure that such Advertiser data is kept very separate. The power of the holding group tends to fall with the price it can get for publication ad space, the economies of scale of such enterprises drives down the price of ad space, with the promise of business on an enormous scale.

Who are the big Agencies?
There are plenty of Up-to-date sources online that can give a more recent and thorough coverage of the breakdown of the Agency groups. As a very high level overview:

- **Publicis Omnicom group** houses the media Agencies formerly of the Omnicom group: OMD, OMG, PHD and Manning Gollieb and the media Agencies formerly of the Publicis group such as Starcom Mediavest and Zenith Optimedia.

- **Dentsu/Aegis** brings to the table Agencies such as Iprospect, Carat and Vizeum.

- **WPP** offers the industry GroupM and its heavyweight's Mindshare, Mediacom, Maxus and MEC to name but a few.

- **Interpublic group** (commonly shortened to IPG) includes Universal McCann and Initiative

- **Havas group** houses MPG/MediaContacts and Havas

Running a Media Agency
Media Agencies are typically made up of account teams (an account being an Advertiser). Each team will be made up of planners, buyers and account managers. Media Agencies have supplier contracts with technology providers including third party technology providers. These agreements vary considerably and can differ between region and country. Media Agencies also have contractual agreements with Publishers that outline payment terms. Such terms are usually confirmed in writing before each advertising campaign via the Insertion Order (IO) a document which also clarifies the amount of media space purchased as well as conditions of the campaign. Larger Media Agencies are occasionally affiliated with creative Agencies or more often have

their own in-house creative developers and designers. Much more common is a contractual relationship between the Advertiser and the Creative Agency directly. Media Agencies usually work with Advertisers in a long term capacity by pitching for their business by responding to and winning the chance to respond to a brief issued by the Advertiser. From an online perspective Media Agencies take a big burden off of the shoulders of the Advertiser. The work required to plan and buy media to reach the Advertiser's stated campaign objectives requires many hands and larger advertisers will rarely fill out their marketing teams with the headcount to undertake these tasks. It is for this reason that third party ad serving technology is most utilised by Media Agencies, who report their successes to the hiring Advertiser.

Creative agencies

There are an enormous number of creative agencies and the landscape is very competitive. A creative agency will usually produce a mock-up of how a campaign could look with lots of creative ideas, when pitching to an Advertiser to build a relationship with them and attain their business. Advertisers usually have preferred Creative Agencies that they will utilise for building creative across various media channels including TV and Print. The majority of Creative Agencies are small companies employing just a few designers and developers but some have reached enterprise sizes and fall under the same holding groups as the Media Agencies.

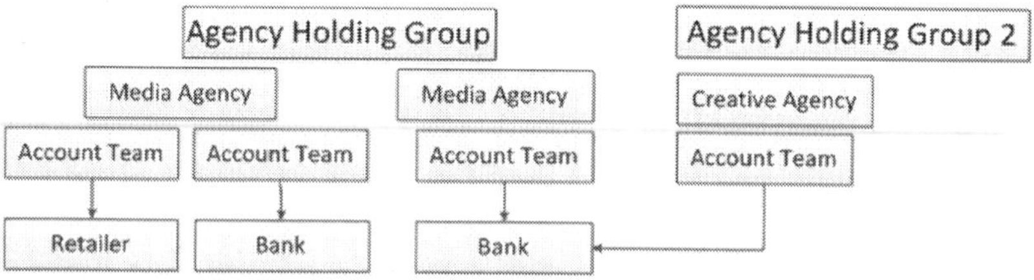

Figure 2.1: *A single Agency holding group may have clients operating in the same vertical but the teams are kept separate, often in completely different buildings. The Advertiser themselves*

has the freedom to select a Creative Agency which might work in a completely different holding group or operate independently.

Publishers

Publishers are the content providers. They are web sites that attract a large number of users. To give up your day job and just live off of the advertising revenue from a website your site would need to attract in excess of one hundred thousand "unique users" per month (depending on the quality of these users: also called "the quality of the traffic"). This means that if the users are coming to the Publisher website for a purpose, and the ads shown are relevant and well-targeted to those users, then the quality of those users is more valuable. This quality traffic raises the price of the ad space on the Publisher website and would mean the Publisher can make a tidy profit from the money that Advertisers would be willing to spend to have ads on a Publisher website. Big Publishers (such as *Facebook, Google, MSN* and *Yahoo!*) attract a vast number of users and in turn are almost always included on Advertiser "Media Plans". Smaller Publishers, although not necessarily attracting big crowds have the added benefits of either a more niche audience or cheaper ad space. Publishers are the home of ads; they control the greatest cost to any ad campaign (the cost of the ad space) and at times view all technology in terms of their own properties.

The remainder of this chapter will be spent focussing each of these stakeholder groups. Each group spends more time using a different piece of ad technology therefore third party ad serving is more important to some and less to others.

Chapter 2 - Section 1
Advertisers and Marketers

- Who is the Advertiser?
    - The Marketer
    - Agency pitch
    - Relationship with the Media Agency
    - Relationship with the Creative Agency
    - *Figure 2.2.1*
- Controlling the page content
    - Controlling the pages of the Advertiser Site - the CMS
    - Landing Page
    - Basket Page
    - Confirmation Page
    - *Figure 2.2.2*
    - CRM Platform
    - Onsite Behavioural data
- Tracking the users on site
    - Site Side Analytics
    - Click to Land
    - Passing the tokens in the click-through URL
    - Referral

Who is the Advertiser?

Advertisers can be loosely divided into two buckets in the online world: "Brand" and "Direct response". Brand Advertisers tend to utilise the web to grow awareness and generate interest and engagement but rarely have something tangible to "sell" online. Direct Response (DR) Advertisers are usually much more complex in their advertising needs. They will have an e-commerce site to sell goods or services online and often need to produce ads and campaigns with objectives to target users at each stage in the purchase process. There are of course Advertisers that cross into both definitions. These are usually very large DR Advertisers who need a little of everything. In this section we will begin with an overview of Advertisers, followed by their relationship with Media Agencies and then Creative Agencies. This is followed by an exploration around the predominant technologies an Advertiser will be working closely with; including the makeup of their e-commerce site and how to integrate such technologies effectively with third party ad serving.

The Marketer

Advertiser marketing team brings together the overall marketing strategy marrying up the available digital advertising budget with the right resource to get the best return.

For Brand advertisers, marketers are concerned initially with ad delivery and verification. If the ads have been served they should have been delivered at an optimal "reach and frequency" with the ultimate aim of hitting the targeting audience with a memorable creative message. In Chapter 5 we will look at how the ad server reporting can deliver this information.

For Direct response advertisers, marketers are concerned with ROI and want to demonstrate like for like or incremental sales from a set marketing budget. With the right combination of delivery techniques, reporting and optimization; digital is a very fertile ground for DR marketers with an ever increasing budget, to invest in.

For the marketer to ensure the advertising budget is best spent, the campaign goals are clearly laid out before a campaign begins.

Agency Pitch

To choose an Agency the Advertiser releases an RFP (Request for Proposal) to a shortlist of Media Agencies. This RFP details the advertiser's marketing objectives over the next few years and asks the Agencies to come back with the best strategic pitch for the work. The process can take quite a long time as the Advertiser is usually looking to sign a contract with an Agency over a term of a few years; departing from such contracts can be very costly to the Advertiser, so the right decision is imperative. Once an Agency is secured, the relationship can begin to grow.

Relationship with the Media Agency

Once an Agency has won over the Advertiser the Agency account team begins the process of transitioning the "campaign workflow" process (the operational practices an Advertiser is familiar using) to align with the practices of the Agency or the needs of the Advertiser, where the Agency sees fit. This stage can involve moving the Advertiser from one set of technologies to another depending on the conditions of the contract with the Agency. This process can also take several weeks if not months but, done correctly, sets the stage for a blooming relationship in future campaigns. In the next section we will look in closer detail at campaign management, a process which is Agency-led.

As campaigns are processed the Advertiser and Media Agency learn which processes and practices work best for them and find ways of sharing and using the third party technology between them to suit everyone's needs. For instance some marketers prefer a more hands-on approach to the reporting data which the Media Agency is able to grant as long as expectations are clear about how decisions around campaign optimization are made.

Relationship with the Creative Agency

Unlike in the world of TV advertising, the Creative Agency takes a back seat to the role of the Media Agency in campaign setup (and usually the Advertiser will have a long term existing partnership with either a preferred Creative Agency or a myriad of them). The marketer will usually take a keen interest in the development of any creative to maintain a consistent brand image (the word "creative" is used to describe the state of a digital ad before it becomes an actual ad that can be used by the ad serving technology). This means there will be a back and forth of communication between the Creative Agency and the Advertiser right up until the ad is fully developed, and it is mutually agreed that its visual elements will not change before the ad is seen by a public audience. Some big Brand Advertisers are more detail oriented than others when it comes to adhering to brand style guidelines and the sign-off process can get extremely lengthy.

For this reason, ad serving technology is designed to allow the Creative Agency to share a preview of the ads with the Advertiser directly and receive their approval before the ad is processed in the ad server for trafficking. The ad preview environment is particularly useful for Rich Media and DCO (See Chapter 3).

With its partners on board (Media Agency and Creative Agency) the stage is almost set to begin running an ad campaign. The final piece of the puzzle from the Advertiser's perspective is to ensure that users arrive at a website that extends their interest towards an eventual purchase.

Technical staff working on the Advertiser marketing team tend to place all their focus and attention on the Advertiser's site which can be pretty simple (for big brand advertisers that do not offer the chance to purchase online - perhaps having less than ten pages on their site) or vastly complex (such as in the case of a DR Advertiser like a retail catalogue website - where the number of pages to manage may be in the millions).

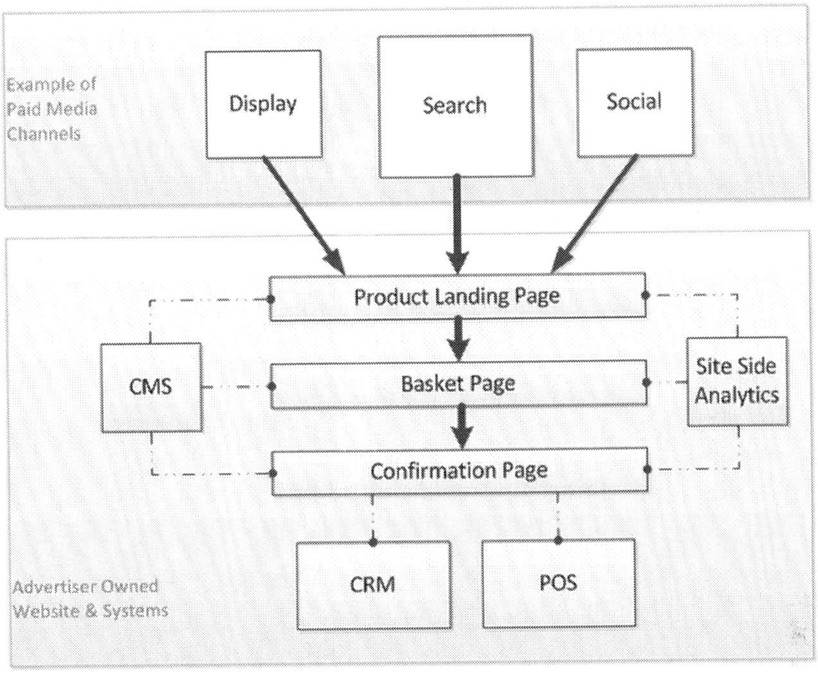

Figure 2.2.1: *In Advertiser-world, the Media Agency ensures that users get to the Advertiser site through various paid-for channels (tracked across the board only by the third party ad server). Once the user arrives on the Advertiser site there are several tools doing the measuring.*

Controlling the Pages of the Advertiser Site - (the CMS)
There are lots of types of pages on the Advertiser website but only a few of them are useful to the marketer. Pages which help demonstrate that a marketing objective has been fulfilled need to be carefully controlled, watched and measured. A CMS tool fulfils this first function.

An Advertiser website that has something to sell online is invariably going to contain a lot of individual web pages and a lot of information, to better inform the consumer on their journey to purchase. Web pages which are built in basic HTML code alone are severely limiting. Thousands of live pages require a solution that will allow the web developer updating the Advertiser website to make changes in seconds. A Content Management System (CMS) allows for the creation and update of thousands of pages in seconds by providing a backend user interface for the web developer to change the site. The user of the website does not see the presence of a Content Management System but instead sees an illusion of "static" webpages. One of the crucial functions of the CMS is that it allows the marketing team to append the live pages with additional pieces of third party tracking technology to monitor page-level "conversion activities", these are called "Conversion Tags" and Chapter 4 is dedicated to explaining their purpose and uses in detail. Some marketers and Agencies need frequent access to the page code to change these tags but not all Advertiser sites (despite the presence of a CMS) allow for frequent changes. This can and often does directly impact the successful and timely completion of an online ad campaign.

In **Figure 2.2.1** the three core page types which best reflect the fulfilment of marketing objectives, are stated. Each of these page types is significant to the marketing effort and can be fully recognised as campaign yardsticks or "conversion events" in third party ad server reporting:

- The Landing Page (or Product Landing Page)
- The Basket Page (or pre-confirmation page)
- The Confirmation Page (or Thank-you page)

Landing Page

The Landing page is the first page that the user arrives at in the Advertiser's online domain. Being the first page, it needs to be designed to the user expectations. Thanks to the connected nature of today's search engines, a user can type in a keyword into the search bar, see a link to the Advertiser's site and click through to the landing page (more information about the Search Channel in Chapter 3). The landing page should therefore reflect the very search term that the user inputted into the search engine and the Advertiser should customise the look and feel of the page to reflect assumptions about the user's reason for arriving on that page.

Basket Page

The user journey on an Advertiser's ecommerce website leads down, what marketers refer to as a "funnel", a lot of users reach a landing page, but many drop out en-route to the final purchase page. This analogy is often used in online marketing to describe the channel strategy for an online campaign. The consumer is attracted into the top of the "purchase funnel" with impactful brand ads that capture user interest, this is followed by capturing user intent and finally the user is drawn through the Advertiser site right up to final purchase at the end of the funnel.

The penultimate step is to load up the "shopping basket" with the intended purchase. Although the "shopping basket" element of the website itself may have many pages, the collective reference for one or more of these pages is a "basket page". Since a user can undertake various behaviours in the basket page, such as dropping out of the process, it is important for the Advertiser to monitor these pages with ad server tracking technology and make sure that the users are not lost forever (see Chapter 7).

Confirmation Page

The actual sale takes place somewhere between the basket page and the thank you page. The last key Advertiser page type is therefore the "thank you" page (which is also is referred to as the confirmation page); where the Advertiser confirms to the user that the product has been purchased.

Tracking activity on the confirmation page is crucial for DR Advertisers; a consumer only becomes a consumer once they arrive here, so the very arrival onto this page (which is not accessible by any other means other than by buying something) is logged in the CRM and POS (as shown in **Figure 2.2.1**). These systems log a unique identification number related to the transaction called an OrderID. It is this same number which ties together the CRM, POS and ad serving data sets as they can all be setup to track the same value when an order is completed. The ad serving data exposing the journey the user went on to arrive on the landing page and complete the sale - allowing the marketer to see exactly which customers respond to which ads and how much they spent.

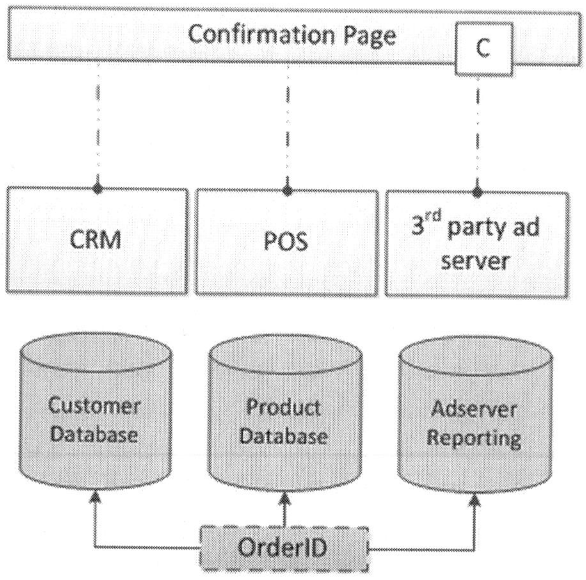

Figure 2.2.2: *The Advertiser can have the web development team working on the Advertiser site setup the Confirmation Page to pass the value of the OrderID field (declared on the page by JavaScript code) to the ad serving conversion tag. As the OrderID is common to multiple systems it can be used to connect a user's behaviour together both on and off the site to determine how the decision to purchase is made.*

CRM Platform

In addition to product data, collecting customer data is vital to the success of the business. Customer data comes into the Custom Relationship Management tool from customer surveys and data collection points to the POS (Point of Sale) system. The data reveals seasonal buying habits, trends, price driven spending and it builds profiles of customers so that existing customers with certain buying habits can be modelled against new customers to predict buying behaviours.

Onsite Behavioural data

To enhance CRM databases, and add extra value to their businesses some Advertisers present opt-in tick boxes in their sign up processes which allow the data they collect, about those users on the site, to be used again for other purposes. Sometimes it is sold to third parties data providers to aggregate with other data sources before being sold on to other Advertisers. Marketers, who fail to do more than collect user details off the back of a campaign, could fund future campaigns by selling on the data. Of course a well-nourished CRM will pay dividends later on when answering crucial marketing questions.

From controlling the point of entry and the pathway through the site to the point of sale, marketers obtain data about the "order" itself but less so about the consumer behaviour in the confines of the site. The second platform that the marketer will spend lots of time in on the Advertiser side are the Advertiser or Site-Side analytics system, something that the marketer will have almost exclusive access to use.

Tracking the users on the Site - Site Side Analytics

Some technologies get more press coverage than others and "Site Side Analytics" tools are often confused with third party ad servers because they are one of the few technologies that have their own entire shelves in large book stores. Established Site-Side Analytics providers include *IBM's Core Metrics, Adobe's Analytics Suite* (formerly called *Omniture*) and the popular, free alternative; *Google Analytics*. Site Side analytics technologies work by the Advertiser placing a snippet of code on every page of the Advertiser website and the tool measures the incoming and outgoing site traffic (mapping the journey users take through the site).

Click to Land

Since the first time the Site-Side analytics tool sees a user is when they first arrive at the landing page, it is common place for a marketer to try to match up the users clicking through on ads (as reported by the third party ad server) to those users landing on the landing page (as reported by the site side analytics tool). Unless the two systems are integrated this is a flawed exercise and will raise many discrepancies because the counting methodology between the two systems is inherently different.

Passing through Tokens in the click-through URL

Integration is possible where the click-through URL of the ad contains an additional variable that the site side analytics tool can recognise when the user arrives to the page. These variables are referred to as "tokens" and when setting up the campaign, the trafficker will append the click-through URL to either carry through a fixed or a dynamic token. To keep matters simple, let's focus on the fixed token scenario:

A click through URL might look like this:
http://www.advertiser.com/productpage1

A click-through URL with an appended token might look like this:

http://www.advertiser.com/productpage1?campaignname=campaign1

In this example the actual click-through URL was changed by the trafficker in the ad server interface (to see how this is done head to Chapter 3 - Ad Serving Operations). The site-side analytics tool could be setup to recognise the variable called "campaignname" and use the information passed through attached to this variable to get more information about the incoming user (such as the campaign name for the ad they just arrived to the page on). In this instance *campaign1* is a fixed value; it doesn't change unless the trafficker changes it. In the scenario of providing a dynamic token the ad server might be clever enough to have some backend "macros" or shortcut pieces of code that will dynamically add a value into a field.

In this instance the trafficker might insert:

http://www.advertiser.com/productpage1?campaignname=%campaignname%

The macro is shown with a percentage symbol either side, and when the user clicks on the ad, the clickthroughURL is formulated in real-time so that the macro-portion pulls in a master-value from the ad server backend called "campaignname". This feature is a huge time saver for the trafficker.

The trafficker can add:
?campaignname=%campaignname%
to all click-through URLs in multiple ad campaigns for the same Advertiser and the campaign name will dynamically change for the site side analytics tool to read the information and correctly attribute the user and their arrival to a campaign name which matches the master list of campaign names in the ad server.

Referral

Either way, the site-side analytics data makes for compelling analysis. Essentially these tools measure user journeys through the site from entry to purchase. The data is then used by the web development to structure the website and by the marketing team who use the data to enrich the CRM database. Site side analytics reveals important information about how users arrive at the website. This is known as "referral" information and can disseminate between traffic arriving from paid search vs. natural search. Where these tools fall short are in identifying user behaviour before the user arrived at the site which is where site - side analytics reporting marries up nicely with third party ad serving data.

It is the role of the marketing team to match data from:

- The CRM
- The POS
- The third party ad server
- The Site-Side analytics tool

...to answer some or all of the following questions:

- Which ads are driving the highest return? And what is the optimum customer journey?
- What affect do campaign optimizations have on customer behaviour?
- What are the behaviours of the most valued customers and how can this data be used to create a bigger and more loyal customer-base?

We have looked in detail about the world from the perspective of the Advertiser and Marketer. It is now time to turn our attention to the role played by the Media Agency.

Chapter 2 - Section 2
Agency Planning and Buying

- The role of the Planner
    - How to plan?
    - *Figure 2.3*
    - Research Tools
    - *Figure 2.4*
    - Demographic Digital Media Consumption by Publisher Website
    - Unique Audience - Site Overlap
    - Research through Benchmarking
    - In-Agency planning solutions
    - *Figure 2.5*
- Technology for Buying
    - Agency Trading Desks
    - *Figure 2.6*
    - The Agency-side Media Plan
- Selecting an Ad Server
- What technology-based Services do Media Agencies offer?
- Media Agency data analysts

Media Agencies bring a wealth of expertise to the table but not all Advertisers employ them to manage and run digital ad campaigns. Those Advertisers that feel they have the talent and buying power, utilise technologies and outsource some functions (such as trafficking) to achieve the same goals as hiring a Media Agency. The risk inherent in this approach is that the full scale of the work undertaken by the Media agency is cloaked by design as a positive customer experience so that Advertisers can spend media budget without getting their hands dirty with the day to day operations. The following section looks at the predominant roles and functions undertaken by the Media Agency.

The role of the media agency can be divided into four key areas, which we will look at in more detail:

- Planning Campaigns
- Buying Media space
- Managing Campaigns (locally, regionally and globally)
- Reporting and Optimizing to Advertiser KPIs

The role of the Planner

Deciding where to spend marketing dollars to meet Advertiser campaign goals, is a tough chore and takes considerable experience to get it right. Agencies employ "planners" for this very role. The process starts by having the planners dissect the campaign brief received from the Advertiser. They then decide which sites and channels will yield the best results.

How to plan?

The channel recipe for campaign effectiveness is not an exact science owing to the buying behaviours of the consumer. Strong cross channel planning strategies are balanced by the marketing principles of "the purchase funnel", suggesting that Display advertising is effective at the top of the funnel for consumer awareness and research, while the Search channel is more effective lower down the funnel where there is an intent to purchase or click. In Chapter 3 we look in depth at each channel at its merits and how to manage campaigns via the ad server effectively.

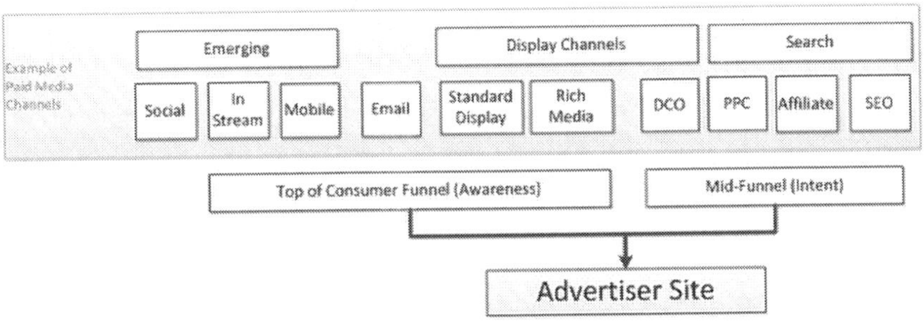

Figure 2.3: *A generalisation of the paid digital marketing channels available for the Media Agency to plan and buy ad space across. Broadly speaking the right mix can be formulated through careful research and succinct planning, although new channels and Publishers make the optimum mix a challenge to get right. More on Campaign Setup by Channel in Chapter 3.*

Research Tools

Planners and buyers use research tools to establish which sites in a preferred channel mix will meet the demographic targeting and audience reach criteria to satisfy the Advertiser objectives for the upcoming campaign. *Neilsen* and *ComScore* are the two dominant research technologies in digital advertising. These two companies closely track a panel of individual web users across the globe with their consent (identified as true individuals rather than anonymous cookies), and use this panel as a sample of the overall internet population. The sample is then scaled-up to the predicted total audience size of the internet (called the "internet universe") and the demographic details of the unique visitors present on each large Publisher web site.

The output could be compared to a league table of websites where comparisons can be made across sites with the greatest reach (called a "unique audience"), the count of users and the "page views" for each site (the number of times all users are loading individual pages). Given that we are talking about sample sizes the numbers are not precise reflections of all users on these sites, but they do give a clear enough indication about Publisher website traffic for a planner to make some decisions. The planner will log into the research tool before the start of a campaign to decide that the audience they are aiming to target with a particular campaign brief; uses a certain Publisher website. The next step is to pass such information along to the buying team at the media agency who instigates the purchase of available advertising space on that site.

Autos		A	B	C	D	E	F
		Nielsen			**ComS core**		
		18-25 m	25-40 m	60+ m	18-25 m	25-40 m	60+ m
1	Autos.microsoft.com	80%	70%	25%	90%	65%	30%
2	Autotrader.com	75%	75%	20%	80%	80%	20%
3	Webuyanycar.com	70%	40%	10%	75%	40%	15%
4	usedautos.net	50%	20%	5%	40%	20%	7%

Figure 2.4: *An agency that uses both the Neilsen and ComScore research tools can export reports from those platforms and compare the data for the two systems.*

Demographic Digital Media Consumption by Publisher Website

In the example in **Figure 2.4** the top sites for a given time period for websites classified in an automotive vertical show that for the first site on the list (microsoft.com) that 80/90% of the total audience of 18-25 year old males on either of the measured audience panels for the two technologies visited this site. If it is the intent of the Advertiser (that the media planner on the

Agency account team is servicing) to try to reach as many 18-25 year old males as possible, it would be wise for the planner to inform the media buyer to contact microsoft.com to try to secure ad space for an upcoming campaign. If the planner was trying to reach one hundred per cent of the 18-25 male audience, both of the research tools agree that it is not possible to do this with a single site.

Unique Audience - Site Overlap

To reach one hundred per cent of the right audience, still using **Figure 2.4** as an example, the Agency would need to consult a different report exported from these systems called a Unique Site Overlap report. Such a report would show the uniqueness of the audience on each site in the right demographic bucket. At this early planning stage the purchase of the media space that results from making decisions by looking at this data is not a one hundred per cent accurate reflection of what will actually occur when the campaign goes live. Only once the campaign is live and all users are tracked (as opposed to using a panel) will it be clear where there is overlap in unique users. The ad server can report on this directly (see Chapter 5) with its own version of the Unique Site Overlap report, but the actual delivery of the ads to the demographics stated in this table needs to be verified. *Neilsen* and *ComScore* offer additional tools based off of their panel data to verify the delivery of ads to the correct demographic group (see Chapter 5 - Verification)

Research through Benchmarking

Data collected in the third party ad server from previous campaigns can be extremely useful in determining the best Publisher sites to choose for planning as the historical data can be viewed in a way that allows for Publishers to be ranked by performance across all of the metrics available in ad server reporting. Big Agencies may amalgamate all the data for all the Advertisers they service to give a good indication of publisher performance by Advertiser vertical. Agencies that have run enough campaigns historically can find out if a combination like the ad dimensions will give better performance on one site over another. Such tools might be developed in house by Agencies but some independent technology providers have alternatives. *Mediamind's Smart Planning* tool is an option for Agency planners looking to improve on a pre-campaign planning strategy. This ad-server owned research tool offers benchmarking across Publisher websites for a large pool of Advertisers, thereby giving a more accurate picture of where certain ads might perform effectively, long before the media space is bought and paid for.

In-Agency planning solutions

Informed decisions about the campaign plan, lead to conversations between the Agency buying team and the Publishers. The Agency buying process has evolved from its origins by traditional methods of buying media is still used alongside the new technology-supported buying methods. In traditional buying, the Agency buyer makes a call to a contact they have acquired at the Publisher site where they are interested in buying media space. On both sides of the phone, the Publisher and Agency agree on a particular "buying-rate" or "cost model" for the Advertiser's campaign. The Agency buyer may negotiate a position so that the Publisher is responsible for performance of the campaign and in doing so the final price of the ad space may be tied to this figure (more on actual cost models and costs in Chapter 2 - Publishers). The relationship between the media buyer and the Publisher seller in most instances will have been formed over many months in which time the Publisher would meet with the buyer to provide updates about the Publisher's media space and technology integrations. In instances where Publisher performance may not have reflected well in research tools like *Neilsen*, such relationships win the Publisher repeat business.

The request for ad space or media "inventory" from a Media Agency to a Publisher is recorded in an "insertion order" or IO (essentially an invoice). The signing of the IO secures the deal and the campaign can begin.

Technologies have surfaced, created by either the Media Agency themselves, or by third parties to automate the setup of a campaign following the confirmation of a deal and keep a record of the negotiation proceedings. These are called "planning tools". The *Donovan Data System (DDS)* product called *iDesk*, is a good example of one such technology. *iDesk* allows the Agency to quickly input the details of the purchased ad space, connect this to their billing system and automatically "setup a campaign" inside the third party ad server interface. *iDesk* is currently setup to automate this process with all the major ad servers (see Chapter 3 - Display Ad serving for more information about how this works). In addition to this Agency buyers can come back to the records in this system in the next campaign or buying cycle and make sure that throughout negotiations that the Publisher does not attempt to charge a higher price than previously.

There aren't a huge range of options for Media Agencies that are looking to upgrade, replace or install a billing system that communicates well with planning tools and outputs data that allows an agency account team to keep an eye on the pacing for marketing budget spend across the campaign. The future promises to bring these kinds of budget management capabilities directly into the ad server (partly managed through the ability to input cost data in the ad server interface in the trafficking process as explained in Chapter 3) but for the time being the most widely adopted system for literally issuing payments to Publishers and keeping track of all costs: is *MediaBank* (also part of the *DDS* family under the brand name *Mediaocean*). This is crucial because the marketing budget must not just cover off the cost of the advertising space, it must also cover the cost of using technology like 3d party ad serving and additional Agency fees.

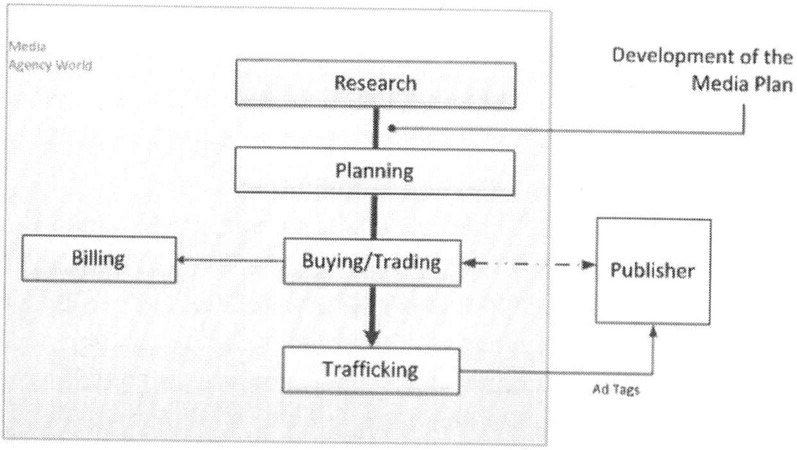

Figure 2.5: *the bread and butter of Media Agency world consists of Research, Planning, Buying and Trafficking in a straight-forward campaign development workflow. As the plans for the campaign begin to take hold and IO contracts are made with the Publisher team, the Media plan develops as a living document, referenced by multiple parties over the campaign's lifetime.*

This buying process is key to Media Agency involvement in digital advertising. The size of larger Media Agencies mean that on paper a large number of IO's will be double-signed with the largest Publishers. Buying more ad space affects the price as Publishers attract Media Agency dollars through economies of scale. At a certain volume commitment, prices are lower for media Agencies than they would be for Advertisers because Advertisers will almost always be buying less ad space.

Technology for Buying

Buying from Publishers and Publisher networks directly is now referred to as a "traditional media buy" because as we allured to before: technology has changed the buying process. Getting on the phone to secure ad space (inventory) from a Publisher leaves too much of a dependency on human contact, relationships and it takes too much time. Automatic buying technologies now allow for the purchase of mass reach inventory known as a Publisher "remnant inventory" (literally the ad space which is unsold). The processing and placing of orders for inventory is now done through "ad exchanges" which are trading marketplaces for media inventory (not wholly dissimilar from the stock market) which can also occur in real time with the correct enabling technologies in place (RTB). The traditional media buying conversations still occur for the "biggest deals" such as large Publisher homepage takeovers; the purchase here is for ad spots with a higher value or larger audience known as "premium inventory".

Agency Trading Desks

There are a limited number of known and popular Ad exchanges where the inventory is grouped and classified by the Publisher by the audience expected to be exposed to that ad space. At the most basic level it can be said that the exchange advertises the sale of an audience. Accessing the Exchanges is hard work and the technology that allows the purchase of these ad spaces and audiences are DSPs (covered in Chapter 8). The "Agency Trading Desks" (ATD's) are specialist buying teams that are part of the Agency that utilise the DSPs to access the Exchanges. They have close ties to the Agency buying team and are utilised to purchase audiences on the Exchanges, a process undertaken when the traditional buying method is not used. This is a fairly rich topic so I am going to save the details for Chapter 8. The basic premise is that Agency buying teams don't just have to pick up the phone to Publishers anymore; they can buy the ad space through in-house technology teams which utilise the DSPs now. Big business agency trading desks include *WPP GroupM's Xaxis* and the *Publicis Audience on Demand* (*AOD*) platform.

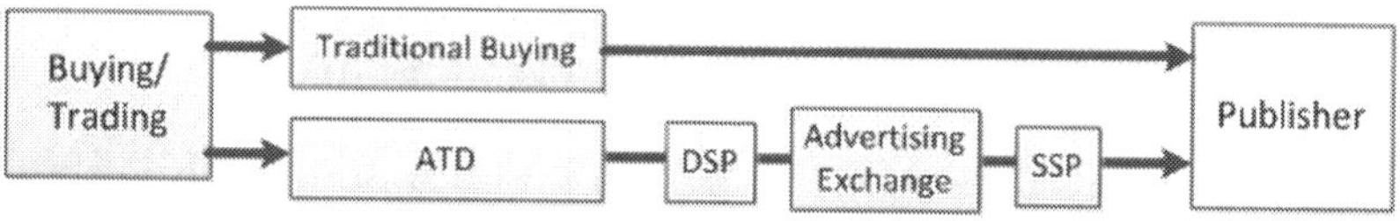

Figure 2.6: *The process of Media Agency buying and securing media inventory is possible down two pathways. The traditional method is a direct relationship-based selling opportunity. The new methodology; predominantly used to trade remnant inventory utilises Advertising exchanges. Expertise in automated trading is managed by the Agency trading desk team. More on this model in Chapter 8.*

The Agency-side Media Plan

Once the buying process is complete the account team will have in their hands a copy of the "media plan". The media plan is a single document which clearly shows which ads are due to run and when. As the document is only completed when all parties are satisfied with the inventory purchase, it contains all the relevant information required to begin the construction of the ads themselves. This is due in part to the supply of the Publisher specifications (details of which can be found in Chapter 2 - Publishers) and will include information like ad dimensions and when the campaign is due to go live. Once complete, the media plan is supplied to the "trafficker" on the Media Agency side as well as the Creative Agency. The process followed by the Creative Agency is detailed in the next section. As for the trafficking process, the complexity of the proceeding processes is dictated by the make-up of the media plan. For instance the media channels that the campaign is planned and booked to run on will determine on what processes and considerations need to take place in the trafficking process (such as for trafficking ads due to run in *Google* search versus those due to appear on *Facebook* or the *MSN* homepage. The nuisances of this channel by channel trafficking have been fully documented in the Chapter 3 – Ad serving Operations.

Once trafficking is complete, a campaign is active and the Media Agency account team will share the responsibility to monitor the delivery of the ads and report on campaign performance using the reporting functionality in the third party ad server. The specific reports that Media Agencies can see are demonstrated and explained in Chapter 5 - Reporting. Finally the Media Agency will complete the process of "campaign management" by either optimizing the ads in the existing campaign (See Chapter 6 - Optimization) or will utilise the information collected to run a second campaign or extend the existing campaign (See Chapter 7 - Retargeting).

The campaign setup process, from research right through to trafficking should be a carefully considered operation, but time constraints around the availability of inventory and the timelines of the Advertiser's own marketing plans can mean a rushed process. From speaking with Creative Agency, Publishers, Media Agencies and Advertisers involved in daily campaign management over the years I have managed to determine that any digital ad campaign needs at least two weeks to get the planning and setup just right. Rarely will a campaign get such a generous window and parties are often rushed on delivery. Every experienced trafficker can tell stories about 'Friday night' trafficking, a well-known burden of the trafficking role in which media plans for the weekend are received at the last working hour of the week, but a rite of passage for working in digital advertising.

During the stages of campaign setup and management (research, planning, buying, trafficking, reporting and optimization) the Agency account team will continually check in with Advertiser, bringing them up to speed on how close to those marketing KPIs, the campaign is. On some occasions the planners and buyers will manage to secure more marketing budget to deliver more ads on the media plan to reach a goal. The optimization process is also strongly connected to buying and Agency buyers may have to revise their IO's with Publishers if the ads are not performing.

This concludes the common roles of the Media Agency account team. As we have seen Media Agency's sometimes have trading desk teams as well. Quite common are also Trafficking and Technology teams. Such a team would be made up of Agency employees that are technical and skilled working within the environment of the third party ad server. Where these teams exist, the in-Agency trafficking process is slightly different and this team might take on the full process of trafficking a media plan instead for all the other account teams and their campaigns. Such teams also handle the troubleshooting of problematic campaigns, ads and provide advice around solving technical queries. It is also common for this team to conduct the selection process for choosing new technologies to use including ad servers.

Selecting an Ad Server

As this book will reveal, choosing an ad server is not an easy task. The selection process should be careful considered based on both the needs of the Agency and the needs of the Advertiser. As third party ad serving technology is rapidly evolving, traffic and technology teams on the Agency side will typically invite third party ad serving companies to pitch for new business (which tends to be more for on-boarding new Advertisers or migrating whole Advertisers from a different ad server, rather than going through the consideration process for each new campaign). After a period of research the traffic and technology team will issue an RFP which contains a list of technical questions about capabilities and higher level business questions about costs and plans for the ad server in question. If the RFP and the pitch that follows meet the Advertiser needs the Agency will formalise the relationship and complete an ad serving contract with the selected technology provider.

What technology-based Services do Media Agencies offer?

Media Agencies sometimes own technology solutions and sell these on to their Advertiser clients as services. Technologies which report on campaign performance are drawing in data from the third party ad server and other data sources. Technologies for buying or trading, which connect to exchanges and Publisher networks, are built by Agencies for exclusive use by their Advertisers and are used to attract more Advertiser business. Technologies such as Agency-owned planning tools are integrated with third party ad servers to speed up the process of moving from planning to trafficking. Such tools add a competitive advantage to one Media Agency over another and are an important consideration for any Advertiser selecting a new Media Agency to work with.

Media Agency data analysts

The Media Agency roles and responsibilities in campaign setup and management from research and planning through to buying and trafficking help demonstrate why most Advertisers choose to employ the expertise of such stakeholders. The role of the Media Agency does not end when the campaign begins but goes on to add strength through expertise in optimization, reporting and the on-going trading of advertising space. It is important to state that all media agencies are different, even within the same holding group Agencies are known to follow different processes and workflows. Some Agencies have account teams but then split out the responsibility of campaign management by channel by having additional teams in place such as a search team or an affiliate team. Further to this some Agencies who have a particular focus on data-heavy strategies, employ a team of expert analysts; who build data processing systems and retrieve the most granular type of reporting from the ad-servers during and post campaign. Media Agency teams that have analytics resources are on the rise as the industry ventures towards greater use of what has been termed "big data": making use of large datasets such as ad server cookie level reporting to make business decisions.

It is at the Advertiser's discretion to employ the Media Agency and by the same token, the Advertiser chooses a Creative Agency. Creative Agencies are also not essential to every digital campaign; campaigns which run on channels like Search do not require a designer or developer to produce an aesthetic visual as an advert. Those channels which do have this need such as Video or Standard display bring the Creative Agency into the campaign setup process at the point that the Media Agency issues the media plan. Since this document details the specifications that the creative Agency will need to build to, the Creative Agency cannot begin their work without it. The next section will go into detail about the role and workflows undertaken by the Creative Agency.

Chapter 2 - Section 3
Creative Shop

- The Creative Shop
    - Relationship with the Advertiser
    - Relationship with Publishers
    - Relationship with the Media Agency
- Marketing budget for Creative development
- Roles and Responsibilities
    - *Figure 2.7*
- Getting the Design right
- Development and Production
- Flash authoring
    - *Figure 2.7.1*
- Actionscript
    - *Figure 2.7.2*
- Components, building and publishing ads
- Ad storage systems (Asset Management Systems)
- Localisation
- Standard QA
    - *Figure 2.7.3*
- Uploading Creative
- What's in a name?
- Creative Inspiration

This section defines the role of the Creative Agency and examines the responsibilities that exist there to support the digital campaign setup process. In addition we will take a deeper look into the definition of an ad or creative to understand the skills, tools and systems that are mandatory for the Creative Agency to support the Advertiser, Media Agency and Publisher.

The Creative Shop

Visual ads are designed and created by a "creative team". Such a team can either sit inside a Media Agency or more commonly sits within an independent Agency of its own right; the "Creative Agency" (sometimes referred to as a "Creative Shop" in the US). When a media agency or advertiser chooses to plan or setup a digital ad campaign that does not utilise complex visual elements (such as with campaigns setup in the search channel) the services of the creative Agency are not required. As the possible digital advertising channels have evolved, so has the role of the Creative Agency: as we will see later, channels like Dynamic Creative Optimization (DCO) have completely changed the perception and the expectation around Creative Agency involvement throughout the campaign.

Creative Agencies build their predominant relationships with the Advertisers who employee them. Relationships with Media Agencies and Publishers, which are just as crucial to maintain for successful ad campaigns exist for different purposes with separate dialogue required. Let's look at this balance more closely:

1. **Relationship with the Advertiser**
   To first work with an Advertiser, a Creative Agency will attempt to advertise the skills of their designers and developers by obtaining the Advertiser campaign brief and preparing mock-ups to showcase to the potential "client". Mock-ups will be the creative realisation of the brief into the story-board of the campaign in an aesthetically innovative way. This work is undertaken for free at cost to the Creative Agency that can hope to win the attention of the Advertiser and if successful; their business for the campaign and beyond. Such tactics make the creative Agency work very competitive and the protection and limited distribution of the campaign brief, crucial to the existing Creative Agency.

Independent Creative Agencies have very close relationships with the Advertiser, more so than they would have with the Media Agency in fact and this all comes down to the development of a brand. In brand development, the Creative Agency is employed to birth the Advertiser's brand standards and guidelines. By keeping a consistent loyalty to those guidelines the consumer experience of the Advertiser and the ads that they encounter enable far stronger brand and product recall. The Advertiser therefore invites the Creative Agency to approve and develop all creative in digital ad campaigns as well to adhere to the creed of the brand. Having developed such standards, the Advertiser will look to use the Creative Agency to approve work undertaken by the Media Agency that may impede on the perception of the brand. Alongside this auditing process the actual output delivered by the Creative Agency is referred to in the digital world as "the creative" and consists of images and content in the form of digital files.

2. **Relationship with Publishers**

Publishers own the infrastructure of the web, the sites and ad spaces themselves. The Publisher can restrict the type of ads that can be used on their websites. These limitations or "specifications" and mostly unique to each website and legally must be observed in order for the creative to "go live" on a Publisher website. The legal agreement to adhere to such specifications is laid out when the Media Agency commit to the purchase of the inventory.

Publishers will check the creative thoroughly before the campaign goes live. Creative developers that may try to side-step the specifications using clever coding will have their creative caught by the Publisher operations team. On the one hand the inclusion of any limitations to the Creative Agency may seem like a barrier to expression and creativity, but the Publisher must look out for its own interests. These interests include the preservation of its own design and the specifications ensure that the creative is as visually effective as it can be in the publisher created environment of their webpage.

Creative Agencies and Publishers will often work hand in hand on expressive and elaborate executions that, for one campaign or two, are granted permission to breach Publisher specifications. Such exercises can mean good publicity for both parties, as well as impactful branding for the Advertiser.

3. **Relationship with the Media Agency**
   Commission an artist to paint and he will paint until the masterpiece is complete, his own interpretation and style at the helm. For the artist at the creative agency, a party that is not doing the commissioning could be viewed as a hindrance to the creative process. However, when a Creative Agency develops the "creative" without *some* collaboration from the Media Agency, things go wrong, crucial details are missed or the intent of the campaign goals could be misunderstood.

   The answer is not to involve both parties at every step in the creative development process. The relationship between Media Agency and Creative Agency is a balancing act, because the Creative Agency needs to retain creative directorship while still inviting feedback and contextual campaign information from the Media Agency. The right balance is best struck by working with both a Media and Creative Agency that have a strong *existing* relationship. These optimum relations give success to a campaign far beyond the use of the traditional Media Agency-Creative Agency engagement; the use of the Media Plan.

As we have seen, a media plan is an important tool to align the Media Agency" buys" with the creative that needs to be developed for them. Laid out in a template that might be foreign to a new Creative Agency, a weak relationship can truly impact the timelines for the campaign. Problems that can arise from not collaborating include:

- The Creative Agency may not deliver completing ads in time, meaning a late start to the campaign
- The Media Agency could make last minute demands for creative specifications that the Creative Agency didn't plan for; the changes can lead to a late start to the campaign
- The Media Agency could add Publishers, sites and placements to the media plan at the last-minute, making the Creative Agency late on delivery, can lead to a late start of the campaign.

The best advice for all parties is to maintain a consistent contact with all stakeholders before campaign launch and during campaign delivery, to ensure that the booked advertising space is utilised effectively. If new creative can be developed within the marketing budget and media plan timelines then the process to build more creative will go ahead. [As a side note: these situations are as relevant to creative teams at creative Agencies as they might be to creative teams working within the Media Agency.]

In an ideal world, Media Agency and Creative Agency should work hand in hand through the whole campaign. Creative Agencies often request that the Media Agencies create the Media Plans with more input from the creative developer. Ideally, the workflow should be that the Creative Agency and media agency work together to come up with the creative idea and then the Media Agency would book the suitable placements for that creative execution.

Let's now look closer at the work being undertaken by the Creative Agency and what sorts of roles exist there to facilitate that work.

Marketing budget for Creative development
Visual ads, animations and images are some of the most expensive components of a digital advertising campaign. The campaign budget is set aside early on for the development of creative to the specifications of the final media plan. In turn Creative Agencies can charge hourly rates or fixed costs reflecting the output of ads, either by tallying them up or by charging based on complexity or a combination of both. Campaigns which have more ads or more complex ad functions can therefore cost a lot more and hit the campaign budget harder before the campaign has ever begun.

Since campaigns can also change over time, the need can arise for more assets and ads, so it is sensible to set aside part of the marketing budget for additional, unforeseen creative costs. In addition to this creating new ads for every new ad campaign can get very costly for the Advertiser. Over an Advertiser's lifetime, millions are spent on building ads from scratch.

Third party ad serving technology can assist in this area: the technical solution is to develop creative that utilises DCO (Dynamic Creative Optimization). We will cover this off in full detail in Chapter 3 but Creative Agencies that aim to develop DCO ads can provide a very significant saving in the long term for Advertisers looking to run numerous digital campaigns over the course of a year or multiple years. Millions can be reduced to hundreds of thousands of dollars without sacrificing creativity.

When the budget has been set aside, the Creative Agency teams can begin working on the creative for the campaign.

Roles and Responsibilities
A creative "build" requires the efforts of two distinctive roles at the Creative Agency. These roles are the designer and the

developer (or producer). The full Creative Agency's structure is formed as follows:

- The **Account Management Team**: This is the team that handles the relationship with the Advertiser directly and creates the briefs for the creative team. This team is in charge of managing expectations between the Advertiser (referred to as the client) and the creative team.

- The **Creative Team:** Formed of the Art Director and the Copywriter. The Art Director (designer) is in charge of producing the graphics and leads the designing of creative containing animation. The copywriter has the responsibility of coming up with the text (or "copy") in the ads. These roles collude to come up with the overall concept for the final creative output, "story-boarding" them for the production team to develop.

- The **Production Team:** The production team's structure varies from Agency to Agency. Some big Creative Agencies (like *Saatchi & Saatchi*) tend to outsource most of their production work to specialist "Production Shops". In general, a production team would have front-end Developers and back-end developers. Front-end developers would in charge of coding the "look-and-feel" part of the Advertiser's websites using Flash, JavaScript and HTML among other languages. The back-end Developers in charge of coding in server side languages for Advertiser websites or in complex in-ad languages like Actionscript - which we will cover off in more detail in the next few pages.

  The Developers would receive the "art" or "creative" from the creative team, have a discussion to agree on feasibility, to code and develop the finalised output which is usually a Flash file called a *.swf

In some instances, standard display campaigns are easy enough to be developed directly by the art directors in the creative team who generally have the required Flash animation skills to do the work. Here there is no need to employee the work of the production team, who might just be involved in more complex executions like Rich Media.

The creative Agency teams work together in the creation of creative for the campaign. At a high level the process is as follows (this process may differ from Agency to Agency):

1. The Account Management team solicits the campaign brief from the Advertiser
2. The Account management team receives the media plan from the Media Agency
3. The Account Management team supplies these documents to the Creative team
4. **The Creative team design the creative and build out the assets**
5. The Creative team supply the assets to the Production team
6. **The Production team author, develop and build the final functioning creative**
7. **The Production team QA the creative**
8. The Production team upload the creative to the third party ad server
9. The Production team supply the reference to the creative, to the Media Agency for trafficking

The Account Management team tend to have less engagement with the technology; it is the Creative and Production teams that undertake the production-line style processing bringing a digital display ad to life. The journey is one from Design to Development to QA (testing) and then to upload, the remainder of this section will explore the technologies that support this creative process.

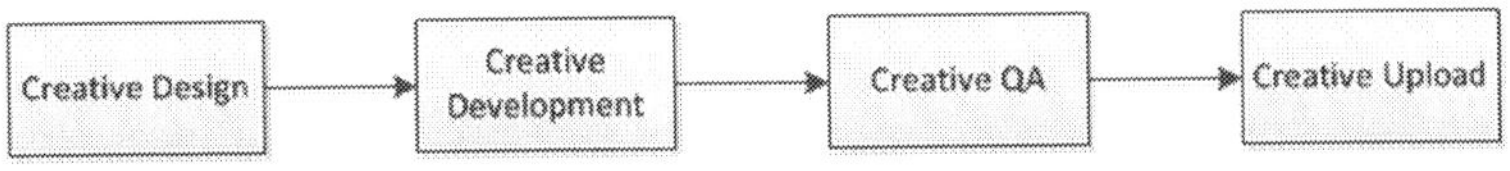

Figure 2.7: *The four crucial stages in the creation and purposing of the Creative Agency output.*

Getting the Design right

The creative team design and create the images and assets for use in the final piece of creative. Images are often created to high resolutions so that they can be used for multiple ad dimensions. Designers achieve this feat using what is referred to as vector-based design. Vector based design allows images to be scaled down or up without a loss of image quality. Designers will use programs like Adobe Photoshop to produce these assets but they are not free to develop very high quality images for all ads. As we touched on earlier, this is due to Publisher specifications and almost all Publishers across the web universally agree that standard display ads should be no more than around 40-50kb in file size. The creative designer needs to be very careful tweaking images and assets to ensure that the creative remains aesthetically pleasing while still meeting the requirements on file size.

Rich media offers designers a more liberal opportunity to include much higher resolution imagery as the constraints on file size are lifted (although these too will be subject to some upper limitations). Video creation also falls into the remit of the designer and the combinations of images, video and even high resolution imagery are the resulting creations that the designer will pass along for development or animation to the production team.

The final output of the creative development process will be one of the following file outcomes depending on what the media plan requires:

Standard Display Campaign - A minimum of one *.gif file per ad required. A maximum of one *.gif file and one *.swf file per ad required.
Rich Media Campaign - A minimum of one *.gif file and one*.swf file per ad required. A maximum of multiple files of many different types including video files.

In Chapter 3; Campaign Setup by Channel, we will look at why these precise configurations are required. For the this section we will focus on exactly what *.gif files are and what *.swf files are and how they are created.

Gif's as most readers might be aware are just ordinary images. They are used as a file type because they have a legacy for having good compression rate and pack nicely into a small file for the Creative Agency to work with and deliver. The gifs would be built by the creative team in a program such as *Photoshop*. The creative team will work on other images and drawings as well but these are not outputted to a final file. Instead they make up part of the production process known as creative authoring. It is the full process of authoring which outputs the other file type mentioned: the *.swf file.

Development and Production
The production team work with the functionality of the creative images that have been passed along by the creative team. Creative for ad campaigns is rarely a static (still) image; it has lots of moving parts, it might be animated or contain controls for interactivity. It may respond to external stimulus or information, and behave accordingly under certain conditions. The production team produce the final files, typically working inside Adobe's Flash

authoring program so that the ad contains this functionality. So what is flash authoring?

Flash authoring

As we touched on briefly in Chapter 1, *Adobe Flash* is a program that allows the creation of dynamic multimedia; typically outputting an animated file that can be played in any browser where the flash player "plugin" has been installed. With vast dominance on almost all web accessing machines (although less so in the now growing tablet and mobile spaces): Flash has been the development environment of choice for digital advertising.

The production team developers will have copy of Flash installed on their local machines and will spend many hours using it to create the desired functional effects inside the creative. The area designated for the assembly of the creative is referred to as the "stage", which displays the current "frame" that is being worked on. Frames can be layered on top of one another or become hidden and as a default the Flash animation would contain a series of frames representing the progression of the animation. Just as with an image created using *Photoshop*, the program has a selection of artistic tools, visual filters and effects. Among the most useful of these effects are "tweens" (pre-coded animation paths to change shapes or provide motion) and the availability of Actionscript.

The authoring tool also utilises a special storage area of imported images, shapes and code called the "library" which can be unique to each animation. Items in the library used in the animation are formally called "assets". Today these are the atoms of the ad serving and building world, there is no entity smaller to play with, move and transport than "assets" but today these are mostly trapped into the authoring tool and cannot be released from the cage of the resulting creative. In Chapter 3 - Dynamic Creative, we will look at how new forms of creative development are changing this.

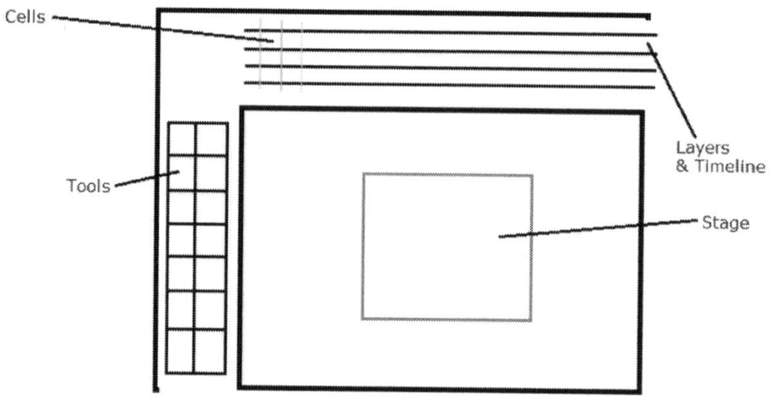

Figure 2.7.1: *A mock-up of the Flash authoring tool, the creative developer's workshop. Many hours will be spent inside this interface to compile the creative in an *.FLA file before it is published inside the same tool to a *.SWF file. The tool is very flexible allowing for the use of designer-ready tools as well as Actionscript code, which can be trigger by anything from the passage of time to the clicking of a button.*

Actionscript

Actionscript is a cousin of JavaScript, much of the code looks similar and with a good grasp of JavaScript, Actionscript is not hard to pick up. It is a very versatile language that can be used to mathematically produce images and animation rather than importing creative assets. The advantage of this method is that the overall file weight of the final creative will be reduced (to leave room for creative flare with more code or more assets).

The creative flare that Actionscript provides the developer with should be met with the objective to offer a user experience that meets what we call in the industry: "the lowest common denominator". Stolen from the pages of a high school maths textbook, Lowest Common Denominator means that creative should be developed to allow even users with the slowest computers and internet connections to have a great experience. The Publisher specifications are designed to ensure this so when building to those specifications the developer compares the specifications across all of the sites on the media plan and produces creative that adheres to the strictest guidelines. For instance; if the strictest specifications demanded a 2mb file but other publishers were more liberal, allowing file sizes up to 5mb then the developer would build the creative to a 2mb specification so that the same file could be used across all of the publishers. This is far more efficient on the creative side that creating a version for each Publisher to corresponding specifications.

On top of the Publishers demands, the developer is recommended to consider guidelines that all Publishers have missed from their specifications but do affect the user's experience with the ad. One such example is the reliance on Actionscript within the creative to "draw" objects and shapes in the creative in real-time when the user encounters the ad. Although this method reduces file weight, it can be a hefty drain on the RAM of the user's machine and slow down the performance of their browser. Such ads look outstanding on high specification computers, but as a best practice the Lowest Common Denominator of the user's own device is an important consideration.

So far we have described the design and build of the creative as a freehand operation, undertaken by the developer inside the Flash authoring tool. Third party ad servers have always given this freedom to flash developers; allowed them to use raw code and start the build process for the creative from scratch for each project, providing help files, training and manuals to assist the build. As the industry has evolved, the skills required to work with code in this manner have become ever more demanding and complex so the number of developers in the industry has shrunk while the number of designers has increased. As we have seen this has resulted in the out-sourcing of the development work to other Agencies. Another growing trend is to outsource to freelance developers.

To assist less-skilled or busier developers, the third party ad server provides assistance inside the Flash authoring tool itself by supplying pre-built templates and using small modules called "Components" to give the Flash authoring tool a direct connection to the third party ad server. This applies to all the processes we have looked at already: Design and Production, but also extends to QA and facilitates; an easy upload into the third party ad server User interface.

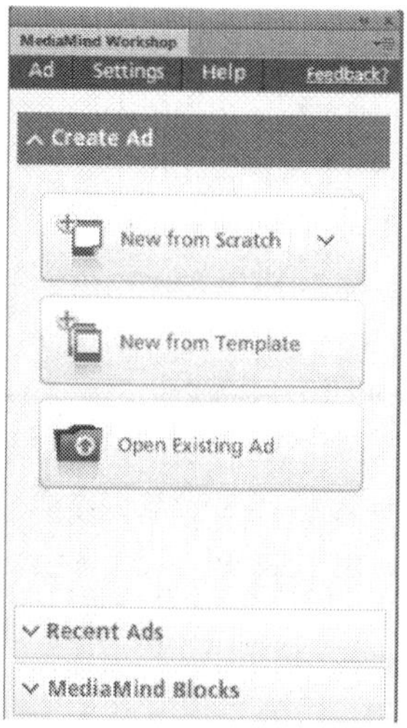

Figure 2.7.2: *Components open as a separate panel in the Flash Authoring tool and allow for the fast creation of creative to ad server specifications quickly and at scale for campaigns where creative needs to be produced in bulk. Creative producers that are already familiar with components like DG/Mediamind's workshop tool can be expected to deliver creative faster than those creative and developers that are not.*

Components, building and publishing ads

Third party ad serving providers offer a range of components to make it easier for developers to build ads. Components come in packages which are usually free to install and use. The *DG Mediamind* package is called "the workshop" and installs onto the developers machine. Updates are usually supplied every few months just like any other computer program to ensure the best creative kit is available to the developer. Among the components will be a pre-built video player as well as a pre-built data capture form. Perhaps the most useful among the components is a library of pre-designed templates (something that *DG Mediamind* refers to as "Blocks"). Loading one of these templates will unpack onto the authoring stage a near-complete Flash project. Clicking a few settings and making some adjustments allows the developer to tweak the template to match the Publisher specifications for the creative. The developer will then drag and drop the assets or images created by the design team into the same project and assemble them so that the frames of the final creative can be played through in running order.

The described project that the developer is working on is actually a file called an *.FLA file. An FLA file cannot be used outside of the Flash authoring tool but stores the designers work in the design stage and when the file is passed along to the production team, it stores their work too. When the creative has been finished, the developer can choose to "Publish" the creative which allows the Flash Authoring tool to save the file to the developer's machine as a *.SWF file. The *.SWF files are the creative output that are sent on to the next stage in the setup of the ad campaign. *.FLA files should not leave the creative developer's machine but they should be retained in case problems arise later on (more information on this can be found in Chapter 3- Rich media). *.SWF files cannot be adjusted later on without opening up the *.FLA file and choosing the "publish" option in the Flash authoring interface. FLA files are useful to keep hold of. Should a *.SWF ever be misplaced by any party, the FLA can be used to generate another copy of the *.SWF file.

Sometimes an Advertiser will run campaigns quite scarcely and to lower costs, will use and adapt old creative for future campaigns. For flexibility to use other developers and Creative Agencies the Advertiser should ensure that all files used in the creation of the creative are supplied to the Advertiser directly at the end of the development process. This includes all FLA's, SWF's, Images, Videos and Fonts. (Font's, which facilitate the design of written content in a creative actually only display that way on the developers machine because they are loaded into the FLA file separately). When the production team converts the files from FLA to SWF the fonts become embedded in the SWF so that they display correctly. If a production team were to out-source development work to a freelancer who supplied all files except the Fonts at the end of the project, were the production team wish to make adjustment to the creative by "re-publishing" the SWF from the FLA file, any text used for an uncommon font would display incorrectly. The freelancer would have to be sure to supply the font file he had used at the end of the project.

Ad storage systems (Asset Management Systems)
High performing creative production teams are those that are most organised when so many files come into play. If each creative has three files for instance, and ten different dimensions are created, in ten different languages, there are 300 files being designed and built. This doesn't take into account the more raw assets like original video files that the design team may have been working on. Clearly there is a need for intelligent file storage systems and in the world of ad development these are called Asset Management Systems.

Some parties unfamiliar with the inner workings of an ad server may be unfamiliar with the storage facilitates that it has available. The third party ad server is not designed as a storage facility for creative. Creative uploaded to the ad server cannot easily be downloaded again, and the ad server does not support the upload of file types used for development such as FLA files or PSD files (the files used by the designer in the creation of layered images in Photoshop). There is however an area called the "creative library". This is tree of folders inside the third party ad serving interface that can visualise and arrange creative before it is picked up for the trafficking process (more on trafficking in Chapter 3 - Display ad serving). The creative library can be seen as 'the drop off point' for the creative, but it is an area relatively rudimentary compared to true Asset management systems.

Asset management systems are not designed for mass ad *distribution* like the third party ad server but provide secure archiving so that historical ads can be retrieved later. These systems also provide the ability to tag or label creative in intuitive ways (which is called the application of "meta data") so that they can be easily retrieved, recovered and assembled later on. Assessment Management systems are also essential to Creative Agencies that work across many borders in many different countries.

Localisation

Big advertisers with campaigns that run in multiple countries and languages will employ one Creative Agency to produce a selection of core templates at a central point globally which is then distributed to Creative Agencies in local countries where the ad campaign will be running. This process is called "Localisation". The Assessment Management system allows for controlled storage and distribution to these local teams where the local creative designers will adjust the creative both for language and to local Publisher specifications. This way nuisances in the media plan at the local country level are not completely restricted to stringent branding guidelines but have some flexibility. The Asset Management system allows the globalised Advertiser to retain a degree of control by feeding brand guidelines through to local teams and approving localised creative to minimum brand guidelines. Global campaigns co-ordinated in this way often follow a long chain of brand guideline approval from the original global marketing team to ensure that even for the smallest Publishers; creative and brand guidelines are adhered to. Asset Management Systems are still in their infancy but help the production team to keep their desks tidy when the number of files in development escalates.

Standard QA

Once the production team have finished developing and "publishing" the *.SWF they must test it to make sure it works accordingly. This process is called "QA" (Quality Assurance) and it can be a complex undertaking if a lot of files are involved and the Advertiser wants to be very thorough about the final creative delivery. To be thorough there would be four different QA processes that would occur in the lifetime of an ad:

1. Local Machine QA by the creative producer
2. QA in the third party ad server ad preview interface
3. QA by the Publisher (to check it against the Publisher specifications)

The reason to do so many checks is that the *.SWF is being transported and embedded in an environment where there are a lot of other things going on (the Publisher website). Particularly when developing Rich Media ads, more can go wrong so a longer and a more stringent QA process is recommended. When it comes to the creation of Standard Display *.SWFs the development cycle will be much shorter and the ads far less complex. In instances where there are thousands of ads to check, step (2.) might be missed out entirely or the work out-sourced or undertaken by spot-checking the files. Typically a good creative production team will undertake the first QA check on this list.

When performing a QA the production team are checking that the creative is functioning and display as expected. On a local machine this can easily be achieved by publishing the *.swf file and viewing it in the browser window or in the authoring tool preview screen. A true QA involved checks that all the interactive functionality is working, that the ad has no excess loops or glitches and that it meets the lowest common denominator specifications for the Publisher. The most crucial check is the functionality of the ability to click, and the developer will encode this into the Actionscript of the creative. This specific script is called "the clickTag" and the third party ad server components ensure that the clickTag is always embedded in the creative from the outset of the production process behind the scenes. Despite this, the absence or incorrect coding of the clickTag is the most common reason that ads get rejected in the QA process in (2.) and this is because the clickTag code is still not standardised among the ad servers. It is a little different depending on which one gets used.

```
on (release) {getURL(clicktag, "_blank");}
```

Figure 2.7.3: *An example of a clickTag coded in Actionscript 2.0. Ad servers are very particular about the precise usage of their specific clickTag, creative which fails to include the correct clickTag code can be rejected by the ad server. This failure can cause significant delays to the strict timelines of a digital ad campaign.*

Uploading the creative

With the creative QA'd by the production team it can now be uploaded to the third party ad server. Once uploaded the creative will live in the creative library until the Media Agency assigned "trafficker" selects it for use in the setup of the ad campaign. The third party ad-server supplied components have built-in the functionality which allows the creative to upload the final, tested creative to the ad server. To do this the developer needs to have a username and password setup which will ensure the creative is uploaded to a designated private creative library. The third party ad server will issue these details to the Creative Agency with the approval of the Advertiser or Media Agency. The final creative can be uploaded as single files or in bulk. Some ad servers allow creative in several files to be zipped up in an archive file or zip file and uploaded to the third party ad server that way. The upload process causes the third party ad server to solicit a reference number. This is called an "Ad ID" or "Creative ID" and the component which facilities the upload of the creative displays this ID to the developer for their reference. The creative developer will then supply this number to the Media Agency trafficker. Some ad servers offer additional QA services, just to be sure that the creative at least meets ad server specifications (which will mean that the creative contains the specified clickTag and that it contains all the required methods that any creative built using the ad server supplied components will contain in any case).

What's in a name?

In the process of the uploading the *.SWF file, the developer should apply the same naming convention that will be used when naming and uploading all the other *.SWF files to the ad server. The best naming conventions are reached in collaboration between the developer and the Media Agency because the creative file name will eventually find its way into ad server reporting, and ad performance can be analysed by the creative file name. If a *.SWF file name is set up to contain information like "creative message", then the performance of creative using a specific message can be determined later on for example.

The role of production team ends with the uploading of the creative. The assistance of this team may be called upon at a later date to undertake the same tasks and produce further *.SWF files or adapts the existing creative by republishing.

The Creative Agency are occasionally asked to participate further in the setup of the campaign in the ad server interface itself but the role to play here is a negotiation between the role of the Media Agency trafficker and the creative control held by the creative producer. With the advent of DCO (see Chapter 3 - DCO) creative functionality and design can be controlled outside of the Flash authoring environment and in the ad server UI instead. It is the choice of the creative producer to take on more of a trafficking role to control the birth of new versions of the same creative.

Creative Inspiration

The canvas of the ad may not sound like the most glamorous of locations for the birth of a masterpiece but incredible creations are born every day the world over and these gems are increasingly recognised, adopted and copied. Such executions can win awards leading to fame for designers and production teams. The marriage of cutting edge technology and compelling artwork makes for some truly inspiring ads that put campaigns in the history books and make Agencies and Advertisers think twice about employing the most formidable creative talent. This is the reason to make a wise consideration for a Creative Agency and to harness a long term relationship with talented designers and developers.

Now that we have looked at the end to end process of creative design and production it is time to turn attention to the role of the Publishers, they are the last stakeholder we will focus on. Powerful and extremely different in the way they approach and utilise the web, they are the ally that every Advertiser quickly realises it needs to have. After all, without the ad space, there is nowhere to display the art produced by the Creative Agency and no audience to show it to.

Chapter 2 - Section 4
Publishers

- What are Publishers?
    - *Figure 2.8.1*
- How do Publishers sell their ad space?
- CPM
- CPC
- CPA
- Publisher Networks
    - *Figure 2.8.2*
    - Niche Networks
    - Blind Networks
- Publisher ad servers
    - *Figure 2.8.3*
    - Inventory
    - Publisher Specifications
    - Publisher QA
    - Publisher Ad Ops
        - Figure 2.8.4
        - Ad prioritisation
        - Frequency capping
        - Over and Under Delivery
        - Browser Targeting
- *Figure 2.8.5*
- How does Publisher reporting differ from third party reports?
- Discrepancies

What are Publishers?

The online advertising industry refers to the majority of the websites on the world wide web as Publisher websites. These are the websites that attract internet users; they are hubs for both audiences and content, often pumping vast sums of money into creating such content, to attract audiences. The audience has an experience on a Publisher website of mostly free, rich information which brings the internet alive; the illusion is that the internet somehow offers a world of information for next to zero cost. The underlying truth of course is that content of the Publisher sites costs money to create, to store, to manage and it is through the eyeballs of those audience members which generate the true value. The audience attention rests on the content, but within peripheral vision sits digital advertising where Advertisers spend vast sums of money in the hope that ads will be seen, clicked and potentially used as a conduit to make a purchase.

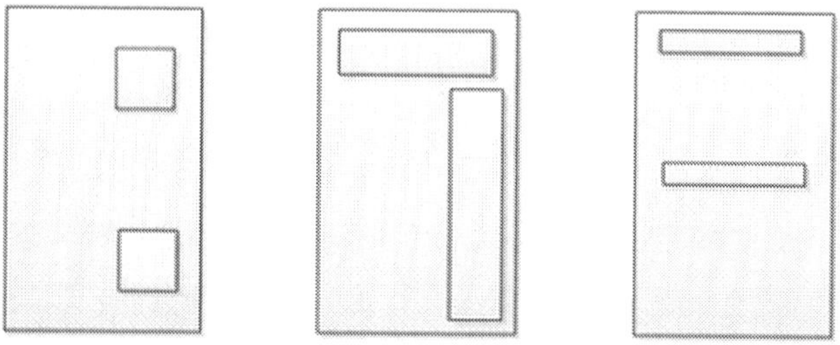

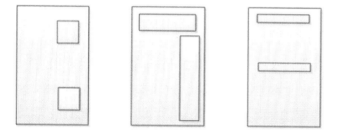

Figure 2.8.1 *: Example Publisher Pages with empty ad spots in varying sizes.*

Figure 2.8.1 shows an example of three webpages making up a very small fictional Publisher site. As a Publisher if I want to monetise my website without charging users to access these three pages then I have a total of 6 ad spots I can sell. If my Publisher site only has one user visit each page once over a period of a month then it’s safe to say that I'm not going to make any money but if my Publisher site is very popular with millions of users visiting these three pages in a month then suddenly I can sell the ad space and make money. How much ad space do I have available to sell? The answer is lots; not just 6 ad spaces, but every time the page is loaded I could show the user a new ad. If each user sees just one page and there are a million users a month then my "inventory" is a million impressions.

The catch to this is that I actually have to predict my how many users or how much traffic I will have in the future to know how much ad space I have to sell and if I want to chop up this inventory and sell it to multiple Advertisers, how can I do it? These questions are solved by Publisher-side ad serving technology. Selling off the inventory impression by impression in this way is just one of the methods Publishers utilise to sell their ad space.

How do Publishers sell their ad space?

The Publisher sells the ad space as "inventory" on to Media Agency buyers (see Chapter 2 - Agency Planning) across three core "pricing models". The models are:

1. CPM or cost per 'mille', offering a thousand ad views or "impressions" at a price. CPM reflects the value of the audience seeing the ads; the further down the purchase funnel they are, the higher value the ad space; if the ad spot is seen more often, by a less targeted audience, the lower the CPM. Also the more valuable the Publisher is perceived to be or the more niche the audience; the higher the cost to buy the space. How does a Publisher decide on the CPM pricing? This is more complex than it may sound. Prices for ad inventory vary enormously between sites, pages and Publishers. Considerations for coming to a reasonable and fair price include any variable that might influence the user's visual exposure to an ad on the final purchase with that Advertiser. This will include: the Format of the ad, the audience type that it is shown to, the total amount of traffic that the ad spot is expected to be exposed to, the total time of exposure, the strength of the content and whether the Advertiser is looking to sell directly through the ad or just conduct an exercise in branding. Beyond these considerations the pricing needs to remain competitive with other publishers. In some cases Advertiser and Agencies help Publishers to determine the final

price based on the pricing of similar ad spots in the market in the process of negotiating the cost of the inventory. CPMs are not an exact science or uniform across the web. For Agencies and Advertisers it pays to get a quote for ad spots with several different Publishers to get a good guide on a market price.

2. CPC models dominated the early internet; forcing the Advertiser to pay for clicks not the number of times the ad is seen. Clicks are more valuable because the user demonstrates some intent to engage with the ad, product or brand. But clicks do not work in favour of the Publisher; if the creative is badly designed the Publisher takes the hit by showing an ad thousands of times with no clicks. As we will see later in this section the Publisher can also track the ad's click by calculating the likelihood for a standard user to click on the ad over the course of a campaign the Publisher can determine what a good price would be to charge per click. If a Publisher can get away with serving just a few ads but expects a click for almost every user, it will be more favourable to charge on a CPC. Where CPC models exist "long tail" Publishers have been known to try and dupe the ad serving counters employing small armies of internet robot programs to mimic users clicking. Such techniques do not take into account that ad servers have filtering layers in place that do not pass fraudulent click activity onto the reporting part of the ad server.

3. The last model is CPA or cost per acquisition. The presence of a conversion tracker on the Advertiser site (supplied by either the Publisher themselves or the third party ad server) ties a conversion back to the ad and publisher which drove that conversion, this can also be extended to a lead or sign up (more details on the pathway to conversion are covered in Chapter 4). For this model a "conversion" just means triggering a conversion tag" so this can mean the completion of any specific action. Due to the flexibility of this definition

there are pricing models that exist like "CPL" (Cost Per lead) where the action of generating the lead will fire a "conversion tag" - so in this sense CPA and CPL are the same.

Running a business selling ad space is never quite as simple as three pricing models. Others which I have encountered: Fixed Price, CPM combined with a frequency cap, FOC (free of charge), CPMV (cost per visual impression), CPE (Cost per Engagement), Rev-share models (Revenue-Share), Sponsorship (a model particularly popular in the Chinese market) and a whole range of deals where online ad space is packaged with ad space for different channels such as TV. New technologies in ad serving will mean lots more options for inventory purchase in the future.

Publisher Networks

With these models in hand the Publisher can approach their the media Agency buyer or Advertiser. Publishers must monetise their websites to offset the costs of producing and maintaining content and without subscription this can only be achieved through the sale of ad inventory. The Publisher typically has a sales team that packages up the inventory based on common knowledge or, on occasion, assumptions about the audience viewing it. For instance the Autos Section of a website is typically classed as inventory suitable for middle aged men in the market to purchase a vehicle. The Publisher sales team might choose to contact Autos Advertisers (or Media Agencies representing Autos Advertisers directly) to sell, closing the deal by having the new customer sign an IO (Insertion Order).

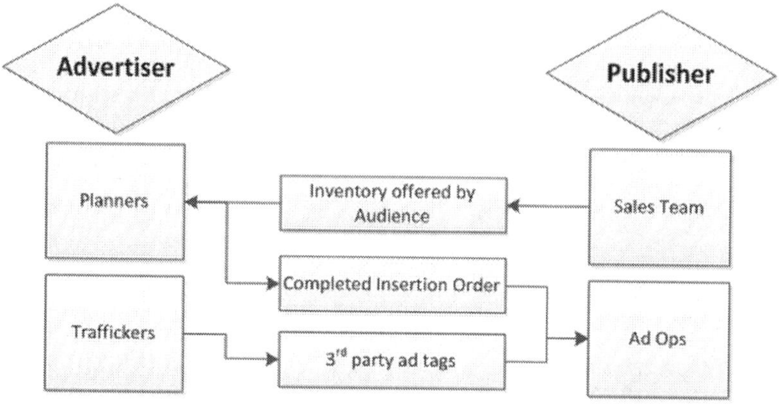

***Figure 2.8.2** : Campaign Setup Workflow between Advertiser or Media Agency and Publisher*

The completed IO is processed by a Publisher ad operations team who use a "Publisher ad server" to load ads and ad tags onto the Publisher website. A Publisher network acts as a sales and operations house for multiple Publishers, and normally only take on Publishers with a certain amount of available inventory and audiences which are in demand by Advertisers. For a Publisher, signing up to become part of a network means the security of outsourcing most of the advertising campaign operations, and in some instances contractual agreements are made to guarantee revenue.

Publisher networks hugely reduce wastage of inventory by being able to select from a greater pool of Advertisers and capping the user's exposure to a particular campaign or Advertisers messages across multiple sites. Networks having been going through big changes in the last two years, The biggest change of all has been the advent of Advertising Exchanges. Advertising Exchanges and SSPs are covered in more detail in Chapter 8 - Programmatic.

Niche Networks

A Network is a term thrown around a lot in the Publisher space. Mobile Network and Video Network are examples of Publisher Networks that are more channel specific which are becoming much more common in online advertising. Another type of network is the Affiliate Network and its complexity gives it a channel all of its own. To understand the difference briefly; Affiliate networks operate under more dynamic cost models than standard Publisher networks and offer a differentiated reach of the online media audience. As affiliation is actually considered a separate channel to both Search and Display; this book dedicates a complete section to it in Chapter 3 - Affiliates.

Blind Networks

Networks sell the available inventory but aren't always completely transparent about exactly which pages the ads will appear on or even which sites in their Publisher network they will be served on. With a blind network buy there is no way for the Advertiser to go to a page to see their ad when the campaign does go live. Only reporting will reveal the delivery statistics which is why using a third party ad server for these "buys" is essential.

The relationship between the Publisher and media buyer is facilitated through the agreement of an IO and since several Publishers will be on the Media plan for any given campaign, the job of determining exactly how much to spend with who can be determined by the relationship that the Publisher sales contact has with that Media Agency buyer. Once the relationship has been established it's time to utilise the technology to assist with the completion of the buying process.

Publisher ad servers

There are two sorts of Ad server. Firstly is the third party ad server (also known as the "Advertiser ad server" which we have been referencing to date) and secondly is "the Publisher ad server". The two are commonly confused but very few companies produce both technologies under the same branding; the exception to the rule is *DoubleClick*, offering *DFA (DART for Advertisers)* as the Advertiser ad server and *DFP (DART for Publishers)* as the Publisher ad server (and merging the two under a rebranding exercise which is taking *Google* some years to achieve).

A Publisher ad server is a platform that measures and manages the ad spaces on a Publisher web site, sites or domains. It is typically rolled out only to single sites or networks as opposed to Advertiser ad servers that have a much larger cross-Network reach. Publisher ad servers are most commonly accessed by the advertising operations team at the Network or Publisher.

Initially the Publisher ad server can be used to establish how many ad spots on the site are available to receive advertising currently and in the future. Sales houses and reps for Networks and Publishers, utilise the technology to package the available ad inventory for sale. Examples of Publisher Ad Servers include *Adtech*, *DFA* and *OpenX*.

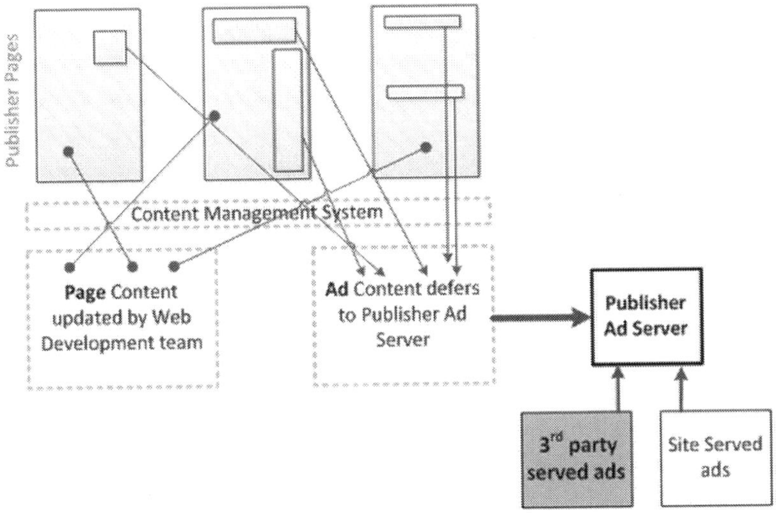

Figure 2.8.3 : *Management of Publisher Sites - Content Vs. Ads. Ads are then served by the Publisher ad server (such as DFA) being served themselves by either a locally served ad or a third party served ad.*

Inventory

Once available inventory has been sold to an Advertiser or Agency; the advertising operations team on the Publisher side awaits the details of the signed IO, including the ad tags "trafficked" from the Advertiser ad server. Sometimes ad tags are not supplied, such as in instances where Publishers have sold inventory and agreed to serve the assets directly from their Publisher ad server or domain. This is also referred to as "site serving" and, in some instances offers a lower overhead to the Advertiser while compromising on the benefits of de-duplication and the third party report verification received from the third party ad server. In 2014 in the UK, some traditional TV broadcasters continue to only site-serve "instream" video ads rather than receive third party tags (more on Instream in Chapter 3). Ads which eventually appear on Publisher pages must be built to explicit specifications so as not to inhibit the user experience on the Publisher site.

Publisher Specifications

Publishers will publicly release specifications according to which ads need to be built by the Creative Agency. Public availability ensures that there can be no excuse for a Creative Agency with the media plan in hand to develop an ad which will not be rejected by the Publisher before the campaign goes live. Available inventory is also sold under the strict conditions that the Creative Agency adheres to the published specifications. For Standard Display ads the specifications usually conform to the industry accepted specifications for Display ads, set out by the IAB (http://www.iab.net/guidelines/508676/508767/displayguidelines). The IAB advise that Publishers place restrictions on file size (40-50kb is a standard file size for a standard Display ad) as well as the number of loops that the ad is allowed to have and limitations on "automatic play" and audio volume. Specifications also clearly provide creative guidelines for the content of the ad, for its suitability on the Publisher site, as well as rules for ad dimensions (please see Chapter 3 - Display Ads and Rich Media ads for more details).

Publisher QA

At the start of the campaign setup the Publisher ad operations team will receive the ads from the Media Agency or Advertiser (either as third party ad tags or raw creative). The first step in the setup process is to undertake a period of testing called the Publisher QA process. This will involve loading the ads into a test environment which will replicate as closely as possible the onsite experience of the loading of the actual ad. This test environment, also called a "staging area" looks and acts very much like the live Publisher site but allows the Publisher to:

a. Check the ad conforms to the Publisher specifications by checking page load speed or performance, looping and sizing
b. Checking that the ad does not contain any malicious code (including malware)
c. Checking that the ad does not have a bad interaction with other elements on the page (failures of the ad to perhaps load onto the correct "layer" of the page can be over-ridden in the Publisher's CMS system).

Publisher Ad Ops
The advertising operations team load the ad tags or assets into the Publisher ad server (providing they have passed QA) and apply various rules to their delivery such the agreed geographic location of the users IP address, ad prioritisation and frequency capping. Specific ad delivery ensures the ads appear where the Advertiser has paid for them to appear. For some agreements this may not be a specific page but rather "run of network" or RON which infers a randomised delivery to any ad spots (of the matching ad dimensions) anywhere on the network of sites connected to the Publisher ad server account. This same collection of settings gives the operations team the chance to ensure that the ad is delivered only to specific browser types or to specific IP addresses (or geo locations).

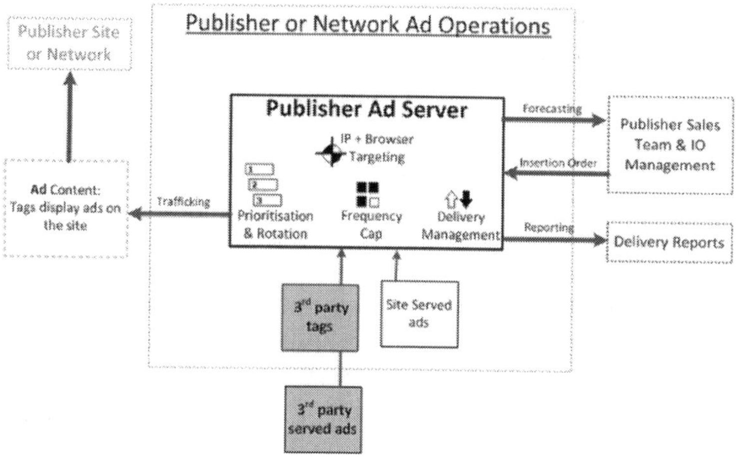

***Figure 2.8.4** : Publisher/Network Ad Operations. On the right of the diagram the Publisher team (sales and operations) liaise with the media buyer to share the available inventory and complete the purchase in advance of a particular date. This same team can access the Publisher ad server interface from their machines to determine what is available and to control what gets delivered and when.*

Ad prioritisation

A Publisher has the power to prioritise which ads to show to users based on how high a priority those ads are compared to other ads on the network. Prioritisation is used to override the delivery of ads which are worth more money to the Publisher over a shorter period of time or to show ads of a lower worth when inventory is unsold. Such ads are referred to as "house ads" and may not be ads at all but visual assets used to direct users to particular parts of the Publisher website.

Frequency capping

Frequency capping is a more powerful feature in the Publisher ad serving world than for the third party ad server. Set the frequency cap in the latter, and backup images will be displayed when the cap is reached (as the third party ad server always needs to serve something). But set the frequency cap in the Publisher ad server and upon hitting the cap, the user will be shown an ad for a completely different Advertiser; therefore more effectively capping the user exposure to a single Advertiser. Frequency caps are usually set to limit the user's exposure to just a campaign to a handful of "impressions" over a given time period of twenty four hours or less. Publishers are able to use such settings to their advantage to push more ads for a particular Advertiser over a shorter period of time. It is important therefore for the Advertiser to specify to the Publisher when booking their campaign the requirement of an effective frequency cap. Here the third party ad server plays a strong role by allowing the Advertiser to report on the effective number of times a user should see an ad in a given time period to ensure they convert, click or perform a desired function. Not enforcing a frequency cap can see the agreed purchase of inventory "burned through" in a very short period of time. Also setting the cap too long may impact the effective reach (users may not see an ad often enough) so it is an essential balancing act to set the cap correctly.

Over and Under Delivery

A Publisher ad server is supposed to be an effective tool in making sure that the number of ad spots sold to the Advertiser matches the number of ads displayed to users during the agreed time frame. Due to the complexity of many different ad campaigns (inventory lookups, page dynamics and sudden site traffic spikes as well as ad load discrepancies) a campaign can under-deliver (which is a burden to the Advertiser who is looking to display all the ads they paid for) or over-deliver (a burden on the Publisher which may see their agreed margins on sold inventory, diminish). Over and Under delivery can have knock-on effects to future booked inventory by cannibalising available space or leaving valuable gaps where there were previously booked campaigns. Contractual compromises between Publishers and Advertisers are common place and now an accepted, but still a frustrating occurrence in the planning and buying of campaigns.

Browser Targeting

Publisher ad servers have the ability to target users based on their browser and IP address. The most common use for this functionality is to ensure that the ads are being delivered to IP addresses in the country where "audience" sold to the buyer is described as being located. This ensures that users that arrive to the Publisher site from somewhere else in the world are not shown ads by Advertisers that may have little or no presence in that country.

Once the Publisher ad operations team has processed the IO and inputted the campaign details into the Publisher Ad server interface, the ad campaign will go live at the set time and the Publisher Ad Server will work to deliver the ads evenly over the given time period (or however the delivery has been setup). At the last stage in the setup of each ad, the ad operations team will include small pieces of code called "macros" which allow the Publisher ad server to track clicks and prevent ads from caching on the local or remote machines as the ads are delivered. [As a side note: caching is a concept whereby a computer will store a copy of an image to save time and bandwidth by having it load from local memory rather that pulling the information down from the server for each load. It is important to prevent this from happening with ad serving because if the trafficker makes changes to the setup of the campaign or the ad itself, the change will not appear everywhere because the historical image will still be displayed]. The mechanism used to prevent caching is a concept that exists in the third party ad server as well as the Publisher ad server. Recording clicks is also something duplicated in both systems. When the ad operations team is finished with the trafficker's ad tag it can end up looking like this (nuances of this particular method of adding macros differs among the various Publisher ad servers so this example is not accurate for all Publisher facing systems):

Before
<a href=”http://altfarm.mediaplex.com/ad/ck/1234-12345-1234-1?mpt=[CACHEBUSTER]“>
<img src=”http://altfarm.mediaplex.com/ad/bn/1234-12345-1234-1?mpt=[CACHEBUSTER]” alt=”Click Here”></a>

After
<a href=”%chttp%3a%2f%2faltfarm.mediaplex.com/ad/ck/1234-12345-1234-1?mpt%n”>
<img src=”http://altfarm.mediaplex.com/ad/bn/1234-12345-1234-1?mpt=%n” alt=”Click Here”></a>

Figure 2.8.5 *: In this example the ad ops team receives the ad tag from the Media Agency trafficker (the trafficker has sent this tag from the third party ad server Mediaplex onto the Publisher in question) The ad ops team amends the tag with a cache buster (%n) and a click tracking macro (%c) other character amendments are made to make the tag suitable for serving from the Publisher Ad server DFA*

To ensure that clicks are tracked accurately, some Publisher sites and networks include instructions in the Publisher specifications that the clickTag is coded in a particular way. We have touched the issue of clickTag inclusion the previous section in this chapter (The Creative Agency) but it is possible that the Publisher requirements regarding the use of the clickTag and the ad server requirements conflict so that it is not possible to fulfil both requirements. In this instance the Media Agency must inform the Creative Agency as to which set of specifications to build to, essentially allowing the reporting of clicks on the ad server type (the third party ad server) to overall the counting of clicks in the

Publisher ad server. When in doubt it is always recommend to build to the ad server specifications on the use of the clickTag. As the campaign gets underway, the ad servers (of both types) begin to store data and generate reporting.

How does Publisher reporting differ from third party reports?
As with the third party ad server, at the end of a campaign or during, the Publisher ad server can deliver a report to show how the ads performed and what was delivered to the user. The actual technical mechanism that counts these statistics actually counts them at slightly different times between these different ad server types (differing anywhere between one hundred and several thousand microseconds). This means that if you were to collect a delivery report from the third party ad server and compare it with the one from the Publisher ad server you are likely to see a discrepancy between the numbers. It is the role of the Publisher Ad Operations team to supply the reporting to the Media Agency (who may or may not use as a reference to optimize their campaign). The Ad Operations team can also pull the reports from the Publisher ad serving interface to check that the campaign is delivering correctly and make manual adjustments to the delivery settings to bring the actual delivery closer to the numbers promised in the IO.

Discrepancies
The IAB has created standards around acceptable limits of discrepancy (between the figures reported between different counting systems) which stand at five to ten per cent (plus or minus). Larger discrepancies can either be investigated, or the Advertiser can contractually agree with the Publisher to always pay out on the third party ad serving figures where the counting methodology of the third party ad server has been verified by the IAB. Discrepancy investigations by the support team at the third party ad server alongside the Publisher can take a long time, as the data sets need to be as comparable as possible and the

technologies may need to be tested side by side over time to uncover potential issues. The most common cause of discrepancies between Publisher and Advertiser technology is human error, where tags are implemented incorrectly or reports are pulled against the wrong tags, dates or placements, all of which are easily remedied by tighter processes and better communication between all parties involved in the campaign. Many third party ad servers will allow Publisher to have their own access to third party reporting directly so that they can keep an eye on delivery that way. Publishers accessing third party ad server reporting systems will be able to see all of the campaigns running on their network or site which may include multiple Advertisers, campaigns and Media Agencies.

Providing the ad campaign goes off without a hitch, the ads get delivered to the Publisher's audience over the agreed time frame and under the agreed conditions, the Media Agency is a step further towards meeting the advertiser's campaign goals. We have begun looking into the setup of a digital advertising campaign by examining each of the four major stakeholders and their connection to each other. The underpinning technical detail that achieves the feat of digital ad campaign delivery requires a much deeper understanding on technical detail, flushing out the work that the trafficker must undertake. Each channel is setup differently but for a third party ad server to be used to its full potential it must be used to track all channels that make up an Advertisers marketing mix.

Part B

Campaign Setup by Channel

Part B
Campaign Setup by Channel

- *Figure 2.8.6*
- How does the end to end Campaign Management workflow work?
- Billing, Electronic IO and Ad serving rates

We have looked at each of the stakeholder groups associated with an online advertising campaign and some of the technologies and processes they use in the lead up to the campaign setup, most of which occurs outside of the third party ad server. The actual process of setting up the advertising campaign and distributing the ads and creative through to the Publishers is done in a channel by channel process by logging directly into the ad server interface. But what does it mean to setup a campaign channel by channel?

Channels evolve, change and mature over time. There has been an effort on the side of the technology providers and Agencies to try and identify the properties which distinguish channels from one another and although on the surface they seem to be different, the underlying tracking technology is essentially the same. Essentially there are three types of basic tracking technology which allow for reporting in the ad server, these are impression tracking, click tracking and interaction tracking. In various combinations and implementations these trackers can be used to track advertising in all media channels but it is the properties of these channels which ad to the complexity behind the setup. The rule is that the more complex the Media Agency would like to have their data reported by the ad server, the more complex the setup needs to be.

With these complex insights it becomes easier to overcome new tracking challenges to feed advertising campaigns with more data to attain higher ROI. The features available to accomplish precision tracking in the ad server are now highly evolved and allow for vast changes from a single switch or adaptations to tracking in channels that might spring up literally overnight.

Which channels does an Advertiser need to run a digital ad campaign across to be successful? The quick answer is that there is no magic mix. Channels which have yielded the best results in the past become familiar territory to planners and buyers and are over-used, driving up the price of media (such as in the Search Channel). Constant channel experimentation is recommended since the right mix will requires an adaptable strategy.

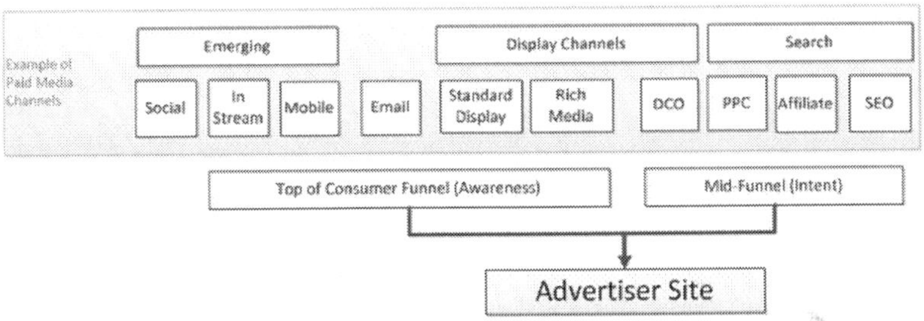

***Figure 2.8.6** : A reminder of the current state of play for the channels available to media planners and buyers on which to plan and buy inventory and drive the target audience down the purchase funnel. This example diagram is a guide rather than a rule.*

How does the end to end Campaign Management workflow work?

To review: the overall campaign workflow looks like this:

1. the Agency or Advertiser will typically make a deal with one or more Publishers for their inventory
2. the Creative Agency will build the ads.

3. The Agency/Advertiser will then take the reins themselves to manage the campaign, channel by channel.

It is on this last item that the third party ad server comes into its own; carefully tracking the whole ad campaign and with it tracking potential customers as well as delivering the ads to user machines, churning out the tracking data into reports (to understand performance) and then giving the Agency the option to adjust or optimize the campaign setup for the best return. This process is cyclical throughout the lifetime of the campaign and then the same lessons can be applied for future campaigns until the Agency/Advertiser treats the process as a KPI hitting production line, and great expertise can be born out of rinse and repeat.

Apparent exponential technology growth means that this production line changes dramatically every three years or so and therefore a hunger for learning and adaption (trial and error) makes for the most successful Advertising campaigns and the best digital media Agencies.

Billing, Electronic IO and Ad serving rates

Third party ad serving is a cost that sits on top of costs for the media space and although it is essential to keep costs down for every campaign, selecting a new ad server is not something that typically happens on campaign by campaign basis. Getting the best deal on "ad serving rates" is understandably important for all parties that have to bear the cost, but ad serving rates themselves are contractual and reviewed over a period of a few years. Ad serving rates are usually set a price on the delivery ads across the ad server reporting metric "impressions". However, compared to media costs, ad serving costs are significantly lower and for the most basic ad serving and tracking should very rarely take a sizable percentage of total campaign spend. Bolting on other technologies to improve insights, performance and to lower costs (such as DCO) will raise costs higher, but then the gains are significant. Media Agencies managing campaigns on behalf of Advertisers sometimes pass the cost of ad serving directly along to the Advertiser but this is not a rule for all Media Agencies so it pays to shop around and ask questions about ad serving rates when an Advertiser is selecting a Media Agency to work with long term.

Now that the bills are out of the way, it is time to introduce the concept of "trafficking".

Chapter 3

Ad serving Operations

Chapter 3
Ad serving Operations

- Trafficking
- The third party ad server user Interface
- User Access for campaign setup/ Permissions
    - Using multiple third party ad-servers (double-tracking)
    - *Figure 3.0.1*
    - *Figure 3.0.2*
    - The golden rule of ad serving
- How does the trafficker check the ads are working? (Setup verification using an HTTP tracer)

Trafficking

The campaign setup process is referred to as "Trafficking" and is undertaken by either:

- The Media Agency
- The Advertiser
- The third party ad server support team (outsourced)
- A specialist trafficking company (outsourced)

The emergence of specialist trafficking companies is not a new concept in the world of ad serving. Big players include *Theorem, Traffic Rich*, and *Operative*. At these organisations large numbers of technically trained staff (usually based in countries where staff can be hired at a low cost) will complete the trafficking process according to the media plan supplied by the Media Agency. These companies provide support for most of the known ad servers and can be essential for large Advertiser marketing teams who do not employ an Agency and do not have the resources to complete trafficking themselves.

The speed of the trafficking process depends on the complexity of the campaign and the experience of the "Trafficker" (the person doing the trafficking). Media plans supplied to traffickers on a Friday afternoon for a campaign live date of the weekend all too commonly experience a delay owing in part to problems such as incomplete Creative Agencies supplied creative or problems meeting Publishers specifications.

The third party ad server user Interface

The rest of this Chapter will make reference to the Trafficker using the third party ad server to setup and control the tracking of the digital ad campaign. The third party ad server has a universal user interface which can be accessed on any computer connected to the internet. Once logged into this interface the trafficker can perform the role necessary to conduct these tasks. Although the interface itself differs in look, feel and design between the third party ad servers on the market, the features available in the tracking setup for each channel are almost identical. Where such features are unique to a particular ad server, this book will make reference to such facts and indicate which third party ad server the feature is unique to. As iterated in the introduction to this book, some of these features may be universally available in all ad servers or adapted by the time this book goes to print or in the future. It is important to check with third party ad server technology companies to get the most up to date information about feature availability.

User Access for campaign setup/ Permissions

A trafficker has the appropriate access levels inside the third party ad server interface to make changes to all aspects of the campaign. It is advised for Agencies and Advertisers to be fully aware of the trafficker's access permissions before they embark on the trafficking process. It is important to be aware of what parts of the setup could be subject to human error, if tasks are completed inadequately. It is for this reason that these technologies have very specific levels of enabler permissions in place, so that some settings which may be tied directly to a fee or charge, are out of reach of inexperienced traffickers.

Now before we explore into the intricacy of each setup by channel there are two topics to touch on that apply to trafficking regardless of which channel is being tracked:

1. Double Tracking
2. Setup Verification of live ads

1. Using multiple third party ad-servers (double-tracking)

Sometimes Advertisers will employ multiple Agencies to work on a campaign by dividing the work up by the channel that they belong to (for instance some Agencies might be specialists in running Search campaigns where others usually manage Display). When these Agencies are using different third party ad servers or site serving through Publishers directly, it is important to ensure that each ad server (or the main ad server used for reporting) can track all of the online activity as clearly as possible to prevent the duplication of audiences and users.

What this means in practice is that a third party ad server will drop a third party cookie on a user when it serves them an ad (see Chapter 1). If two separate Media Agencies are reporting their campaign results back to the same Advertiser from two different ad servers, it will not be clear if they are describing the behaviour of the same individual. Furthermore it will be very difficult to describe how a user came into contact with both sets of activity over the same time period in order to distinguish which ad or Media Agency was responsible for pushing the user further down the purchase funnel.

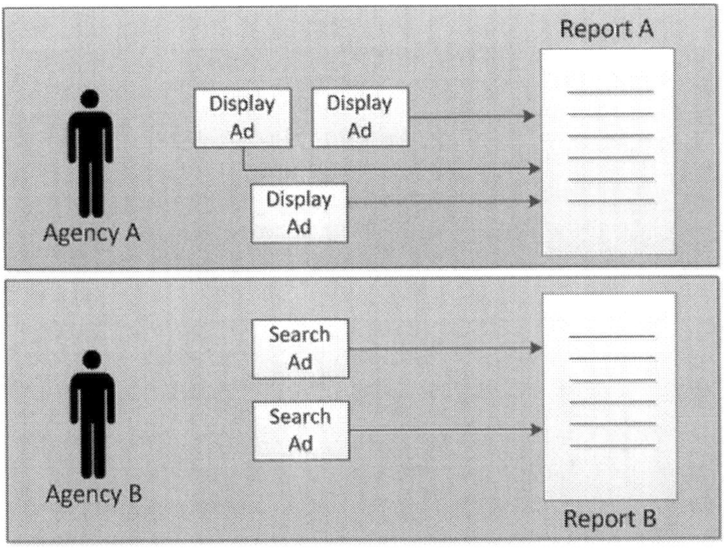

***Figure 3.0.1**: The problem at hand; working with two separate Media Agencies or at least two separate ad serving systems means that ads existing outside of the system are essentially invisible to that Agency and a true picture in single report, with a consistent methodology, does not exist. Building the results from multiple system reports is extremely challenging.*

Essentially the activity tracked in ad server A is invisible to the activity tracked in ad server B and visa-versa. On several occasions I have sat down with puzzled media planners who cannot understand why the search channel activity is being controlled by their sister media Agency, is not showing up in their standard third party ad server campaign reports. The answer is of course that the sister Agency is using a different third party ad server (or a section of the same third party ad server which is cut off from the main ad campaign tracking).

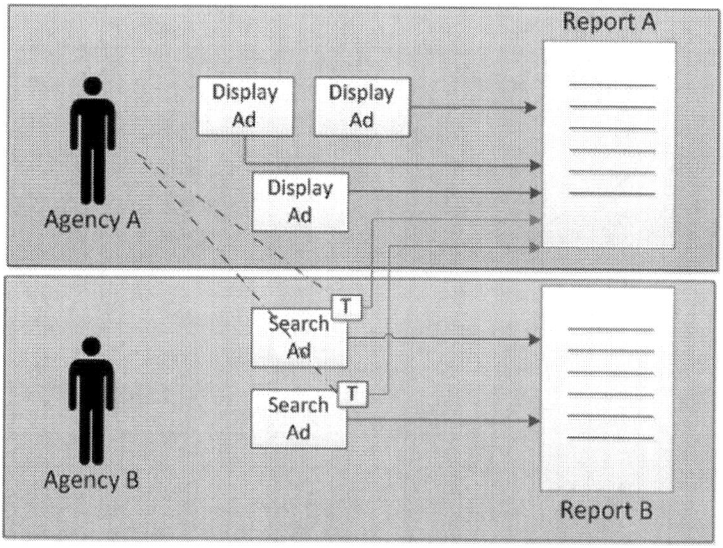

***Figure 3.0.2**: The solution: double-tracking. Cheap tracking pixel technology is generated and subsequently implemented to reveal the invisible ad activity to one of the Agencies(Agency A) who will now be in a position to represent all activity in a single report (Report A).*

To resolve this problem the traffickers will need to make sure that the ad server from which the final reports are being generated, creates extra tracking code to go into the activity being completed by the secondary ad server.

This way all the activity is tracked together (because embedded tracking code from the primary ad server in the second ad server reveals those ads so that they are recognised by the primary ad server as native ads belonging to the ad campaign).

The same should be done for Publisher served creative (the code needs to be created in the third party ad server and added to the ads when they deliver form the Publisher ad server if site-served). To allow for this tracking, the trafficker creates a series of tracking pixels in the ad server (a process we will cover in more depth in the next section). This whole process makes de-duplicated reporting available (also called "De-duplication") but there is an ad serving cost to tracking things in two systems referred to as "double-tracking".

De-duplication is a golden rule for successful ad serving; always making sure that the entire audience for all ads belonging to an Advertiser, are tracked in a single system.

Double-tracking is a more advanced concept but an everyday reality for Advertisers who have a lot of digital activity to run and a need to bring their reporting data together to make sense of it. This is one of the advantages of using a single system for data management, although a single third party ad server does the trick, new technologies are now emerging that appear to facilitate this need such as Data Management Platforms (DMPs). This issue with such a method is that the tracking methodology between two wholly different ad serving systems will cause unseen errors in the collection and measurement of the data. This is much more advanced so we will save further discussion about DMPs until Chapter 8 - Programmatic.

2. **How does the trafficker check the ads are working? (Setup verification using an HTTP tracer)**
   It is important to know once the trafficking process is complete that the ads are in place and being served as expected on Publisher pages. This can be done without having to access the reporting interface in the third party ad server and for peace of mind some Advertiser will want to be able to perform this check themselves.

An HTTP Tracer is a small program that runs alongside the browser and monitors the packets of data travelling to and from the user's browser. This is enormously useful when checking to see if code has been implemented on a page correctly. By loading the publisher page up where the ad is displayed and having the tracer open the server calls can be viewed in real time, demonstrating that tracking is indeed in place.

Most tracers are free. *Fiddler* (a standalone program) and *Firebug* (a *Firefox* add-on) are popular choices. As well as seeing if ads are clicking, redirecting and loading up parameters or other files, the tracers can note if event handlers are being fired for Rich Media ads and display variables that are being passed on to the server (for further details about setup verification please see Chapter 3 - Display ad serving).

On day one of campaign launch, the trafficker can utilise monitoring tools and then pull reports from the third party ad server to check on delivery, performance and total sales or conversions (see Chapter 4).

These are two generalised (non-channel specific) considerations for the seasoned trafficker, but the full display trafficking process lies ahead.

Chapter 3 - Section 2
Display ad serving operations

- Day in the life of the trafficker
- **Foundation Level trafficking for standard display**
    - Creating a place in the ad server to setup the campaign
        - Third party ad server hierarchy
        - *Figure 3.1*
        - Settings at Agency and Advertiser levels - Silo Capabilities
        - *Figure 3.2*
        - Settings at Agency and Advertiser levels - Sharing Capabilities
    - Structuring the campaign setup to replicate the Publishers on the media plan
        - Media Plan
        - *Figure 3.2.1*
        - Trafficking Sheets for outsource trafficking
        - Sites
    - Identify the formats of the ads and creating the placements
        - Ad Formats
            - Banner
            - Leaderboard
            - Skyscraper
            - MPU
            - Roadblock and Skins
        - Placements and Packages
        - Cost Packages
    - Assign the creative and setting rotation controls
    - Naming Conventions
        - Ad & Creative
    - Automated QA
    - Ad Preview
    - Adding the click-through URL: clickTag

        - 302 Redirects
    - Adding multiple click-through URLs
    - Ad classifications / Custom Categories and searching
- Ad Duplication
    - *Figure 3.2.2*
    - *Figure 3.2.3*
- Readying the Ads for Assignment
    - Backup gif
- Possible Placement Assignments
    - *Figure 3.2.4*
- Ad assignment
    - Multiple ads to a single placement
    - A single ad to multiple placements
    - A single ad to a single placement
    - *Figure 3.2.5*
- Adjusting the Ad Controls
    - Frequency Capping
    - Ad Rotation
    - Sequencing
    - Weighting
    - Ad Prioritization
    - Time Based
- Post Cap Gif
- The two levels of control
    - *Figure 3.2.6*
- Trafficking the Tags to the Publishers
    - Ad Tags and Tag Formats
        - *Figure 3.2.7*
    - Flighting
    - Thoroughly Checking an Ad is live
- **Intermediate level trafficking for standard display**
- How does a trafficker manage campaigns with hundreds of Ads?
    - Bulk trafficking through Excel templates
    - Bulk trafficking with Excel as the UI
        - Automated trafficking setup via ad server API

        - *Figure 3.2.7.1*
    - The JavaScript carriage capability
    - Survey vendor Code and third party scripts-in ads
        - *Figure 3.2.8*
    - Tracking but not serving
        - Is it possible that a Publisher cannot support third party ad serving?
    - *Figure 3.2.9*
    - A note on Click Commands
- Ad Replication
    - Ad Delivery and Replication
        - Server-Side Caching
    - What exactly is a tag?
- Making a bigger impact with Display Campaigns

This section runs through the trafficking process from end to end, using the Display Channel as an example. Campaigns for Mobile, Instream, Rich Media and DCO generally follow the same workflow (i.e. the creation of the Media Plan, the adding of Sites, the creation of Placements, the assignment of Ads, the additional of Ad Controls or Weighting rules and the sending of the ad tags to the Publisher). As we are focussing on the Display Channel, and the majority of the legwork is done by the trafficker, it is this role that will undertake the majority of tasks that follow.

Day in the life of the trafficker

Prior to the trafficking process, the media plan makes its way around the Media Agency, before being handed over to the designated trafficker. In an ideal world when this document is completed: the Publishers sites are listed, the number of booked impressions is highlighted against each one and the creative names are filled in to an agreed convention. Media Agencies are rarely able to bring together so much concise information in time, and more often than not will pass along the media plan to the trafficker incomplete. Media plans should come as close to a standardised document as possible (being the same document layout used in all Agencies around the world) but currently media plans come in lots of shapes and sizes. For this reason trafficking companies and some ad servers issue a template called a "trafficking sheet". The trafficking sheet is just a media plan, filled out in a specific layout and the benefit is that this allows for high speed human or machine processing.

The trafficker will work from the layout in trafficking sheet, attempting to replicate the required setup in the user interface of the third party ad server. Information missing from such a document slows down the trafficking process and ultimately the campaign. Adhering to the strict instructions coupled with the trafficking sheet to aid its completion, should be followed to the letter to keep the correct pace for the digital ad campaign delivery timeline.

The trafficker will keep to the following workflow:

Foundation-level Trafficking for Standard Display

1. Creating a place in the ad server to setup the campaign
2. Structuring the campaign setup to replicate the Publishers on the media plan
3. Identify the formats of the ads from the supplied plan and create the placements to match
4. Assign the creative to these placements and set rotation controls
5. Traffic the tags

The rest of this section will focus on this simple workflow and then look at the trafficking of more advanced media plans, showing how the trafficker can take advantage of bulk trafficking technology, working directly from excel.

<u>Intermediate-level Trafficking for Standard Display</u>

6. Bulk trafficking and 4th party tracking
7. Ad Replication
8. Making a bigger impact with Display Campaigns

1. Creating a place in the ad server to setup the campaign

The success of a campaign and the data that the third party ad server collects, not only depends on a clean and effective trafficking process and campaign setup, but also on considerations made by the trafficking team long before a campaign begins. These considerations include the organisation of all campaigns at a higher level in what is termed "the ad server hierarchy". Planning and implementing an optimum hierarchy setup will save hours of work later on.

The third party ad server hierarchy

The hierarchy of the third party ad server is regrettably not uniform across all third party ad servers and is a reason that many Media Agencies have a preferred third party ad serving provider. Switching to another ad server can mean a re-education into how the ad server hierarchy is constructed.

To review from the beginning of this book; when a trafficker first logs into the user interface of the third party ad server they will note that the whole interface is divided into Campaign Setup versus Reporting/Analytics. Some ad servers issue different access credentials to the trafficker to divide these areas up, restricting access to those that do not need to see particular parts of the interface. Should the trafficker wish to begin the process of Campaign setup, they navigate to the campaign setup section.

The first thing to note about campaign setup is that access is limited to the Advertisers and Campaigns that the trafficker has been granted permissions to both read and append. To coin a phrase from the world of computer programming, the trafficker is said to have "read and write permissions". With the correct permissions in hand, the hierarchy that the trafficker initially arrives at has many levels. Each of these levels serves a purpose.

DoubleClick (DFA) hierarchy is structured so that the highest level is called "Network", the next level down is called "Sub Network". The traditional *Atlas* hierarchy begins with the level "Company" followed by a level called "Branch" before moving down to "Client" and then to "Advertiser".

Mediamind offers an "Advertiser" and "Advertiser-Brand" level at the top of the hierarchy. Each of these folder-like entities has a rather unique set of rules. The more folders there are in a hierarchy (both horizontally - across to multiple Advertisers and vertically, down to campaign level), the more situations that a third party ad server can cater for, these include very advanced use cases.

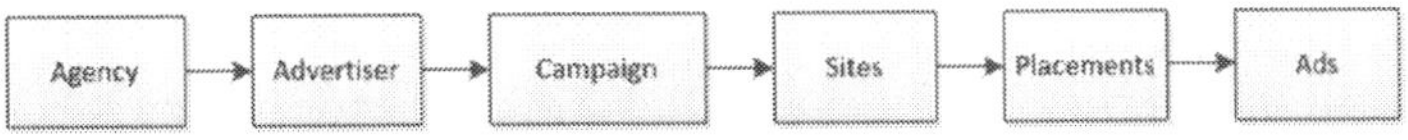

Figure 3.1 *The trafficker initially logs into the third party ad serving campaign management and setup interface and drills down into the standardised hierarchy. The very top levels of the hierarchy are commonly hidden from the trafficker so the trafficker appears to begin the journey in a folder for their own Agency displaying all the Advertisers that they manage. In turn the Advertiser folder contains all of the Campaigns that have been setup or are being managed under that Advertiser. Please note that we are focussing on the setup for Standard Display campaigns in this section. Hierarchy navigation is not completely consistent for all channels, most notably the arrangement is different for the "Search" channel..*

Settings at Agency and Advertiser levels - Silo Capabilities

The top level entities in the third party ad server interface, offer their own settings which can be applied to the folders and entities that they contain. This is useful for applying bulk settings to the hierarchy that sits below. Examples of the unique capabilities of these top level entities are as follows:

a. Allowing for the classification of the whole Advertiser into a vertical definition such as "Automobile" or "banking" (this information is fed into benchmark reporting and publicly published by the ad server on a rolling cadence - See Chapter 5 - Reporting)

b. Billing Settings (so that all activity associated with the account can be captured by the ad server billing systems and the ad server costs can be invoiced to the paying client)

c. Contact Settings (usually Publisher contact details for the distribution of ad tags - see later in this section under 'Flighting')

d. Bulk application of third party tracking or third party applications (such as the deployment of the Ad Choices badge to all ads - more detail of which is available in Chapter 7 - Retargeting)

e. Advertiser Universal settings such as Verification settings, Time Zone or location settings

This last item applies a rule to the Advertiser as a whole to establish how data should be collected, stored and processed by the ad server. The presence of these settings constricts the data collection process which informs the reporting system. In essence they act as filters and have a big impact on reporting when adjusted. Given the more complex nature of these settings they are discussed in more detail in Chapter 5 - reporting, and are omitted from this section.

Ad server hierarchies that silo their data and tracking are more common place than those that offer the alternative sharing model.

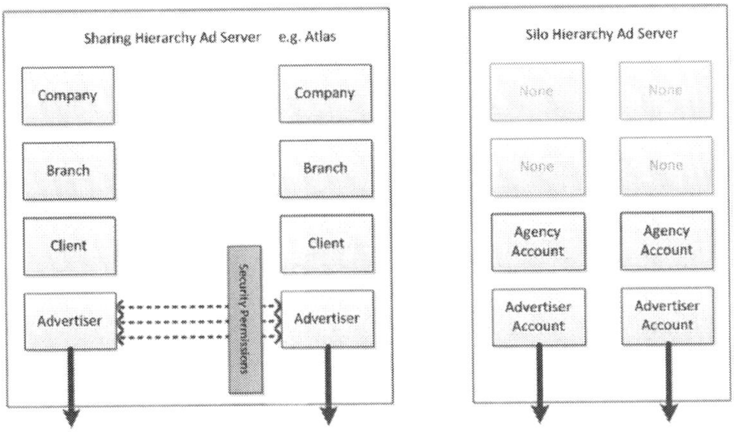

Figure 3.2 *The two types of account structure or hierarchy are shown: The Silo model and the Sharing Model. Siloed models; although more simple, are a little restrictive when big Advertisers need to extend the influence, control and counting methodology across to other Advertisers and Agencies that may be working together under a joint venture.*

Settings at Agency and Advertiser levels - Sharing Capabilities

Under the sharing model, the top of the hierarchy can be customised to share information with other top level entities. This is a feature common place in the original *Atlas* third party ad server structure and allows for campaign-collaboration between multiple Agencies and Advertisers. The most common settings which are shared utilising this 'bridge' are:

- Conversion Tags (see Chapter 4 for description; this is an alternative method of data-sharing to the more popular "piggybacking" method)

- Double Counting (Duplication and De-duplication settings) The presence of this setting allows for the tracking of channels like Natural Search (see Chapter 3 - Search)

- Threshold and Time-zone Settings (porting Silo settings across to other Advertisers that may benefit from standardising a particular setting amongst them).

Control of these shared settings and entities is given to the source entity/account. It is seen as a benefit to be able to use a single account to control settings in a remote and separate hierarchy. Issues can occur where a trafficker amends a particular setting, unaware that the adjustment affects other (seemingly disconnected) accounts. It is an important feature of the Ad Server user interface therefore, to clearly broadcast to the trafficker if any part of the hierarchy is being shared to other accounts, and precisely where that is occurring.

2. Structuring the campaign setup to replicate the Publishers on the media plan

After the trafficker has logged into the ad server user interface (and is presented with a list of all the Advertisers that they have been granted access to), the correct Advertiser folder is selected and clicked on, bringing the trafficker to a list of Campaigns that are stored under that Advertiser.

In these early rafters of the ad server hierarchy, the trafficker will not have the required permissions to created new Advertisers or Agency's. This work must be undertaken by the ad server support team (to prevent hierarchies from being crowded with new Advertisers). Owing to this, Advertisers new to Agencies or new to third party ad servers take extra days to be setup for the first time. Only once an Advertiser entity is in place, can campaigns be created within it.

Media Plan

As covered in Chapter 2, the media plan is a manufactured documentation keeping the record of all Publisher bookings for multiple Publishers within a single campaign. From the Media Agency's perspective, the Media Plan is that documentation; however "media plan" is also a third party ad server hierarchy entity in its own right. This means that the Media Agency version of the media plan needs to be processed by the trafficker (or adapted into a trafficking sheet) so that the plan is fully replicated in the ad server.

The trafficking sheet, is predominantly in a spread sheet format with each row representing the relationship between a Publisher website ad location/spot (called a "placement") and the creative/ad that is to appear in that spot. The media plan also looks much like a project plan or Gantt chart as it features a timeline which clearly demonstrates how long the ad will be assigned to the placement and displayed on the Publisher site for.

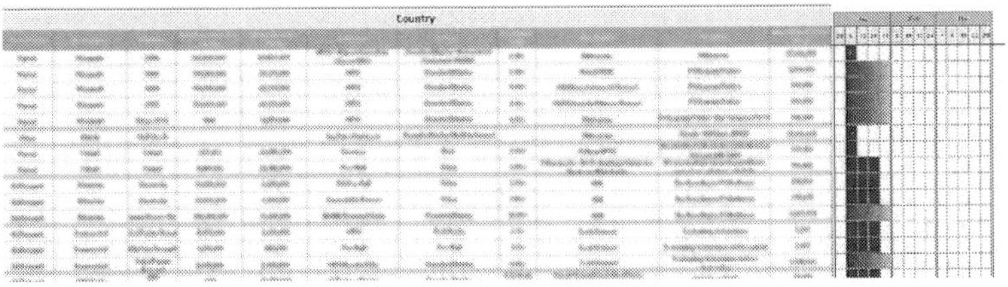

Figure 3.2.1 *A example of a media plan.*

Since physical media plans rarely look like the end result in the ad server user interface, some Media Agencies are asked to convert their media plan documentation into the "trafficking sheet" layout or template referenced at the beginning of this section. Such sheets are particularly useful because they can be fed into automated systems, which can generate the required setup without utilising the time and resource of a trafficker. Some in-agency planning tools covered off in Chapter 2 are capable of undertaking this role, side stepping the need for as much trafficking headcount on the Media Agency side. These systems (such as *Adazzle*) have an API connection with the third party ad server in order to enable such automated processes. (So as not to diverge from the core trafficking process this is explained at the end of this section under this section in *Automated and Bulk trafficking*.)

Trafficking Sheets for outsource trafficking

When outsourcing trafficking to an external trafficking company, supplying a completed trafficking sheet will be more assistive than supplying the original media plan. This is because the traffickers at these organisations will be processing the media plans of a large number of Agencies and Advertisers in a day. This requires uniformity to complete the work effectively. Agencies that do not employ traffickers and rely on account teams to construct the media plan, are responsible for completing the trafficking sheet in full or face the rejection of the documentation by the outsourced trafficker. Incomplete media plans and trafficking sheets continue to play havoc with digital campaign delivery times where such rules are not strictly enforced and rejection, due to incomplete sheets, is commonplace.

Sites

Since each row of the trafficking sheet references a particular Publisher website, this information must be replicated in the campaign setup. The trafficker begins by creating a new media plan entity and then drilling into that entity to add a new site to the media plan. A master list of all known Publisher sites appears on the screen and the trafficker makes the correct selection.

As rosy as this may sound, the master-list of all known Publisher sites is a centralised database of the third party ad server that requires regular maintenance. A universal agreement between all traffickers, ad server users and Agencies exists through the enforcement of anti-replication rules in the ad server so that only one of each site appears on the list (those sites that appear to be absent can be added upon request to the ad server support team, but this process can take a day or more and should be factored into the timelines for the campaign setup).

The duplication which realistically appears in these databases (because each master list of sites database is unique to each third party ad server) is chaotic. Some popular sites have so many names to represent them it is impossible for the trafficker to decide which one to choose. The best practice? To pick a single name and continue to use that same name every time media is booked on and ads trafficked to that website.

Why can't the site master-list be unique to each account, Agency or Advertiser? If it was, there would be far less clutter, the data would be far "cleaner" and it would take less time to setup and traffic a campaign. The reason to retain a single consolidated list is because Publishers also access the third party ad server. When Publishers access the third party ad server they see a list of all of their sites and the activity being run across them by all Agencies and Advertisers. Traffickers that select the wrong site when setting up the media plan (despite the fact that the name might look right) are inadvertently messing up Publisher-reporting from the ad server interface (as seen from a different user perspective). If the trafficker is unclear about exactly which name to use when setting up the Media plan they should contact the Publisher for that site and check in with them to see which site names listed in the ad server interface match with the media bought and listed on the plan.

A typical media plan contains upwards of one Publisher website, some big campaigns feature twenty or more sites and may also include Publisher networks (which also are selectable as ad server "site" entities when setting up the media plan). Once the Publisher and sites are selected, the foundations of the media plan are complete. The next step is to copy the trafficking sheet further which will show that each site has at least one corresponding "placement".

Placements are dependent on one piece of information above all others and that is the dimensions. Without the correct dimensions declared, ads will always be displayed incorrectly; the placement must be considered to be the frame of the ad and the ad must always fit into the frame. To get the dimensions of the placement right, the site needs to be matched up with what the Creative Agency developed. The collective name for all the creative produced to standardised sizes is called "formats" and the correct formats need identifying to proceed with an accurate trafficking setup.

3. Identify the formats of the ads and creating the placements

When Publishers decide to sell ad space they take a long hard look at the their website and establish the opportunity to package the available inventory to sell to Advertisers of Agencies. By limiting the dimensions of the ads so that across a site there are thousands of ad spots available with dimensions of type one and thousands available by dimensions of type two, there are only two total sets of dimensions and therefore only two pieces of creative that the Creative Agency needs to build. These two sizes, are referenced by the Publisher as its "available formats". Dimensions however are just a single property of what defines a format. The most basic format is an ad with dimensions 300 pixels wide by 200 pixels high but more complex properties to these dimensions (such as the ability for the ad to cast the whole screen to one side) changes the name of the format from the industry recognised "MPU" to the industry recognised "sidekick". It is the standardisation of formats for all Publishers right across the web which has made ad campaigns manageable and scalable.

Ad formats

The web is full of ad space but in major markets like the UK, the *IAB* has defined most of these spaces as being capable of occupation by "standard formats" which are represented by various creative dimensions as well as other properties as discussed. This standardisation has helped Creative Agencies to build ads faster (and more effectively). It has also helped Publishers easily monetise their inventory offerings in the wider marketplace. Ads built to the IAB specifications and dimensions of a standardised format can easily be trafficked to all sites supporting IAB approved formats, with the standardisation escalating the overall process.

As previously mentioned in Chapter 2- Creative Agencies, the *IAB* also issues guidelines for ad creation and acceptance, to maintain a good user experience on Publisher sites:

- Standard flash ads for instance are advised not to "loop" their animation more than three times (repetitive messaging inside a single piece of creative) which has been shown to deter the positive engagement of a user with a brand.
- For ads that might contain video, it is advised to keep the audio of the video muted when the ad loads, even if the Publisher permits the video to begin playing through without it having been initiated by a user (sometimes referred to as an "auto-play" as opposed to a "user initiated video play")

- High contrast colour usage and flashing imagery which may pose a risk to users with photo sensitive epilepsy have vanished
- And perhaps most famously is the strict guideline against the use of JavaScript "pop-ups" and "pop-under's" which plagued the early web and had a significantly negative impact on user experience.

Although the IAB do not get involved in the ad development process with the Creative Agencies; the Publishers themselves have adopted these guidelines into their own strict specifications so that ads containing too many loops for instance are rejected before the campaign can go live.

The use of the term "format" can be understood by considering a "pop-up" ad format. The properties of the ad are almost the same, such that when the "pop-up" format is run on any site, everyone knows what it is and how to get rid of it. This is the ad format standardisation that the IAB have been largely responsible for; bringing order to an immature internet circa 2004. Format names are one of the most important concepts to grasp before the trafficking process can begin because they are the content of the media plan or "trafficking sheet".

Banner

The banner format or 468 x 60 was very popular when it was originally coined as a standard format but today, as screens have grown in size, this format has become less and less popular because the ad itself is really too small to push a creative message and remain impactful, on a computer and remains too large for more portable devices.

Leaderboard

The leaderboard is a 728 pixels by 90 pixels ad format, and has taken the limelight away from the banner format as it increased in popularity, simply because there is more space to work with. Some Publishers offer a super leaderboard format which will typically be more than 900 pixels across and is sometimes referred to as the "masthead".

Skyscraper

The skyscraper (120 pixels by 600 pixels) remains a very popular ad size on Publisher sites although it is beginning to be overtaken in popularity by the larger "super skyscraper" at 160x600. Once again because screen sizes in non-mobile and non-tablet devices are growing, so the super skyscraper just presents more information.

MPU

The MPU (mid page unit) is the squarer sized ad format at 300 pixels by 250 pixels. Still a very popular format, the MPU is very commonly used as a space to host Rich media video as the square size lends itself nicely to building a video player. MPUs are commonly more expensive spaces as well, as they are more likely to appear closer to the top of page content as a single unit, than the Leaderboard and Skyscraper formats (which often appear multiple times on a page and are more likely to drop below the fold of the browser window).

Roadblock and Skins

A Roadblock is the name given when a Publisher page has all its ad spots taken over by the same Advertiser and ad campaign. Roadblocks consisting of two or more ads can be synced together using Rich Media (see Sync Ads), but even when unsynchronised, still offer more impact by repeating the same message multiple times on the same page. Sometimes web pages also centre all of the content of the page (more common with the major Publishers) which leave the sides or "gutters" of the page available for advertising. A "skin" is giant image or collection of images that cover these areas: also referred to as the "Wallpaper."

Perhaps we have taken something of a detour from the world of trafficking into the universe of formats but to bring the story home, each row of the trafficking sheet or media plan will list out a *placement* of a particular size, (this is the housing for the format of the creative it will be paired with and display, when the ad loads). The trafficker selects the site in the media plan in the ad server UI and is taken to a new blank screen which the trafficker will populate with all the placements under that site which appear on the media plan.

Placement & Package

Inside each site or Publisher entity in the media plan the trafficker creates a series of "placements" which will match the corresponding ad formats purchased from the Publishers in the plan. The trafficker can check the physical Publisher campaign IO to check the setup correctly matches with what was purchased and what appears on the Media plan.

Placements belonging to Publishers at the media plan level in the third party ad server interface, can be grouped together by the trafficker into "Packages" if required, so that some bulk settings can easily be applied to a large number of placements. These settings usually refer to the monetary value of the media cost of each of the placements which are *labelled* as "Costs" in the ad server. To allow for added flexibility, packages support different cost models and are the reason most traffickers decide to keep a pocket calculator handy on their desks during this portion of the trafficking process. For this reason Packages are sometimes referred to as "cost packages".

Cost Packages

The inputted information in the cost fields in a cost package is for reference purposes only and does not carry through to the Publishers themselves. This means that if the trafficker were to set the costs of a placement and then amend them later - the agreed IO cost and contract with the Publisher is not changed or broken: this information is never conveyed to the Publisher themselves. Instead it is used to calculate extra cost fields in the ad server reporting, based on information like delivery and performance statistics. For instance, the cost field can be aggregated across all of an Advertiser's campaigns running over a given period and then broken down by country to calculate the cost amount being spent in all countries across all campaigns at a set period in time. In this example the Agency or Advertiser could pull this information from the reporting section of the ad server interface (more information in Chapter 5 - Reporting)

As cost information additions are extra work for the trafficker they often omit this but then find the need to - rebuild reports manually later on to calculate these post-campaign costs. It is highly recommended therefore to include these figures during the trafficking process so that the ad server does the leg work of calculation. Some ad servers also have the option of displaying ad serving costs and Agency mark-up costs to reflect the true cost of each package to the Advertiser.

For some ad servers, placements cannot be created without first creating a package to put them in, and the media plan screen looks like a compressed version of the trafficking sheet. Here, placements are hidden inside the packages as folders and it is the packages which are assigned to the sites. Once package settings are created they are rarely changed, so packages are often hidden to the trafficker in the trafficking screens after creation (to remove clutter on the screen).

Once Publishers, Packages and Placements have been setup in the ad server interface by the trafficker, the next step is to match up the creative with the ads.

4. Assign the creative and setting rotation controls

In parallel to the trafficker setting up the campaign in the ad serving interface, the Creative Agency connects to the ad server via the supplied components in the flash authoring environment. It is here the Creative Agency can name the files that the developer supplies. A successful upload will return a confirmation message inside Flash with a unique identifier for each uploaded file.

These identifiers can then be sent on to the trafficker, who is able to retrieve the creative. In *DG/Mediamind* for instance these identifiers are called "Ad ID's". Ad ID's themselves are a poor indicator for what a creative actually looked like or where it came from, so the file-name supplied by the developer is quite significant. Despite the fact that the creative developer will supply the creative with a certain name, this name can be altered by the trafficker at the start of the trafficking process, so as to filter down effectively to reporting later on.

Naming Conventions

Creative naming conventions (as in the filenames given to the Flash creative and GIFs) can mean the difference between efficient and inefficient trafficking. Creative naming conventions should be agreed between the Creative Agency and Media Agency before the ads are created, so that when they are uploaded, the context of the files supplied is perfectly clear.

Some information that the name could be made up of might include;

- the creation date
- a brief description of the creative
- the campaign name
- the Advertiser name
- the name of the Creative Agency developer
- information about the intended location of the final ad (if known) such as placement or site information
- an indicator of some of the functionality of the creative such as "expand" for a Rich media expandable ad
- an indicator of the ad's intend KPI (such as "service signup" or "brand awareness")

Although most of these data points reference things that are added later in the campaign, such information really helps the trafficker working in the third party ad server to match the ad to the correct site, ad spot and creative folder.

Down the road the creative naming convention is also a lifesaver in reporting where the "creative name" field can be added to any kind of report revealing information about an ad that had been misplaced, or even a creative theme that was more successful than others. In many instances, the creative name can be used as quick fix where perhaps a third party ad server has reporting limitations (the naming convention is used to 'carry' creative information through to data analysts to improve campaign optimization).

To demonstrate the effectiveness of this, a creative name can be transformed from:

| ***Creative3_1108_dave***
| to
| ***Unilever_Lynx_Axe_brandawareness_summer2015_akqa_themealpha***

Any analyst reading a report containing any information about this creative will now at least have an indicator about the Advertiser and brand it is referring to owing to the references in the naming convention.

Ad & Creative

To use Creative in a campaign it must turned into the entity referred to as an "Ad". Some ad servers do this automatically, others require a couple of extra steps on the part of the trafficker to create the ads. This will be the first time that the trafficker has exposure to how the ad will look and behave, and as such, the trafficker can conduct some basic testing to ensure that the Creative Agency has built the ads to the requirements of the brief.

Automated QA

Some ad servers automatically process the creative when it arrives in from the Creative Agency. These checks for Quality Assurance (QA) check a short list of creative properties that should be present in all creative supplied, so these are standardised properties and not checks for unique functionality. Checks will include locating the presence of the clickTag, checking the creative for malicious code and ensuring that the click portions of the ad actually click when such user action is taken. Once ads have passed this automated QA they can be used for further testing by the trafficker. As a side note: some ad servers are not using machines for this process but hire teams of individuals to manually check each and every creative that passes into the ad server interface, as such the initial QA can take up to around twenty four hours before the rest of the trafficking process can be undertaken.

Ad Preview

The newly created ad can be viewed in the ad server interface as it would be displayed when live. This preview area comes close to simulating how the ad server will display that ad once it is live on the Publisher website. The preview screen allows the trafficker to visualise the finished ad for the first time, check that interactions are firing (see Chapter 3 - Rich media) and that the ad is behaving as expected. The ad can then be viewed against the backdrop of a live Publisher page. Finally, a copy of the preview can be sent to any other Advertiser or Agency contacts for final sign off (it is not common for the sign off to be a mandatory process as this has proven to slow down the trafficking process). This shared preview produces a URL which often remains live long after the campaign has ended so that it can be used as a reference to what the ad looked like. This same URL can be supplied to the Creative Agency who would store it for their own on-site creative archive records so that the creative could be re-viewed as an ad at any point in the future.

Once the trafficker is satisfied that the ad is behaving as expected it is time to add a location for the click.

The main difference between 'Creative' and 'Ad' is that a usable ad has a corresponding URL so that when the user clicks on the ad when it is on a Publisher page, the user we are redirected through to the destination designated by the trafficker.

Before moving forwards it is worth restarting this claim: A completed or "finalised" ad (as it is referred to in the *Atlas* third party ad server) is the marriage of the creative and the clickthrough URL. The trafficker of course will take the URL from the one supplied on the media plan. This is why creative is not assigned directly to placements, since creative does not carry a click-through URL.

The recommendation for any Advertiser is that the landing page (that the clickthrough URL directs to), should in some way be contextually relevant to the user. Some traffickers work with Advertiser website management teams to ensure that the clickthrough URL is dynamically populated with a value that the user may have inputted into the ad (such as zip code). The corresponding Advertiser site is then setup to process this value and amend the landing page in some way, such as by using the zip code to conduct a search and then displaying the search results specific to that zip code as the landing page. These more relevant experiences are a campaign consideration which will undoubtedly show improvements in campaign performance if set up correctly.

Adding the click-through URL: clickTag

Remember the clickTag concept from Chapter 2 - Creative Agency? As a reminder, all creative needs to be embedded with the correct clickTag by the Creative Agency to be approved for use inside the third party ad server for the campaign.

The clickTag is actually a very simple piece of technology that prevents the Creative Agency from "hard-coding" the clickthrough URL into the creative itself. Now, when a user clicks on an ad, the clickTag in the flash file queries the ad server, sending the user to the complete URL inputted by the trafficker rather than any address inputted by the creative developer.

The purpose of removing the power of the click-through URL from the creative developer and placing it instead with the Media Agency trafficker means that, should the click through URL change during the campaign, the SWF file produced by the Creative Agency does not need to be adapted and "re-published".

This time-saving functionality is one of the reasons a clickTag is so important and also means that creative can be developed and published even if the final click-through URL is not known until the day before campaign launch. It allows for the flexibility of changing a URL midway through campaign. The other primary reason for the clickTag is that without it, the 3d party ad server would not record a "click" when the user clicks on the ad - more on this in Chapter 5 - Reporting.

302 Redirects

The response delivered from the ad server back to the browser commonly carries the HTTP status code of 302 (most readers will be much more familiar with the code 404 from the same family indicating a missing web page). By comparison 302 is used to inform the user's browser that the web page has been temporarily moved. This instruction allows the ad server to use the 302 call to log an impression on the counting module component of the ad server while serving the creative or 1x1 from the content server or CDN (see Chapter 1 - Ad Serving).

Adding multiple click-through URLs

As a side-note, the big third party ad servers consider a standard flash ad to be one that contains a single piece of animation or flash file, with a single click-through URL to correspond with the click-able areas. In some instances there are:

1. multiple locations within an ad to click, directed to the same page (which is still considered a single click-through URL)

2. multiple locations within an ad to click, directed to different pages (multiple click-through URLs)

In the first instance all the clicks will be attributed to the same "clicks" bucket when reporting on a single ad, to break out which click-location inside the ad was generating the most clicks the second scenario has to be adopted (ii). For (ii) rich media technology is usually utilised so that the second click is actually a custom interaction and the supporting report either reports "other" clickthroughs as custom interactions or redefines them in a custom report as an additional set of clicks alongside the same ad.

Alongside the click-through URL, it is worth the trafficker adding extra contextual information to the ad so that the performance of that ad and others with the same properties can be generalised in the reporting interface later on.

Ad classifications / Custom Categories and searching
By converting a creative entity into an "ad" entity, new options become available, options which are available to all ads said to sit at the "ad-level" unique to the Advertiser account. One of the key options available at the ad level is the ability to add fields to the description of the 'ad' in the ad server. One of the most useful of these fields common to the big ad servers is called the "ad classification" field. This may not be a single field but multiple fields. Each ad classification field is designed to carry a new piece of information about the ad entity, with that ad, on its journey from creation through to reporting.

For instance "ad classification field 1" may contain a creative message type. If I am a big automobile Advertiser my possible creative message types might range between 1) Model awareness 2) Model interest 3) Model detail. Each ad created from a creative can be classified into one of the three types. It is up to the trafficker during the trafficking process therefore to classify the ads by appending the text written in "ad classification field 1" to suit one of these options. When the time comes to report on the performance of the ads in the ad server analytics interface it will be clear by displaying this field, which creative message was most effective regardless of other factors such as the ad size, the Publisher or if the ad contained any video for example.

Current ad serving technology offers ad classification fields as open text fields that the trafficker is in charge of updating. It is important to offer this flexibility which has been used creatively by many of the industry's problem solvers to improve the quality of reporting.

Other fields which sit at the ad level include the length and width of the creative. In older ad servers these fields also need to be manually updated by the trafficker to reflect the correct size of the creative but some accurately detect the size and populate these fields automatically. As with the ad classification field, the length and width of the ad can be added to reports to determine if ads of a particular size are better performers.

There are a whole selection of other fields which can be populated manually at the ad level and it is this data inputting task for each ad that is responsible for taking up so much of the trafficker's time.

Now that the ad has been well described in the ad server interface, any member of the Media Agency team that might go into the interface will be shown information about that ad and find it far easier to identify. The next step will address how the ad will relate to the Publishers on the media plan. This rests on ensuring that there are enough ads to go round.

Ad Duplication

In order to keep campaign costs down a minimum amount of creative will be produced by the Creative Agency; after all, what is the point in paying the Agency for a creative for each Publisher on the media plan, if the ad to be displayed will look exactly the same on every site?

In such an instance the creative is first transformed into an ad entity by the trafficker and then replicated so that each ad assigned to each Publisher's placements is unique (even if the only visually unique thing about it is the ad ID, generated unique for each ad created). Unique ad assignment is important because if the unique ad ID is analysed by itself later on for its performance, the unique properties of its assignment will reveal where it sat in the media plan and therefore which Publisher the performance could be attributed to.

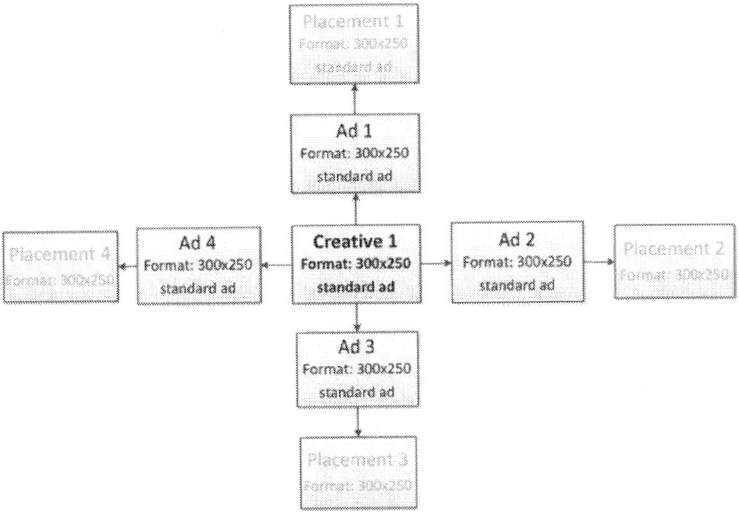

Figure 3.2.2 *making full use of an expensive Creative-Agency produced creative in a specific format. The Creative is simply duplicated as an Ad entity. In this image each ad is then unique to each Placement.*

In turn the trafficker is required to assign each ad to a single or multiple placements based on the information supplied by the Creative Agency (a creative name or ad ID) and the media plan in front of them.

It is not unheard of for the Creative Agency to side step any connection to the third party ad server entirely and just send the creative assets directly through the to the trafficker. The trafficker can log into the ad server interface and upload these files to an area within the Advertiser's "account" called the "creative library" at any time. This is the same location that the Creative Agency would upload their files to if they were using the automated upload facility available in the flash-based authoring component.

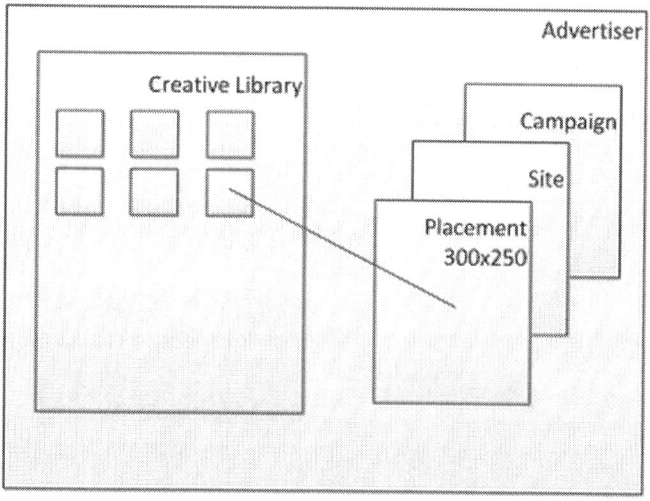

Figure 3.2.3 *The Creative library is present at the Advertiser level. Creative can be archived, arranged and stored in the creative library facility of the ad server. In the placement creation and ad assignment screens the trafficker choose the creative of the right dimensions and marry it with a corresponding placement.*

Readying the Ads for Assignment
Once ad entities have been created and the classification fields have been completed, the ads can be assigned to or coupled with a single or multiple placements. To enable the process of assignment, the placement needs to meet mandatory requirements:

- The ad has a corresponding click-through URL
- The ad is the same dimensions as the placement requires it to be (there are caveats to this for Rich Media ads)
- The ad has a fall-back display option, in case the user's browser cannot display a flash file.

The suggestion of a fall-back option is a new concept, but one worthy of further explanation:

Backup Gif

Standard ad serving and Rich Media offer a fail-safe, so that user machines or devices that do not have a flash player installed (or have an older version than the one required to play the creative) still see an ad. The fail-safe ad is a "backup gif" and must be supplied whenever a flash file is supplied by the Creative Agency. Since the third party ad server must always serve something if an ad request is received by the server, it will show the backup gif when the conditions of absent technology on the local user machine or browser are met (such as the absence of the flash player plugin).

Serving backup gifs is a more relied upon failsafe in recent times with the lack of flash support for mobile devices. In instances where a mobile-specific campaign is not setup, and a user browsers to a Publisher site intended for a PC user; an *iPad* for instance, fails to receive the flash file and a backup gif is displayed instead. Such failsafe or fall back technologies are to play a wider role in the development of ads for mobile and flash alternatives such as HTML5.

When the campaign goes live the placements should rarely be showing the backup gif since the whole point is to be showing the best possible type of creative to the end user. It is possible to monitor these occurrences from within the third party ad server reporting interface; occurrences might be confined to a single placement or Publisher which would require further investigation in conjunction with the Publisher ad ops team directly.

Possible Placement Assignments

As a rule, the assignment of ads to placements is not exclusive to the setup of 'an ad (with click through URL) with backup image'. There are other setups that can be assigned to Placements, the backup image can be assigned on its own without a better ad in place and the campaign can still go live.

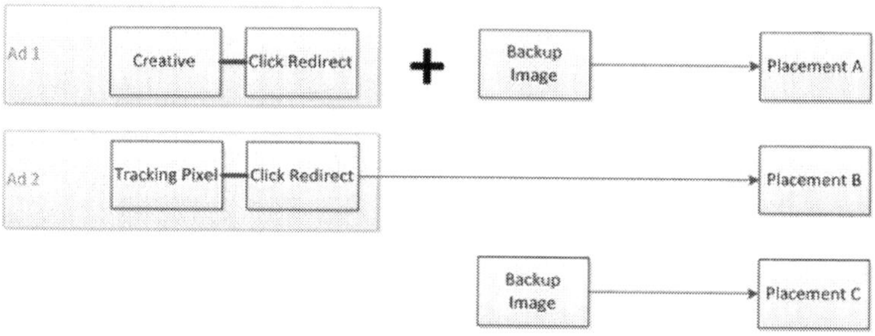

Figure 3.2.4 *So far we have discussed the setup shown below for Placement A (the ad to placement assignment for Ad 1). Placement B shows the setup for channels and sites requiring more a tracking only solution without full third party serving. This will be covered off later in this chapter under 'Tracking but not serving'*

The assignment shown for Placement C in **Figure 3.2.4** is an absolute last resort for any trafficker to have to do; to allow them to move forward with the trafficking process they may be forced to only assign a backup image to the Placement with no corresponding Flash creative as an ad. In this instance the Placement would still require that the backup gif be supplied with a click-through URL. The result is that the user will see only the most basic backup gif. This can occur when a Creative Agency fails to supply the Flash file to the correct dimensions in time but a backup image (perhaps from a previous campaign) is available for the trafficker to select from inside the ad server interface.

Ad Assignment

In **Figure 3.2.4** (assigned here to Placement A), it is now mandatory for just a single ad to be assigned to a placement. Indeed the flexibility is built into the ad server to allow for multiple ads to be assigned to a single placement and vice versa, saving the trafficker a lot of time:

Multiple ads to a single placement

A placement displays within it, an ad of the same dimensions but it is not always the same ad that is displayed. Refresh a Publisher page and the same placement might be displaying another ad by the same Advertiser with a different piece of creative. This is achieved through the manipulation of the controls on the placement level to change which ad is displayed inside the placement. By having multiple ads assigned to a placement the trafficker only needs to send a single tag to the Publisher at the end of the trafficking process. This might be supporting a whole heap of ads behind the scenes, controlled by the trafficker in the third party ad server interface.

A single ad to multiple placements

In some instances the same creative needs to be used across multiple Publishers but few ad servers are proficient in allowing traffickers to apply the same creative to multiple placements. Instead the ad server forces the trafficker to create a copy or duplicate ad before assigning it to subsequent placements with the same creative dimensions, even across multiple Publishers. The downside to this limitation is that any "changes" made to the creative (such as the creation of a new creative message or the building of a new creative entirely) mean creating a whole new ad and un-assigning the old ad across multiple instances.

A single ad to a single placement
A simple sounding assignment, but one that at scale can spell trouble for the trafficker, who may have to spend hours making the assignments in accordance with the supplied media plan.

To serve the interests of time-saving, ad servers supply tools which allow the trafficker to perform these (laborious on a large scale) tasks in a short space of time across hundreds, thousands or hundreds of thousands of ad assignments (see bulk trafficking section later in this section)

A lot of ground has been covered, so here is a summary of the trafficking process so far.

a. The trafficker has logged into the third party ad server interface and navigated from the Advertiser level down to the campaign level
b. The trafficker has set up the media plan at this level by selecting the correct sites
c. The trafficker has created placements for each of the sites
d. The trafficker has found the creative supplied by the Creative Agency and created ads from them where they do not already exist as ads
e. The trafficker has added information to the ads including click-through URLs
f. The trafficker has assigned these ads with backup images to the correct placements, following the requirements of the media plan

Figure 3.2.5 *The basic trafficking workflow undertaken by the trafficker inside the interface of the third party ad server.*

Before moving onto the last step in the basic trafficking process, as shown in **Figure 3.2.4** (traffic ad tags to Publishers), the trafficker has the option of adjusting a series of the ad controls, after which it is recommended to conduct a "QA" (quality assurance) or test the placements as "tags" before they are sent to the Publisher.

Adjusting the Ad Controls

Ad Controls are essential for placements that have more than one ad assigned to them. The placement will not be displaying all of the assigned ads at once so they must be shown in turn. Ad controls are a set of logical rules that the ad server can follow when a request is received by the server to display an ad.

Frequency Capping

By limiting the number of times a user sees a particular ad the trafficker ensures that the user is not over-exposed to the same images. When combined with "ad rotation" (definition shown below) this ensures that users only see a particular creative a set number of times (called a "frequency") over a particular period of time. Frequency capping can be applied at different levels, for the purposes of this section it can be applied at the ad level but it can also be applied to the collection of ads on a single placement (called a delivery group in *DG/Mediamind*) or even across an audience (as in the *Atlas* Ad server). Although usually seen as the feature of a Publisher ad server, frequency capping on the third party ad server allows for the controlled delivery of more expensive formats such as rich media ads, balancing format delivery to best manage advertising budget while still delivering impactful executions.

Ad Rotation

The Advertiser ad server allows the trafficker to ensure that the user is not seeing exactly the same image all of the time. By putting several images or creative into rotation on the same placement, the user has the potential to be exposed to different images and fresh content each time the same placement loads. The following describes different types of ad rotation:

Sequencing

Sequencing is the ability to storyboard a series of ads so that users that have seen the first ad in the sequence are exposed to the second in a series. Sometimes this is restricted to ads of the same dimensions and format, but ad server improvements are allowing for more flexibility in this area in the future. Sequencing uses information stored in the ad server against the user's cookie to determine which ad to show based on what ads have been delivered to them before. Sequencing is recommended for Advertiser who like to storyboard their ads, taking the user on a journey through effective creative messaging.

Weighting

Ads in rotation can be weighted so that those with a higher weighting are seen more often. Weighting is expressed as a percentage and the total weighting for all of the ads on a placement must always equal one hundred per cent. Weighting is particularly useful when optimizing a campaign to ensure better performing ads play more often.

Ad Prioritization

For some ad servers weighting can be expressed as a whole number rather than as a percentage. The lower the number, the more often it will be shown. Typically ad prioritisation exists within the band of one to one hundred. This is especially useful when ads are commonly taken out of rotation and not always replaced, if weighting was used in this situation then the new ad weights would need to be calculated each time.

Time Based

A day-part analysis of a campaign (See Chapter 5 - Advanced reports) will reveal temporal trends about best performing ads broken down hour by hour. The time based setting allows certain ads to be shown at certain times of the day. This can help significantly in avoiding "wastage" (ads being delivered to an irrelevant audience) by setting an ad to serve during quieter serving periods that perhaps costs less to serve (such as a GIF or a standard ad showing at 4am instead of a rich media ad). Also, performance may improve on different days such as at the weekend so this feature can be useful then. It is important to make a careful consideration about performance when adjusting day part delivery. Ads that fail to receive clicks at night may still be providing a hidden contribution to final sale (see Chapter 4 - Conversions).

Post Cap Gif

Some ad rotations are balanced: in which, if one ad is not shown, another is shown in the same rotation (such as with Weighting) but others like Frequency capping present situations where a user could have seen the presented ads in a finite series. Ad Servers offer the presence of an "other bucket" in this situation (also present in Targeting) where, if the ad request is made by the Publisher page and all the ads have been shown in the series, then a backup image is shown. This image is typically a GIF and is always required in such setups. Some ad servers do not force the Advertiser or Agency to upload a single backup or default image for each placement, but instead allow them to upload a universal backup image at the Advertiser level (a non-campaign-specific piece of creative) which is just shown whenever the conditions are met.

The two levels of control

Ad controls control *only* what ad is displayed in the placement. The Publisher also has such controls in their Publisher ad server as explored in Chapter 2, but the ad ops team are using these controls to choose which advertiser's placement should be displayed. This is an complex concept but vital to the understanding of ad delivery, these are facts that often need to be re-stated during a troubleshooting process because the terminology used to describe the Media Agency traffickers ad controls and the Publisher ad ops team's controls are the same. For instance there are a minimum of two frequency caps that can be set for a placement; one in the Publisher ad server and one in the third party ad server.

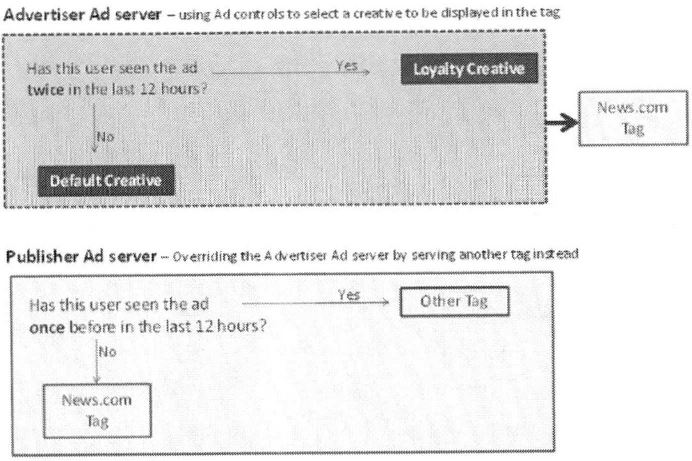

Figure 3.2.6 In the above example both the Advertiser ad server and the Publisher ad server are using frequency capping to control which ad will eventually get seen by the end user. The Advertiser Ad server can only control what goes on in the Placement (referred to in this diagram as a "tag") that it delivers to Publisher ad server. The Publisher ad server cannot change the setting inside that tag but it can choose not to serve that tag and serve another instead. In this example it doesn't matter what the trafficker on the Advertiser ad server included in the ad controls because the default creative will never get seen as long as the frequency cap in the Publisher ad server is shorter than it is on the Advertiser's side.

The ad control interface in the third party ad server is where the rules for ad delivery are managed so on top of these options is the ability to set which ad is shown to which specific type of audience.

As audiences are not a requirement for the basic setup of a display ad campaign it has been omitted from this section and added to Chapter 4 - Audiences.

After the trafficker has set the ad controls; the ad, the placement and the completed settings are ready to be used as "tags".

5. Trafficking the Tags to the Publishers

Ad Tags and Tag Formats

The creative has been turned into an ad and the ad assigned to a placement, now the "tags" can be generated and sent to the Publisher. The "ad tags" themselves are short pieces of code that simply reference the location of the ad on the third party ad server. This code is most commonly generated as JavaScript although it can also be generated as an iframe (more HTML friendly script) or for added flexibility, standard HTML.

Tags typically have a reference number located inside them which normally reflects the placement or Ad ID and are a fast track method to identify the tag for troubleshooting purposes, should problems occur later on. (The individual troubleshooting would simply take the ID and input it into a search box inside the ad server interface to locate the placement regardless of where it was located within the hierarchy).

An ad tag can be generated for each placement on the media plan within the ad server interface once the placement has been populated with ads.

```
<script src="http://bs.serving-
sys.com/BurstingPipe/adServer.bs?cn=rsb&c=28&pli=6
222360&PluID=0&w=300&h=250&ord=[timestamp]&u
cm=true&pcp=$${gmttu}$$"></script>
<noscript>
<a href="http://bs.serving-
sys.com/BurstingPipe/adServer.bs?cn=brd&FlightID=6
222360&Page=&PluID=0&Pos=2894"
target="_blank"><img src="http://bs.serving-
sys.com/BurstingPipe/adServer.bs?cn=bsr&FlightID=62
22360&Page=&PluID=0&Pos=2894&pcp=$${gmttu}$$"
border=0 width=300 height=250></a>
</noscript>
```

Figure 3.2.7 This code will render the ad inside the placement for which it has been generated when it is passed onto a web page and loaded from within a browser. It is possible to run a check on the tag on a local machine by generating the ad tag and then opening the resulting plain text file in a web browser. Both rendered image and click portions of the placement are represented in this code.

Flighting

Once ad tags have been created, the trafficker working in the third party ad server needs to get the tags to the Publisher ad server and the Publisher operations team. Few technology companies offer an integration between the Advertiser ad server and a Publisher ad server (with the most notable exception being DoubleClick) so ad tags created in the Advertiser-side technology do not automatically appear inside the Publisher technology. The ad tag code is therefore delivered to the Publisher operations team via email and the operations team receive the ad tags and put them into the Publisher ad server interface.

The third party ad server interface offers a screen at the end of the trafficking process to attach the ad tag to an email sent from the ad server directly. The trafficker inputs the contact details (email address) of the Publisher ad operations team and may attach a note, more code or other files to the email containing instructions for implementing and testing the ad tag. The instructions also contain reference information such as the placement dimensions and naming conventions, so that there is no confusion about the ad tag that is being sent.

Once the trafficker sends the tag, the third party ad server keeps a record of the send. These records are utilised by large trafficking teams on large scale display campaigns to determine which tags have already been issued. By comparing reporting data to these records later on it is possible to determine which Publishers have neglected to implement the sent tags on time.

Upon sending the tags, the Publisher ad operation team receives the ad tag to their inbox and will copy and paste the ad tag code into the technology on their side (the Publisher ad server). This will set the ad to go live in-line with the information they have received on the IO from the planner/buyer at the Media Agency or Advertiser. This information will match the line item on the Media Agencies in-house media plan. If the ad tag is not received; some ad servers offer Publishers the flexibility to log into the third party ad server directly to re-download the ad tags for their sites. In doing so the Publisher ad ops team will have third party ad server login credentials, with different permissions to the trafficker.

Thoroughly Checking an Ad is live

Once an ad tag is put into a Publisher ad server and is live on a Publisher site, traffickers are keen to check how the ads look in the live environment on the site. Some Publishers return screenshots or send over the URL of a page back to the trafficker where the live ad can be seen. To check a correct implementation it is advised that the trafficker load the Publisher page in question while running an HTTP tracer program on their local machine. Programs like *Fiddler* or *HTTP Watch* are suitable to reveal if the correct tag is loading onto the page (by cross-referencing the Placement ID) and that both the loading of the image (or flash file) and use of the click-through URL are generating real-time server calls. Server calls which make requests referencing the placement or ad ID usually clarify that the right placement is on the page. If the wrong placement ID has been implemented onto the page the ad server reporting will not report back accurate results and the Publisher ad ops team should fix the tag on the page with the correct placement ID.

In addition to running these manual checks, the trafficker can use the third party ad server to verify actual delivery to the right user audience such as users in the correct geography. This is called Verification and further information about this and the monitoring of delivery information is available in the third party ad server reporting interface (see Chapter 5).

Once the correct tags are live on the Publisher pages the campaign setup is complete and the trafficker will access the reporting interface on the third party ad server to begin the process of Optimization (see Chapter 6).

7. How does a trafficker manage campaigns with hundreds of Ads?

Bulk trafficking through *Excel* templates

With thousands of ads, placements, sites and many assignments, un-assignments and amendments to be made, bulk trafficking tools are indispensable for the trafficker. The trafficker can download the ad server's trafficking sheet from the media plan level to a local computer and fill it in row by row before uploading it back to the ad server via an error checking and queuing system. The trafficking sheet is designed so that it can be read directly by a machine. At any time the full media plan can be exported from the ad server interface and appended before being re-uploaded so that bulk changes can be made. The ad server makes a log of changes at scale by specific traffickers so that if multiple traffickers are working on the same media plan at any time, there is little confusion about which trafficker made the last changes to the media plan.

Bulk trafficking with *Excel* as the UI

Some tools like the *Atlas* 'Media Add-in' mean the trafficker can complete almost every task of the trafficking process from inside Excel including exploring the ad server hierarchy. Like the Flash components supplied by the ad server to the Creative Agency developers; an additional piece of software can be downloaded from the ad server and installed locally on the trafficker's machine to enable the use of the bulk software. Essentially a skin or plugin accessed directly from the excel interface, permits the execution of various operations when trafficker credentials are verified. The gain in operational scaling is very apparent but the downside is that the interface of an excel spread sheet is a tenuous replacement for the usable designs of ad serving interfaces. As of publication, the marriage of a true bulk trafficking solution and an ad serving interface has yet to announce their effective engagement beyond a spread sheet-style design.

Automated trafficking setup via ad server API
It may seem strange that it is possible to transform Excel into a user interface for the ad server, but as long as a connection is established with the correct user credentials, excel and other programs can be used to replicate the actual ad serving interface. This is made possible due to the ad server "trafficking API".

An API (or Application Programming Interface) allows an ad, web page or program at a distance (external to the server in question) to request only a select piece of information from the server and have that information returned in order to fulfill a function.

Services that offer an API quickly ensure the propagation of their information around the internet and soon become indispensable to the workings of the web. Take for instance *Facebook* which allows developers to sign up to their API to retrieve information about users (with their consent). Or *Google Maps* which allows anyone who has requested a free developer 'key' (a type of password) to display a *Google* map based on the longitude and latitude information supplied, passing the developer key in a request to the server directly.

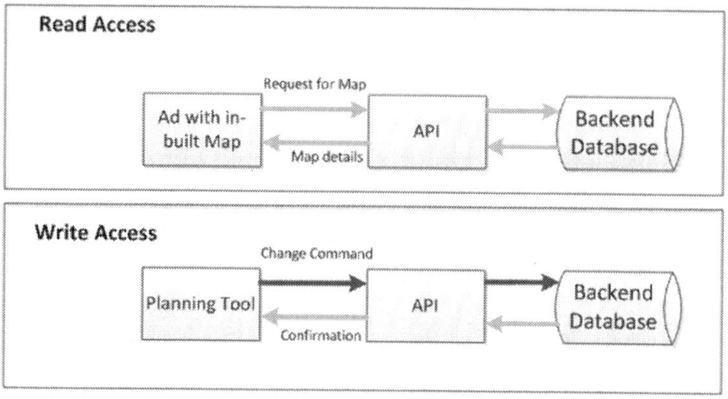

Figure 3.2.7.1 With just read access an Ad or any other application can make a request to the backend database via the gateway of the API. The Request for Map is joined by the API key which grants access to the backend database. The backend database processes the request and if the API command is correct and the key is accepted, it returns the required details which in this instance are the details of what the map looks like which are subsequently shown in the ad. With write access an application such as a Media Agency planning tool can issue a command to the ad server database via the API such as to have a new placement trafficked. If the API key and the command are accepted then the database makes the amendment to the setup of the ad campaign and returns a confirmation to the planning tool that the task has been completed.

As **Figure 3.2.7.1** shows, with an ad server trafficking API, the external program can issue commands to the ad server from a distance to request that an action be executed or for the submission of information into a particular section of the hierarchy. This two-way functionality of both affecting setup in the ad server media plan and returning confirmation of the changes is a step further than the "read-only" access of public APIs offered by *Google* and *Facebook* in the previous examples.

The ad server trafficking API supports a multitude of commands and can return useful pieces of information about the campaign setup. This is how it is possible for a remote copy of excel to make requests to the ad server and fetch a current copy of the media plan without requiring the trafficker to leave the trafficking interface of the excel environment. In the future, strong ad server APIs supporting all functions of the ad server will permit application developers to create simplified user interfaces and dashboards which could be installed on mobile devices allowing traffickers to traffic, monitor and control campaigns on the move. For the time being trafficking APIs are predominantly utilized by in-Agency planning tools and tools like *iDesk* (as touched on in Chapter 2 - Agency Planning).The media plan created in *iDesk* makes the relevant calls to the ad server using it's API and entities such as the placements can be created from afar. In turn the ad server can return information such as a list of available "site" entities so that *iDesk* can select one and return that request back to the ad server: trafficking at a distance.

Other API capabilities exist to support the ad server capabilities such as for reporting. More details can be found in Chapter 5 - Reporting.

The JavaScript carriage capability

Another of the more common advanced capabilities of the standard display ad is its capability to launch additional code on the condition of certain JavaScript based activities resulting from real-time user action. Such activity may include the JavaScript parameter of "Unload"; whereby on the condition of the ad being abandoned (such as by leaving the page or closing the browser) the JavaScript can in turn launch an on-screen survey. This particular example is the delivery of what is referred to as "Survey Vendor code", but there are many actions that can be taken, allowing the trafficker to manipulate the JavaScript capabilities from the comfort of the ad server interface.

Survey vendor code and third party scripts-in ads

Survey Vendors emerged in the world of ad serving technology because true Advertising effectiveness is a subjective concept. Although an ad may have performed well according to ad server reporting (receiving clicks, interactions and even conversions (see Chapter 4) it is still not one hundred per cent clear if users were influenced by the ad itself to perform these actions. It is entirely possible that if the ad was shown in the right place at the right time, that that ad merely acts as a convenient pathway for the user to complete an action they had every intention of doing anyway.

Furthermore it is not clear if the message inside the creative itself had an impact on the user. Since we cannot see what is going on in a user's head, collecting this information requires some qualitative surveys to be conducted.

Research companies or Survey Vendors such as *Dynamic Logic* create short surveys that can be launched as part of the delivery of the ad, to collect this information from users. When the ad loads, is clicked or closed a small survey loads onto the screen. This survey overlays the rest of the information on the Publisher page and is designed to quickly ask the user about ad effectiveness, without disrupting the user experience.

This information, once submitted in the online-form, is sent on to the Survey Vendor's database on an external server. In order for the survey to load up in the first place, a small piece of code needs to be provided by the survey vendor to the trafficker long before the campaign goes live. The trafficker then loads this code into the third party ad server interface at the ad level when trafficking the campaign (adding the code to which ads it is required to fire off against). Pre-created fields in the ad server interface allow for these codes to be fired during one or more of the JavaScript activities on the placement.

To setup a Survey from the outset of the campaign, the Agency/Advertiser needs to reach out to the survey vendor when the campaign is being devised and the supplied code by the vendor should deliver some unique identifier in its return ad-call that will allow the data from the vendor to be tied to the data from the ad server later on. A Placement ID is suitable for this purpose. Therefore an optimal setup process would be:

a. The Placements should be created by the trafficker first
b. Then the trafficker should export the media plan in the bulk trafficking tool (displaying all of the Placement IDs) and send it along to the survey vendor
c. The code corresponding to each of the placements should be created in the Survey Vendor interface (not found inside the ad server), with a matching Placement ID
d. The survey vendor should update the "survey vendor" field in the supplied exported media plan before sending it back the trafficker
e. The trafficker should ensure that the code is set to fire at the right time (by either adding the information in the media plan and then uploading the media plan back into the ad server interface, or by making the necessary adjustments on each placement once the media plan has been uploaded).

The various nuances of the trafficking workflow are designed to facilitate clever additions to the process, such as the addition of survey vendor code. The availability of the bulk media plan functionality makes it much easier for the trafficker to work with these additional trafficking requirements.

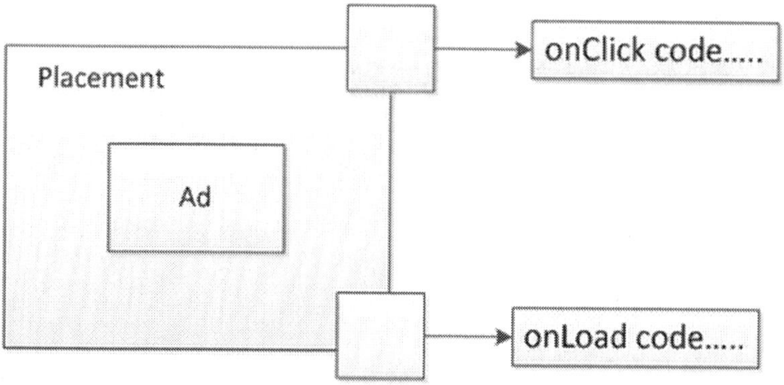

Figure 3.2.8 Placements and Ads all have the capability to support or provide a "piggyback" to other blocks of code. These codes can be added by the trafficker during the trafficking process and appear to the end user as seamless functionality to the ad, if they are seen at all. These methods allow ads to act as channels which can pour information to more external sources. Publishers often keep a keen eye on ads for this exact purpose because ads pouring information to other networks can tarnish the Publisher's own valuable audience - a process known darkly industry-side as "data leakage" (see Glossary).

We have touched on the ability of the ad or the placement to support the "piggybacking" of additional code (albeit the survey vendor code for now). The same fields in the ad server interface which allows a JavaScript activity such as "onLoad" to be selected on the ad level, before firing additional code, exist at the ad level, placement level and higher up levels such as the campaign level. The campaign level allows the same code to be applied to all ads in the campaign. The Advertiser level allows the code to be applied to all ads in all campaigns for the whole Advertiser. If the trafficker pastes code in from a different system, like Survey Vendor code (called "third party code" or "4th party code") into these higher levels of the hierarchy, their use allows for the bulk implementation of such code, feeding the fields in the entities that trail below. This paves the way for a concept touched on in Chapter 1 - Double ad tracking.

Recalling from Chapter 1; double ad tracking means that a single ad server can have a view over activity running in more than one ad server. This is made possible because the ad tag code from one ad server is exported and implemented by the trafficker into the same third party code fields that would be used for survey vendor code.

It would not make sense to have two whole pieces of creative from a both ad servers appear in the same ad spot at the same time, so the trafficker in the lesser ad server needs only to supply the most basic type of tracking. The creative will then just be served from the one system, but the reporting of the activity will appear in both. In this sense an ad server's primary function is to serve the ad but in a close second is the function of tracking. This same method can be used when a Publisher decides to serve the creative from their own system.

Tracking but not serving

It is quite common in display ad serving to have a fragmented media plan; where the trafficker has creative for most of the setup but must use "tracking pixels" for the rest. The creative is usually served from the third party ad server directly, but some Publishers 'do not support third party ad serving' and instead permitting the Media Agency trafficker to supply a tracking pixel (for each of the Publisher-hosted ads) so that the trafficker can be sure that the activity is tracked or represented in the third party ad server.

> **Is it possible that a Publisher cannot support third party ad serving?**
> Publishers have less to gain from the use of a third party ad server in a campaign than Advertisers or Agencies do. Implementation of code requires operational resources, extra training and ideally the presence of a Publisher ad server. These may not be available to small scale Publishers or Publishers with content housed in very unique environments (such as the emergence of ads in mobile apps created without a standardised SDK - see Chapter 3 - Mobile Ad serving for more information). Clashes between code supplied from an external system could in theory also conflict with the Publisher page, particularly if there is a poor CMS in place. However given the demands of Advertisers to utilise third party systems to verify delivery and performance, poor systems in place on the Publisher side are bad excuses for not offering total transparency. Publishers which refuse the use of third party ad serving tags are risking deeper investigation by the wider community to uncover reasoning to avoid transparency.

Permanent tracking pixels need to be created in the ad server by the trafficker and their ad tags sent and inserted into creative (served by the Publisher directly by the Publisher ad ops team, from the Publisher ad server). This brings the counting methodology as close as possible to the third party method. In this instance the trafficker can still send the ad tags to the Publisher at the end of the trafficking process, but since it is not strictly displaying the ad, the code looks a little different. Some ad servers refer to this code package as a "Tracking Placement" and it is made up of a tiny 1x1 tracking pixel image and a single line click through URL (a click redirect). The trafficker will need to create one for each corresponding item on the Media plan, where the ads or assets are being served by any system other than the third party ad server. To keep things nice and tidy, the tracking placement should be treated like any other placement in the platform and be assigned to the correct site. Given the nature of tracking placements it doesn't make sense to add the "ad control" options to these entities.

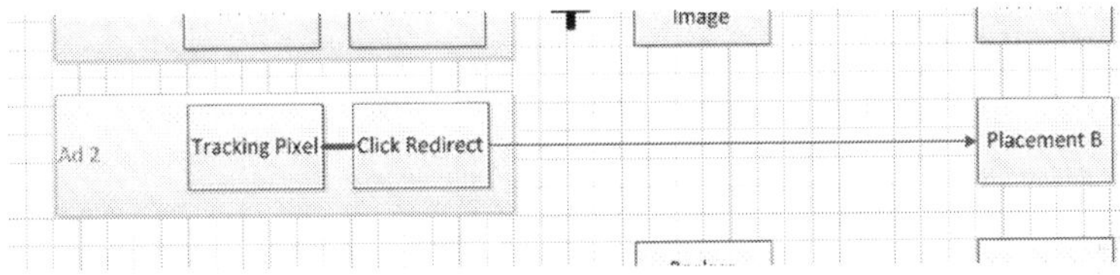

Figure 3.2.9 another ad assignment option for the trafficker: assign a tracking placement (a tracking pixel with click redirect) to a placement. The flexibility of a tracking placement allows the tag to be trafficked to a second system where the actual ad or creative might be hosted. When the tag for the tracking placement is trafficked it is consider to be a "4th party pixel" in any third party system.

A note on Click Commands

DFA (the *DoubleClick* third party ad server) allows traffickers to create multiple "click commands" (Click Commands are just click re-redirects) but crucially allows the assignment of many of these entities to a single placement. When these tags are trafficked to the Publisher, the Publisher has the freedom to choose just one of these click commands from the supplied tag (where the Publisher may be site-serving the actual ad). As each of the click commands might point to a different landing page the Publisher can use the power of the Publisher ad server to rotate the click commands across the site-served creative for the purposes of optimization and landing page testing.

Since all of the click commands are assigned to the same placement, *DFA* records these "click" metrics under the same placement in ad server reporting. This gives the Publisher more freedom in determining which ad to display while site serving while still counting clicks in the correct place in the *DFA* platform. Ad servers which limit the creation of one click command to one tracking pixel in a tracking placement format do not force the Publisher to use both image (pixel) and click portions of the tag. The tag will work and the metrics will count even if only the click portion or just the pixel portion is used.

With the combination of these more advanced tactics in the trafficker's arsenal, most display campaigns can be setup and managed. Before closing out this section let's focus briefly on the mechanisms at work here which are useful in determining why an ad that may have been trafficked already and implemented onto a Publisher site is either not reporting or displaying as expected.

7. Ad Replication

Ad Delivery and Replication

To get an ad to deliver all over the world requires several technologies working together. The ad server itself will normally do the complex calculations and decision making about which ad to display as well as storing the images and flash ready for distribution, but getting the ads from the ad server and its hardware to billions of pages (and eyeballs) requires the support of a CDN or content delivery network (See Chapter 1).

The trafficker has the correct access to the ad server interface to swap in and out new ads even when the campaign is live but this action does not have an immediate result. The time it takes to swap a creative over (or replacing an old ad with a new one) and have it appear all over the world in a live campaign is referred to as "ad replication", and for far reaching global distribution campaigns should take no longer than around fifteen minutes (after saving the changes in the campaign management screens of the ad server).

For those looking to check that such changes are now "live" it is possible to go to a Publisher page and refresh it until they see the change live, but it is recommended to clear browser cache and cookies (and waiting fifteen minutes) before refreshing the page. This ensures the old ad has not been cached locally and removes the restrictions placed by frequency capping at the Advertiser or Publisher ad server.

Finally if the ad is still not displayed, it is wise to check the settings for IP (geographical) targeting since a tester sitting in the wrong geography will not see the correct creative if the campaign is working as expected (more on this in Chapter 4 - Audiences).

Server-Side Caching

In addition to this there is a caching mechanism on the ad server itself, meaning that if a tag that looks the same is served frequently, the ad server will make and store its own temporary copy for faster delivery. To eradicate the temporary copy in the ad server, most tags include a string or token in the pixel portion of the tag code itself. This string is simply a random number that changes every time the ad is served out, and since the random number is never repeated, the cache on the ad server is eradicated. The string is normally represented with something that looks like:

"***?rand=RANDOMNUMBER***"

When the trafficker is piggybacking a 4th party tag, the instructions in the third party ad server will explain that RANDOMNUMBER in capital letters can be over-written with a system-friendly macro which, when the pixel is fired, will insert a random number in automatically. Inside *DG Mediamind* this macro is: %RAND%

What exactly is a tag?

When the tag code is sent onto the Publisher the implemented tags are conduits for information being sent to the ad server for reporting and creative delivery purposes but the tag itself is a very small a light piece of code and stand-alone it does not contain all the code it needs to perform certain functions. As such, the tag calls upon one or more JavaScript libraries which contain more complex commands (and are a touch heavier in terms of file size). The construct of these libraries is unique to each ad server and some make better use of various coding methods than others to ensure a slicker and smoother experience with say; video ads, for instance. Understanding how these parts work, detracts from the more immediate focus of this text but third party ad serving providers will be able to supply this information. The important thing to note is that more complex capabilities are only possible through the enabling of these libraries, therefore any tags implemented in a more simple tag format such as a simple tracking placement as opposed to a fully-fledged JavaScript tag will have certain functions missing (including viewability).

9. Making a bigger impact with Display Campaigns

The best advice to improve knowledge and skills further in standard display is to undertake some trafficking in the ad serving interface itself. Most third party ad servers provide a wealth of training materials and support to guide the trafficker through the campaign management process in their specific system and will be happy to assist in the setup of a few test campaigns for training purposes. The good news is that all the concepts covered are common to all the big third party ad servers, those absent features in one system will soon crop in the others, play a game of catch-up with one another to provide more and more standardised features.

The next section will look at the Rich Media channel. Rich Media is an advanced form of display advertising, designed to engage and attract the user. It is especially popular with big brand Advertisers and is the gateway to Video ad serving. Due to its powerful impact Rich Media is likely to see a "come-back" in the next few years, emerging in innovative ways through video players, mobile and through more advanced forms of reality augmentation, but its technical setup is in some ways a little more challenging than the setup for standard display ads.

Chapter 3 - Section 3
Rich Media

- What is Rich Media?
- Why use Rich Media?
- Core Formats
    - Expandable ads
    - *Figure 3.3.1a*
    - Floating ads
    - *Figure 3.3.1b*
    - Video ads
    - *Figure 3.3.1c*
    - Pushdown and Sidekick
    - *Figure 3.3.1d*
    - Data Capture
    - Home Page Takeovers, Wallpaper and Page Skins
    - *Figure 3.3.1e*
    - *Figure 3.3.1f*
    - Polling
    - State Based ads
    - Local Connection ads or Sync Ads
    - *Figure 3.3.1g*
    - Print ads
- Standardisation and Publisher certification
- From the top: Building Rich Media ads
    - Training the creative developer
    - Two schools of Rich Media specs: Publisher and Ad server
    - Parent and Child files - the polite load
    - Expansions and Floating -the declaration of state
    - Interaction tracking: Default and Custom Events
    - Interactions as additional clicks
    - Building Custom Rich Media ads
- Qaing and Testing Rich Media ads
- Trafficking Rich Media ads

- Publisher Troubleshooting
- Rich Media for Mobile & Rich Media for Instream

The following section looks in depth at the full campaign setup process for Rich Media ads which are served and tracked by the third party ad server and trafficked to Publisher websites.

Strictly speaking Rich Media is not a channel but a subset or evolution of Standard Display ads. This means that a large margin of the trafficking process covered in the section on Standard Display also applies to Rich Media. With this new territory comes new terminology and concepts that begin right at the moment of creative conception and trickle down to the delivery of the ad in the user's browser.

What is Rich Media?
Technically Rich Media refers to an ad that contains one or more of the following features:

- Video
- Expandable panels
- Interaction Tracking
- Polite Loading
- Floating Effect*

(* Floating ads are sometimes referred to as "Out of Banner "ads, although this phrase has also been coined to describe all types of Rich Media ads in some ad servers)

Why use Rich Media?
As outlined at the tail end of the last section, Rich Media offers Advertisers the chance to make more of an impact with creative that is more engaging for the user than standard Display ads or Search ads. Rich Media is really collaboration between the third party ad server and the Publisher. Implanting a Rich Media ad onto a Publisher website is going to draw user attention towards the ad due to the nature of its animations, in doing so it is

possible for ads to be created that completely hide the Publisher's content. This is where the phrase "out of banner" comes from as some Rich Media ads literally spill out of the space they were designed to fit inside.

Since Rich Media causes a longer loading time on a page and potentially could conflict with the Publisher's own content and code, the Publisher must be on-board to accept Rich Media before it is inserted into the Media plan for an Advertiser campaign. Typically a Publisher will offer Rich Media at a higher CPM to Advertisers and Agencies for specific ad spots. Ads occupying these spots will need to adhere to set of specifications defined by the Publisher which will have been created to ensure that within the confines of the specifications, the page and the user will not be overtly affected by the engagement with these ads.

At a higher cost of CPM and a bigger drain on the marketing budget for the campaign, one might question how to prove that Rich Media is offering more value than standard display. The answer comes from the possibility of tracking interactions. As detailed in Chapter 5 - Reporting, Rich Media goes beyond impressions, clicks and conversions to provide metrics that explain both what the user is engaging with and for how long. These triggers and timers allow the Advertiser to determine how a user engages with the creative (allowing for improved creative optimization) and provides a new window on effectiveness by looking at "engagement" on interaction as opposed to clicks to assess performance. It is safe to say that when looking into the working parts of a Rich Media ad, there is more complexity than there is for a standard ad which means a greater opportunity for creativity. Greater creative paves the way for awards for creative developers and designers which in turn attract good PR for Advertisers and for Creative Agencies. The most impressive designs eventually become adopted at an industry level and it is thanks to the standardisation of formats by the IAB and collaborating publishers that we now have formats such as the "Rising Star formats" which circumvent the standardisation of Rich Media from becoming too diverse and unmanageable from both a development and testing perspective.

Core Formats

Formats are the core of what makes Rich media so scalable. By focusing on the features of the most common rich media formats it is possible to identify what kind of format a Rich Media ad is just by looking at it or playing with some of the controls. Formats are really just descriptions of advanced functionality within a Rich Media ad but the presence of established format names moves allows planners, buyers, marketers and traffickers to have meaningful conversations about rich media campaigns with little or no knowledge about how the ad works.

With an established set of format names, it is possible to use the naming convention used by the creative developer in the creative file name, or the name on the media plan or Publisher IO, to ensure that all parties have a mutual understanding about the formats used in a campaign. Formats are not universally priced, more advanced functionality typically means a higher end cost to the Advertiser.

The following is a set of the most common formats found in Rich Media:

Expandable ads

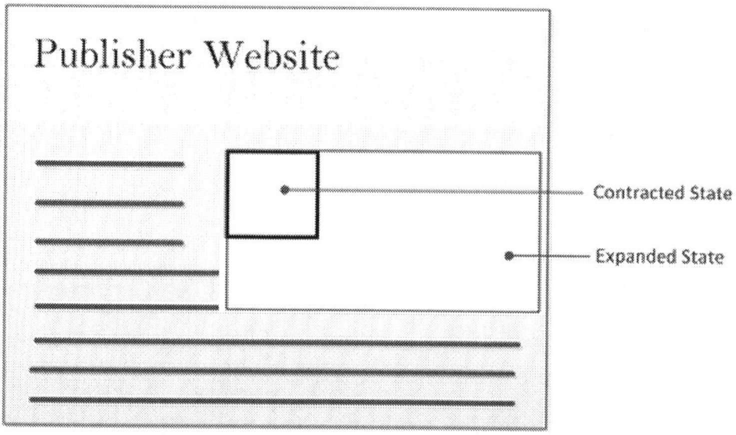

Figure 3.3.1a *an expandable ad grows in size over the publisher content, overlapping it briefly while the ad content is delivered to the user. This figure depicts Rich Media Ad states of expansion and contraction which are covered in more detail later in this section.*

One of the most commonly used formats in Rich Media is the expandable (hopefully in time a word that will find itself a place in the Oxford English dictionary following ten plus years of industry acceptance and use). This is a format that grows in size ("the expanded state") and then contracts ("the contracted state") down to a fixed ad position (called the "ad location") on the page. Expandables can "auto expand" (if Publisher specifications approve) meaning that they start playing in the expanded state rather than requiring a user action to cause the expansion. An expansion can also be triggered by a click or mouse rollover. They can also expand in any of the four directions or expand in all directions at once. Expandables can have a transparent background so that in the expanded state the animation appears to interact with the content of the page itself.

Floating ads

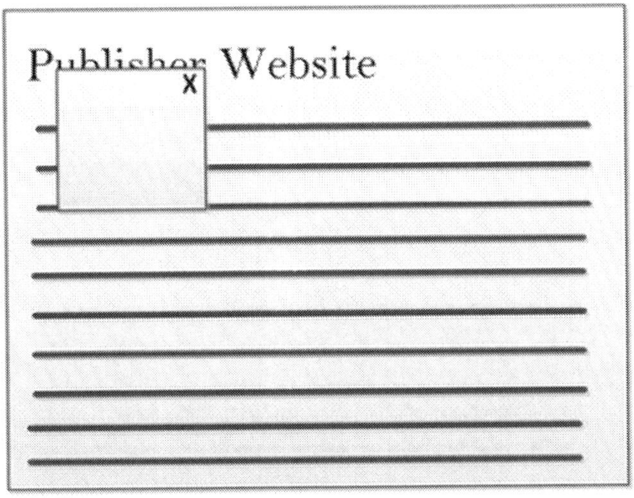

Figure 3.3.1b *The floating ad format loads over the Publisher page content, sometimes tinting the page behind it grey until it is closed with the X shown in the corner. Once closed, floating ads do not strictly return to any fixed point on the page.*

A diminishing format in both the UK and US markets; the floating ad appears on top of the page content, not tied or anchored to a fixed ad spot. The ad itself does not open in a new browser window but often comes with the same qualities as a new browser window (it can be dragged around and closed). The floating ad goes through various states of play during which a user can choose to close the ad via an X in the corner. Coming across a floating ad as a user without an X denotes a failure on both the part of the creative developer and the ad server for failing to notice its absence (this helps explain why the Rich Media QA process is so important). Floating ads are typically frequency capped at the Publisher ad server level, so that if the user loads the same page several times they will eventually stop seeing the floating ad so as to sustain a reasonable user experience and not risk "creative fatigue".

Video ads

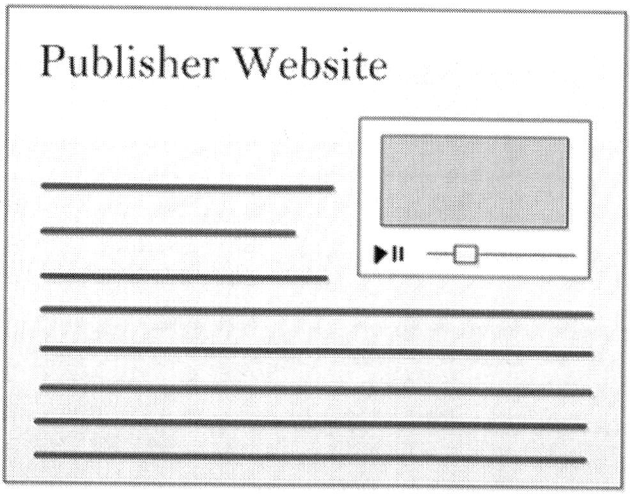

Figure 3.3.1c *Video ads appear in a standard ad spot on a Publisher web page typically playing a short video clip with controls for the user. Most commonly used by film studios to display trailers.*

Video ads are one of the most commonly used Rich Media formats and can be combined with the expandable or floating features. Video ads look like standard ad units but play video (usually with some controls) from inside the placement. Video ads should not be confused with Instream ads (which are typically traditional TV ads purposed for online video broadcasters and purpose built video players - See Chapter 3 - Instream and Video). In Rich Media Video, videos can start automatically but the muting functionality is dictated by the Publisher specifications for which the requirement is most common on mute. HD video, green screen video, full screen video and multiple video play (where many videos appear in the ad at once - like in the case of the format called "the video cube") are all supported by most third party ad servers. Video can also be streamed into the ad live, and the stream itself can be loaded in real time or pre-loaded into the ad by a method referred to as "progressive streaming". Specialist technologies and players have emerged to support unique Advertisers needs such as live video feeds: one such example is *Brightroll.*

Pushdown and Sidekick

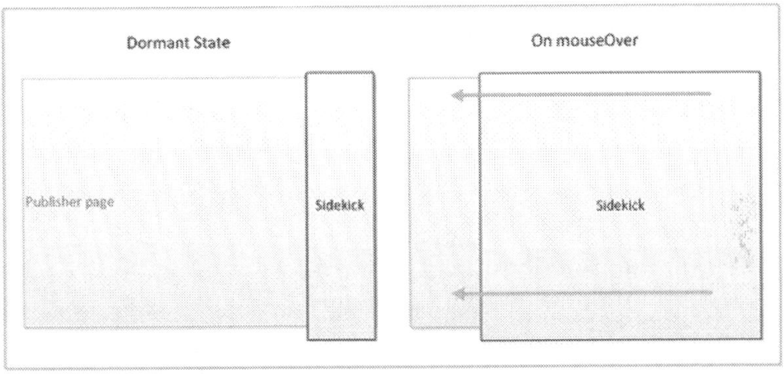

Figure 3.3.1d *A Sidekick format before and after the user rolls over the ad with the mouse. The rollover causes the side kick to expand, seemingly pushing the content of the Publisher page to one side rather than rolling over it as it would normally do in a standard rich media expansion.*

Innovative Rich Media formats are constantly being developed but finding ones that are engaging and not obstructive to the user experience can be a challenge. The pushdown and sidekick IAB approved formats allow the ad to physically push the page content down or to the side in a hybrid of the traditional rich media expandable ad. The user is exposed to the larger canvas of the ad temporarily until they request the content be returned by a button or slider. Such formats are even more effective on devices without a mouse where a sweeping action on a touch screen is more intrinsic to the user experience with the ad. Ad Serving providers and specialist Rich Media technologies such as *DG Mediamind* and US-centric *Pointroll* work with major Publishers to develop new formats with the aim of better monetising the Publishers inventory. Formats chosen by the Publisher can often be made with a contract of exclusivity with the technology company that developed the format for a fixed period. In such instances any Advertiser or Agency running their ad in a new and exclusive format might have to ad serve their ads through the advised technology to have it accepted.

Data capture

Owing to their larger file size, Rich Media ads can do more than standard flash ads, even going so far as to replicate the full Advertiser website in the confines of an ad. A good example is with a Data Capture form which passes or collects data about a user via a form in the ad and sends it off to an Advertiser database in real time, potentially returning information like a voucher code. A use case would be for a mobile provider like the European mobile giant *Telefonica* offering free sim cards to users.

Since no payment details are required, the user completes a form in the ad and submits it before they are given a confirmation message in the ad. The confirmation message contains a conversion tag (see Chapter 4) which logs a conversion without needing to direct the user to the Advertiser site and by returning the confirmation, the data capture form has spoken in real time with the *Orange* database clarifying that the free items will be sent to the address details supplied. Data capture forms of this nature are not meant to store Personally Identifiable Information (PII) on the ad server, but instead encrypt the supplied information and send it to the Advertiser database directly in line with local data protection laws.

Home Page Takeovers, Wallpaper and Page Skins

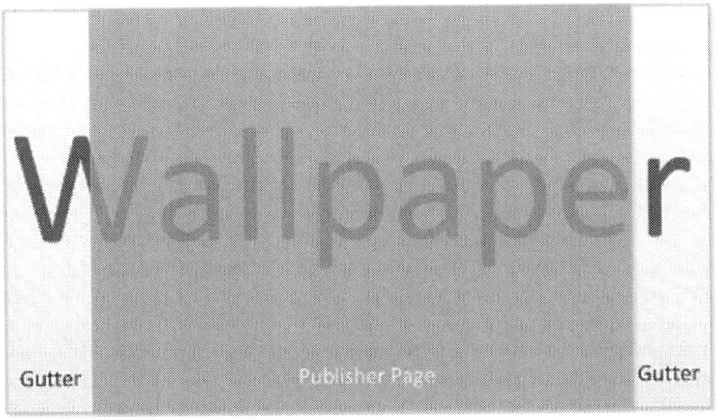

Figure 3.3.1e *a wallpaper execution sits behind the Publisher web page stretching from the left to the right gutter. When further Rich Media functionality is added to the default execution the effect is engrossing including animations which appear to pull the whole of the Publisher page apart in its entirety. Less sophisticated versions simply place very large images in the background. Typically the Publisher page is not transparent as shown in this diagram.*

Modern Publisher site designs centre the content on the users screen producing large "gutters" of empty space down the sides. These can be filled with a giant image, images or a playing video (a very nice effect on a big screen). This format is referred to as a Wallpaper. In comparison a Page Skin tends to mean advertising in every possible ad space and even sponsoring Publisher content working in close collaboration long before the campaign is due to begin (sponsored content is not yet served by third party ad servers but is referred to as an "Advertorial"). The presence of a Page skin is also referred to as "skinning" a page although when it comes to skinning a homepage, it is referred to as a "home page takeover" (HPTO). Home page takeovers are a big deal - they are usually more expensive than any other formats because of the enormous reach they have (think *MSN* or *Yahoo!* Homepage) and rarely last longer than a single day. HPTO's alongside Instream ad units are the cream of what is referred to as premium inventory (the most valuable ad space money can buy).

HPTO's bring a wealth of requirements and needs to the third party ad serving technology (such as real time reporting and optimization, as well as the need for the ad server to have strong relationships with big Publishers to ensure that technologies work in harmony with one another, even when Publisher pages are re-designed).

HPTO's are not as simple to formulate as they sound. For instance the Homepages of a major Publisher like Yahoo! differ in each country, therefore the HPTO format for an international campaign, may have to undergo an extended period of development to suit the homepage of each country.

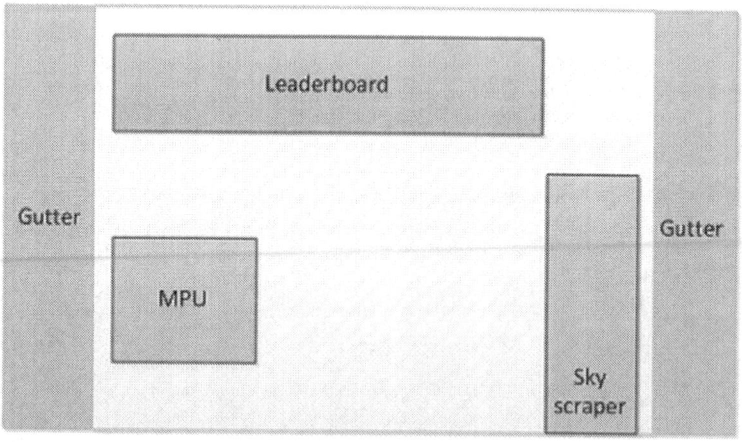

Figure 3.3.1f *The Homepage Takeover is a complete unification of all of the available ad spaces on a single Publisher web page used in a single campaign by a single*

Advertiser. Homepage takeovers are usually high cost executions that require strong collaboration between the ad server, the Publisher and the Creative development team.

Polling

A poll ad can take user information entered into a single ad and display the results of that collective input in real time inside the ad to all other users. Behind the scenes, the ad server is often powering a small database which collects the results purely for the poll.

This collaboration effect combined with a high reach campaign, can achieve poll results that are completely unattainable by a poll on an Advertiser site alone. Some clever manipulation of this technology can connect thousands of users together in real-time collaboration. So instead of collecting simple survey results from individual users and displaying a graph to the collective, users can take webcam photos of themselves and collectively build a collage.

State-based ads

Not strictly a format but rather a feature of Rich Media ads is the concept of "State-based ads" which are a more flexible way of performing creative sequencing than using the in ad-server sequencing options alone (see Chapter 3 - Display ad serving). State based ads simply remember what "state" the user last put the ad into (such as leaving an ad halfway through the playing of a video) so that should they encounter the ad or campaign or even Advertiser again, the next ad which follows could pick up from where the user left off or perform another action.

State based ads work by dropping an additional cookie on the user machine so that the "state" can be recalled later or utilise a reserved area of local memory available for which both Flash (Flash Cookies) and HTML5 can take advantage.

Local Connection ads or Sync Ads

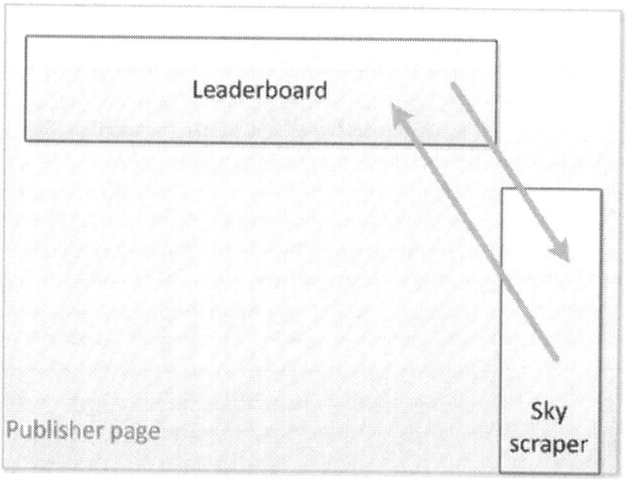

Figure 3.3.1g *Sync ads appear to communicate with each other on the page creating an affect that the two separate units are really just one ad. A clever manipulation of the Flash Actionscript code combined with the capabilities of the ad server allows the ads to appear to be completely synchronised.*

Local connection ads, also called "Sync ads", create the wonderful effect of the leader-board or masthead and the skyscraper unit speaking to each other in tandem. The surprise dawns upon the user when the seemingly separate ad units both displayed on the Publisher page at the same time, suddenly interact with one another such as passing an object between them or syncing in time with each other. For the Publisher ad operations team it is just a case of implementing two separate ad tags on the page at the same time. Rich Media templates created by the third party ad server allow the Creative Agency to swiftly and easily reproduce this effect for those Publishers that support a matching layout. Sync Ads are more commonly used in the process of skinning a whole page, since two of the major ad units are already taken care of in a unique way.

Print-ads

As explained later in this section rich media ad units can contain a number of hidden away files as "child files" which are initially displayed to the user. One of these so called "child files" could be a full size print version of a retail voucher, which inside the confines of a small or even standard rich media unit has trouble being displayed for printing purposes on a small screen. The rich media unit can be coded to allow the user to take advantage of the voucher offer from inside the rich media creative and hit a print button, to print out a copy of the hidden child file and thus the voucher. Again this is more of a Rich Media feature but gives a good indication as to what else can be stashed away utilising the much larger file sizes granted with the use of Rich Media capabilities and specifications. Whole brochures in PDF format are not uncommonly used to stash away more information for the user to expose later on, inside a child file.

A run through of popular formats is rather like browsing a menu in a restaurant. Different dishes suit different Advertisers at different times. There is no hard and fast rule for what to use for the right impact or message. Often the skill of the creative developer or agency has the biggest influence in this area. It is all well and good knowing what is available but it is important to ask two key questions before moving forward with a Rich Media campaign:

a. Can my chosen format be run on any site or page? (Specifications and Certification)

b. How are these culinary delights created? (How are Rich Media ads built?)

These considerations will be broken down in sequence in the following paragraphs:

Standardisation and Publisher certification
In the early days of Rich Media, even with the *IAB* trying to standardise formats, many high volume traffic sites on the internet had just not encountered Rich Media ads in the past and although they were keen to run new formats, these had to be tested with test creative and tags before the campaign could go live. Rich Media technology providers and third party ad serving providers employed teams of people to contact Publisher sites well ahead of a campaign launch date on their very first engagement regarding a specific format to test that it would work on the Publisher site before the campaign went live. With rigorous testing the formats could be run and the same format would not need to be re-tested for future Advertisers and campaigns. The Publisher site was therefore "certified" to run the format.

Today big Publishers have gotten far more efficient at this process and Rich Media certification for formats deemed as standardised by the *IAB* no longer require certification in this way. What this means it that as long as Publishers and technology providers (including third party ad servers) serve the *IAB* Rich Media formats in the way laid out by the *IAB*, the standardised method means that no further testing is needed.

This industry development made Rich Media scalable and the process of standardisation and certification means that any Publisher subscribing to the standardised practices of the *IAB* can run *IAB* Rich Media formats. The same goes for the ad server. The practice of certification still goes on where standardisation and adoption has not reached full industry backing because the channel in question is too new: today this is true of certain formats for Instream and certain formats of Mobile (see Chapter 3 - Instream and Chapter 3 - Mobile). These newer formats are the living evolution of traditional Rich Media so it makes sense that the industry will return to the certification processes that worked so well in the past.

From the top: Building Rich Media ads

The building of Rich Media ads follows the same development cycle as building standard display ads generally speaking. The differences are building in and testing the more complex elements of the functionality. The final part of this section will cover off the additional considerations that need to be made when building Rich Media ads.

1. Training the creative developer
2. Two schools of Rich Media specs: Publisher and Ad server
3. Parent and Child files - the polite load
4. Expansions and Floating -the declaration of state
5. Interaction tracking: Default and Custom Events
6. Interactions as additional clicks
7. Building Custom Rich Media ads

1. Training the creative developer

Creative developers who have built ads for ad servers within the Flash authoring environment in the past will still need to be introduced to the realm of Rich Media ad creation since the various Flash elements (Expansions, Floating, Video, Interactions and Polite loading) utilise different aspects of the components supplied to the creative development team by the ad serving technology. When it is first clear that Rich Media will be used in a media plan, the technology provider hosts what is referred to as a "kick off call" between the Media Agency and the Creative team. This meeting is used to allow the Media Agency to explain to the Creative Agency what execution or format had been agreed to run with a given Publisher and the creative developer is subsequently asked if they need additional training on the available tools in order to build the required format. Creative developers should usually be trained an absolute minimum of a week before the ad needs to be completed, to allow the developer time following the training to get familiar with the new aspects of the supplied components and to work out how to get creative with the code. The kick off call is used to allow the Media Agency to explain what their expectations are from the execution in terms of ad server reporting during and after the campaign. In some instances this will require the developer to undertake additional work implementing what are referred to as "custom interactions" or "custom events". Before the work can start however the creative team always needs to know one thing above all else: what are the limitations to the creative? This is vital since Rich Media opens the doorway to more advanced creative executions, so it is up to the Media Agency and third party ad serving provider to lay down the ground rules or more advanced specifications from the outset.

2. Two schools of Rich Media specs: Publisher and Ad server

Ad Server Rich Media Specifications

Creative developers and designers approaching rich media commonly ask for the ad server "specs". Essentially the request is to determine what needs to be done to the Flash file creative so that is accepted by both the third party ad server and the Publisher. Third party ad servers and rich media technology providers make the work of a developer easier by supplying a set of Flash Components which can be installed in the developers local version of Flash (just as for Standard Display ad serving). The components along with a supply of templates, allows the developer to "build" the ad, containing the code required to upload the creative to the ad server. This code is the majority of the "specification". Casting one's mind back to Standard Display, the only code required by most ad servers is the presence of the "clickTag". With Rich Media this is often such a lengthy chunk of code siphoned into multiple locations inside the flash file that it is simpler to supply a template rather than code it all in from scratch.

Other requirements are usually around the supported formats (the restrictions for which can be gleaned from the Component package: and by looking inside the ad server interface). Sometimes the ad server specifications restrict the number of supported child files, and the file weight of the overall ad unit, so rarely will a rich media creative exceed ten child files, and file weights of over 30mb are still a rarity (although most ad server can handle more if pushed to do so). In fact the best response to a query about specifications is to look at the Publisher specifications first, as these contain much tighter restrictions than ad server specifications themselves.

Publisher Rich Media Specifications

User experience on Publisher websites is greatly impacted by the speed at which users can navigate and load the site. For this reason, Publishers spend time carefully choosing what the file size limits should be of objects and content pulled into a page (as this directly impacts the page load time). Standard flash ads and Rich Media alike need to be limited to certain available ad dimensions and file sizes and Publishers release "Publisher specifications" to media and Creative Agencies to keep the user experience at its optimum (most Publisher specifications are publicly available).

It is imperative to have the creative developer build the creative to these limitations so that ads and ad tags are not rejected when tested by the Publishers ad operations team, before the campaign goes live. Publishers across the board have varying Publisher specifications and this means checking before a campaign to ensure the development team have received specifications from all Publishers. Invariably to save time, Creative Agencies build to the "lowest common denominator" of specs, meaning that the most restricting specifications dictate the build, so that the same ads can be distributed to multiple sites without issue. This is all the same for standard display as it is for Rich Media but Rich Media specifications will be more complex and flexible than those for standard display; particularly with regards to ads utilising methods that do not disrupt the user experience. The most common of these is the parent and child file method; known as the "polite" load.

3. Parent and Child files - the polite load

Parent and Child files

Unlike the vast majority of standard banners (which consist of a single ".swf file"), Rich media ads can be made up of many different files. The parent or master file loads first on the Publisher page (containing the core code required for the ad to pass the rich media specifications of the third party ad server). A rich media ad can be made up of a single master file and a number of child files, where the master file makes a reference to the child files by name so that their content can be pulled into the ad as it plays.

For example a master file containing the controls for a video player, references a child file called "video.flv" (where the child file just contains a video) and could not be played in the browser without the controls and code from the master file. Child files come in many different varieties; from different file types of video to PDFs, word documents, sound files and XML files. When the Creative Agency uploads the multiple files to the ad server, the ad server uses the names of the child files to link them to the master file; commonly dictated by an intelligent method of pairing, such as by uploading the files together or into the same storage folder in the "creative library" section of the ad server. More advanced members of the Media Agency can take a look inside the parent file to determine which order the child files are referenced in (this can be done either in the Flash authoring tool or in various freeware programs designed to peer into the code directly). The order of the child files, just like the naming of them, is imperative to have the ad working correctly. Sometimes a trafficker uploading a rich media ad into the ad server will see an error when a child file is missing and opening the parent file up to see which file is missing in the order of files, will reveal the file's name and allow the trafficker to chase up the creative developer for the absent file.

Polite Download

Why have one parent file and many child files? Why not simply have a single parent file and be done with it? Looking back to the Publisher specifications and the discussion about the user experience; polite download means that the master file loads first, usually with the rest of the Publisher page and then the child file "politely" loads in afterwards (often as a background process), so that the user does not experience a slow page load time. A common polite download situation would see a master file of 40kb and a child file of around 2mb. The polite load prevents a disruption to the user experience and the effect is often undetectable by the user. An example would be instance of an in-page video ad where the parent file is simply displaying the holder image of the first frame of the video file with a play button watermark over the top. When the user clicks the button the video begins to play but the buffering has already started and completed before the user hits play so there is no disruption to the video. Video and polite download Rich Media ads commonly utilise this functionality but the parent files of expandables and floating ads would be found to contain references in the code to the ad's rich media "state"; an essential concept in Rich Media reporting.

4. Expansions and Floating -the declaration of state

For both expandables and floating ads the more advanced functionality is enabled owing to the presence of what is referenced to in the development and build cycle as the "state" of the ad. (This is not to be confused with "State-based ads", which allows the user's interaction with an ad to be remembered for subsequent encounters with the campaign) Hidden away in the code of a Rich Media execution for both these two formats is the ad's state. When the ad changes its state, further actions can be undertaken by the code. For example with expanding ads, the ad has two key states: Expanded state and Contracted State. The creative developer can insert commands into the core code of the ad, to run as the it enters or returns to these states, such as the command to being playing a video or sound file. This freedom is also granted to the trafficker who can (as with standard display ads) piggyback extra code to execute on a change of state such as the firing of a piggybacked pixel or conversion tag (see Chapter 4). States are important for reporting as well, since the change from one state to another fires off default interaction tracking such as counting the number of times the ad has been expanded.

5. Interaction tracking: Default and Custom Events

Rich Media can support the tracking of interactions which means that apart from the usual tracking of impressions, clicks and conversions; the rich media file can send information to the ad server when the ad registers any action at all and these appear in reporting classed as "interactions".

Interactions can be timers, rollovers with the mouse, changes in the ad's Rich Media state, clicks, user gestures and the pressing of keyboard buttons. Rich Media templates supplied by the third party ad server to the Creative Agency will pre-code a number of default interactions. A good example might be that for a video ad, the ad server records when the user is 25% through the playing of the ad and then 50% and 100%. Each of these interactions will have its own column in ad server reporting to aggregate the number of times they occurred; which assists in understanding creative performance. For example with the trailer for a film, a creative that is never recording "100% plays" may contain video that is too long. Other default interactions include total number of expansions and a timer for interaction duration. It's worth noting that default interactions are not industry standardised meaning that there is no list of all default interactions that all ad server and Rich Media tech providers will supply.

It is therefore worth checking with the third party ad serving provider exactly what comes as a default (an example Rich Media report will display this). Furthermore the methodology behind default interactions is different. One to watch out for is knowing when the interaction timer begins: some ad servers do not track "accidental" rollovers as part of the ad engagement while others do. This can explain quite varied differences between interaction rates between different technology suppliers. A useful default interaction for Advertiser utilising TV as well as online delivery mechanisms is the "brand exposure duration" metric. This can make a rich media ad comparable to an ad for TV campaign for the marketer on the Advertiser side, where the total viewing hours nationwide are captured and tallied. All such metrics are simply default interactions and appear in ad server reporting (see Chapter 5).

Thankfully Advertisers are not left just with the default interactions but have the ability to inform the creative development team to add custom interactions. Custom interactions can be added by the creative developer to any part of the ad during the ad build process. This could mean the pressing of a custom button, the user hovering over the brand logo, or even the measurement of time between interactions of different types.

Custom interactions although useful have limited application so it is important not to have the developer go overboard when implementing them. During the kick off call, as the Agency or Advertiser advises the creative developer of the interaction requirements it is worth considering what actions can be taken as a result of high or low figures collected for these interactions. For instances, tracking and reporting on the number of times a user scores a goal in an interactive Rich Media football game ad will not inform either the Advertiser or Agency about user brand engagement and may only serve to append the goal scoring functionality in future iterations of the updated creative.

6. Interactions as additional clicks

Custom interactions add almost unlimited flexibility when it comes to tracking. Another key component for Rich Media ads is that they support multiple click-redirects. So, different elements of the ad can click through to completely different Advertiser web pages. The ad server allows all clicks taken by the user in this manner to be recorded as clicks but reporting can break out the increment of clicks by their click through URL to discern which page received the most traffic while still accurately reporting on the "total number of clicks". More on this in Chapter 5 - Reporting.

7. Building Custom Rich Media ads

It is all very well and good standardising the most popular and well used formats but the whole concept of Rich Media is based on creative impact. To stand out in a crowd one must look different and in Rich Media, such an achievement sometimes literally means 'thinking outside of the box'. To achieve executions that look incredibly impressive, such as those that shake the whole page and seem to dismantle elements that remain functional (such as search boxes and navigation), the creative developer must work alongside the Publisher. Often the ad serving provider will liaise with the Publisher directly to cast aside the Publisher specifications for a single high impact execution that, like a firework, is very dramatic but shorty lived. Most home page takeovers utilise an element of customisation which ads longer to the development time of the ad and will come out pricier than sticking to standard formats.

Once the creative developer has completed the work of adding functions to the design team's creative, the ad (just like with standard display) is ready to upload to the ad server. This can be undertaken in most instances from within the ad server supplied components inside the Flash authoring environment. Unlike standard display ads, Rich Media ads tend to be made up of several files (at least one parent file and one child file). Some ad servers allow developers to zip all the files up together in a *.zip file or folder before uploading them to the ad server for the trafficker to work on them. Before the trafficker completes the trafficking process, the complexity of the Rich Media ad requires it be more thoroughly tested and QA'd.

QAing and testing Rich Media ads

Building rich media ads to specifications takes some time and some Creative Agencies have not worked with some ad servers before, and so will take time to install and get used to their components. The kick off call, as described earlier in this section helps ensure creative developers are fully trained before undertaking the work. However, as with using anything for the first time, progress will be slower than allowing the Creative Agency to work with tools that they are already familiar with.

This is an interesting discovery for ad serving providers because last minute campaigns require fast creative processing and Media Agencies and Advertisers will sometimes defer to the Creative Agency's preferences when selecting an ad serving technology provider. This decision can be solely based on the usability of the tools and how comfortable the developer is with support received from the ad server directly in times of trouble.

Development time varies dramatically, but a single ad concept with rich media elements from scratch never takes less time than a single working day (if you find a Creative Agency that can do this; check the quality of their work and then stick with them!) In fact the longest part of the process for any rich media campaign setup is the development/coding stage.

The Creative Agency is expected to test their own creative locally and potentially even in a simulated Publisher environment on the third party ad server (something that the Media Agency can also do) before the ad is invariably tested manually by the third party ad serving support team as well.

Once the creative passes these checks (a process called QA - for Quality Assurance), The Publisher will also test the ad via the received ad tags before putting the ad live. The ad can fail to pass QA at any one of these checkpoints either for specification failure, or functional failure and the creative is pushed back to the developer to amend or rebuild; sometimes with assistance from the support team at the third party ad server. Ads can also fail even once a campaign goes live despite rigorous checks so QA becomes ever more important.

Trafficking Rich Media ads
Apart from the extended trafficking time required for QA, rich media ads are treated the same way as standard display ads, so that once the ad is created in the ad server, it can be assigned to a placement and the tags can be sent to the Publisher.

As Rich Media ads can be more expensive than standard ads to serve through the ad server, the temptation is for some Media Agencies is to go directly to the Publisher. The danger here is that the Advertiser loses the ability to de-duplicate the user to understand their life time interaction with a brand when the wider picture of a pathway to conversion is considered. In addition independent third party reporting is unavailable and complex interaction reporting is not commonly available in publisher side rich media serving technologies.

Creative Agency and cross Publisher support would also vanish meaning that small problems can quickly escalate beyond repair. Third party ad servers conveniently offer tools to make sure that Rich Media ads are not wasted such as through on-interaction retargeting (Chapter 7) or with ad controls that ensure Rich Media is reserved, deeper in user sequencing or manipulating frequency capping to ensure Rich Media ads are shown frugally to users or displayed at more effective times of the day. No one is denying that Rich Media is a cheap alternative to other channels but the value of the impact can be harnessed through effective trafficking by manipulating clever ad controls. As explained in the previous section, the experience of the trafficker would add enormous value to media budgeting by being aware of all of the ad server capabilities.

Publisher Troubleshooting

As mentioned even after QA and trafficking, the Rich Media ad could fail on the Publisher website owing to an oversight in the technology or human error in setup. In such instances technical support are bought in via the third party ad serving provider to work with the Publisher to fix the problem. This is an additional operational cost that Publishers must bear in mind before offering to allow Rich Media ads to be implemented on sites to utilise greater income on the inventory.

> But how after so many checks can a rich media ad fail? The most commonly reported types of failure on a Publisher site are to do with how the different elements of the page are layered, such that the ad appears underneath or on top of the web page content. Generally speaking, the cause of the problem is a wonderfully exotic CSS element called the "Z-index". Z-index refers to the layer that each part of the web page lives on and there are thousands of such layers that could potentially exist.
>
> Although the ad is designed to appear on the upmost layer, sometimes this does not occur and the ad server may have to use a few JavaScript tricks (where able), to influence the layering of the elements around the ad so as to push them down on the Z-index and raise the ad upwards. This is made available by piggybacking additional code onto the existing ad or even inserting it into the creative itself. Publisher troubleshooting, although time sensitive for live campaigns,

can be a process of trial an error; especially with limited Publisher support, so patience is mandatory while a conflict is being resolved.

Often the support team handling the request will require that the ad tag be loaded in the live page or an exact replica inside a publisher "staging environment" so that through trial and error with code, the issue can be resolved and the campaign put live again. Rich Media ads put live on " blind networks" face the troublesome conflict of having to supply a URL to the support team to resolve the error while crucially not exposing the site name to the Advertiser or Agency. For this reason it is not recommended to run Rich Media through such agreements.

Due to the open ended nature of Rich Media (to express creative flare through technology) there can sometimes be unforeseen technology conflicts which may result from updates to browsers, updates to the core Flash player technology from *Adobe* and other anomalies in JavaScript and Flash elements on the same page. All of which can take a thorough investigation to resolve. Thankfully Publisher troubleshooting issues rarely occur and the Advertiser's return, for high impact formats, are both rewarding to the user visually and facilitate campaign goals for effective reach and greater interaction for the campaign.

Rich Media for Mobile & Rich Media for Instream

Thankfully once one has mastered Rich media, most of the other capabilities of the Display channel seem like child's play. Beyond Display, Rich Media has begun to penetrate the channels of Mobile and Instream too. These nuances are covered in the remaining sections in this chapter. But before leaving Display advertising behind completely there remains an elephant in the room, one which has allowed giants among web technology companies to thrive. This would be the ability to create display ads which are Dynamic in nature, circumnavigating the need to have the creative developer build quite so many ads. The next section focusses on what is referred to as DCO Channel or "Dynamic Creative Optimization" and it unlocks a universe of true creative optimization.

Chapter 3 - Section 4
DCO

Standard Display and Rich Media ads could be described as "Static" ads so that once the creative developer has completed building the ads and has uploaded them to the ad server, the content of that creative does not change. The elements or assets that make up the creative are rigid and cannot be moved without republishing the master file. If an Advertiser or trafficker wanted the ad to look different, for whatever reason, the creative developer would have to adjust the creative on their side and then upload it to the ad server so that the trafficker could replace the existing with the new ad. This process can be a costly undertaking for Advertisers with regards to creative costs and for almost ten years ads created for ad serving for display existed only in this construct.

Creative that can be visually adjusted with content controlled by the trafficker and not by the creative developer means that costs all remain on the media side (Agency and Advertiser) as opposed to on the creative side (creative developer and Creative Agency). Controlled costs or lower costs are more attractive industry wide and mean more can be spent on buying the ad space. The creative can be designed so that its elements are more fluid and not "static" and this is called "Dynamic Creative". The utilisation of dynamic creative for the purposes of improved campaign performance in the third party ad server is called "DCO" or "Dynamic Creative Optimization".

DCO began life when creative developers realised that if they used an XML file type when they created ads that it would save them a lot of time if they wanted to make changes remotely later without having to republish the flash files . This section starts off by looking at these early XML driven dynamic ads before focussing on DCO, looking at the capabilities of this 'channel' and the bright future which lies ahead for its application across Display, Mobile and Instream.

Standard XML Display

As a .swf file is near impossible to break into without heading back to the original .fla file and republishing the ad, creative developers found it too frustrating and time consuming and resolved the access problem using an XML file instead. Unlike .swf files, the XML file can easily be edited in a program like *Notepad* or *Word*, so a creative developer's flash skills and premium access to the flash authoring tool are not requisites to changing the content of an XML file which in turn is used to make adjustments to the .swf file. By coding the .swf file to look for its instructions in a neighbouring XML file, the XML file is suddenly an easy-access gateway into the ad to change the content; be it a price-point, a tag line or even a background colour. Using this method a creative developer could build one piece of creative with an empty text field; the creative could reference an file called "content.xml" which could contain the English-written text to populate the text field, written out in full.

Providing these two files to the trafficker (advert.swf and content.xml) they could upload both files to the ad server for one campaign and then replicate the two files and replace the content inside the content.xml with the same content written in French before uploading the two replicated files into the correct place for the French campaign.

Before XML files came into use the creative developer could have been paid to produce two pieces of .swf creative instead of the one .swf produced today, thus creative costs come down.

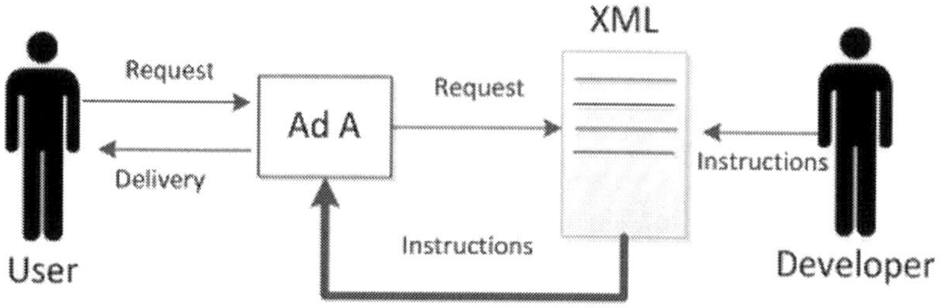

Figure 3.4.1 *the developer can update the ad indirectly with an Ad purpose built to receive instructions via an additional XML file. When the user's browser requests the ad from the server (Ad A) the ad looks for its XML file which provides the latest instructions to update the Ad. The user then gets delivered the updated Ad.*

This example suggests that an XML file can be populated with content but it can also be populated with URLs or references to the location of images or additional content. An .swf file could appear to contain a series of images but behind the scenes, the .swf file is referencing a file that might be called pictures.xml and pictures.xml could contain a list of the location of all the images set to appear the series in the ad. To change the images displayed in the ad, the traffickers could edit pictures.xml to introduce new images or remove old ones. In addition a .swf file could be coded to reference an additional section within pictures.xml that contains a number used to control the speed at which the images in the series rotate (perhaps the higher up the number, the faster the rotation). An XML could contain a whole series of remote controls to adjust just about anything going on in the ad. Each set of controls exists in separate section of the XML file called a "node", referencing the right node in the accompanying XML file maps the control to the function.

Even the XML does not need to sit alongside the creative it is updating. The XML can be completely remote so that in an ideal world an XML file can in theory sit on the desktop of a planning manager from a Media Agency and they can update the ad from their local machine. (To perform this feat the creative needs to have the URL of the XML setup to look for the user's local machine as a unique IP on a network). More commonly the XML can sit on the Advertiser's own site but in either case there are security settings in place to ensure that the XML cannot be remotely accessed or adjusted. A "Cross-Domain" file is a very small file that sits on the Advertiser's top level domain and grants access to the third party ad server to allow it to grab the XML file to make changes to the creative. With this direct connect to the XML file, creative can be changed in real time (and at scale the change will be live everywhere within 15 minutes thanks to ad server ad replication).

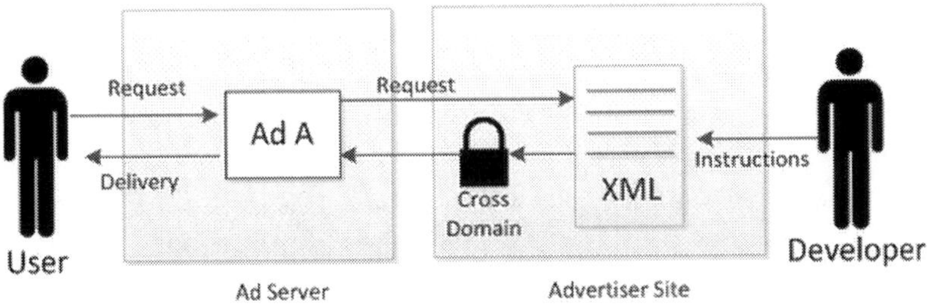

Figure 3.4.2 *With a cross domain file in place, an ad can securely call an XML on an external server (such as on an Advertiser site) and as long as the ad server has been granted access, the XML is free to deliver the information back to the Ad without opening up an unsecure communication channel to the external server.*

As great as this sounds, creative developers very quickly encountered a problem; changes made to the XML file could not be previewed in the flash ad before the amendment was permanently added. Without a preview, new text could bleed into the rest of the creative unintentionally or images could be referenced that don't exist and incorrect settings, set remotely, could cause the ad to become unstable. Furthermore allowing the XML to be changed so easily meant that it was near impossible to track changes made to the ad (when republishing from a flash file, developers typically append the name of the file, creating a new version of the same ad). Whole tools were required for developers to really make the most of the XML remote capabilities and these were to arrive on the scene in an interface as DCO.

DCO - Design Phase

Creating the dynamic template

The modernised workflow for Dynamic creative requires that the creative developer only produces one creative for each ad which can be better off considered a 'template' creative (containing all of the ad possible designs and functions). A separate template would be constructed for each of the required placement dimensions for the campaign. The template essentially a blank canvas which contains elements or assets which are dynamic in nature, meaning that they have the capability of changing the way they look and behave.

To build such creative, the creative developer utilises the third party's component pack inside the flash authoring environment to create dynamic text box's and empty image slots in which text of a fixed length or images of a fixed size can be dropped into at a later date. The dynamic elements can technically be anything that can be built in the Flash environment which includes text, images, videos, sounds, special variables, files, strings and integers. The rich ability of Flash to offer the flexibility to work with so many multimedia formats means Creative Agencies still have the opportunity to get very creative despite the fact that they may only be producing one template.

Figure 3.4.3 *An Ad can be re-designed as a template by making the areas that were previous static assets into dynamic areas which can be populated with similar content. The template, when plugged into the XML describing the location of static assets or static content can be used in conjunction with the template to reproduce a new Ad. This is called an Ad Version rather than an Ad since it is a version of the original.*

Dynamic Creative Planning

At this early stage planning is very important; for instance, how many dynamic elements should the creative developer put into the template? If one element is reserved for a tagline as text based copy, one element for the price point and one for the image there are three elements which can be changed utilising the XML, but is that enough? Some creative developers go the extra mile by making dynamic the image placeholder for the Advertiser's logo and even the small print terms and conditions.

Planning ahead about which elements will be created dynamic is essential, since once the template is created, it could be dynamic enough to be used for an almost infinite amount of time, even reused for several campaigns, without ever reaching creative fatigue by the browsing user.

Planning and identifying the dynamic placeholder is the first step, the second is to consider the possibility of text copy leaking into the rest of the creative. If copy is replaced with a longer piece of copy later on, or if images need to be used that do not fit the dimensions of the ad, then the creative planning process must make such considerations and the dynamic capabilities of DCO creation will accommodate such needs. For instance, the developer could add code to the template so that the creative automatically resizes text or images to fit the dimensions of the template.

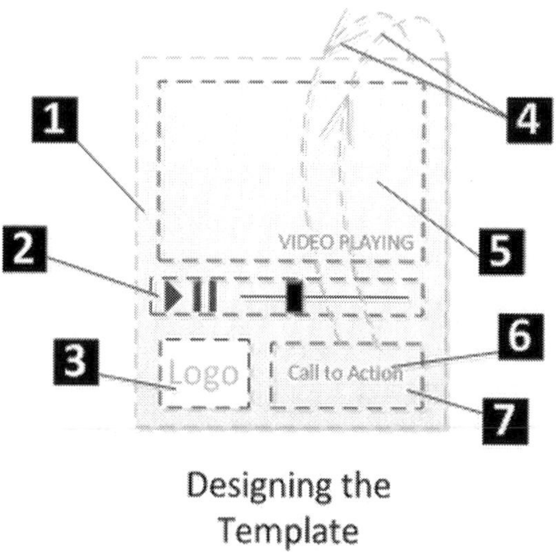

Figure 3.4.4 *Dynamic Templates should be designed for the long term so that an XML can be mapped to any of the Dynamic features and thus control them. Should the Advertiser wish to control anything that was not made specifically Dynamic later on, a new template needs to be published by the creative developer so building for most eventualities makes sense. Each of these dynamic elements are: (1) The background colour of the version (2) The player controls; perhaps there are several sets of controls to choose from loaded up as an additional dynamic SWF file (3) A*

dynamic spot for the logo for those particularly long term templates that might outlive the brand logo. (4) Particularly innovative developers that might animate part of the ad will consider adding additional tweens or paths that can be activated by the XML later on (5) A dynamic video (6) The call to action itself could be adjusted for the actual click-through URL or the text (7) A dynamic field for the font type so that it can dynamically adjusted via the XML later on.

Once the template is finalised the creative developer can upload it like any other ad to the third party ad server. The ad server will detect the use of the dynamic component used by the developer to create the dynamic elements and the trafficker working in the third party ad server interface will be given the option to decide how many "versions" of the creative to create. Third party ad servers and specific dynamic creative technologies can support the creation and management of hundreds and thousands of versions: true scaling for standard display. Subsequently these versions can be assigned to placements directly (just as standard ads would normally be assigned) or for scaled personalisation and targeting versions can be assigned to specific audience types.

DCO - Ad Creation Phase

Versioning

Versions of ads adds two new levels to the hierarchy in the third party ad server. Under the ad level exists the version level and beneath this, the asset level. (At time of writing, ad servers could not offer reporting or tracking capabilities below the version level to the asset level but the industry is expected to adapt quickly to accommodate the asset level as well). To focus now on the version level, there are three common ways of creating a version (also called "variant") ad from the template creative supplied by the creative developer:

1. Single Versioning or Manual Creation

Some ad servers which support the creation of Dynamic Creative, provide an interface on the platform which allows for the basic dynamic template supplied by the creative developer to be adapted into Dynamic versions, version by version. Such interfaces are essentially creative tools which can be used a trafficker to allow for the input of copy into the new ad version, the ability to upload or reference an image from within the version, insert a price point and also to change the colour of the text, the ad background colour, the size of the text (in some instances to even spell-check the copy), before the version can be previewed and saved.

The preview option is popular with Advertisers who like to proof read or view every version of each ad that potential customers will see, so that they can provide their approval before it goes live on the web. As with the preview option for standard display ads in trafficking standard display campaigns, the approval option was removed from many ad servers as the Advertiser approval chain became a bottleneck to campaign delivery timelines.

Despite a variety of supporting features, the essential point of manual version creation or "single versioning" is to undertake the design and build of a manageable number of versions, typically for a very small campaign or at least a campaign with very few ad versions. Single Versioning is not a scalable method and has its merits when an Advertiser is playing with DCO for the first time. More seasoned Advertisers and Agencies move things up a notch to "Mass versioning".

2. ***Excel* Mass Versioning**

Ad serving providers have listened to big Advertisers and Agencies running large scale campaigns with many placements and sites by providing bulk tools which utilise the easy replication of rows of data to scale. The same methodologies have been extended to Mass Versioning in the absence of a better designed UI for creating a large number of unique ad versions. Using a spread-sheet layout inside the ad server interface the trafficker can begin to make new ad versions, row by row from a single supplied creative template. The columns are already pre-defined by the ad server interface which identifies the dynamic elements of the creative and converts them into columns. Each new row represents a new version of the ad and each cell can therefore be customised with a value (such as a whole number for a price point, a text for the copy and URLs to point at external content like images). A spread sheet view quickly allows for the update of many existing versions and adds 'copy and paste' capabilities to create new versions. As with Single versioning there are checks in place for spelling as well as preview functions for each of the rows so that on mass, preview links can be generated and sent over to the advertiser for them to approve.

3. **Mass Versioning from a Feed**

The creation of hundreds of ads is a common demand for Advertisers and their Agencies where a vast product line is being supported. To build separate ads features different products in each one is completely unattainable for the likes of retail Advertisers which is where DCO can come to the rescue. Such product catalogues are usually already aggregated on the Advertiser website and therefore a product list or "feed" exists (behind the scenes of the Advertiser website). Such a list might even be as complex as a database with information that might be updated very frequently such as the colour of the product in question and the number of items left in stock.

In turn this feed allows the CMS to dynamically generate web pages and the same method can be used to build out versions of ads in their thousands. The ad server contains controls in the interface which allows the trafficker to connect to an external database or feed and generate ads from it. The controls also permit the trafficker to map variables such as the stock control to the version and create a rule that removes the version from ad serving when the product runs out of stock. If the price point or stock number is manually changed in the feed it should reflect in the served version. In general the available DCO solutions coupled with ad server in the market range in complexity. *Flashtalking* for example allows the trafficker to browse to the Advertiser site from within the ad server interface to select a product feed that might already be displayed on the Advertiser site. *DoubleClick* allows the trafficker a much more integrated setup when connecting to Advertiser feeds that have been setup using *Google's* own stock control database tools.

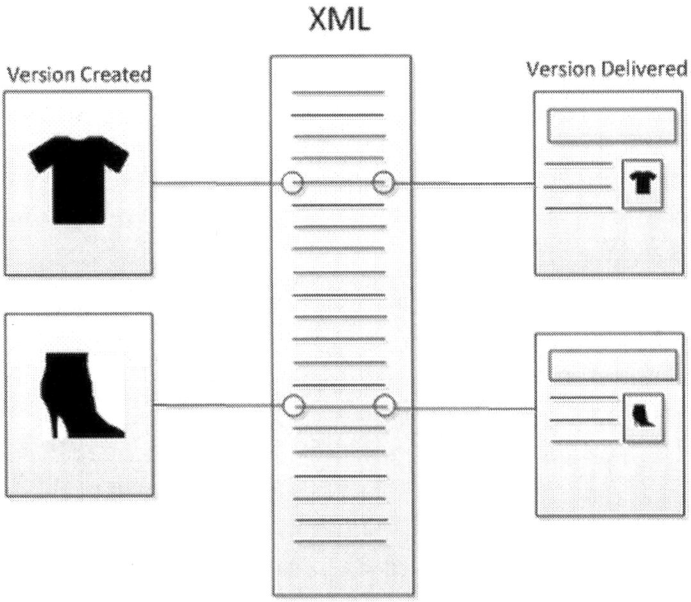

Figure 3.4.5 *a feed (such as an Advertiser's product feed) can be used to generate a mass number of versions. Versions delivered to Publisher sites are those generated from the feed.*

Sometimes product feeds and databases are complex or partitioned out and require ad serving provider support to build out a new feed from which to create versions. In addition if product feeds are likely to change frequently, the DCO tool needs to be configured to 'check' the feed with the same frequency so that dynamic variables like price changes are reflected as close to real-time as possible.

Using a Web Service to restrict load on Advertiser hosted Product images

A mass versioning campaign with a product feed will typically pull the images of the product into the ad version from the Advertiser website directly and not necessarily the third party ad server. This is done by having the URL location of the image included in the product feed and mapped to a corresponding dynamic image placeholder inside the master ad template.

Hosting images and content is a common query that comes up in the DCO setup. After all, with so many images to reference thousands of products; can the Advertiser not simply direct the ad version to retrieve the image direct from the Advertiser site each time the ad is called?

A couple of considerations need to be taken ahead of time. The first consideration is that an ad server is a piece of technology that is purpose built for mass traffic. If the versions and images themselves are expecting to be referenced by every end user on the same scale then the Advertiser site needs to be setup to handle just as many ad calls or risk being taken down by users, demanding content from the Advertiser's own servers.

To get around this, the images themselves can be pulled from an Advertiser site and cached by what is referred to as a "web service" technology sitting between the Advertiser site and the ad server. Images are cached by the web service which takes the risk of high volume traffic away from the original host URL. Caching images in this way comes with its own risks so it worth fully exploring this topic with the ad server in question before setting up and running such a campaign. In such a scenario, an adapted feed would need to be appended to the existing product feed so that new URLs for the product images are referenced by the dynamic field in the ad template.

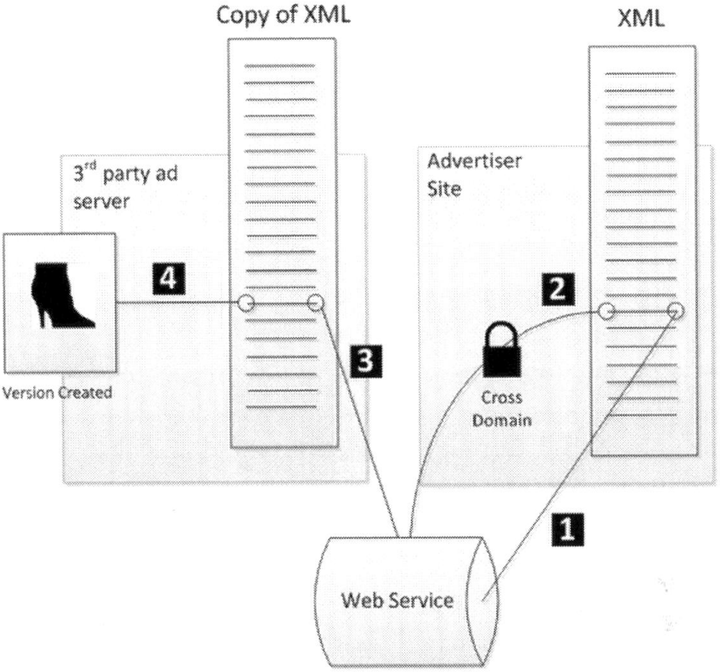

Figure 3.4.6 *Hitting product feeds frequently to keep the versions up to date can be a heavy strain on some Advertiser sites or servers. To get around this problem a Web Service can be setup to replicate the product feed on the ad server. The web service would make a request the core XML on a limited frequency (1) for example once per hour instead of for every ad call. The request returns a response from the feed via the cross domain (2) for security purposes. The web service then updates the various part of a copy of the XML (3). When ad versions are requested by the user the versions are up to date which what is in the copied XML on the ad server (4).*

Feeds themselves are also rarely ready to plug directly into a DCO setup on the ad server side so Web services can be used to scrape the original product feed at different times and act as an adapted feed for the creation of the DCO versions. Feed Scraping is not usually a free service so it is worth an Advertiser or Agency fully investigating feed adaptation and scraping when working out how much it will cost to create and setup a mass versioning campaign.

As with legacy XML creative setup, if a feed sits inside an Advertiser's domain or firewall it will require the presence of a cross-domain which accepts the calls to and from the ad server to work correctly (adhering to the required security protocols to accept the ad server traffic). The use of a web services eradicates the real-time element that was so attractive about XML dependent creative, the amendments to the version will only change when the web service updates a copy of the feed or re-caches the stored images. This process of scraping at the time this book was written was around one hour maximum, so a change to the feed, should It change a version (such as with an update to the amount of available stock on a product) would only be reflected up to an hour later. Some ad servers have even longer time lags on this.

With the freedom to create so many versions, comes the responsibility of identifying each of those versions individually. Each version is assigned an ID in the ad server for reference purposes, since the only other real unique identifying marker is literally the unique combination of dynamic variables that make the version unique in the first place. If a version is changed or adjusted, its unique combinations of dynamic variables no longer matches the original configuration and this is a problem for reporting. In truth any adjustment of a version should create a wholly new version so that the versions can be discerned in ad server reporting. In turn the creation of a new version as with the creation of a new ad requires a certain amount of re-assignment to placements or audiences which on a large scale (such as using a version across a large number of placements and sites) can prove to be a trafficking headache. The most recent upgrades to DCO interfaces for third party ad servers are building in the functionality and logic to cope with assignment on this scale such as by associating versions that have been adapted from one another, together.

DCO - Assignment to Placement Phase

Just as with standard ads, ad versions can be assigned directly to placements. Once the versions have been created in the ad serving interface the trafficker ensures there is the correct configuration of placements, sites and delivery groups in order to attach the ad versions.

Placement vs. Audiences

Being able to scale creative means that very deep personalisation becomes possible, since a version of an ad can be created which has more relevance to a user, than a run-of-the-mill standard display ad (designed for mass reach) would have. Relevance generally brings an improvement in campaign performance especially when DCO is combined with a source of audience data, which brings about highly customised targeting (see Chapter 4 - Audiences and Targeting).

As explained, inside the ad server the trafficker has the opportunity to assign ad versions to placements (as is possible with Standard display and Rich Media) but with DCO, the capability for assignment extends so that across placements the same version can be displayed to multiple audiences.

By assigning versions to audiences the trafficker exposes a single ad version potentially to a much larger group of users that might be exposed to a single placement. This is particularly true when a media plan features a large number of sites and within that a vast number of placements.

All users arriving at a single Publisher site and seeing a single placement will be a smaller number of users than an audience of users encountering ads across several placements on several sites. Since an ad server can identify users in an audience group, whenever the ad server serves to the audience member, their presence in the audience can over-ride the default capability of serving the ad designated only for that site and placement.

This will only work if the definition for an audience is fairly broad. If the audience is too granular (such as users that live in a certain Zip Code who have visited an obscure page on the Advertiser site) then the rules setup by the trafficker on the placement will not find the matching audience and will therefore serve a non-targeted ad or ad version.

Setting up thousands of very specific audience groups with corresponding ad versions is very time consuming and if only a couple of users ever encounter a version, there will not be enough data to suggest that the versioning of the ad is having an influence on their decision to click for instance. If a couple of users also click on a version which is almost identical, how would one workout which creative version is the best performer?

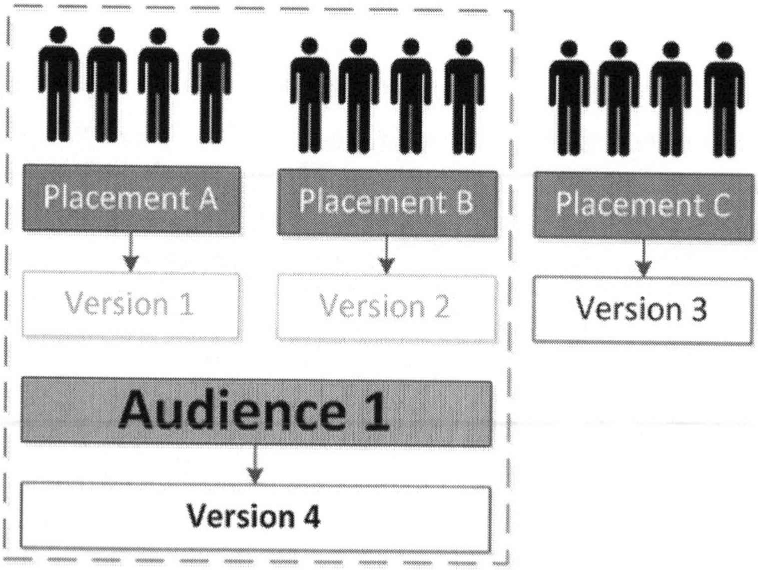

Figure 3.4.7 *if versions are assigned to placements (where one placement is on each Publisher site for instance) then the number of individuals seeing each version will be low and deciding what*

the best version is becomes more challenging as the sample is smaller. Apply a version to an entire audience and a version is shown to a wider group. This is not always the case (sometimes audiences are smaller than the traffic going to a single placement) but to get the most meaningful data set, the version should be applied so that it is seen by as many users as possible with as few versions created as possible.

Targeting different Versions to different Audiences
As Mass versioning allows for a vast combination of dynamic elements to be turned into ads of their own, the next step is to involve the media planning team from the Agency to decide which of those ad versions are suitable for which audience type (since the assignment to placements alone is circumvented). This means defining the effective audiences in the ad server and then assigning the correct versions to the correct audience. The media planning team are important in this step since the media is often bought to match the audience targeting requirements provided by the marketing team.

Audiences can be assembled or defined in a variety of ways for both dynamic creative and for standard creative. Chapter 4 deep dives further into the available audience groups for targeting inside a third party ad server (something that differs from the audience targeting capabilities offered through a Publisher ad server). Of these types, the "retargeting" audience is the most common for which a single ad version might be highly relevant to a user.

A retargeting tag (as will be further explained in Chapter 7) can, for example be placed on an Advertiser's product page: invisible to the user and allow the user to be targeted again later if they leave the Advertiser site without purchasing. The result is that an ad version (created using mass versioning) matching the last product the user saw, can appear to effectively chase them around Publisher sites until they make the purchase. To enable the chase the media planners procure the inventory required across Publisher sites. Pure DCO solutions like *Criteo* do all this legwork for the Advertiser in question, buying the inventory on their behalf with the intention to chase down such a sale, using mass versioning to keep the creative relevant.

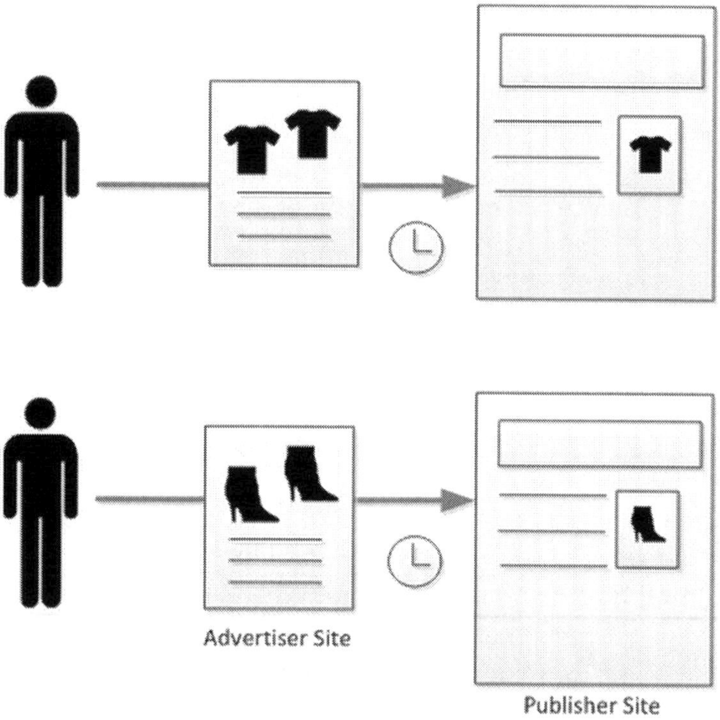

Figure 3.4.8 *Audiences visit the Advertiser site, in this example the product page where a retargeting pixel adds their cookie to a cookie retargeting pool. When the audience later encounters an ad spot bought by the Advertiser on a Publisher site, the ad checks to see if the user belongs to a retargeting pool and if so shows them the relevant version. This is all possible with standard ads but DCO allows for this at scale.*

Connecting DCO with Audience Buying

The ability to deliver a customised version of an ad based purely on a user's actions means that DCO can be used in conjunction with machine-based audience buying systems in the RTB space. This is a significantly more advanced concept, which is covered off in more detail in Chapter 8.

Pinpointing a user and showing a relevant piece of creative in the form of an ad version has spun off into two core technology features Dynamic Retargeting and Carousel Ads. To digest both of these two technologies requires a deeper understanding about retargeting tags (and though these are features of DCO ads) the detail about their setup and implementation are detailed in Chapter 7 - Retargeting.

DCO - Optimization Phase

Auto-Optimize vs. Manual control

Once the versions are created and assigned to placements and audiences there comes the question of how to decide which versions to show the end user. Although personalisation comes into the game for versions created using corresponding product feeds; in the case of building out hundreds of versions of ads that have different creative nuances (such as different font and background colours) it is less clear what version to show to who and when. Sophisticated rules are required because optimizing many ad versions is a bigger task than optimizing standard ads. With versions en-mass it makes more sense to allow machine-learning to "optimize" the versions so that those that are performing well are exposed to a wider effective audience and those that are not doing so well simply disappear. Having said this it is worth checking that the third party ad server that supports dynamic creative allow for both manual and automatic optimizations since these features are not universally available.

The control of weighting or sequencing ads, or running different ad versions at different times with various frequency caps, are options that remain open in DCO as they are in standard display and are effective tools in refining a campaign (with a small enough amount of versions for the target audiences seeing those versions to not become too granular).

Once a DCO campaign is setup manually by the trafficker; the automated approach can prove to be a powerful tool if well managed at arms-length. Auto optimization has some core facets.

1. First of all the setup needs to consider how to optimize
    a. Will the machine learning adapt according to an A/B style test (see Chapter 4)?
    b. Or use multi-variant testing (see further on in this section)

2. Then a consideration needs to be made on the core success metric which may for example:
    a. prefer a lean towards clicks over conversions
    b. or favour a higher basket value in conversions
    c. Or converters from a particular geography.

3. The last consideration is the effective pool for the optimization, so this would be to display the version or collection of versions to be shown just to users arriving at a given placement or opting for a wider group by taking learning's across a complete audience.

The trafficker selects the placement from the site in question in the ad server interface and attaches the versions in a group, after selecting the preferred success criteria from the above. When the campaign goes live, those more successful ads will be shown more frequently or receive more valuable user engagements and this can all be displayed in reporting. The machine does need time however to learn based on the user activity, which creative is the best to display. This can take a couple of weeks or more depending on the complexity of the campaign.

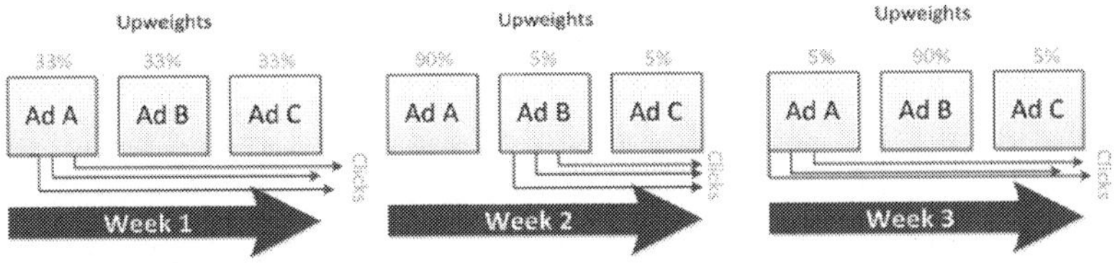

Figure 3.4.9 *Auto-optimization at work. The success metrics is the total number of clicks. High number of clicks in this example tells the optimizer what % of the audience should see the specific ad version in the following week. In the first week the weights are balanced but by the end of the week Ad A is getting the most clicks so in Week 2 most users see Ad A. However by the end of week 2, the small portion of users seeing Ad B are clicking on it at a higher rate than the users seeing the other Ads. Therefore in week 3 the up-weight is set to Ad B. By the end of week 3 Ad A seems to be getting the higher rate. The learning from this auto-optimization that Ad C can probably be dropped from the campaign as a version.*

Auto-optimization as a "Black Box Technology"

Some Advertisers ask to see the output of the auto-optimization engine making its decisions but not all ad servers offer this as an output. This is a controversial point since the learning's made by the auto-optimizer are not something that the Advertiser or Agency can retain and apply to other brands (in some instances the learning's cannot even be transported to new campaigns since the creative versions used may be different). There is merit in being able to export this data although as yet DCO ad serving technology has been slow to visualise the learning's and give the trafficker the control to over-ride the auto-optimization process to improve it based on manual optimization knowledge once it has begun optimizing.

Multi-variant testing

Get really granular with DCO and the focus is not on the creative as a complete entity but rather the tiny fragments inside the creative otherwise known as Assets. Multi-Variant testing allows the Advertiser to make decisions about the effectiveness of individual assets (for example; if a blue background on any version is always more effective than a red background). This granularity allows the Creative Agency to build a much more effective ad from the ground up without necessarily opting for DCO but requires continuous testing across a large control group to remain relevant. Multi-variant testing is popular where the creative development team is much closer to the trafficking and reporting process. The effort required to maintain something so subjective in nature is too high a price to pay for a very small improvement in conversion uplift. A direct response Advertiser may claim that every additional sale matters but if the work required to bring that sale hikes up the operational costs of developing the DCO template or the work of the trafficker past that of the gain in a couple of sales then it is not worth the effort.

We have dived into the setup of DCO campaigns that both use a few versions and those that operate across mass versions. Trafficking and optimizing these campaigns is also fairly simple providing plenty of testing and practice goes on before the campaign goes live with DCO activity for the first time and the campaign goals and audience targeting requirements are clear. DCO adapts well to both brand Advertisers (to improve and scale creative copy and content) and for direct response Advertisers (for personalised audience targeting, retargeting, and creative optimization for the purpose of driving more valuable user engagements). In the next section we begin to drift a little further a-field still from Standard Display ad serving and even beyond Rich Media into the campaign management for Video otherwise known as Instream and Pre-Roll; a certain future for an internet infrastructure that provides users with an ever more immersive advertising experience.

Chapter 3 - Section 5
Instream Video

- What is Instream?
- *Figure 3.5.1*
- Pre Roll Mid Roll Post Roll
- *Figure 3.5.2*
- Site Served Video
- *Figure 3.5.3*
- Where do Video Ad Networks add value?
- VAST - the video tag standard
    - Companion Ads
    - *Figure 3.5.4*
    - Ad Skipping and TrueView
- VPAID - Standardised Interactive Video
    - *Figure 3.5.5*
    - VPAID Authoring
    - *Figure 3.5.6*
    - DCO for Instream
    - *Figure 3.5.7*
- Beyond VAST and VPAID
- Publisher Certification
    - *Figure 3.5.8*
- Trafficking Instream ads

Third Party ad serving providers consider Instream video to be the fastest growing channel in digital. Instream Video is perhaps the distant cousin of Standard Display and a closer relative to the Rich Media channel. The trafficker actually has a much easier job trafficking Instream Video ads than the job required to undertake DCO or Search for example, the more complex legwork sits with the Publisher.

This section will start out by explaining what Instream is before explaining how it is still in its infancy before providing an understanding about the tag structure, the capabilities of the ads in terms of tracking and reporting as well as the complete picture for campaign management from the perspective of the trafficker.

What is Instream?

Instream ads can be thought of as the evolution of TV advertising in many instances, Instream ads are literally an Advertiser's TV ad embedded into the video player of a Publisher website designed to play out video content. The ads are usually shown before the featured video content shown by the Publisher.

> Referring to Instream as VOD (Video on Demand) is a little inaccurate since VOD encapsulates the ability to stream video whenever required and would include playing video content from set-top boxes and paid for streaming services such as *Amazon's Lovefilm* or *Netflix*. None-the-less it is still common to hear those working in online advertising to refer to the Instream channel as "VOD".

Figure 3.5.1 *an example of an Instream Video ad. The Instream ad plays as a TV ad would play, before the featured video content in the same player. As with most Instream ads, some of the main video controls are disabled to prevent the user forwarding through the ad to the content faster than it is playing.*

Publishers offering Instream content are on the increase but the globally available inventory is still somewhat limited. The biggest sites for Video at time of writing include Google's *YouTube* and in the US sites like *Hulu*. All of the major broadcasters also offer in-browser video players and grant ad spots to Advertisers often in conjunction with deals designed to buy TV ad space.

To create the Instream ads, Advertisers will typically use the very same content which was filmed for TV but some are convincing their production teams to create video specifically designed for the web. The ads which are produced today tend to be fifteen seconds, thirty seconds or a minute long in play time and are converted by specialised production houses (often the function of more advanced Creative Agencies) into digital video suitable to be used online. Pure TV video is usually created at a very high definition which needs to be converted before it can be more easily transported around. There are several companies operating in the TV asset management, distribution and delivery space; big players include *Extreme Reach* and *Adstream*.

Once the video is digitised it needs to be fully adapted to Publisher specifications as one would expect from ads in both the display and rich media channels. Then it can be uploaded to the ad server and trafficked out before appearing in front of a user as a pre-roll, mid-roll or post-roll.

Pre Roll Mid Roll Post Roll

Despite the fact that video ads served before the featured video are the most commonly used Instream format (otherwise known as the Pre-Roll), there are also in use Mid Rolls (middle of the featured video) and Post Rolls (shown after the featured video). These formats all exist in the "stream" of the video itself and are referred to as "Linear" Instream ads meaning that the ad and the video content all seem to play in one continuous stream from beginning to end.

"Non-Linear" Instream ads allow the user to perform additional actions so as to potentially extend the possible engagement period within the creative beyond the fifteen seconds of the core video. Providing that the Publisher specifications permit non-linear, this can be achieved by introducing interactive elements into the ad.

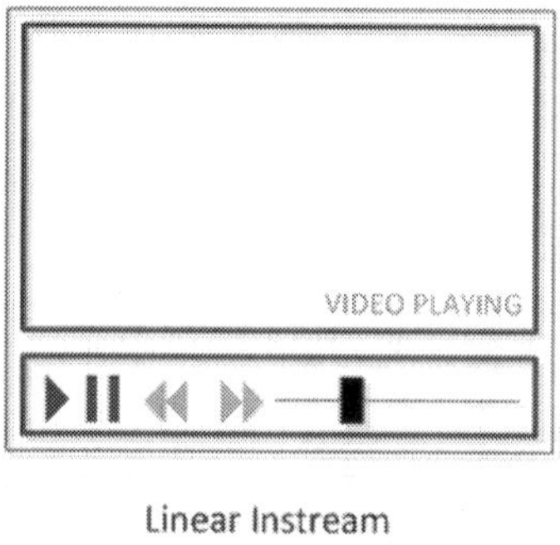

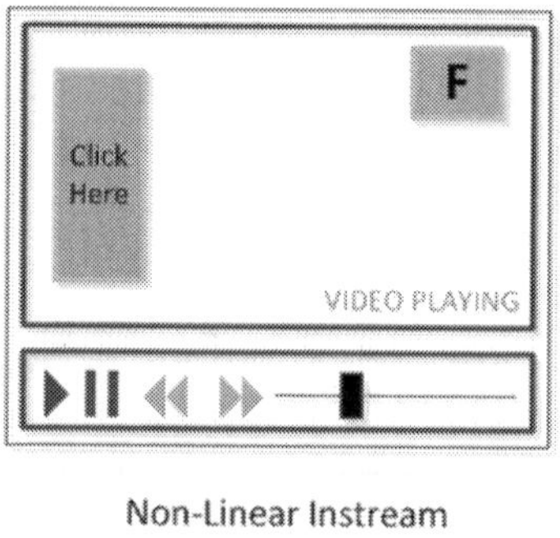

Figure 3.5.2 *Linear Vs. non-linear ads. Linear ads play through from beginning to end, only the video itself when clicked will take the user through to a landing page in a new window. With non-linear there can be additional clickable and interactive regions which, when rolled over or clicked might pause the video opening panels to a mini-website for the Advertiser inside the video player itself. The area labelled as 'F' might click through to the Advertiser's Facebook fan page for instance.*

To guarantee that videos are suitable for the Publisher or Broadcaster, media planners at Agencies and some Advertiser marketers have been circumventing the use of third party ad serving and passing the video assets directly to the Publisher site for implementation, distribution and serving. This behaviour gives little regard for the damage it is doing to the understanding the true value of the inventory in question and identifying the ad campaign value beyond single sites or the Instream channel in isolation.

Site Served Video

Video heavy Publishers and digital broadcasters have been notably resistant in granting permission to have video ads served by an independent third party. This thinking and practice is reminiscent of the internet in the early years when many Publishers. Some broadcasters may not even be aware of the value that third party ad serving offers to the Advertiser's funding their valuable content and with a well a more well established industry in TV ad trading than in online it is no surprise to find some resistance to change.

To remind the broadcasters, third party serving allows for the de-duplication of cross-Publisher reach, frequency and the de-duplication of conversions (see Chapter 4), independent tracking and auditing as well as standardised IAB approved reporting methodology across Publishers and video players. The Publisher's excuse to site serve says more about what that Publisher is thinking and practicing than they might realise.

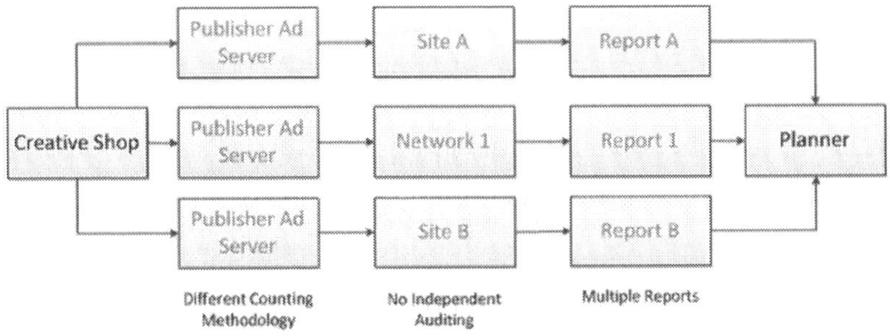

Figure 3.5.3 *Serving direct to the Publisher or broadcaster's video player without a third party creates blindness in the data and an operational nightmare to collate the generated data at the end of the campaign. The flaws are listed following this diagram: 1) there are different counting methodologies for the video because different Publisher ad servers have different counting capabilities, 2) there is no independent auditing of the collected data so it could be tampered with by the Publisher in their favour without the Advertiser knowing and 3) the process generates multiple reports in various formats that make life difficult for the planner/marketer/analyst reviewing the resulting reports.*

The trend among Media Agencies for some time was to serve Instream from third party ad servers but cut costs while still retaining some degree of transparency; by implementing tracking pixels and click trackers where the video itself is site served. This method still creates a degree of blindness and does not preserve the independent verification of the ad delivery in the ad server. A tracking pixel for instance cannot confirm if a video ad was ever seen, ever played or ever skipped. The demand from the industry has been for better standardisation and the *IAB* arrived in support of two technology standards for Instream which ensures:

- Consistent tag implementation among diverse Publishers and players
- The ability to standardise Instream metrics and core functionality among compliant video ad servers

Where do Video Ad Networks add value?
If an Advertiser chooses to run a campaign across a single network then there is no query of de-duplication because users are confined to seeing ads served from one place and tracked by a single system. For this reason Networks try to have as much reach as possible and in the Video world this is entirely possible. *Videology* is an example of a high reach Video Network. Third

party ad-serving continues to be useful on just a single network to independently verify the delivery and tracking of these ads.
Until very the very recent standardisation of Instream ad tags and technologies, third party ad serving ads was near impossible because of the many differences between Publisher players and the way they handle, process, play and track video. The standard passed by the IAB was VAST and if a Publisher video player is not certified to run VAST or VPAID ads it is best to avoid planning and buying their video inventory because it cannot be effectively managed with a third party system.

VAST - The video tag standard
VAST stands for Video Ad Serving Template, third party ad servers will output a VAST tag (which looks like any other ad tag) telling the player it is implemented in, what to display. The broadcaster's digital player will send an ad request to the third party ad server which will respond to the player by supplying an XML file that it can read. Reporting is then aggregated in the ad server as usual. VAST supports Linear ads, Non-Linear ads and "companion ads".

Companion Ads
Instream ads in the player can be accompanied by ads on the same page which tend to appear near the video content. Like Rich Media Sync Ads, companion ads are used to complement the video creative or to make it appear to be more interactive. The Publisher can use different parts of the ad tag code for the trafficked Insteam tag to assemble the companion ad next to the video content when it plays.

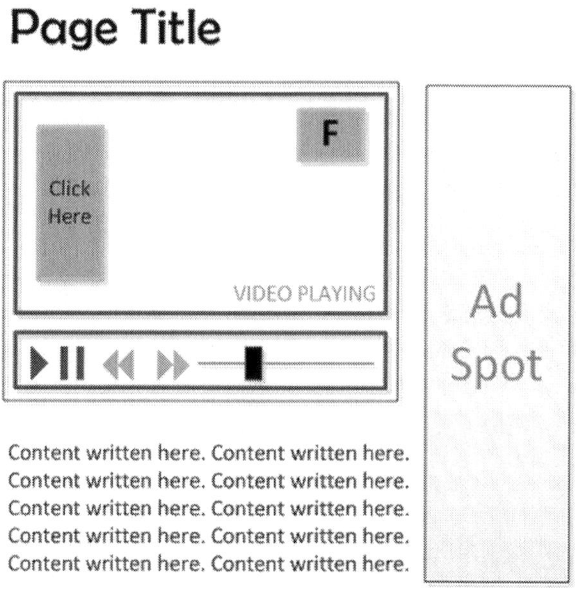

Figure 3.5.4 *A companion ad is served on to the same page as the Instream video, commonly in a reserved ad spot next to the player.*

Ad Skipping and *TrueView*

Some of the ads produced can be skipped after a few seconds while other ads play all the way through, disabling the video player controls that would usually allow the users to fast forward. In recent years *Youtube* has presented users with a button allowing the user to skip the whole ad. This technology is rolled up into a product offering called *Trueview* so that Advertisers only pay upon an entire viewing of the ad. The innovation of *Google's* skip functionality has been included in the standards for VAST 3.0 which means that increasingly, deeper interaction, starting with a skip will be available for Advertisers to implement on all ads, even outside of *Youtube*.

In addition to VAST tag standard there is an advanced player communication standard called VPAID.

VPAID - Standardised Interactive Video

VPAID stands for Video Player Ad Interface Definition and is a standardised method of communication between the video ad and the Publisher's player. Once the tag is embedded on the Publisher side, the video player calls the ad server to request the delivery of the video ad itself which is then streamed in. The Video player than performs an on-going communication between the ad and the player until the ad plays all the way through. If left untouched by any user engagement, the VPAID ad will typically play through as though it were any other linear ad but engage with it and the video might slow or pause to present new information to the user. Through engagements and video plays, the ad returns metric information to the ad server. Unlike VAST which contains around fifteen standard metrics, VPAID (like Rich Media) adds almost limitless customisation as custom metrics on top of additional standard metrics as well.

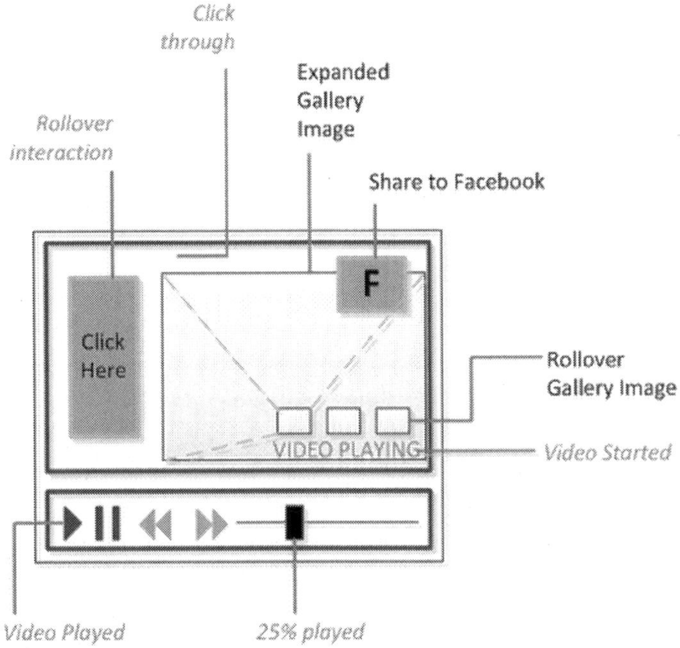

Figure 3.5.5 *A example of a VPAID ad. Collected metrics are stated in grey italics, additional functionality beyond standard linear VAST shown in black text. With VPAID there is a lot of data that can be gleaned about a user's interaction with the video ad as it plays, many of such actions can disrupt the linear play to pause the video. Functions such as image galleries might open new images in the video but on top of the playing video. Share to Facebook may open a new mini window within the player to allow the user to push a post to Facebook. Tracking for VPAID opens up the sort of options previously only available in Rich Media such as interaction tracking and more granular video completion metrics.*

VPAID Authoring

The development of VPAID ads sounds complicated to some Media Agencies and Advertisers who are unaware of precisely how standardised these formats have become. Elements among VPAID ads are so common (such as adding a call-to-action, adding a like to a *Facebook* Fan page, *Youtube* page or *Twitter* feed) that a creative developer does not even need to be involved in the process of converting a TV ad into a fully functioning interactive creative. This is down to a whole heap of available tools which are in fact small authoring environments (mimics Flash-like authoring capabilities in some instances). Ad servers are now beginning to market such tools to Agencies and Advertisers to cut down on creative costs but the same sort of tools are extended to specialist video Publisher networks as well, these include *Videology* and *Innovid*.

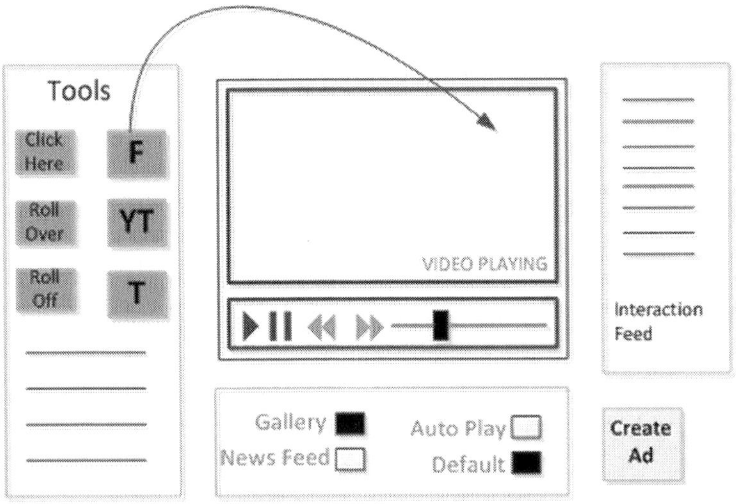

Figure 3.5.6 *A VPAID Authoring tool; allows the trafficker to transform an existing video creative into an interactive one. No coding experience is required since the interface allows elements to be dragged onto the video stage where they can be customised and the resulting data outputs can be tracked via an interaction feed panel. The completed project can be made into an ad at the click of a button.*

DCO for Instream

As with other forms of Display advertising (Standard Display, DCO and Mobile) the ad server can be used to make a decision to serve a particular creative to a particular audience type (see Chapter 4). If a flurry of audiences can be deduced, how does one go about amending a fixed piece of video to create differing versions of the creative?

The easiest solution is to use VPAID authoring tools to produce static frames in the video that appear to carry a different creative message such as different price point or written reference to a location. Some tools have emerged however, that allow the trafficker to append the video creative by layering text, images and additional video footage both on a layer which appears to sit above the rest of the video or deeply nested in the video itself. The latter of these options produces an astounding effect, most easily implemented when layering text or images onto a blank canvas such as a wall that might appear in the background of the video.

The addition to the video appears to display in multiple frames and in multiple angles because the text or image is carefully mapped to other moving objects.

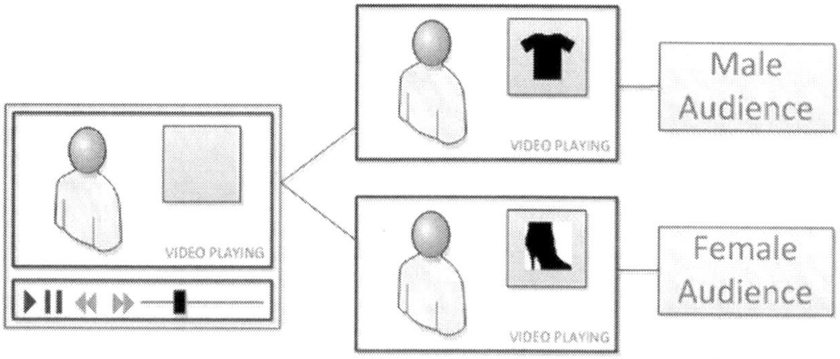

Figure 3.5.7 *DCO is available for Instream. Even with video that has already been filmed or made, the footage can be adapted by inserting a dynamic area into the video that even changes with the light and movement of the footage. This area can be mapped to other images or 3d objects as assets; the outcome is new versions which can be applied to audiences or placements just as with DCO for standard Display.*

Technology permits scalability by allowing the user to create many versions, inserting different, relevant messages into these subtle locations and exporting different versions of the video in doing so. Such technologies are in their infancy and therefore are not altogether cost effective at this advent. On example in particular: *Impossible Software*; have the ability to plug such a feature into ad serving technology. In this workflow the creative developer would pass the single video (which would be used as the template) into the user interface of the video versioning tool and the trafficker would control the output of the versions into the third party ad serving interface. Subsequently these versions would be assigned to placements and audiences (see Chapter 4).

Beyond VAST and VPAID

Digital Advertising is overly ripe with acronyms and confusingly a VPAID ad can be served through a VAST tag. The important thing to remember is that VAST is a tagging standard whereas VPAID is more like a format or a standardised way to describe the functionality of an interactive video ad. As of publication the so-called standardisation effort has given birth to a brood of numbers and letters that without explanation have little logical labelling:

- VAST 1.0
- VAST 2.0
- VAST 3.0
- VPAID 1.0
- VPAID 2.0

Without getting too technical each is a significant improvement on the other but since there are several standards for video in circulation, third party ad servers need to certify that ads will display and function when run with premium Publishers and broadcasters. This is both to check that the claims that a Publisher can support both VAST and VPAID and if so to see which version they are supporting. In turn the ad server needs to ensure it supports the output to the corresponding standards.

Just as Rich Media Publishers used to require certification the process remains the same. When a media plan becomes available from the Advertiser direct or the Agency media planner, the list of

Publishers should be supplied to the third party ad serving provider so that, if required, a certifications team can perform certifications. Certifications are only required on new sites and players but where these exist, the timeline for the campaign management and setup process will increase to accommodate a full certification.

Publisher Certification

In Instream ad delivery, the video player environment on the Publisher site that renders the ad tag is not standardised, not everyone is using the same kind of player technology. Therefore each Publisher site needs to be certified to ensure that third party served instream ads are fully functional in terms of delivery, verification and reporting.

Efforts have been put in place by the *IAB* and other interested parties to standardise the delivery of Instream ads industry wide with limited success, a claim of usage of the VAST standard by a Publisher is no guarantee the practice is being undertaken. Unfortunately due to the sheer volume of video player technologies in use, even the third party ad server has extended processes around running video campaigns and media plans must be checked. If new sites and new video players appear on the scene, testing and certification are sensible undertakings.

These processes are common place when a channel is in its infancy (and the mobile channel requires similar certification to ensure that the third party ad server tracking will work. The key is to test ad tags so that there is no discrepancy between ad server and Publisher reporting before the campaign goes live. This way Publishers can optimize ad delivery so that there is no over or under delivery with almost identical reporting as the third party ad server (where the Advertiser or Agency will be monitoring the delivery independently).

The certification process is actually very straight forward and with responsive parties, the process need not take more than a few days. Having said this, in practice, up to three weeks is recommended between the announcement of a new video Publisher on the media plan and the completion of the long term certification of that Publisher.

- Third party ad serving providers have a Publisher certification team in place who, once alerted to the presence of a new site on a plan, make contact with the Publisher verbally and send over test tags in an email to the Publisher contact.

- The Publisher takes these test tags and loads them up onto the Publisher-side ad server, displaying the resulting ads in a test environment.

- The location of the test environment is supplied to the third party ad server certifications team who run some tests to check that the metrics are collecting correctly and that the ad server calls are all taking place at the right time.

- When both Publisher and ad server satisfied with the metrics they are seeing the Publisher is labelled as certified and the Advertiser can go ahead to run activity on this Publisher in this channel.

- Certification usually means that any Advertiser from that point forwards can skip this process to run video on the Publisher site in the tested player.

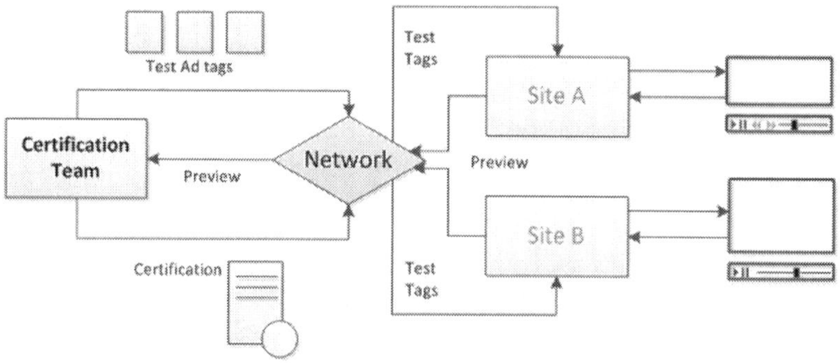

Figure 3.5.8 *Certification for Instream remains a requirement in digital advertising. The certification team at the third party ad serving provider sends test tags to the Publisher direct or the network for the site operations team to implement the test tags in the correct player environment. The preview of this implementation is sent back to the Certification team who assess the preview, awarding certification if the preview passes various tests.*

Certifications can be lengthy processes, especially when the certification reveals discrepancies and errors. For this reason it is recommended for the media planner to supply the list of sites and publishers for the video channel to the third party ad serving provider long before the campaign live date. Owing to the last minute building of media plans, Media Agencies can sometimes find themselves in trouble trying to push video to uncertified sites. It is therefore very important to be aware of the full scope of the certification process for Instream before ever buying the video ad space.

Publisher certification as a process is nothing new. Rich Media was also once an infant channel and used to follow the same process. Eventually all the established publishers and players supporting video certified in full and although re-certifications need to occur when there are big site changes, the certifications all go on quietly in the background without disrupting media plan timelines too much. Rich Media as a channel has now matured and Instream will follow suit and standardisation improves; ridding this extended campaign process in the coming years.

Trafficking Instream Ads

As mentioned earlier in this section; Instream video ads tend to be simpler to traffic from the third party ad serving interface than Display or Rich media ads which will come as a relief to all traffickers. Linear VAST ads mean the simple vetting of and placement assignment of core flash files (*.mov, *.flv, *.avi are examples and all of which are very common video file types). With VPAID the process is more complex but as an immature channel VPAID in Instream is still rarely made up of complex interactive executions.

Traffickers are encouraged to obtain the highest video quality available from the video producer or Creative Agency. With a higher definition video asset, the ad serving interface can transcode the video into lower quality videos for sites and Publishers that prefer to work with a lower video bit-rate. Ads are created, assigned to placements and placements to sites in the same way as with Display trafficking before the tags are generated and sent to the Publishers. With VPAID, the process of testing interactions in a preview environment is also adopted.

With some ad servers the trafficked ad tags look a little different than Display ad tags when the code packages are opened on the Publisher ad ops side. The ad tags contain links to various qualities of the video to allow the Publisher team to select which version they would prefer to serve to their users. More advanced Publisher ad servers assess the suitability to serve a certain bitrate (usually based on the speed of the internet connection) and serve the video with the bitrate deemed more suitable by the Publisher ad operations team.

With Instream ads trafficked, the tracking feeds down into the third party ad server when the ad is served and the metrics are recorded (see Chapter 5 - Channel Specific Reporting for details regarding these metrics). As with all other channels, the unified tracking and reporting opens up the possibility to understand how Instream ads add value to campaigns running in other channels. Hopefully such insights justify the higher cost to serve. The consensus remains that this channel provides a more engaging impact upon the user which will encourage better performance of the campaign as a whole.

Channels which can deliver visual creative are hotly sought by big brand marketers who use the impact associated with imagery to draw user attention. With such creativity there is limited call-to-action within the creative except for activities that might encourage better education or awareness about the product or service. Rich Media and Video digital advertising are very well suited to this need and on the periphery sit Display and its maturing cousin; Mobile. The next section divulges the campaign management process for Mobile, disclosing the key concepts behind its gradual refining and why as a channel it is so intangible. Unlike Insteam which might be a relatively simple chore for the trafficker, mobile continues to produce headaches for Agency operations teams the world over in the context of third party ad serving.

Chapter 3 - Section 6
Mobile

The Mobile channel presents the greatest upcoming opportunity for Advertisers. The growing volume of internet traffic coming from mobile devices is staggering providing a channel of enhanced reach. Since the ratio of devices to humans is reaching a level playing field, devices have become unique to each human which means the eradication of the assumption that a whole household is accessing the internet from the same place. Further in this section we will see how this resolves in data collection. Beyond improved reach, the features of what were originally called "smartphones" are standardised enough that creative developers can assume that ads can be developed to make the most of these features. Examples include:

- Gestures
- Geo-location
- Accelerometer

This would suggest that the mobile channel should be an exciting area for growth and creativity but it is fraught with challenges that many technology providers, Agencies and Publishers have been accused of not implementing consistent standards as have been created in the other digital channels.

This section begins by looking carefully at what it means to ad serve to "mobile" devices, the challenges with serving to both browser and in-app environments and the process of trafficking to certified mobile properties. Finally we settle on the politics of mobile as a narrowly controlled media channel and the importance of supporting independent tracking mythologies to disclose reliable reporting metrics.

The Connectivity Consideration
Even with the introduction of Smart Phones, internet connectivity and bandwidth remain an issue for delivering high quality creative to mobile devices. For instance, most Advertisers and Media planners will rule out the possibility of running rich media with video formats on mobile Publishers because it puts a heavy drain on the user: the need to download a lot of information to display the ad. To avoid the user suffering a bad experience on a Publisher site, high file size ads have been discouraged, which limits creativity. Where technology is still catching up is finding a way to identify those users using a mobile device on the move versus those that are stationary and are downloading data through a Wi-Fi connection. If connected the Wi-Fi, suddenly bandwidth and data downloading does not need to be restricted but ad servers are not currently providing device level targeting that distinguishes between Wi-Fi and connection via a mobile provider. This feature may never be needed in the ad server itself owing to the improvements in wireless data transmission. 4G

promises internet speeds that will rival Wi-Fi and if data costs come down over the next few years there will not need to be an ad server feature to separate out the users by their bandwidth speeds. For the time being it is advised for creative developers to build the frugal Publisher specifications available, since this makes full consideration for users who might not be able to download large ads.

Internet Enabled Device Divergence

Since there is a whole plethora of internet-enabled devices and the distinction between what is a mobile device and what is not, is a conundrum. In order to separate out media inventory, Publishers began by creating different properties in the hope that the browsing user would head to the property most suited to their device. With this methodology a user arrives at the standard site from their "desktop device", chooses to download the app from their mobile device or uses their in-built mobile web browser to head to the purpose built mobile web site. Larger Publishers such as newspaper publications have taken this a step further and developed applications designed for use on tablets to give a brighter, larger and more engaging experience. Here the distinction is clear, ads must be created for the browser environment and for the "in-app" environment:

- Desktop browser
- Mobile Browser
- In-app for Mobile
- In-app for Tablet

Making the distinction between the user's arrival is an easy task for the Publisher, the browser type can be detected by the JavaScript design of the Publisher site such that mobile users are re-directed to a mobile site while others land on the usual desktop browser page. For apps, the distinction is made when the user first downloads the Publisher's app; choosing the app meant for tablets versus the one meant for other mobile devices.

Publisher Certification for Mobile
As with Instream Video and originally rich media, both apps and browser Publisher properties need to be fully tested and certified before an ad campaign can go live. Without certification, the Advertiser runs the risk that the data collection and actual ad delivery might fail. As a best practice, when a mobile campaign is being booked and inventory purchased, the third party ad server should be alerted so that if required, the certification process can begin. Just as with the other channels, the certifications team at the third party ad serving provider contact the Publisher directly and send over test versions of mobile ad tags. The Publisher implements these on the correct properties and the certifications team check the ads deliver and function and that data is collected in reporting.

Just as with Display inventory, Mobile inventory is partly held by large Publisher Networks that tend to be mobile-specific and certifying through the Networks means that much of the mobile web is Publisher-certified to run third party tags. As with Display it is recommended that should any new Publisher sites or Networks crop up on a media plan, that these details be supplied to the certifications team around three weeks before a campaign start date. Rich Media and DCO ad formats are enabled within most third party ad serving interfaces and open up the options for what kinds of ads can be delivered and tracked at scale but the use of these will extend the period of certification. Thankfully the IAB has started to standardise some core Rich Media formats specifically for mobile which, as with the Rich Media channel for non-mobile devices has been a huge help in eradicating the need for certification almost altogether.

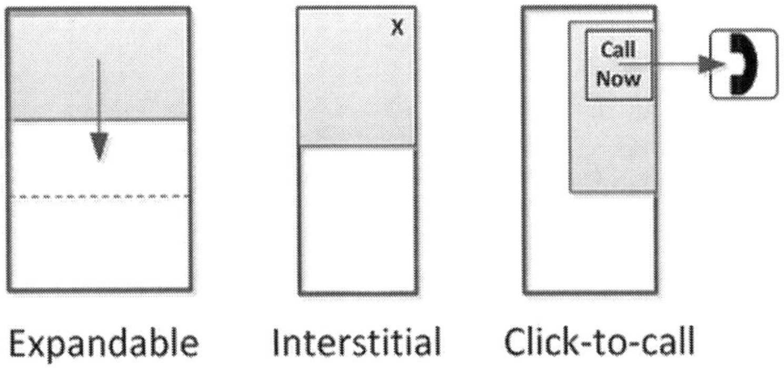

Figure 3.6.1 *Examples of Rich Media units for Mobile campaigns which include expandable ads (simply ads made up of two core panels), Interstitial ads (which fill the screen to cover the content much like a floating unit from Rich Media for Display) and the Click-to-call functionality (unique to the mobile space driving the user through to a phone number which connects from the device instantly).*

Beyond certification the mobile landscape is diverse and technically speaking, cumbersome and complex. The distinctions and challenges faced in delivering ads to mobile browsers and in-app environments is great enough to have slowed the spend in mobile channels for media space.

Challenges within the browser

Within the same ad campaign the creative developed for these environments will be consistent in design so as to keep the costs of creative development down. If there were only four possible environments things would be relatively simple but mobile devices differ in screen size significantly. This wasn't always the case, so developing a standard 300x250 meant the same ad could be used on the desktop Publisher site and in the Publisher mobile site. That is until the a user arrives to the mobile site with a small screen and sees just half a 300x250; not an effective execution and essentially a wasted delivery. When the user arrives at the Publisher site the JavaScript can be used detect the screen-size to request an ad of the most suitable dimensions from the third party ad server by firing off the corresponding ad tag. This still means that the Creative Agency needs to develop many ad sizes and will use the Publisher specifications to determine which ones to build out. The Publisher ad operations team and the trafficker would have a big task on their hands if they had to create hundreds of tags to do this job. Thankfully technology has come to the aid.

Responsive Design

Responsive Design is a new concept but essentially means that with a single ad tag implemented on a Publisher page that the screen size can be adjusted and as the screen enlarges or shrinks, the delivered ad unit changes. The effect is that the same placement appears to deliver a leader-board on a tablet but on a mobile device that spot shows a banner format. The Publisher ad operations team can celebrate, receiving just one tag from the Agency trafficker and yet all users seeing only the ad dimensions most suited to their device. Discouragingly the Creative Agency still needs to design ads to each of those dimensions and although third party ad servers are now offering creative templates in Flash to assist with building responsive ads, there is still likely to be a higher cost to the Advertiser than there would be for developing a single format for a desktop-only campaign.

Whatever happened to Flash?

Flash, the cornerstone of the creative development process is being phased out across mobile devices. But it is not the browsers which are not supporting the plugin required to play the Flash animations, it is Adobe themselves who have opted to stop offering the plugin for mobile browsers. The challenge to adapt the plugin to an ever divergent technology landscape without profit put the nail in the coffin for Flash. Instead HTML5 presents an opportunity to have the same (if not a better) visual experience than Flash on a mobile device.

The fall-back Mechanism

Within standard display a fall-back mechanism has long been the standard: serve the flash animation, and in instances where Flash is not supported, show a backup image. This method does not serve mobile campaigns very well at all. Since the vast majority of mobile devices do not support flash, users are seeing static images as ads instead of the costly animated creative that was developed for a better user experience. The demand today looks like this:

- If the user's browser can support Flash, show the Flash ad
- If the user's browser cannot support Flash, show the HTML5 ad
- If the user's browser cannot support HTML5, show the backup image

As mobile internet traffic grows further it is likely that the demand from Advertisers will be that the HTML5 version is the one at the top of the food chain. At time of publishing, HTML5 is being treated as an inferior coding environment (where in fact its capabilities are better supported and superior to those of Flash). Although fall-back mechanisms have become integrated into the delivery of ads by third party ad servers, for mobile campaigns, it is still a best practice to look at device delivery reports and to see how many backup images are being delivered by a campaign.

Trafficking ads for Mobile Browsers

The Agency buyer or marketer procures the mobile inventory from the Networks or Publishers and supplies the Media plan to:

a. The third party ad serving provider to check the sites for the purposes of certification
b. The creative developer who builds out the required creative based on the media plan, taking into account the Publisher specifications.
c. The trafficker, who sets up the campaign in the same way as a display campaign

Once the trafficker identifies that the sites being served to are mobile, the ad server grants the ability to attach creative to the ads to support both responsive design and a fall-back mechanism. The trafficker then traffics the ad tags to the Publisher ad operations team who implement them on the mobile site. The total number of tags being kept to a minimum thanks to responsive design.

QA for mobile browser-based ads

To QA the ads the trafficker needs to use a different method than is used in other Display channels since the actual ad needs to be tested on as many mobile device types as possible. In order to check the ad thoroughly and monitor the ad calls, the trafficker can use an HTTP tracer like Fiddler and adjust the proxy settings on the test mobile device so that all the traffic to and from the mobile device runs via Fiddler running on a local desktop based computer. The trafficker can then create a preview URL of the ad inside the third party ad server interface and send to the mobile device from where the URL should be accessed via the mobile browser.

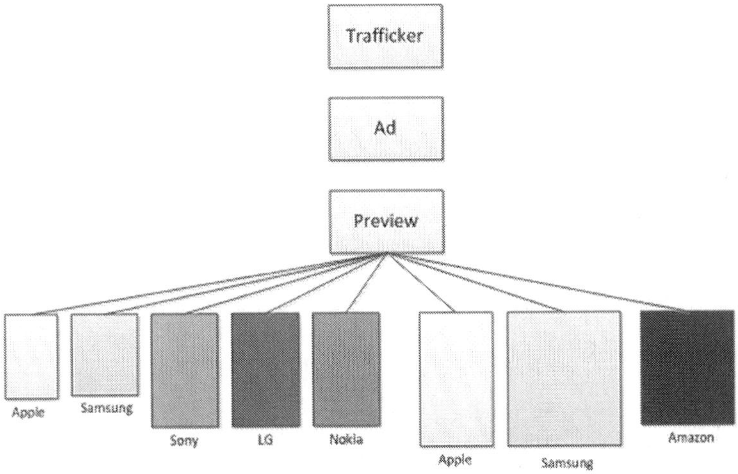

Figure 3.6.2 *Owing to device divergence, a thorough QA process would mean testing a preview link generated by the trafficker on all available mobile devices to check that the ad loads and is at least clickable before the mobile campaign launches. This goes for mobile phones and tablet devices.*

There are some web-based mobile browser emulators available to check ad tags across a range of devices without performing a QA across every device type available but where possible it is recommended for the trafficker to QA the ad on each physical device type.

Challenges within the app

The app space has a growing number of ad formats cropping up and these are predominantly owned by the dominating Mobile Ad Networks. These ad networks control the delivery of ads to the apps making it easy for app developers to monetise their applications by signing up to the networks, deploying a piece of code in the app and having the network serve up ads whenever the app pages load. This has assisted in supporting wholly free apps, providing developers with a revenue stream.

To third party ad serve an ad into an app means channelling through the network but also delivering the unit and gathering the data into a non-browser environment, so here is where things get a little tricky. Apps are rarely designed to allow for multiple calls into and out of a uniquely developed code structure, so apps much originally be developed using a template that produces a standardised communication channel in and out of the app environment. This template is referred to as an "SDK" (Software Development Kit) which, when supplied by the ad server ensures the basic ad calls will occur sufficiently for accurate counting in ad server reporting. Encouraging Publishers to build applications with such an SDK for the purposes of third party ad serving (and thus greater and fairer monetisation) means working with Publisher-side development teams to have them understand the benefits of putting more work in the development of the application.

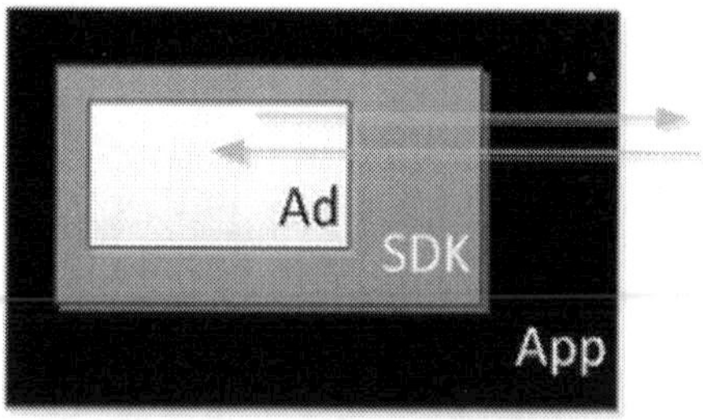

Figure 3.6.3 *The SDK circumvents the problem of the black-box environment of the App, facilitating calls into and out of the ad to the ad server or measurement technology.*

Trafficking ads for In-app ad campaigns

Whether a Publisher chooses to work with an SDK or not will still require the third party ad serving provider's certification team to test ads in the application before certifying the environment and approving the app for third party ad delivery on a media plan. Even without the SDK in place, other technologies have emerged on the Publisher network side to facilitate ad tracking called "Ad Enablers". The trafficking process for in-app ad campaigns is the same as in-browser for mobile, where either the direct app or the mobile network are listed as the site in the campaign management workflow in the third party ad serving interface.

To QA how an ad will behave in an app environment is more complex that QA for mobile ads in the browser. The trafficker must work with the Publisher to provide a test page when the actual ad tag is implemented. Very few mobile apps offer emulators which can be used by the trafficker on a mobile device to emulate the in-app environment for the purposes of testing. Without the test the risk is the ad will not function as expected.

Where do Mobile Ad Networks add value?

As mentioned in the Instream Video section, if an Advertiser chooses to run a campaign across a single network then there is no query of de-duplication because users are confined to seeing ads served from one place and tracked by a single system. For this reason Networks try to have as much reach as possible and as in the video world, in the mobile world this is entirely possible. *InMobi* is an example of a high reach mobile network. Third party ad-serving continues to be useful on just a single network to independently verify the delivery and tracking of these ads.

It is clear that the delivery of third party served ads to both the browser and the in-app environments, offer their fair share of challenges. Only certification at its most thorough can come close to the guarantee that the ad will deliver with the support of a fall-back. Data collection for these ads is not quite as standardised and straightforward as for the other display channels and this comes back the device itself (more detail on this in Chapter 5 - Channel Specific Reporting).

As Mobile matures it will take pride of place among channels that are more purpose built to drive specific actions like sales. Channels which drive specific actions like sales are referred to as Direct Response channels. The most significant among these is the Search channel. The next section in this chapter unwraps Paid Search (also known as PPC) which is a much more mature digital channel that is fully third party ad server supported and is seen as the gateway to performance marketing.

Chapter 3 - Section 7
Paid Search and Natural Search

- SEM and PPC
- Creating Campaigns and Keywords in the Engine
    - *Figure 3.7*
    - *Figure 3.7.1*
- Connecting a Bid Management System to the Engine
    - *Figure 3.7.2*
- Why track paid search through a third party ad server?
- How to track Paid Search through a third party ad server?
    - Manual Search Tracking
        - *Figure 3.7.3*
    - Automated Search Tracking
        - *Figure 3.7.4*
- Ad Server tracking integrated with Bid Management
    - *Figure 3.7.5*
- Extending tracked Paid Search to the long tail
    - *Figure 3.7.6*
- Extending tracked Paid Search to Mobile
- Search and other Channels
- What is SEO?
    - *Figure 3.7.7*
- Referral URL to trigger a click
    - *Figure 3.7.8*
- Ad Serving costs for Search

The next areas of this chapter provide reference information for what are called the "Performance Channels". Performance Channels are highly measurable channels marrying reach with effectiveness; specifically designed to drive audiences through to conversions (see Chapter 4). Performance Channels are located lower down in the strategic marketing funnel because they are explored and used by consumers that have predominantly come closer to finalising the purchase decision. This can be compared to the display channels which often better serve the needs of the Advertiser further up the funnel to create brand and product awareness.

Search is effective when users have already built up an awareness of a product or brand through more visual channels such as display, as they use the search engine to research the internet for more information. In this sense Search engines are the navigation hub of the web experience and as such are valuable places for the Advertiser to attract attention.

Search can be divided into two channels Paid Search and Natural Search. The two channels are almost never managed by the same team but both channels can technically be tracked by a third party ad server. It is worth noting that for the Search channels, the ad server is not considered to "serve" anything since there is no image displayed but rather can attend to a portion of the user click path for tracking. The ad server's position is still wholly relevant because internet users that might take actions with any other channel, may also perform an action in a Search channel and capturing this pathway is essential for conversion and attribution reporting (see Chapter 4).

This section begins by looking at how paid search is used as a channel by the Advertiser and how the third party ad server connects to the search engines to seamlessly integrate for tracking purposes. This process has evolved over the years and has taken a big workload off of the trafficker's shoulders. We will touch on how the shady past shapes the process today and why the future of campaign management for paid search looks so strong. This section will also touch on bid management solutions; which assist the core ad search programs to scale the implementation of keywords. More controversially this section will end by explaining how natural search can be tracked as a channel in its own right and how the setting up of this channel from a tracking perspective must be carefully considered so that more directly paid-for channels do not appear to lose their effectiveness.

SEM and PPC

Paid Search is often given the acronym "SEM" which stands for Search Engine Marketing, however, Paid search channel is also commonly referred to industry-wide as PPC, which has the potential to confuse those new to the world of search since PPC actually means Pay Per Click. It is true to say that the paid search channel is predominantly funded through a PPC or click-based pay model, as opposed to the CPM dominated model for the Display channels, but it might not be the best name for this channel as a whole.

Defining Paid Search is fairly straightforward but this section will not dwell too much on its intricacies beyond the intermediate educational requirements of the Advertiser to third party track its activity, since there are a great horde of how-to textbooks already written on the topic.

Paid search is essentially the sponsored search listings that appear on the search results page in the search engine. These traditionally appear along the top (just under the search bar) and down the right side of the page. They are usually presented on an off-colour background and the ads presented usually match the keyword typed in, in some way. The search engine algorithm for the paid search listings is meant to ensure that Advertisers that have paid more for their keywords to display will appear higher up the results list or more frequently across more users search results pages.

When referring to the paying of keywords it is useful for us to loop back to the term PPC. The search keywords themselves cost the Advertiser money only when there are clicked on (the delivery of the sponsored listing itself is essentially free). Advertisers arrive into an auction to offer up the maximum price they would pay should a user click on their ad. Winning the auction will trigger a charge in the Advertiser's account.

In its most basic form, the Advertiser is permitted to enter into this auction by creating an account for buying keywords with the Search Engine. For instance *Google* offers a program called *Adwords*, *Microsoft's Bing* offers *Adcenter*.

Creating Campaigns and Keywords in the Engine

Paid Search activity is usually managed by a specialist search team which belongs to the marketing team on the Advertiser side directly or sits in the Media Agency (separated from the Display operations team). Some Media Agencies have carved off a decent portion of their staff to create new search specialist Agencies (a good example is *Performics*; an SEM Agency under the *Publicis Group* umbrella). These teams access the SEM interface belonging to the engine by navigating to their site and logging in.

The first step to setting up a search campaign for the first time is adding bank details and funding the search account. Once funds have been deposited, the team can begin by creating or uploading keywords. Keywords are basically anything that a user might type into the search engine to find something. Search engine marketers are encouraged to create as many keywords as they can think of and many user specialist tools and programs to generate keywords in their thousands and millions.

Once the keywords are determined they need to be coupled with a short description and the URL where the user should be directed to once they click on the ad, essentially like with ad serving; a click-through URL. Keywords coupled with the description, title and clickthrough URL make up the search ads themselves. To help manage these ads they are sorted into buckets in the SEM interface: called "Ad Groups" which in turn are clumped together to form campaigns. The most common way to mass produce millions of search ads involves using spread-sheets on a local machine to couple the generated keywords with their component parts and the name of the ad group to which they belong. The sheet is then loaded up into the interface underneath the correct campaign.

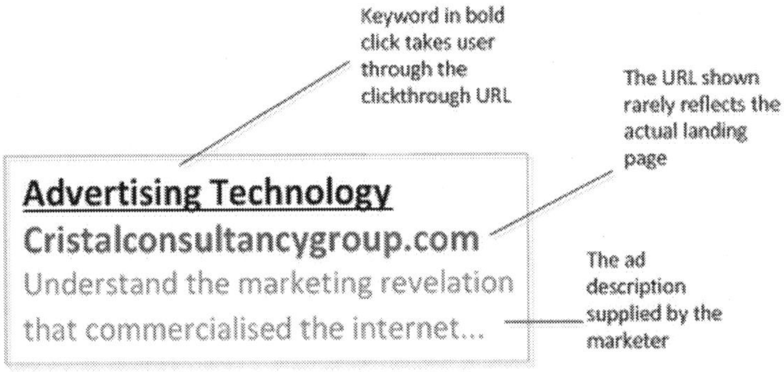

Figure 3.7 *Components of the now standardised Search Ad include the Keyword as the header underlined in bold followed by a URL (which does not have to reflect the true landing page or the clickthrough URL). Both are accompanied by a short description.*

Campaigns in the SEM interface can be defined at the marketer's discretion, many marketers are following a convention of having a new campaign for each brand, product and marketing campaign. The campaigns listed in the interface may not need to all be active at the same time, so it is simple to activate and deactivate the activity. Also alongside each keyword the marketer needs to determine how much they are willing to pay for the keywords so the maximum bid price is entered. The spread-sheet as a whole is then uploaded to the interface and the campaign can be put live.

Inside the same SEM interface in the engine, it is possible to get reports to show which keywords were clicked on and how much was eventually paid. Despite its simplicity there is a whole range of options available to enhance the performance of the search campaigns, from adjusted messaging at different times of day to utilising retargeting strategies (see Chapter 7). What is actually happening to the user when they click on a sponsored search result in the search engine, is that their click activity sends a count to the SEM reporting server so that the information about the click such as the keyword clicked on and the timestamp of the activity is stored just as the user arrives at the landing page destination.

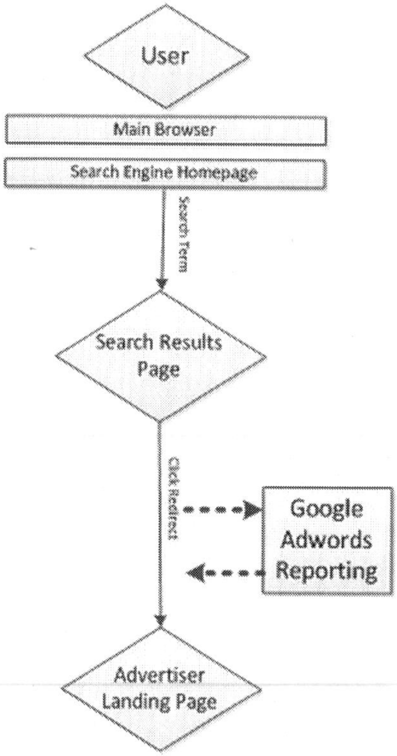

Figure 3.7.1 *The click-path that the user is taken on as a result of the action of searching. In this example the user navigates in their browser to the search engine homepage (in this instance Google) where their search term is carried to the search results page. Here the SEM Search Ad is displayed. The user clicks the ad (which is*

labelled as a sponsored listing) and appears to land directly on the homepage. The user is in fact redirected through the Google Adwords reporting server so that the click is registered and the Advertiser is charged for the activity.

Connecting a Bid Management System to the Engine

The search engines have developed their own APIs to allow other systems to connect and control this keyword and campaign management environment, at a distance. What these systems have that the search engine SEM interfaces do not, is more complex ways of deciding what keywords to pay more for over others. In the context of the auction model in which PPC is determined requires that at scale, prices be set according to the value that each keyword is bringing. Since a multitude of factors determine this, these external systems are commonly referred to as "Bid Management Systems" and pull on various data sources to make decisions.

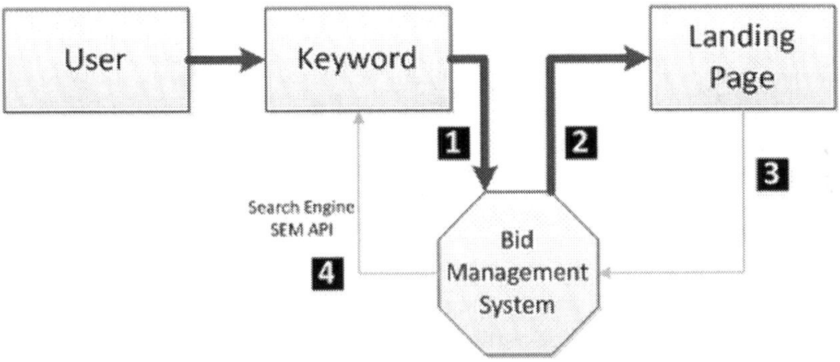

Figure 3.7.2 *The user would typically input a search term into the search engine such as Google and the ad clicked on (represented here by a keyword) would take them to the landing page (redirected through the Adwords reporting server). With a bid manager involved the user's click-path will still route via the Adwords reporting server but will also route via the reporting*

server for the Bid Management System. This is represented by (1) and (2). Information about the user's journey is also collected by the Bid Manager's technology (also embedded on the Advertiser's landing page) and this is also fed in the Bid Management System's reporting server. With information about clicks and conversions (see Chapter 4) the Bid Manager can update the bid price on the keyword via the Search Engine's SEM API.

Bid Managers track the user as they click on the keyword to determine how far that user goes down the purchase funnel and adjusted bids for keywords based on this as a starting point. To this extent, when the bid manager is setup on the Advertiser's SEM account, the bid manager connects to the search engine via the API and adds a "code wrapper" around the click -through URL of the keywords listed there. The wrapper is portion of code that sits either side of the click-through URL and when the user clicks the link, the bid manager is now tracking the user independent of the search engine.

Despite having their own SEM interface; *Adwords, Google* has its own Bid Management tool which makes up part of the *DoubleClick* suite; the latest iteration at time of writing is called *DS3* which evolved out of the legacy tool *DARTSearch* which was one of the first ad-server integrated bid management tools. Other popular and powerful players in the space are *Marin, Kenshoo* and *IgnitionOne*.

> Bid management tools have begun evolving in recent years so that they take on new data from the Advertiser side and begin acting a little more like a DSP or a DMP but leading with bidding on the search channel (see Chapter 8 - Programmatic). The difference here is that Bid Managers are built for enormous scale for the handling and processing of millions of keywords where bidders in the Display space are working with far fewer ads.

Having looked into how campaign management works for search marketing campaigns; both smaller scale inside the SE (Search Engine) interfaces and at a larger scale with bid management systems there remains an important space for the independent tracking and counting of the data by the third party ad server.

Why track paid search through a third party ad server?
Owing to the scale and dynamics of Paid Search, it is considered to be a wholly separate channel from Display advertising. This means that in order to track users that:

1) clicked on paid search
2) were influenced to search by display ads

..there must be a common technology tracking both channels at a single point. The regular use cases for using a third party ad server still stand; such as the case to have an independent tracking technology, kept separate from the Publisher/Search Engine provider. It also becomes possible to compare and contrast the costs of paid search across multiple products, brands and countries to other channels in a single system of record with the same counting methodology.

How to track Paid Search through a third party ad server?
To the trafficker working inside the third party ad server interface, the search engines can be classed as Publishers and the keywords as the ads or placements. The trafficker navigates to the Advertiser account in question in the ad server hierarchy and there are two methods to then connect the third party ad server from there.

Manual Search Tracking
Manual Search tracking is how things used to be done in the world of ad serving for paid search. This method is now reserved for very rare instances in which the Search Engine

API fails or for connecting to smaller more obscure search engines. The trafficker undertakes the following steps:

1. Sets up a new campaign in the third party ad server interface with the correct naming convention (that might mean the advertiser is naming different campaigns according to which channel they belong to) or accesses an existing campaign that contains activity for all channels
2. Generates a tracking pixel with single click tracker for each keyword in the engine inside the campaign
3. Inserts the same landing page URL as can be found alongside the existing keywords in the engine into the click trackers.
4. Traffics all of the click trackers, so that the ad tag code for the clicks becomes available
5. Downloads the keyword list from the Search Engine SEM interface for the campaign in question
6. Replaces the click-through URL column in the keyword list spread sheet with the matching code for the click from the ad server
7. Uploads the completed spread-sheet back to the Search Engine SEM interface and puts the campaign live from there

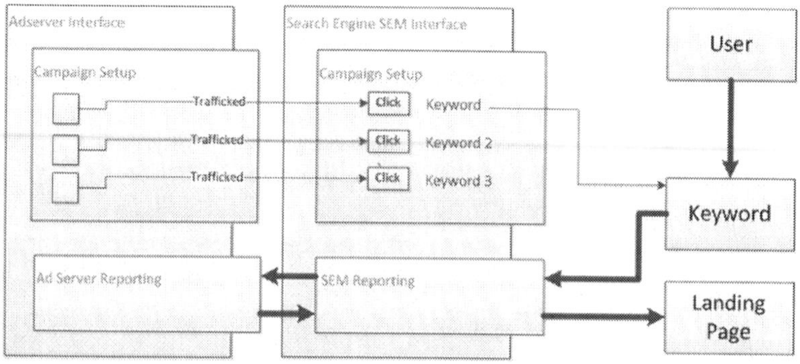

Figure 3.7.3 *Manual Search Tracking involves a heavy operational burden on the trafficker. A tracking placement is created for each keyword to match the keywords in the engine. The click redirects are then trafficked to the Media Agency who replace the click-throughs on each of the keywords with those generated by the ad server. When the user clicks the ad for the keyword in question, the user click path is routed through the Search Engine SEM reporting (such as Adwords) and the third party ad server reporting before landing the user on the landing page.*

This manual process is enormously time consuming and problems occur when trying to differentiate the click trackers in ad server reporting from other kinds of ad servers if a naming convention has not been set up to divulge the channel type. Thankfully the Search Engines themselves came to the aid of marketers whose total number of keywords was becoming unmanageable with this system.

Automated Search Tracking

The search engine API allows the third party ad server to connect directly to the engine and write the click-through URLs to the keywords themselves directly. The trafficker then:

1. Logs into the search engine from a slightly different screen inside the third party ad server but still sitting within the same Advertiser account. This login will be the same as the one used by the search marketers to access the SEM interface in the search engine directly.

2. Sees the campaigns as they were created in the search engine and selects the right one to track all keywords in that campaign so that the tracking is fed into the ad server under this account.

The third party ad server will then automatically 'wrap' the landing page URLs in the engine with ad server click tracking with no additional effort required from the trafficker.

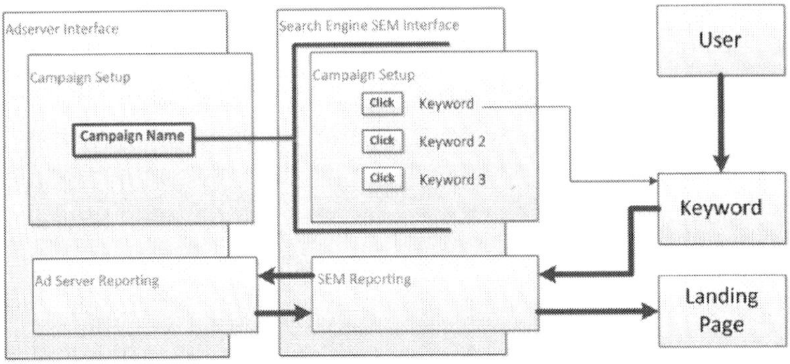

Figure 3.7.4 *The automatic search tracking option presented by some third party ad servers is much more favourable operationally speaking. Here the trafficker only has click "track" by selecting the right campaign name in the third party ad server and the corresponding name in the Search Engine SEM interface has all its keywords wrapped.*

Once the keywords are being tracked the ad server connects to the engine at least once per day via the API to request reporting information which is pulled down into ad server analytics so that the trafficker can pull reports about the cost of the keywords and their performance. This means the Advertiser or Agency does not need to log into the various engines to extract the results but can get them all combined in ad server analytics. More information on this can be found in Chapter 5 - Channel Specific Reporting.

Ad Server tracking integrated with Bid Management
Bid management systems can be used in conjunction with third party ad server reporting and at a deeper level the two technologies can share data independent of the search engine itself. Operating bid management systems and ad-serving is easy for those ad servers that claim to have a basic level of integration. Essentially both bidder and ad server work separately but harmoniously in that their code wrappers both wrap the keyword in the engine via the Search engine API and the two code wrappers do not disrupt the different systems from tracking and reporting separately. To achieve this state the ad server needs to have worked with the bid management provider in a process of certification. In some instances the wrappers disrupt one another unless one wrapper is added after the other, this tends to be the case with lesser known bid management providers and less user-utilised search engines.

Sharing data between ad servers and bid managers is a relatively new idea compared to the longer history of search marketing. In this instance the ad server is collecting a vast amount of data about the Advertiser's ad campaigns outside of the search keyword but can tie all this information back to it. With the Advertiser's approval, the ad server can pass data that might show if some keywords are more or less effective depending when the user saw or acted upon them. In turn the bidder can improve its bidding algorithms through a system of learning.

> An advanced example of such an integration would include the passing of E2C (exposure to conversion) or P2C (pathway to conversion) data from the ad server to the bidder using a daily feed (See Chapter 5 - Cookie Level data). Using this method allows the bid manager to apply an "Attribution Model" to users featured in the data to adjust the bid price for certain keywords (more on Attribution Modelling in Chapter 4).

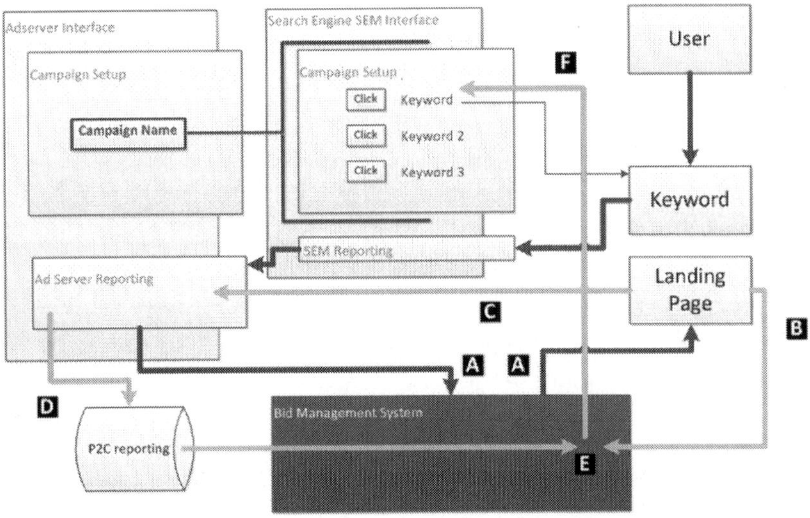

Figure 3.7.5 *Introducing integrated bid management into the equation allows the bids on the keywords to be much more intelligent and the prices to pay to be far better informed. The user click-path now triggers counts in SEM reporting (such as Adwords). Ad Server reporting and Bid Management reporting at point (A). The user lands on the landing page triggering the Bid manager's landing page tag (B) demonstrating that the keyword can be given higher value since it drove a site-side action. The landing page also triggers a conversion tag (C) - more info on this in Chapter 4. The user data about the click and the conversion as well as user data about other engagements across other media on other channels for the clicking users is passed into (D) "P2C Reporting" (see Chapter 5) and the data is collected in the Bid Management system at (E). Inside the Bid Management System, the marketer is free to apply an attribution model (See Chapter 4) to the keyword information to establish its value before adjusting the bid price at (F).*

Extending tracked Paid Search to the long tail
Google Adwords product has a sister toolset called *Google Adsense*. *Adsense* allows small Publishers to attract CPC (Cost per click) revenues through Advertising, which otherwise would be completely unattainable since the amount of user traffic to such sites remains very small. Niche Publisher sites have very specific content that, despite having a small amount of traffic might have a perfectly suited audience for a "contextually targeted" ad.

Adsense works by having the Publisher download *Adsense* code from *Google*'s site (after signing up for an account and inserting bank details) and sees the Publisher embed the code on any page of their site. Users then arrive at the site and the *Adsense* code reads the content of the page. This content is then checked against the *Adwords* databases to see if there are any matching keywords which it then displays to the user. These are *Adwords* paid search ads, appearing in the *Adsense* spot on the page. Since *Adsense* draws from the *Adwords* database itself, *Adsense* uses the same click-through URLs as adwords, if these keywords are tracked in the third party ad server they will also be tracked by *Adsense*.

> Advertiser's should have the option of separating out the traffic coming from *Adsense* supported Publisher sites versus those coming from the Search Engine itself by only applying certain SEM campaigns in the SEM interface to either *Adwords* or *Adsense* since the traffic quality might be different. It is worth the Advertiser checking with the Search engine directly to see if campaigns be separated out. If they can, the trafficker should also separate out these campaigns in the ad server so that it is clear in the ad server reporting.

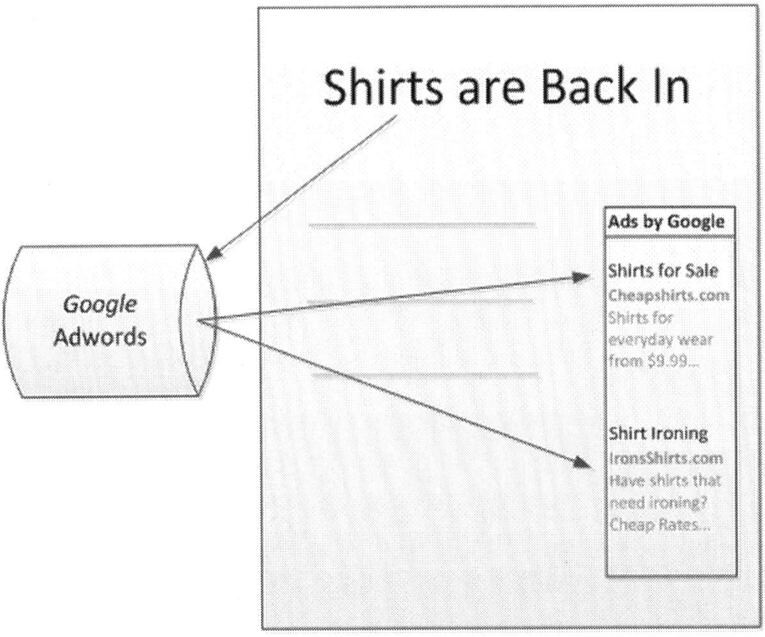

Figure 3.7.6 *Google Adsense is powered by the Google Adwords engine. When the user loads the Publisher page, the Adsense code collects the contextual information on the page and passes it into the Adwords engine before the relevant ads are displayed. This diagram is simplified however Adsense will rarely scrape the page in real time. Rather the Google spiders will have cached the page in the Adwords engine in the past week to associate the URL with the relevant context, then Adsense just sends the URL to engine which checks ads associated with that contextual information which are then served out. The click-through-URLs will still contain the pathway as used in the third party ad server to count the clicks there.*

Extending tracked Paid Search to Mobile

Just as with separating out *Adwords* campaigns from *Adsense* campaigns, the Search Engine should discern those campaigns delivered to Mobile from those delivered to desktop devices. Mobile devices offer the geo location facility and as such, the search keywords are likely to be more relevant to user and therefore more valuable to the Advertiser. When bidding for keywords in the SEM interface or through the bid manager, the geo location relevant ads are likely to cost the Advertiser more if the resulting activity is likely to bring in more revenue for the Advertiser. If the mobile search activity draws from the same database of keywords and click through URLs that the marketer sets up in the SEM interface, in the bid manager and in the third party ad server then it will be tracked in third party ad serving. Again, to break this out into the correct kind of reporting, the campaigns should be sufficiently labelled in the Search Engine SEM interface and created as separate campaigns in the ad server under the same Advertiser account.

> *Google* have utilised their technical ability to allow Advertisers of all sizes to take advantage of advertising to a bulk number of Publishers through "GDN" the *Google Display Network*. This is not search activity but is more closely aligned with Affiliate advertising covered off in the next section.

Search and other Channels

Tracking and counting paid search provides a wealth of data within the third party ad server that can be used to create inventive strategies to improve the optimization and serving of creative across other channels. For instance, if users are searching on specific keywords, those can be paid for through SEM and the traffic can be driven to a specific Advertiser landing page which may house a retargeting pixel (See Chapter 7) which could be used to power a follow up DCO campaign if the user does not go on to buy the product in question.

Paid Search is often cited as being one of the most effective marketing channels for driving performance activities. But from the Advertiser's perspective, any channel that is effectively driving user web traffic through to the Advertiser site should be funded by the marketing team so as to make those channels even more effective. Owing to the way Search Engines work, paying for an expensive website that is Search Engine optimized can be an effective use of this budget and SEO (or "Natural Search") therefore is transformed into a channel that needs to be tracked alongside the other channels. It is clear to see how this channel differs from the others, there is no procurement of advertising space, yet the Advertiser's site appears on the search results page. It is important to touch briefly on how this works.

What is SEO?

SEO (Search Engine Optimization) describes the on-going development of a website for it to be picked up naturally by the way a search engines work such that the pages are displayed in the standard search listings. These "natural search" listings appear in the centre of the search results page and trail down the page onto multiple pages. The copy and links which make up these results are generated by the search engine. As the results page loads information comes from the search engine database which is kept updated by the search engine's web crawling technology which are called "Spiders". Spiders are continuously crawling the web in accordance with the natural search algorithm which ranks which pages are the most relevant to user's search term and returns to the database the right information.

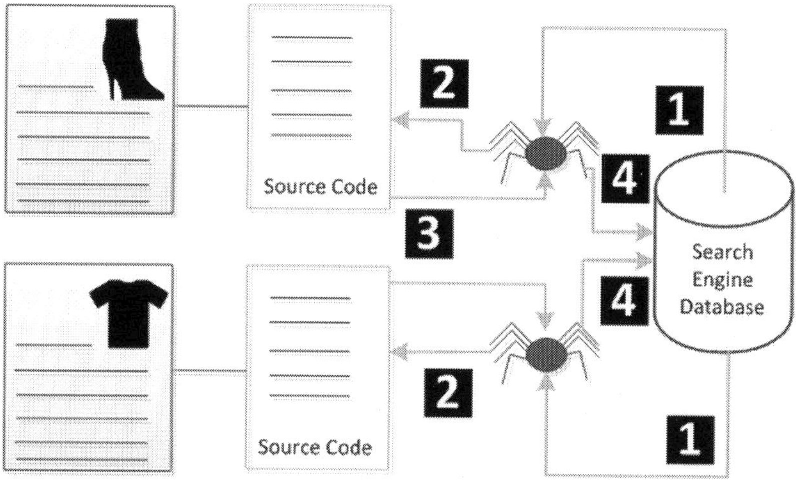

Figure 3.7.7 *The spiders or web crawlers from the Search Engine (1), crawl through the web's URLs to reach websites (2). The crawlers read the source code of the page (3) and pass the required information about that URL back to the Search Engine Database (4). The information is stored as a cache in the Search Engine database. Crawlers or Spiders repeat the process of crawling pages more often depending on how popular they are which can be determined by the number of other domains pointing sending users traffic to the URL.*

Publishers and website owners work very hard to try to get their page seen at the top of these results and because these results are unpaid, the cost to the advertising effort is indirect. As stated, it would not be true to say these results are free since it is the sweat and tears of the website development team that ensure a high "page rank" in the engine. To justify the cost of the man hours put into developing a great SEO strategy, the SEO results need to be tracked to establish the effectiveness of the strategy.

Site side analytics tools such as *Adobe's Omniture* or *Google's Google Analytics* are very effective at detecting the incoming site "traffic" from these engines and understanding where it came from to quantify the effect of the SEO efforts. Having said this site side analytics tools can rarely tie together a user's behaviour with the natural search keywords alongside other paid for channels such as Display and Instream Video. Also such results are better verified by an independent third party so as not to allow for favour with the Publisher owning the media that is driving the traffic in the first place. The third party ad servers were never originally designed to track this kind of activity but this need is in increasing demand from Advertisers and Media Agencies.

Referral URL to trigger a click

As a reminder from Chapter 2 - Advertisers and Marketers, the user that arrives at the Advertiser site leaves a trail behind them for the last action, giving away how they arrived at the site called a "referral URL". The referral URL gives the Site Side Analytics tool an identifier from which the search term (that the user entered into the engine to get to the site) can be obtained. Site Side Analytics tools do this by using JavaScript. This same JavaScript method can be written out by the website developer, separate to the analytics tool and be used to trigger a click tracker. Suddenly the user receives an ad server cookie where they would not have got one from the natural search result itself. This makes it look in ad server reporting that the user clicked on this click tracker to get to the site rather in that the site arrival triggered the click tracker. The result is that the SEO channel is tracked by this simple user action. Such JavaScript code should deployed on all possible landing pages of the Advertiser site that a user might be able to access from a search engine.

Behind the scenes in the third party ad server interface the setup is a little more complex than creating a tracking placement and using the click tracker portion to mount into the script on the page. The trafficker has two options:

1. Either the script can be designed so that each possible keyword triggers a different click tracker. This would mean

the trafficker is given a list of the keywords by the Advertiser website management team (this list can be exported from the site side analytics tool). The trafficker would then create one tracking placement for each keyword and the click portion of the tags be trafficked and sent back to the website management team. In turn this team would tweak the JavaScript on the page so that when the user arrives on the page, the search term that informed their entry point to the site be captured and the corresponding click-through URL be triggered. Reporting for this option is very simple since the trafficker just pulls a standard campaign report and the keywords are already pre-defined in the report. The difficulty with this method is that a JavaScript would not be able to house too many keywords nor would the trafficker want to create or manage too many tags to support it.

2. ..or the script can be designed to pass the exact keyword search term from the referrer URL into a dynamic token in the third party click tracker. This would mean the trafficker only creates one ad in the ad server and having the website management team implementing the click portion on the Advertiser site inside the purpose-built JavaScript. The JavaScript would be tweaked so that as the user arrives to the site the click is fired and the keyword portion in the referrer URL is dynamically inserted into the click call back into ad server reporting. The trafficker would then need to ensure that when reporting on the clicks from this ad in the campaign reports that the contents of the dynamic token is displayed and aggregated so that the most popular keyword entry points can be ascertained. This kind of reporting can be harder to set up.

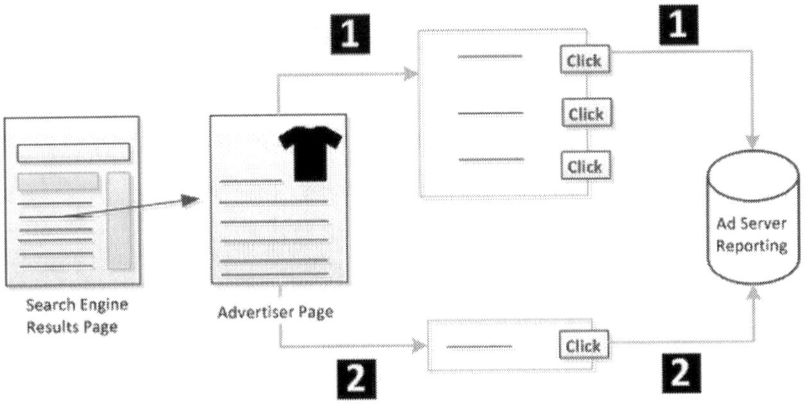

Figure 3.7.8 *The user types a search term into the search engine and is taken to a search results page. On this page the natural search results are listed running down the page which match to relevant sites. The user clicks on one of these results and is taken to the Advertiser site. One the landing page is embedded a script that either fires off the corresponding ad server click tracker for the search term (1) or inserts the search term into a dynamic token in the single click tracker option available to the Advertiser (2). In either instance the information is supplied to ad server reporting.*

If these setups are followed these clicks will be treated like clicks in the Display channel or clicks in the Paid Search channel and this will create a situation where conversions (see Chapter 4) on SEO under the last click attribution model (see Chapter 4) will take the full credit for the conversion and actual paid-for media will be eclipsed by this activity. Although this may sound complex: what it really means is that natural search will suddenly appear to be more effective than other media channels tracked in the ad server: so much so that it might convince the marketer to stop paying for the paid-for channels altogether. This is something of an illusion because if the marketer stops paying for media in paid for channels, the site side analytics tools will report a complete drop off in site traffic altogether and conversions will also fall short (see Chapter 4). Natural search results are very commonly used but they should be thought of as one of the influencers in the user's pathway to their transaction or journey on or to the Advertiser site rather than the only influence. For this reason the natural search tracking activity needs to be downplayed in ad server reporting (see Chapter 5 - Channel Specific Reporting).

Ad Serving costs for Search

third party ad servers usually charge Advertisers and Agencies based on impression volumes for ads served. Since no image is being delivered for the Search channels, the provider will normally charge based on clicks only for the click trackers.

This introduction into the world of paid search and natural search exposes in greater detail the importance and relevance of third party ad server reporting and conversion calculation.

The next section continues with the theme of performance marketing, looking at what happens when Publishers begin to realise that the best way to attain user attention is to utilise the Search Engines themselves. It may be true to say that such Publishers value their ad space over their content and as such transform their sites into conduits to channel user traffic through to Advertiser sites. These Publisher websites are called "Affiliates".

Chapter 3 - Section 8
Affiliates and Affiliate Networks

- Affiliate Sites and Networks
- How the Affiliate Earns
- Auditing the quality of the Long Tail
    - *Figure 3.8.1*
- Tracking Affiliate Activity in third party ad serving
    - *Figure 3.8.2*
- The absence of impression tracking
- Affiliates that grow

This section will look at Affiliate advertising as a channel and put it into the context of third party ad serving. Like Search, ad servers have a greater role to play in tracking rather than serving the physical ads and so the benefits of a marketer, Advertiser and Agency using a third party ad server in this space are the same as apply to the world of paid and natural search. We will begin by describing what Affiliate advertising is before diving into the complexity behind the tracking methodologies required and the reporting capabilities that this provides. Being a performance marketing channel, Advertisers which are considered to be Direct response Advertisers are more common users of the Affiliate Channel than those seeking to do big branding exercises. This is because Affiliate activity at scale can be a cost effective method to drive sales and other conversion activities (see Chapter 4).

Affiliate Sites and Networks

The landscape of Affiliate advertising as a digital marketing channel is made up of two core entities: the Affiliates websites and the Affiliate networks which house them. Typically speaking the Affiliate network supplies the digital creative (core images and *.swf files) and click trackers to a mass of Affiliate websites.

> Large Advertisers, particularly in the gambling and online retail verticals, have their own Affiliate programs so do not always utilize Affiliate networks. Instead act as the network themselves by storing the creative and distributing the click trackers. In doing so, the Advertiser takes on the responsibility to provide the Affiliate websites with their reporting data.

Affiliate sites go on to earn a commission when users click the affiliate links and purchase on the Advertiser site right away or within a given time frame. It is in the best interest of the network to drive traffic that will end with a purchase, so often the Network will encourage affiliates to use the context of their digital publications to incentivize the user to click on the ad. Typically speaking eighty per cent of all traffic is generated by Affiliates that offer an incentive scheme. That is that they offer a discount, a general offer with money off, or some other type of monetary incentive such as virtual points. The remaining twenty per cent of Affiliates tend to keep themselves content focused such that the already niche nature of their websites utilizes the SEO framework of the site design, and this in itself attracts users. The user searches a relevant term in the search engine, finds the Affiliate site perhaps halfway down the page of the search results and clicks to the Affiliate site. Here they find content of interest and a contextually relevant ad, which drives a click and potentially a sale.

How the Affiliate Earns

Networks such as *Trade Doubler* and *Commission Junction* have gradually attracted the attention of smaller Publisher sites that sign up to the network to become Affiliates. Within the interface supplied by the network, the website manager (for the now Affiliate website) browses the ads available to the Affiliates on the network and enrolls in the campaign. Enrollment releases the ability for the Affiliate to implant the ad on the site. Clicks on the ad are usually counted by the Affiliate network and are displayed in that interface alongside attributed conversions (see Chapter 4) so that Affiliates can determine their daily revenues. This method does not work for all small Publishers, since the Publisher is essentially displaying the ads for free and only getting paid when the user clicks or performs a conversion activity after clicking. This can result in the Publisher giving away millions of impressions for free with no return for the use of the ad space.

Auditing the quality of the Long Tail

It can be very hard for a Network and Advertiser to audit these small Publisher sites on a continual basis, which can result in some negative consequences for brand image. Generally speaking an Affiliate site will be tailored towards the purchase activity and therefore will tend to abide by an Advertiser's branding regulations which should be supplied by the Network in the enrollment phase. This lack of control has put some Advertisers off of using affiliates but new developments in verification reporting in the third party ad server are likely to remedy this over the next few years (see Chapter 5 - Ad Verification).

Without using technology solutions there are checks that can be done on the Affiliate sites simply using the operational headcount available either at the Media Agency, the Affiliate network or on the Advertiser's marketing team. There are two processes for policing: "Affiliate Auditing" & "Affiliate Screening"- both of which would be outlined to the Affiliate in the enrollment phase.

Auditing is usually a quarterly process that involves looking over every individual ad that is being shown across all sites and checking copy and ad position to see that it aligns to the Advertiser's branding regulations.

Screening is a process of accepting or declining affiliates who apply to join the program. The advertiser or affiliate network can decide which affiliate is good enough to join the campaign and thus can stop low quality sites from enrolling.

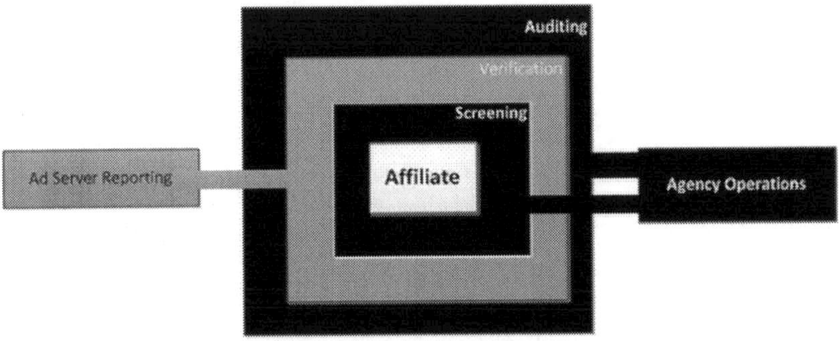

Figure 3.8.1 *Affiliation extends the distance between the planners and buyers, and the inventory that is being procured. To ensure that the final location of the ad is safe for the brand to sit inside there are several safety nets both operationally and technologically. The auditing and screening process is covered in detail here and Verification is covered in depth in Chapter 5. It is worth noting that verification works off of the impression rather than the click metric on which most affiliation is based, so thorough verification reporting is not available for campaigns conducted across a click-based buying model.*

Tracking Affiliate Activity in third party ad serving

In the third party ad server the trafficker will see the name of a whole Affiliate network on the media plan in place of a Publisher site name. In the third party ad server interface, in the usual trafficking workflow for Display activity, the affiliate network name can be selected under the ad server site names. Once the site is added to the campaign in the interface, the trafficker generates a single tracking placement for each Affiliate network listed. Only the click portion of the placement is required and when the tag is trafficked to the affiliate network, it is this portion that the Affiliate network operations team load onto the enrollment page of their network; representing the Advertiser's campaign. The Affiliate network then adds information to the page about brand regulations and in its completion the package is known as an "affiliate program". When the affiliate logs into the interface of the affiliate network, they enroll in the program. Once the ad is on their site, users that click the activity will trigger a count for a click in the third party ad server.

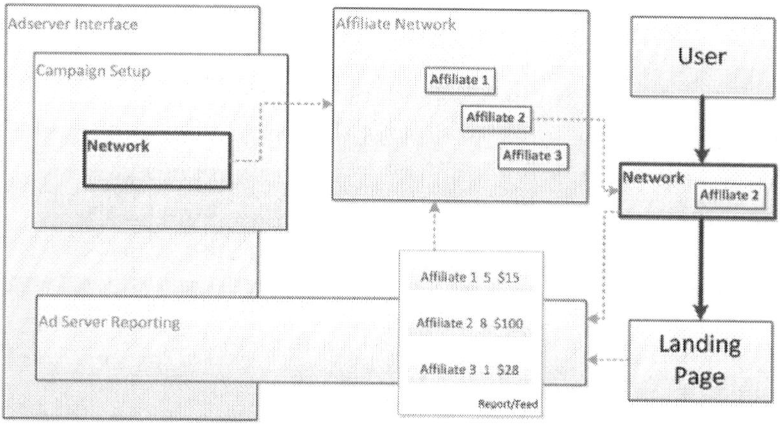

Figure 3.8.2 *Affiliate tracking consists of a single tag or click tracker provided by the trafficker in the ad server interface: supplied to the Agency or affiliate network operations team directly who will set up the tag to load the affiliate identifier into the click tracker as a token when the tag fires. When the user arrives on the Affiliate site, the identifier for that site is passed into the token in the single network tag as the click data is passed into ad server reporting. The user then continues on to the landing page and the conversion data (see Chapter 4) is also captured in the ad server reporting. Within reporting a feed is compiled that shows what activity (clicks and conversions) should be attributed to each affiliate which can include the monetary value of the conversion or total conversions. This information is then used by the Affiliate Network to pay the affiliates.*

Since the Affiliate network mostly pays out on a CPA and not a CPC, the trafficker in the third party ad server interface also needs to ensure that a conversion tag is generated and is implemented on the Advertiser site in the right place (more on this in Chapter 4).

The absence of impression tracking

Advertisers do not use the impression portion of the ad tag in their Affiliate activity because the affiliate program is usually opened up to an unknown number of Affiliates, who will deliver an unknown quantity of impressions of the ad in order to get clicks or conversion events. Affiliates are commonly asked to house the creative or images on their own servers so that even the Affiliate network is not burdened with serving the actual creative. If the impression portion was used or the ad served, the ad serving costs to the Advertiser could be astronomical since it is a very broad base of long tail Publishers driving the traffic to the Advertiser site. It would also be very difficult to contact all the Affiliate sites to ask them to take down their impression pixels to cease ad serving entirely. For this reason is not effective for brand advertiser to use the Affiliate channel for brand activity since clicks and conversions alone are not a good representation of true reach and frequency (see Chapter 5 - Reporting).

Affiliates that grow

Affiliate activity does not just consist of small Publisher sites. Affiliation is a very clever and complex dynamic of shrewd Publishers that use very innovative site designs in order to drive user traffic to Advertiser sites for the purpose of purchase. All such Affiliates start out small but their content is arranged in a method that attracts high volumes of traffic. These affiliates are sometimes referred to as "Aggregators" and often break away from Affiliate Networks to become large Publishers in their own right, attracting Advertisers and Agencies to spend with them directly.

Just as with Search activity, the Advertiser or Agency will just end up paying the ad serving provider based on the click activity. To conclude this chapter we will turn now to the outlying channels of Digital Advertising. From an ad serving perspective there are a number of restrictions placed on these channels which severely limit the existing tracking and serving capabilities of ad serving technology. Such restrictions exist not because the Advertisers do not want to track their activity but that Publisher-side technologies place restrictions on the ability for a true independent audit to occur. These channels will continue to suffer from funding problems unless the Publishers open the doors, and offer greater transparency and a hand of integrity to those with the marketing budget to spend across a wide reach of channels.

Chapter 3 - Section 9
Email, in-game and Social

- Permission Marketing
    - *Figure 3.9.1*
- Sending Emails on Mass
- Email Marketing advertising metrics
- Third party ad server tracking for Email
- In-game and digital outdoor tracking
- Social Media tracking
    - *Figure 3.9.2*
- The versatility of tracking pixels

This section rounds up the email, in-game and social channels for digital advertising. These channels are not small channels by any stretch of the imagination, they get a lot of user attention and vast volumes of internet traffic through them every waking moment of the day. However when trying to use third party ad serving as eyes across all media buys, these channels are outliers and for one reason or another limit the amount of tracking and serving that can be done. Thankfully the meagre technology of tracking pixels and click trackers allows a very independent eye on delivery and click activity, but beyond this Advertisers are essentially blind and must submit to Publisher reporting at the very best.

Email advertising is an old channel in the world of digital advertising. Few Advertisers extend their budget to cover it beyond their own existing user base but if it is a traffic driver to an Advertiser site, users need to at least be tracked for the email channel to appear in the ad server reporting. In-game is classed as standalone software either on a PC or secondary device including console. Along with Email, In-game as a channel suffers the same setbacks as trying to track activities with applications for Mobile advertising. Lastly we will look at social: a dominator in the world of content production but very slow to monetize their properties. Social networks continue to keep their networks locked down to third party ad serving which seems daft, given that it shuts off potential revenue in favour of less transparency for the Advertiser only adding to the speculation that social may not be as effective for Advertisers as initially thought.

Permission Marketing

Email advertising gets a bad rap because Advertisers believe that email advertising is synonymous to Spam. Strictly speaking the difference between email marketing and spam is that the user has provided consent to be sent emails from a third party versus being delivered unsolicited mail. The difficulty with presenting email marketing as a fruitful channel for Advertisers is that the methods to obtain consent for email marketing are lumped into small illegible boxes as a condition to access a service. With such methods the consent is provided but the user never really wanted to receive advertising from a third party.

Email advertising falls into two broad categories: emails that are single page adverts, and monthly subscribed emails from a Publisher directly with ad space around the sides or embedded among the content. To receive either of these two forms of email advertising, a user must sign up to the service and opt in to receive messages from third parties. The strict opt in requirements demanded by regulators such as the DMA (Direct Marketing Association) in the UK mean that the email advertising channel is sometimes known as "Permission Marketing" a phrase also coined by the author *Seth Godin.*

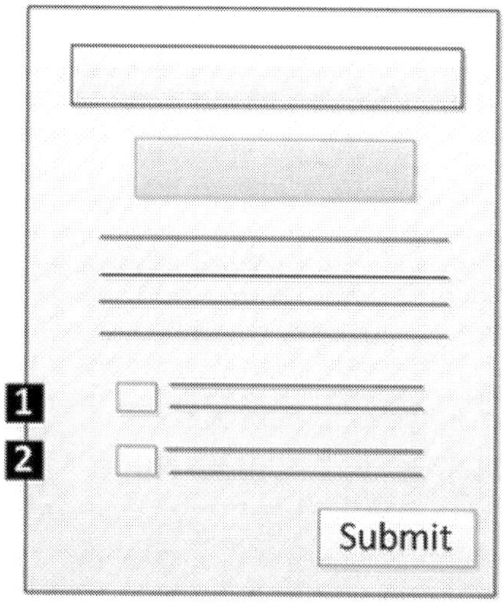

Figure 3.9.1 *The cursed double-opt-in boxes. On a Publisher site a user might be interested into the content as to opt in to a newsletter. On the newsletter opt in page there may be displayed two boxes: (1) is for first party advertising: can the Publisher deliver Publisher-specific ads to the user's inbox? The second (2) asks about third party advertising, upon which email advertising is founded. Publishers regularly try to use the manipulation of language to confuse the user into opting in. Examples include "tick here to not opt out of third party advertising"; which will only serve to de-value email as a marketing channel even further.*

By consenting to receive such emails, the user's email address becomes a commodity that the Publisher or email list owner can sell to Advertisers or, with a user's permission on a second tick box, the "double opt-in" can be sold on to other list owners to receive additional mail where further advertising space is then made available to Advertisers.

Sending Email on Mass

Consented emails from respected Publishers can be commoditised because the emails are opened and read and the ads attract clicks, which can result in conversions (sometimes with better results than standard display - See Chapter 4). In order for a Publisher to send thousands of emails they either use their own list or buy one in from a data provider such as *Axiom*. As such the list of emails becomes the property of the Publisher for a given period of time and it is their responsibility to act in accordance to the wishes of the Advertiser, the user and the original list owner.

Email list quality is a huge factor determining the success of a campaign and it essential that addresses are cleaned regularly by the database owner to ensure that any addresses requesting an unsubscribe or where a "bounce back" is occurring, are removed. To send thousands of emails, a Publisher needs to use a mass email delivery system such as *Email Vision*. The list is simply uploaded to the delivery platform, the HTML email compiled, and then sent as an email over a given period of delivery. To be certain the emails are not blocked, the Publisher needs to be sure they are sending from a whitelisted IP address. They can work with the email delivery platform and major Publishers like MSN or Yahoo! to check that the IP is not on a blacklist where other spam email sender addresses are blocked. Here, the email provider is acting as the gate-keeper for what can and cannot be loaded into emails. If an IP address is deemed dangerous, links or images can be blocked and in some instances emails can end up in junk mail folders.

Email Marketing advertising metrics

An email delivery platform can measure four core metrics.

1. Open rate, detecting how many of the emails sent were viewed in the main reading pane of the email program or web-based application.

2. Click through rate (CTR) for the subsequent clickable areas or URLs embedded in the email.

3. Bounce rate (i.e. the number of emails that were never delivered to inboxes because they received a bounce-back). These email addresses are sent back to the list owner after the campaign ends to investigate to see if they are now wholly inactive.

4. Unsubscribe rate; needless to say a high unsubscribe rate following the launch of an email campaign, is a storm cloud that neither Advertiser no Publisher wishes for. The user that clicks the unsubscribe button, which should appear at the bottom of every Publisher-owned email, will be removed from the original list (which will either be Publisher owned or hired).

Third Party ad server tracking for Email

Connecting the third party ad server to the email marketing channel is important to ensure that this channel is independently tracked and that the email channel is considered as an influence in the user's pathway to conversion (see Chapter 4).

The trafficker in the third party ad serving interface would look on the media plan and might see a Publishers name followed by a mention of the name of a newsletter. This same reference would need to be included in the third party ad serving site list. The traffickers selects this as a site and generates a 1x1pixels and click trackers and sends these on to the Publisher ad operations team to ensure they embed them into the email creative. True third party ad serving (even of images inside emails) is never undertaken. More often than not, the impression tracker is also wholly abandoned and only the click tracker is implemented. Here, the email provider is considering the third party ad servers IP address to belong to a blacklist because there is such a wide usage of the IP across millions of other emails at some point in the past. This means that pixel never loads and therefore never records an impression.

In addition not all email provider interfaces are setup to receive emails that can render images properly. Those that are not 'HTML friendly' will render a text-only version of the email. In such a delivery the image pixel would never load but the user may choose to click through via the supplied link, which would route through the third party ad server before landing the user on the landing page.

Due to the simple nature of email and email delivery there is no possibility of recording dwell rates or interaction rates, but conversion tracking is possible so long as the click trackers are in place on the email creative (more in Chapter 4).

> Email lists have evolved significantly in recent years. Formerly they were large databases of Publisher owned data about users where users were recognised by an email address collected with their permission. Now list owners and Publishers have gone a step further and logged the cookieID of the users using first party cookie information and have also labelled up the users into audience types by logging their interests based on what they are being exposed to and what they are clicking on. Rather than sell these databases to Advertiser's as email lists, they are now being sold as sources of data to be inserted into DSP's and DMP's to improve programmatic buying and trading (see Chapter 8).

In-game and digital outdoor tracking

Despite the promise of mass in-game advertising, high reach games remain a premium offering to players and therefore advertising rarely has much impact in this space. In game ads would deliver creative to an online game via a feed (such as an XML feed). The same is true of digital outdoor advertising as well (content can be kept regularly up to date via an XML feed) but the nature of the games console and standalone gaming applications outside of the browser, mean that the third party ad serving cookies cannot be dropped. This hinders the ability for Advertisers to establish how much value the game environment really provides to the overall cross-channel ad campaign. Until such time as in-game cookies are dropped and can easily be matched with those of the ad server; there is less strength in running such campaigns as the impact of the creative itself in the context of a multi-channel campaign is lost. There may be some hope in second screen audio watermarking technologies but at time of writing, nothing scalable has come onto the market.

Social Media tracking

Digital advertising through social channels is still in its infancy and as yet the link between third party ad serving and these environments is rather tentative. Social media in the context of Digital Advertising can be divided up into three parts:

1. The mass advertising that appears on the right side of the page for Facebook. This is managed by an advertising exchange program called FBX (see Chapter 8). This scaled technology is much more closely aligned to the world of Paid Search than that of display advertising.

2. Ads that appear in the user feed. These ad spots are technically unlimited and depend on the user engagement with the private feed. Ads are purposed from content on fan pages or elsewhere on the web but have limited engagement capabilities.

3. The home of the Advertiser on the social network. In the case of *Facebook*, this is the fan page, where is has been notoriously challenging to embed tracking and tagging technologies such as conversion tags (see Chapter 4). Meanwhile 'tweets' and 'likes'; the measures of user engagement endorsed by the social networks Twitter and Facebook, do not pass this information back to the third party ad server using any reserved method (so officially the metrics are not supported by third party ad servers).

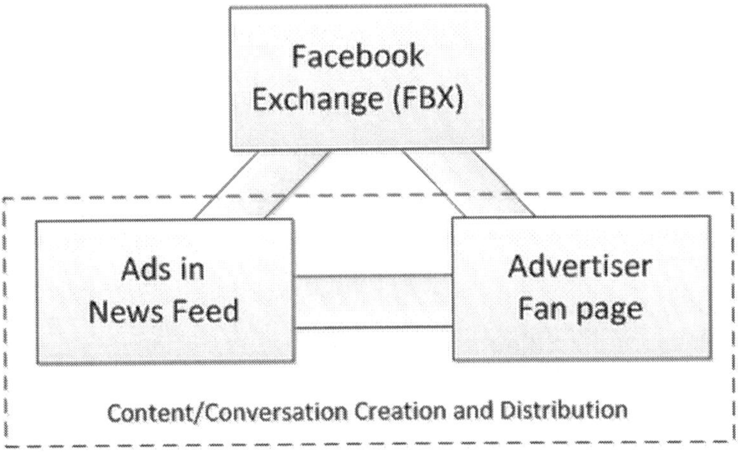

Figure 3.9.2 *Still in its infancy: the ad ecosystem of the popular social networking site Facebook consists of 3 core properties for Ads. FBX (which caters for the paid scaled and targeted advertising on the right navigation: drawing from user data), the Advertiser's Fan Page (for some Advertisers this is more of a hub than their own websites) and ads which appear in the user's news feed (commonly content is repurposed from the Fan Page).*

In all of these situations one fact rings true over all others as a cry of utter restriction. Facebook and Twitter do not allow JavaScript tags from an external source on their sites as a matter of policy. This means that should these sites appear on the media plan, the trafficker merely sets up impression and click trackers for each placement. The trafficker then sends the resulting tags along to the Media Agency to either embed into the FBX access point or work with technology providers that are repurposing Advertiser content as ads (such as *Upcast* or *Experian's Alchemy Social* product suite). This data leaves very limited performance information (clicks and conversions) and delivery information (impressions) inside ad server reporting for the Advertiser and Agency to see.

The versatility of tracking pixels

It is clear that tracking pixels and click trackers are very versatile technologies and allow for tracking in a variety of channels including a majority of the newest channels available to Advertisers. The concern with pawning out a vast quality of trackers and not conducting full ad serving is that there is only the confirmation that a pixel was ever delivered on a site and that a click was instigated. There is no proof as such that the true ad was delivered or who saw it. Publishers that today only accept tracking pixels will need to go a step further and provide greater transparency to third party ad servers and technology providers if they are to attract full investment from Advertisers with big budgets.

This concludes the Channel by Channel campaign setup chapter of this book. We have gone meticulously through the work of the trafficker in the setup of ad campaigns via the third party ad serving interface, from Display, Rich Media, DCO, Instream Video and Mobile, to Paid Search, Natural Search, Affiliates, Email and the Social channel. But the campaign setup for all channels by the trafficker is only complete when the trafficker generates not just the ad tags but also the conversion tags. The next Chapter looks in depth at the importance of Conversion Tags and how the trafficker uses the concept of conversion attribution to discern the optimum targeting and audience settings available in the campaign setup.

Chapter 4

Attribution and Audiences

Chapter 4 - Section 1
Conversion tags and Attribution

- What are conversions?
    - *Figure 4.1*
- Where to place the conversion tag?
    - *Figure 4.1.1*
- Where to have conversion tags (table)
- CPA
- Conversion tag types - Sales Vs. Counter Tags
    - *Figure 4.1.2*
- Extended data/Extended Parameters
- *Figure 4.1.3*
- *Figure 4.1.4*
- How do you test conversions?
- Conversion Tag Functionality - Piggybacking
    - Container Tags
    - Certified container tag providers
    - Which conversion tag fires first?
    - Selective Pinging
    - *Figure 4.1.5*
    - Piggybacking with Extended data
    - *Figure 4.1.6*
- Conversion Tag Functionality - Conversion Windows
    - Window Settings
    - Post-impression and Post-click windows
    - Long and short conversion windows
    - Shadow Tagging
    - Reporting on Conversions
    - Repeat Conversion Windows
- Conversion Tag Functionality - Attribution Modelling
- *Figure 4.1.7*
- Attribution Settings
- Engagement Mapping

    - *Figure 4.1.8*
    - Custom Attribution Modelling
- Challenges in implementing conversion tags
    - Tag Management Solutions
    - *Figure 4.1.9*
    - Universal Tagging Security

In Chapter 3 we explored the campaign setup channel but all the efforts of the trafficker come down to one question for the marketer: What is the goal of the advertising campaign? What does success look like? For big brand clients the goal is usually to a get message out to a target audience, to build awareness and brand affinity but the ultimate goal (as is the goal with more direct response style Advertisers) is to drive sales. This section will go into technical detail about "conversion tags"; a technology that can be used not just for measuring sales but also events that might be deemed a goal for the marketing team. Beyond this it is important to establish exactly what activity drove the use to a conversion; untangling all of their marketing engagements with an Advertiser to establish how to attribute the conversion to a paid-for activity.

What are conversions?

It's all very well measuring the delivery of ads and collecting information about how many unique users saw and clicked ads but the vast majority of Advertisers want to know how many users then landed on their website and how many went on to buy a good or service. This can be ascertained by monitoring the traffic driven directly to the purchase pages of the Advertiser website.

Conversions by definition vary by vertical. Here are some examples of uses for the conversion tag:

- Automotive - Tracking Brochure requests or test drive sign-ups
- CPG/FMCG - Tracking sample requests or coupon downloads
- Retail - Tracking sales through the site or clicks to the sales phone line
- Entertainment - Sales through to ticket purchase or local cinema listings
- Finance - Leads generated through Insurance quotes
- Telco - Form completion for a free SIM card

A conversion tag is a piece of JavaScript code; generated inside the third party ad server interface by the trafficker which is sent to the site management team of the Advertiser website to upload into the source code of the page. The trafficker can output the conversion tag in various formats (such as iframe Vs. JavaScript) depending on what is easiest for the Advertiser's website management team to implement.

Once implemented on the page, the conversion tag will allow the Advertiser to watch for incoming traffic and recognise it as originating from a third party served or tracked ad. The tag, once present on the webpage can recognise the difference between ad-driven traffic to itself which is called is a "Conversion", and non-ad driven traffic (which carries various names depending on which technology is being used; the *Atlas* third party ad server calls this an "Action").

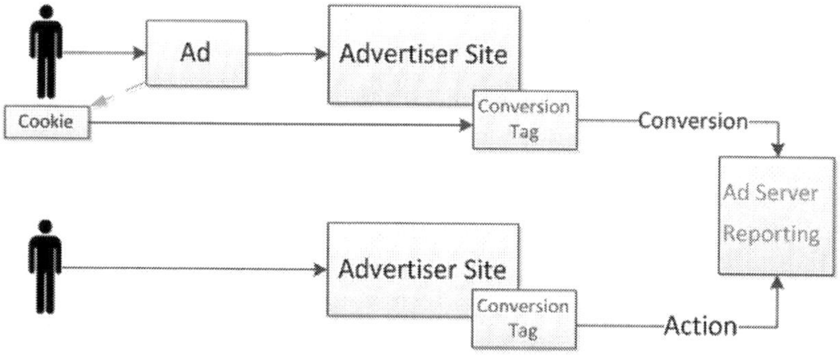

Figure 4.1 *Conversions detect for the presence of an existing third party ad serving cookie on a user's browser. This will have been dropped onto the user's browser by the delivery of an ad that the user would have encountered previously. The conversion tag then passes the cookieID to ad server reporting when it loads on the Advertiser site to allow ad server reporting to place the conversion event, marked with a timestamp to the cookieID in cookie level data. In aggregated reporting the Publisher which featured the ad would show a single conversion. In comparison if a user visits the Advertiser site directly, having not previously encountered an ad or having deleted their cookies, will still trigger the conversion tag on the page. This conversion tag will update the ad server reporting with an action instead of a conversion. This will add a record to the conversions and actions database in the ad server and not be marked or any cookie level data against any existing cookieID.*

Once the "conversion tag" (also called a "Spotlight tag" in *DoubleClick* or an "Action tag" in *Atlas*) is generated and placed on a page it begins to work, feeding conversion and action information back to the third party ad server. It does this by looking to the users browser when they arrive on the page and once the tag code renders, seeks a cookie belonging to the third party ad server; a cookie which would have been dropped by a third party ad server via an ad in the past.

If the conversion tag finds a cookie; the ad server matches the cookieID to the action of the conversion tag firing and in the ad server database adds a new row to a master table, to represent that the conversion occurred, when it occurred and which cookie it occurred on. If no cookie is found, the ad server still makes a log that the conversion tag was triggered and at what time, labelling it as an Action.

Where to place the conversion tag?
The Advertiser is advised to place a conversion tag on whatever pages relevant to measure the success of the campaign. Put a conversion tag on a landing page and the ad server can measure the number of users that got through to the Advertiser site. Place one deeper on the pathway to an actual purchase, such as the basket page, and more information is gleaned such as "drop-off rate" which indicates how many users are not making the journey all the way through to a purchase.

The most useful position for a conversion tag is on the "confirmation" or "thank you" page of an e-commerce site. When a user triggers the conversion tag on the confirmation page; the Advertiser knows that the user has purchased; a purchase which can be attributed back to the ad which drove the user to the site in the first place. It is imperative therefore that each conversion tag is unique to its page 'type'; placing a conversion tag on a landing page and then duplicating the code to use on a confirmation page will skew results. This is because the arrival on the two different page types could be counted as marketing success goals but they need to be segregated since an arrival is a less valuable "conversion event" than a purchase.

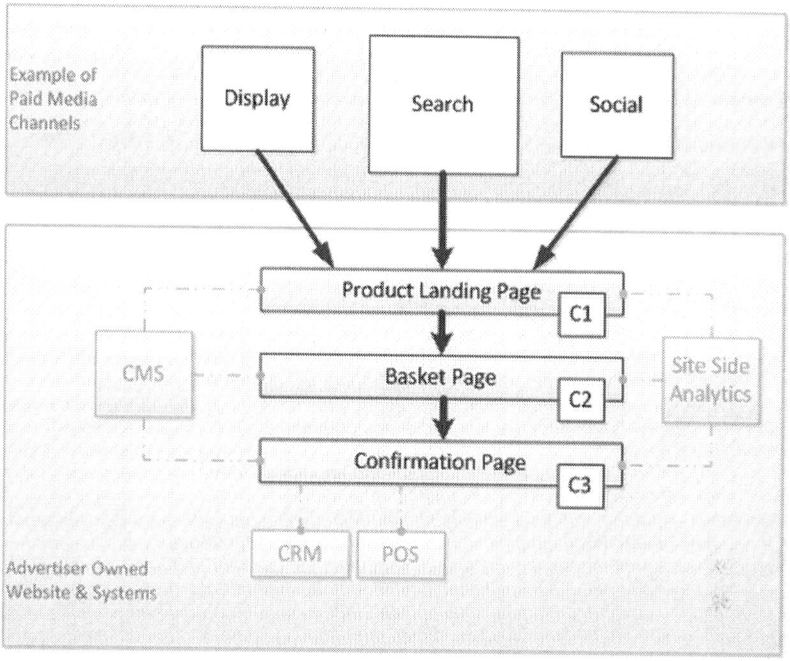

Figure 4.1.1 *The paid-for media channel/Publisher site, drives the user through to the product landing page via an ad. There could be a conversion tag on this page (C1) to assess how many users get this far. Users that make it as far as the basket page could have this conversion event tracked by an additional conversion tag (C2) and those users that purchase will trigger the last conversion tag shown (C3). In ad server reporting it is possible to establish the drop-off of users throughout the process and correlate the difference between users that for example, came in off of a predominantly-social pathway versus those that came in from more of a display pathway. The results might indicate that users that see more display ads rather than social ads are more likely to cause C3-type conversions. Site side analytics can also measure such activity but the ad server factors in the user's engagement with all ads in the campaign to establish an attribution pathway (covered off later in this section).*

The pages on the Advertiser site soon become markers in the marketing funnel for the ad campaign as users arrive to the site. Those that drop off at product pages are conducting research. Those that drop off at the basket page are closer to the buying decision. This progress should be reflected in the naming convention adopted by the trafficker when the conversion tags are created so that it is much clearer in reporting how valuable certain conversion events are.

Conversion tags are also useful in other locations:

Where to have conversion tags	*Why it is useful*	*Why it may not be possible*
Within ads	If the landing page is not accessible, the click within the ad can be used to trigger a conversion tag. If the conversion event is to fill in a form: the form can exist in the ad itself and the submission of the form can trigger a conversion tag.	Conversion tags can be used to carry retargeting tags and if these are fired in locations on Publisher pages then there is the opportunity for an Advertiser to build a cookie pool from the Publisher's audience (see Chapter 7 - Retargeting). This is a condemned practice called Publisher Data Leakage and should be avoided to maintain good relationships with the Publishers.
Facebook Fan Page or **Youtube Channel page** (On Advertiser	Brand Advertisers in particular drive traffic to *Facebook* fan pages or *Youtube* pages.	*Facebook* and *Youtube* (at time of publication) do not allow third party conversion tags on their properties. Advertisers will have to

'properties' outside of the Advertiser site)	A conversion tag here would show the value of the Publishers and ads driving the traffic.	work hard to demonstrate the importance of these technologies to these big Publishers in order to have conversion tags placed.
Amazon or **E-Retailer** or **Supermarket sites** (On alternative purchase locations)	FMCG, CPG, Electronics and Telco Advertisers in particular allow users to purchase their products via other online sites. Conversion tags on these sites will show how many sales are being generated and which ads are driving those sales.	*Amazon* and large supermarket sites (at time of publication) do not allow third party conversion tags on their properties. Advertisers will have to work hard to demonstrate the importance of these technologies to these big Publishers in order to have conversion tags placed in basket and thank you pages.

CPA

The success of a campaign can be measured by the number of completed conversions but in addition the actual sales can act as a trigger to paying the Publishers. A CPA is a cost model that agrees that the Advertiser pay outs a percentage of the value of the final sale to the Publisher that drove the user to the confirmation page. In return the Publisher delivers however many impressions, and thus provides however much inventory will be required to meet the income goal returned through the conversions.

As an example: an Advertiser might need to sell ten thousand suits and have an Advertising budget of £100,000 to do this, but approaching a Publisher site, finds that the CPM is £1. This would mean that every tenth user that sees the suit ad would need to buy the suit through the website. The Advertiser might know that the likelihood of this happening is very small; a conversion is more likely to work for one user in a hundred than one in ten. The advertiser could negotiate with the Publisher to agree instead to pay on a CPA of £1. This way the budget is used to sell all ten thousand suits and the cost is lower for the Advertiser.

Clearly CPA does not work for every Publisher. but will work for Publishers displaying ads to niche audiences for high cost purchases. In such an example the CPA can return more revenue than a CPM.

If an Advertiser site contains more than one product for sale, the conversion tag can be used to work out which product was actually purchased and how much it cost:

Conversion tag types - Sales Vs. Counter Tags

Conversion tags come in a few varieties; most ad servers have the capability of generating conversion tags with the sole purpose of counting the traffic or the number of conversions (called a counter tag). This can be compared to the generation of what is referred to as a "Sales Tag"; which can pick up more information about the conversion in addition to counting, such as value of the user purchase or number of items in the basket.

Technically speaking these tag types are very similar. The differentiation helps the trafficker to remember the purpose of the tag. This gives an indication of the tag location when campaigns are set up without consistent naming conventions.

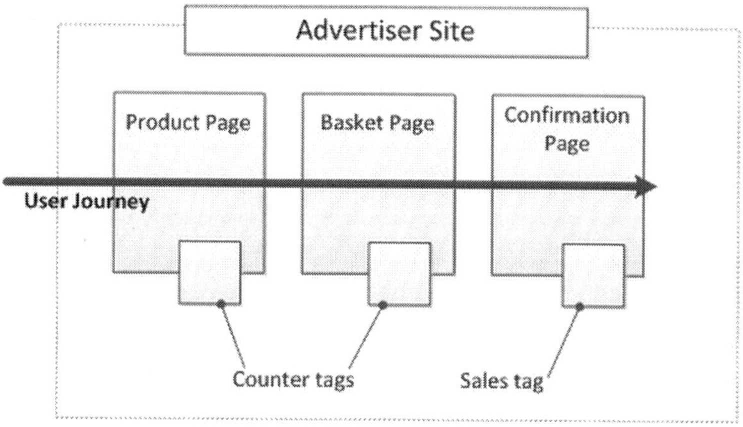

Figure 4.1.2 *The trafficker is best off creating counter type conversion tags for pages where the Advertiser just wants to monitor the user's journey to that page. Sales tags are better created for pages where the most valuable conversion event is occurring such as the point of sale.*

Extended data/Extended Parameters

The sales type of the conversion tag can also be setup to capture specific information about a sale. This information is made up of three groups of parameters referred to as "Extended Data" or "Extended Parameters". In the collection of each of these parameters, the Advertiser site management team pass the parameter into the corresponding field in the conversion tag using a mechanism like a simple JavaScript code, before it delivers the conversion information back to the ad server.

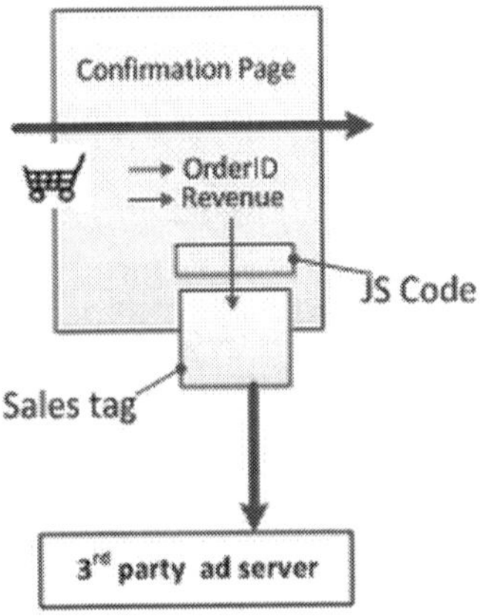

Figure 4.1.3 *As the user makes the purchase on the confirmation page; extended data parameters can be supplied to the conversion tag via a script, and supplied into ad server reporting.*

The three main groupings of parameter are:

1. "OrderID": The OrderID is a unique field generated by the Advertiser upon purchase to differentiate between the sales.

2. "Metric Parameters"; number value associated with the sale. The most commonly collected are two parameter fields called "Quantity" and "Revenue". Quantity usually reflects the number of items in the basket and Revenue reflects the total basket value.

3. "String Parameters"; are available to add context to the purchase. Some ad servers call this information "Category fields". Category fields follow strict guidelines; the Advertiser is permitted to pass information about the sale such as the names of items in the basket or description of the items purchased, but it is strictly prohibited for the Advertiser to collect Personally Identifiable Information.

Some ad servers limit the number of Metric and String Parameters that can be collected but there is rarely a need for more than one hundred fields of data. Most campaigns utilising sales conversion tags will collect between three and six data points.

```
<script type='text/JavaScript'>
// Conversion Name:  Confirmation Page
var ebRev = '%JS_TotalCost%';
var ebOrderID = '%JS_ConfirmNo%'';
var ebProductID = '%JS_RmTypCd%';
var ebProductInfo = '%JS_HName%';
var ebRand = Math.random()+'';
ebRand = ebRand * 1000000;
//<![CDATA[
document.write('<scr'+'ipt src="HTTPS://bs.serving-
sys.com/BurstingPipe/ActivityServer.bs?cn=as&amp;Activity
ID=32932240&amp;rnd=' + ebRand +
'&amp;Value='+ebRev+'&amp;OrderID='+ebOrderID+'&amp
;ProductID='+ebProductID+'&amp;ProductInfo='+ebProductI
nfo+'"></scr' + 'ipt>');
//]]>
</script>

<noscript>
<img width="1" height="1" style="border:0"
src="HTTPS://bs.serving-
sys.com/BurstingPipe/ActivityServer.bs?cn=as&amp;Activity
ID=3299410&amp;Value=[Revenue]&amp;OrderID=[OrderID
]&amp;ProductID=[ProductID]&amp;ProductInfo=[ProductIn
fo]&amp;ns=1"/>
</noscript>
```

Figure 4.1.4 *An example of a Mediamind sales conversion tag. Such a tag is best implemented as close to the top of the source code on the Advertiser page as possible (to ensure the conversion event is captured if the user leaves the page before it is fully loaded). This script would be generated by the trafficker who would send it through the Advertiser website management team. There are a series of extended*

> *parameters that the trafficker has added to the example tag shown which include both Metric Parameters and String Parameters. Product ID is an example of the former and ProductInfo is an example of the latter. The tag shown has two portions: the part labelled <noscript> can be implemented on a page that does not accept JavaScript but only the <script> or the <noscript> portion of the HTML shown needs to be implemented at all.*

It becomes part of the trafficking process for the trafficker to add the Metric and String Parameters as required to the tag before sending it over the Advertiser site management team with implementation instructions.

With regards to the collected data, the ad server simply records the data against a CookieID (which cannot be traced back to an individual's personal details). That CookieID is associated with an OrderID when the conversion tag fires and the detail are recorded in a single row in the ad server reporting database (see chapter 5). Here inside the confines of the ad server, no information at all about the purchaser can be gleaned except the behaviour of the cookie in question by looking in the database to other references to the Unique CookieIDs engagements with other ads or conversion tags. A consistent collection of information for a campaign from a conversion tag, will allow extended data parameters to become columns in ad server aggregated reporting (see chapter 5) and purchases can be grouped so that users that purchase a particular product, can be analysed for their buying patterns, ad engagement habits, expenditure and complimentary purchases.

Once the trafficker has exported the conversion tag from the ad server interface, adding metric and string parameters; the site management team will implement the tag. At this stage, testing out the implementation is crucial to avoid mishaps in data collection down the road.

How to test conversion tags

Conversion tags work right out of the box. Once implemented, they will count conversions in ad server reporting if a user's cookie has encountered an ad for the same Advertiser from the same ad server before. This is not universal; some ad servers allow conversion tags to only count conversions if users have encountered ads from a campaign associated with that conversion tag.

As an ad server begins tracking the conversion data, the reported figures should remain relatively consistent, however if ad server reporting shows a fall in conversions or if the conversions do not start appearing right after a campaign is put live, then the conversion tag itself needs to be checked.

An implemented conversion tag can be visited just by landing on the right page; if the user has not encountered an ad before, the tag will fire; triggering an "action" which will show up in ad server reporting. The user arriving to the page where the conversion tag sits can use an HTTP tracer (which, as a reminder, measures the server calls to and from the page).

If the URL of the ad server appears in the list of server calls when the page is loaded, then the conversion tag is present. To check its functionality deeper to determine if the conversion tag fired off an "action" versus a "conversion" requires to user to know what a successful conversion count from the conversion tag to the server looks like. This information can either be obtained by contacting the third party ad serving provider or in some instances the call is the same and only ad server reporting will show that there has been a conversion count. In this call to the server will be carried the extended data parameters as well.

The problem here is that ad server reporting processes conversions slower than the processing of impressions and clicks, so the conversion activity may not display in ad server reporting for up to twenty four hours. That is a long time to wait to find out that the conversion tag is not firing correctly and that no conversion event was recorded in the ad server reporting. For this reason it is recommended that the creation and implementation of the conversion tag happen at least a few days before the ad campaign is due to go live. If there is a problem with the implementation, it can be tested, remedied and retested before the campaign goes live.

Although it is recommended that the trafficker checks the conversion tag is implemented correctly before the campaign goes live, checking for the "conversion" in ad server reporting for testing purposes has two problems for the tester:

1. The most relevant conversion tags (usually sales tags) will predominantly be housed on a page at the end of the Advertiser site's user journey (also called a "booking pathway"). If this is indeed a thank-you page, the tester will normally be required to undertake a transaction to get there. It is recommended that Advertiser's therefore have 'testing' transactional information that can be inputted into a form (such as a fake credit card number) so that the tester can reach the sales tag without incurring a cost. A surprising number of Advertisers have not foreseen this requirement and as such conversion tag testers (in support teams on the Agency side or working for the third party ad serving provider) undergo personal expense to conduct testing with reimbursement later on. This can result in an embarrassing situation for any Advertiser whose site management team have implemented the conversion tag incorrectly on the thank-you page. Expensive transactions such as holidays can be particularly tough on the tester.

2. If the conversion was actually measured then the reporting will contain the record of a conversion- however this conversion would not really have been a true sale but

a test sale. For this reason some ad servers have conversion tag test functionality built in. This allows the conversion test data to either be quarantined from the actual conversion data for when the campaign goes live or allows the tester to omit their IP address from the collection of campaign-relevant conversion data, so that it only appears in test reporting.

In reporting, a drop in conversions most commonly occurs because the web development team of the Advertiser site are unaware of the significance of the code. A weekend release cycle of the Advertiser site could easily accidently remove the conversion tag and on a Monday morning, when the development team realise the tag has been removed, they would be alerted in ad server conversion reporting and need to replace the tag. The trafficker would need to just export the same conversion tag code again to fix this. It is wise for the trafficker to check conversion reporting in the ad server reporting interface frequently to ensure that the conversion tag has not been removed. Unfortunately despite programs designed to educate the site management teams about the importance of conversion tags, such technical mishaps will still occur.

A conversion tag that is setup and tested as working can be used to support the tracking of conversion events for a whole campaign but there are additional conversion tag settings and functionality that are utilised in almost every campaign utilising conversions. These settings fall into three groups:

a. Piggybacking
b. Conversion Windows
c. Attribution Modelling

The remainder of this section will look at these settings and explain how they work, how the trafficker can set and adjust them and for what purpose.

a. Conversion Tag Functionality - Piggybacking

Container Tags

Conversion tags (spotlight and action tags) can be setup to trigger the loading of other conversion tags. This trigger usually 'fires' when the page with the conversion tag on it is loaded. Conversion tags with this functionality are called "Container tags" or "Floodlight tags" and the vast majority of conversion tags have the ability to perform this function. The container tag can hold a large number of other tags from a variety of sources, it can also be used to carry third party code. If these additional tags originate from another technology provider: these tags are referred to as 4th party tags.

What other conversion tags or third party code would an Advertiser want to "piggyback" onto a conversion tag? Given the usefulness of conversion tags it is not just third party ad servers that want to measure conversions as they happen. Publishers measuring CPA might want to put a small piece of code in the container tag so they know straight away when sales are being made. In addition to this, any technology that drops a cookie on a user's machine at some time, will want to create a connection between that event and the arrival of that user to this key point in the purchase process: the confirmation page conversion tag.

It is also worth bearing in mind that sometimes Advertisers are using more than one tracking technology (double ad serving) and they therefore want the non-dominant ad server's conversion tag to be piggybacked into the container. The aim of the container is to reduce clutter on the page behind the scenes.

When an Advertiser or Agency completes a trafficking sheet for the trafficker at the start of a campaign, it is customary to supply the trafficker with instructions regarding piggybacking. The additional conversion tags to piggyback into the container tag are sent across as code and the trafficker inserts this code into the piggybacking screen in the third party ad serving interface. Some ad servers provide the facility to label each piggybacked tag with a name to identify its origin or purpose. This way when the trafficker makes changes to the container tag, it is clear which tag does what. This is particularly useful when there are multiple tags for different purposes by originating from the same technology provider (therefore having virtually the same code syntax and being difficult to uniquely identify).

Certified conversion tag providers

Some ad servers such as *Atlas*, also employed a process whereby all piggybacked tags needed to belong to recognised and certified providers. To pass certification, the technology providers of the additional conversion tags would need to sign legal documentation to verify that the piggybacked tags would not be undertaking bad industry practices (such as the collection of PII or data collection which could breach Publisher terms such as Publisher data leakage). This process of certification gets a mixed reaction across the industry as some traffickers find that it significantly slows down the process of piggybacking. In some instances technology providers refuse to sign legal documentation which can mean changing plans to use that provider or the ad server altogether for that campaign.

Piggybacking essentially means being able to adjust technology sitting on the Advertiser's site without disrupting the site management team (which will almost always slow down the process of tag implementation). This level of accessibility usually means that swapping tags in and out of container tags becomes a daily activity for the trafficker, sitting completely outside of campaign launch dates.

Which conversion tag fires first?

When a container tag contains several conversion tags, the container will call the third party ad server first, then the piggybacked tags fire off using a random algorithm. This way the piggybacked tags are all treated fairly and priority is not given to a particular one. Sometimes the trafficker may want to over-ride this default which is where selective pinging comes in.

Selective Pinging

On a high traffic web page, such as the confirmation page of a major Advertiser with an ecommerce site, the container tag might house twenty or more third party conversion tags or tracking pixels (the phrase 'pixels' is used because it is typically the <noscript> code in the generated conversion tag code, which is implemented into the container). Calling all of these pixels every time the confirmation page loads, risks the user leaving the page before all pixels have had a chance to load. If the user abandons the page before the container fully loaded then some of those third parties won't track anything at all.

The solution to this is to have particular rules in place on the container tag (controlled from within the user interface of the third party ad server) which have piggybacked conversion tags fire off at different times. The most common method is to limit the firing of those tags which had nothing to do with the sale. For instance, the ad server can check in a matter of micro seconds if the purchasing user cookieID was referred to the Advertiser site from an ad on a specific Publisher site; it then fires the corresponding pixel and ignores the other Publisher-supplied pixels. This method is sometimes called "Selective Pinging".

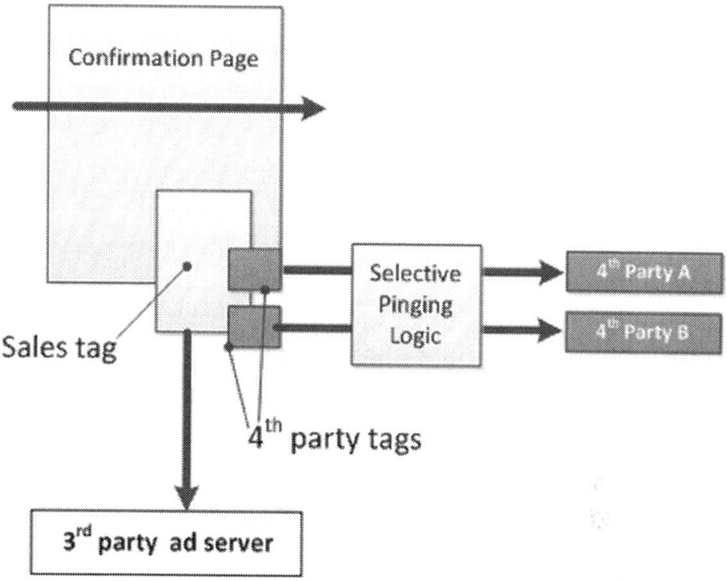

Figure 4.1.5 *In selective pinging the trafficker has received several conversion tags or pixel code from the Advertiser or Agency who have explained that the code comes from a couple of the suppliers on the media plan. These conversion tags (referred to in this diagram as 4th party tags) are loaded by the trafficker manually into the ad server piggybacking interface for the confirmation page sales/container tag. The trafficker than adjusts the selective pinging logic so that if the user arrives to the confirmation page that was originally directed to the Advertiser site by an ad on Publisher A, the 4th party A tag would fire and the 4th party B tag would not.*

Piggybacking with Extended data

Piggybacked pixels can capture information that the container tag already collects such as OrderID or any metric and string extended data. To pass the information through, the ad server utilises an "ad server macro" which is a tiny piece of code, already defined by the ad server which can be placed into piggybacked tags just as a token would be inserted into an impression or click tracker. An example of such a macro would be %orderID% which would be appended to the end of the 4th party pixel code to automatically recognise the Order ID in the container tag and populate the token space containing this macro with the same identifier.

Beyond the extended data, the 4th party tag can also capture pre-defined ad server macros such as the Conversion tag ID. It is worth the trafficker checking with the third party ad serving provider for a full list of the available pre-defined ad server macros.

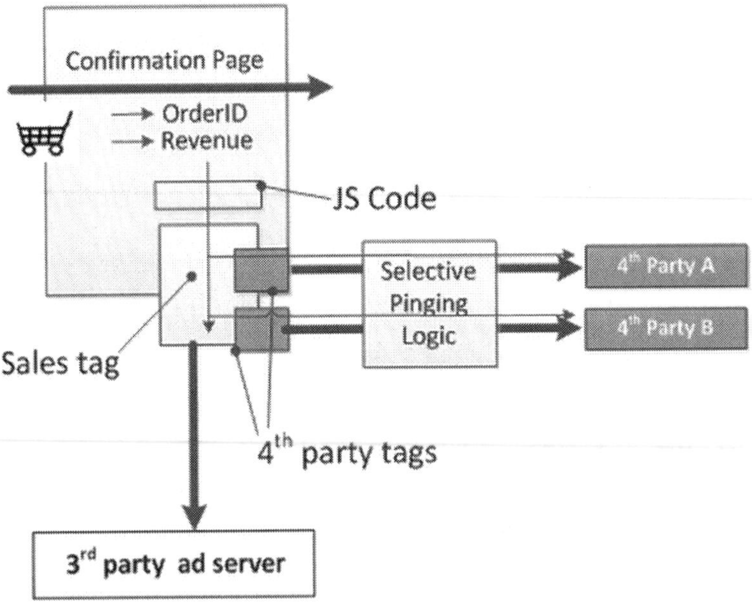

Figure 4.1.6 *The extended data present on the confirmation page is passed into the sales conversion tag by the*

customised code on the page (written by the Advertiser site management team). When the sales tag fires, it carries the conversion information with the extended data through to ad server reporting. The sales conversion tag is operating as a container tag and fires the correct 4th party tag using the Selective Pinging logic. Upon firing the 4th party tag calls the 4th party reporting server, carrying with it the same extended data variables present in the sales tag (namely the OrderID and the Revenue).

The conversion tags described here as being piggybacked in the container and the container tag itself will report data back to the ad server when it is fired but ad server reporting will treat this decide whether or not the activity counted as a conversion event using the conversion window settings.

b. Conversion Tag Functionality - Conversion Windows

Window Settings

A conversion tag sends information to ad server reporting each time it is fired, but the ad server has to decide if this information constitutes a "Conversion" or not. We have seen how the ad server makes a decision between a Conversion and an Action but consider this scenario:

A user sees an ad for product belonging to an Advertiser and then switches off their PC, goes on a long round-the-world trip and then returns to the machine two months later. On their return, the user switches on their PC, opens the browser and types in the URL of the Advertiser website before purchasing the same product and firing the conversion tag on the confirmation page after the purchase.

Is this a conversion? Some readers would say no. Some would say that only if the user clicks on the ad, did they intend to purchase. But in that instance would a two month gap between that click and the final purchase still mean we can attribute the conversion to that click? The answer lies in the ability of the trafficker to customise the conversion tag's conversion window settings.

Post-impression and Post-click windows

There is no "right method" for measuring conversions; but the two schools of conversion measurement are called "Post Impression" and "Post Click" conversion.

- A post impression conversion is when a user has seen an ad but not used that ad as a route to visit the Advertiser site to trigger the conversion tag (the user may have typed the URL into the browser directly to visit the site). The conversion is then classed as a post-impression conversion.

- A post click conversion is when a user sees the ad and clicks on it to arrive at the Advertiser site. The user then triggers the conversion tag from their by visiting the page where the conversion tag is placed.

These two models tend to fit different product types and purchase cycles. Consider the user exposure to a high impact video ad for a vacuum cleaner. The ad server reporting records just one impression to that ad by a unique cookieID. The next event recorded by the same cookieID is a purchase of that vacuum cleaner on the Advertiser site just one week after the exposure to the ad. If no other data exists for the same cookieID the Advertiser can infer that the user converted as a result of only seeing the ad and this is recorded as a post impression conversion.

The time-lag of one week is a consideration that needs to be taken into account based on the fact that the product in question is a high value purchase (a vacuum cleaner) and that the user may have taken some time to come to a decision to buy the item after seeing the ad.

The "Post Impression window" can be controlled and set by the trafficker on the conversion tag sitting on the confirmation page of the Advertiser site. Given that vacuum cleaners have longer purchase considerations that smaller retail goods (say a week or more), the post-impression window should be set to be over 7 days. The trafficker goes into the conversion tag settings inside the third party ad server interface and adds this setting before the conversion tag is implemented. Here, the post impression window should be set to a value over 7 days. In this example let's suggest that the trafficker sets the window at 12 days.

This means that when the ad server reporting receives the conversion event from the fired conversion tag, the ad server would count this user as having made a post impression conversion. If the user had made the purchase on the 13th day after seeing the video ad, the ad server would not count this as a conversion at all.

Post-click conversion windows work in the same way but consider the time lag between the click on the ad and the conversion activity by the same user. Most ad servers default the values of these windows at 30 days for post impression and 90 days for post click. It is also the case that as a default, the clicking of an ad is a more valuable metric that the impression count on an ad by the same user. If a user's activity for an ad campaign leading up to a conversion consists of a click in the first week and an impression in the second (for a conversion window of 3 weeks), then the click will be attributed as the main driver to the user making the final purchase in ad server reporting, once the conversion tag is fired.

Long conversion windows and short conversion windows

Long conversion windows give the user plenty of time to make a consideration before converting but the question is: how long is too long?

> Typically if a trafficker is too liberal and leaves a conversion window open for too long, then user's conversions will be attributed to an ad that may have had no real-world influence on the user's decision to purchase/convert. Here, a user may scroll past a DCO ad and hardly notice it on day 1 and then see a more engaging TV ad on day 20 and convert on day 21. In ad server reporting the attribution for the conversion would be awarded to the DCO ad. Perhaps if the conversion window was shortened to 5 days (so that the TV campaign would not interfere with the online campaign) the DCO ads could be dropped from the campaign since they would appear to provide no direct influence.
>
> However, leaving the window too short means that the true value of the ad campaign may not be correctly attributed. This may be because some users were been influenced by a specific rich media ad but delayed their purchase for too long, meaning that the influence of that ad was not captured in ad server reporting. When the trafficker looks in reporting and sees no conversions for the Rich Media ad (because the conversion window settings were too short) and the trafficker decides to stop serving the rich media ad, the total number of sales may drop.

Ad server reporting can also provide good reports for "time to convert" such reporting shows when most users are converting after seeing or clicking on ads in the same campaign as the conversion tag is associated with (see

Chapter 5). In such reports, considering the collected extended data can help the Advertiser to determine what the conversion window settings should be. Using this method, when the purchases of the product featured in the ad campaign are being made, using a string such as 'Product Name' the Advertiser can spot the difference between conversions for the product featured in the ad from those that were not featured. Those products featured in the ad are more likely to have been purchased as a result of the ads they feature in, so long as the converting users saw those ads in the first place.

Given that there are no hard and fast rules to set these windows; experimentation is key to finding a happy medium, otherwise too many or two few conversions could be awarded to the wrong ads or attributed to the wrong Publishers when paying out on a CPA.

Shadow Tagging

Some ad servers allow the Advertiser or Agency to view their total conversions in reporting by more than one conversion window so that stats can be compared (answering the question; is there a difference in the total number of conversions between short and long windows?). Those ad servers that offer a fixed window on the conversion tag with no option to make changes in reporting need to utilise the functionality of the container tag to see what the effect would be of adjusting the conversion window. In this instance multiple conversion tags are created under the same Advertiser with different window settings. These conversion tags are then piggybacked onto the container. Comparing the conversions across the different conversion tags in ad server reporting exposes the effectiveness of the different windows. This method is sometimes referred to as "Shadow tagging".

Reporting on Conversions

The presence of conversion windows means the ad server has to do a lot of work to calculate conversions as it must look back through the collected data for the entire length of all windows in order to allow reports to be pulled with an accurate reflection of total conversions. The data processing for ad servers which typically process billions of impressions each week means that accurate conversion data (at time of publication) is not currently available in real-time unless the ad serving technology has considerably less information to process. Data is typically available within twenty four hours of collection for reporting purposes owing, in-part, to the processing of conversion window information.

Repeat Conversion Windows

Sometimes users will purchase something and then refresh the confirmation page. To prevent the ad server from counting more than one conversion event, there are adjustable settings in place called the "repeat conversion window" which is usually set at about a minute or more. This way any refreshes of the conversion tag which take place by the same cookie in the same minute, are ignored in conversion processing and are not counted as conversions.

c. Conversion Tag Functionality - Attribution Modelling

It would be unfair to award the conversion to the last ad that a user clicked on, since this would suggest that this last ad was completely responsible for a purchase or conversion that followed it. As consumers we usually experience a number of engagements with a brand before a purchase. These engagements or "touch-points" (a reference used by *Flashtalking*) should each be given some credit for the final conversion. In practical terms this means that rather than paying the Publisher responsible for the last ad that was clicked, (as would occur under an agreement to pay the Publisher for CPA) all Publishers that contributed should be awarded a portion of the CPA. The division of that amount of capital (even at time of this book's publication) very rarely lands in the lap of more than one Publisher, owing largely to the complex payment terms that would need to be met by all parties. This includes the lack of technology to support such payment systems, and a lack of universal industry agreement in any attribution model beyond what is called the "last click" attribution model.

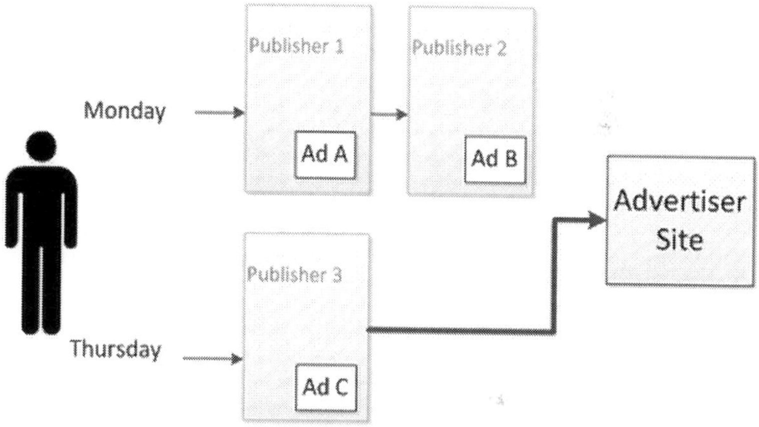

Figure 4.1.7 *If attribution modelling did not exist then only the last Ad touch-point on the user's journey through to conversion is responsible for the purchase/conversion. Here, the user saw three ads for the same campaign across three different Publishers before clicking through to the Advertiser site where a conversion was counted. In ad server reporting, under the "last click" attribution model, only Publisher 3 deserves the full CPA. As a default most ad servers count conversions under the last click model unless adjusted by the trafficker. Using the model can be adjusted under the conversion tag settings screen in the third party ad server interface.*

Attribution Settings

Attribution settings present themselves in third party ad servers as a way to adjust the reporting of the total number of conversions as they appears in ad server reporting when looking at conversions driven by each of the Publishers and channels on the media plan. These settings are typically simple adjustments from the default last click model, to perhaps a model that weights impressions and clicks equally and will therefore award the conversion to the last Publisher (even if that Publisher did not have the user directly click on that ad, but rather the user just saw it - counting a post-impression conversion).

Adjustments to these core attribution settings are useful to reveal the true number of total conversions per Publisher and per media channel, when a last impression methodology does not seem to award enough conversions to a more costly channel.

For instance consider this scenario:

- The trafficker begins by setting up the ad campaign according to the media plan. The conversion tag is generated with a "last event" (click or impression) attribution model selected.
- During an ad campaign for 'ski boots' Paid search was the most expensive channel used by the advertiser.
- Alongside this the Advertiser has retargeting tags on their site and is running DCO ads displaying creative chosen based on retargeting. The DCO display inventory is costing the Advertiser less money to run.

- The user starts by actively searching for 'ski boots', sees a Paid search ad and navigates to the Advertiser site (the ski boots product page).

- The user then leaves the site and considers buying the boots but defers by a day or so.

- The user then checks their email and the DCO ad is served to them featuring the ski boots, the product appears to have followed the user to their email inbox.

- Rather than click on the DCO ad, the user navigates directly to the site to purchase the boots.

- The user buys the boots, on the thank-you page the conversion tag fires to signal a conversion.

- In ad server reporting the total number of conversions on the conversion tag attributed to the DCO ad is 1 and the total number of conversions attributed to the search ad is 0.

If the trafficker had selected a "last click" attribution model, then Paid Search, being the last click before the conversion event, would be awarded with the conversion. Here, the attribution settings can be used to better represent the value that search is driving, awarding the whole conversion to the Publisher and channel responsible for the last click.

If in the same scenario, the user had actually clicked the DCO ad as well, a more complex attribution model would have been required to tell ad server reporting that Paid Search (regardless if it was the last click or not) is always more valuable, perhaps DCO because Paid Search better represents the users intent to purchase.

Engagement Mapping

Some ad servers present more complex attribution settings than just "last click" or "last event". Like the more simple settings, these can be adjusted inside the settings on the conversion tag by the trafficker. Rather than make changes to the "conversions" column in ad server reporting, an additional column is presented alongside the original conversion column. Inside the third party ad server *Atlas*, the trafficker can observe the "e-conversions" column alongside the standard conversions column so that there is a yard stick to understand the context of measuring conversions under new models. E-conversions consider how all Publishers, ads and channels can share part of the whole conversion so that the split conversion, in its parts, are properly attributed to a combination of Publisher, Ad and Channel. In this way Publishers could appear to get 0.2 of a conversion in the E-conversions column in ad server reporting. This is determined by the value of the factors involved in true conversion attribution.

As a result of this information the planner or buyer can better calculate the value of the media space back to CPA since a CPA reflects the value of the attributing media space that drove the conversion event. Where a Publisher agrees to be paid on a CPA, the contractual obligation to pay out on conversions should be tied back to an agreement about the attribution model associated with that conversion. This encourages an industry based around a "last click wins" model, to a model more aligned with how users choose to engage with Advertising and subsequently spend with the Advertiser.

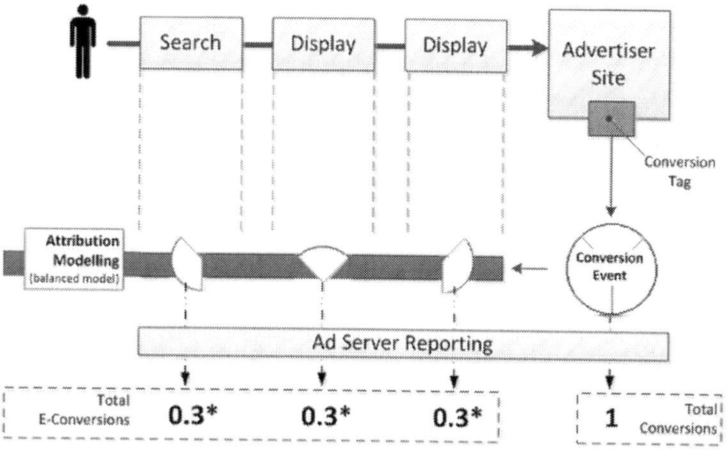

Figure 4.1.8 *On the user's pathway to conversion, there might be an engagement with touch points across multiple channels. Once the user arrives on the Advertiser site and triggers a conversion tag, the conversion event is fed through into ad server reporting for standard conversion calculation. Within reporting one conversion is counted. In addition the conversion might be processed by a layer sitting on top of the reporting interface known as Attribution Modelling. Shown in the diagram the trafficker has set the attribution model for this specific conversion tag as a 'balanced model' meaning that the attribution is evenly split across all publishers and channels. Inside ad server reporting the three touch points receive equal weighting and e-conversions are a percentage of the overall conversion. Here shown at 0.3 conversions for each touch point. Under this model reporting would show that the Display channel is more effective at driving conversions than Search since the total for Display will be 0.6 where Search will stand at 0.3. Without attribution modelling the final touch point was Display which under the 'last click' model means full attribution goes to Display. With this as a reporting methodology, the correct action would be to take Search off of the media plan for future activity. Such action may easily*

be damaging to a campaign since search may be playing an important part of this pathway to conversion, an attribution which is hidden without Attribution modelling being enabled.

Custom Attribution Modelling

Trying to determine which ads are driving actual conversion events is a complex task. On the average media plan, there is a diverse range of Publishers across multiple channels showing different pieces of creative. If a user encounters each of these types on their "pathway to conversion", where does the attribution lie?

In science and mathematics, breaking down a problem into its simplest parts makes it easier to understand. In third party ad serving, particularly inside the Atlas ad server for attribution modelling these parts are called "Factors". Possible factors include:

- The dimensions of the ad
- The format of the ad
- How recently the ad was encountered (termed "recency")
- The quality of the Publisher delivery (see Chapter 5 - Verification)
- The quality of the creative
- The viewability of the ad (see Chapter 5- Verification)
- The Publisher or site name

An advertiser can rank each of these factors in terms of prioritisation in how to determine the value that each Publisher, Ad and Channel is bringing to a campaign. This prioritisation produces an algorithm to calculate what Atlas terms "e-conversions".

These algorithms are heavily scrutinized as being far too subjective, because the Advertiser has the freedom to tweak the algorithm in favour of certain Publishers or formats. This can unfairly weight a campaign based on Advertiser and marketing bias rather than a closer examination of the historical cookie level data.

Seasonal fluctuations in the data should also be taken into account, and for some attribution service providers, machine learning is introduced to make light work of building a complex and dynamic attribution model. Given the complexity of such tasks, various point solutions have cropped up to provide such services which are commonly integrated with third party ad serving technology by receiving a feed of their data or connecting via an API. Examples include *Encore Metrics* and *ClearSaleing*.

Many Agencies and Advertisers prefer to make their own minds up with their Publishers about what attribution modelling means for them and they will typically use the data from the Exposure to Conversion (E2C) or Pathway to Conversion (P2C) reports to do so (See Chapter 5 - Cookie level data). In this reporting, all touch-points can be exposed and the Advertiser can look at the whole data-set to decide where the value is being provided on a case by case basis. Large Agencies sometimes have in-house systems to calculation attribution more fairly.

Challenges in implementing conversion tags

Advertisers find conversion tags exceedingly useful and become enthusiastic about ad server reporting when conversion counting is added to the mix of reporting metrics but there are two hurdles to overcome to make the most of conversion tags:

1. Conversion tags take the site management team a long time to implement and a long time to remove. Sometimes it can take a marketing team six months or more to get new tags placed on an Advertiser site.

2. There are so many pages on the Advertiser site: because each conversion tag is different, coding up a large site can be a nightmare if conversion tags and container tags are created one by one

These two needs alone birthed a new frontier in conversion tag management called "Universal tagging".

Tag Management Systems

To get a complete view of the user journey and get a proper handle on conversion attribution, conversion tags should be placed on as many pages of the Advertiser site as possible. This means a lot of work for the Advertiser website managers who keep dropping these pieces of code, received from the trafficker onto pages. Keeping a log of conversion tags across the site can be a full time job in itself. Although container tags have reduced the work by making individual pages a little tidier (keeping all conversion tags inside one container), a large Advertiser site may have thousands of pages.

Tag Management Systems are single pieces of code that (like site side analytics tools) can be included on all pages of the Advertiser site making the implementation very easy to scale. The site management team can simply deploy the single piece of code using the CMS (which will usually grant the ability to update all pages at once). This single act allows the Advertiser to map any existing conversion tags, new conversion tags, retargeting tags and third party code to existing URLs from inside the ad server interface. The role falls to the trafficker to generate and implement the conversion tags all from within the same system.

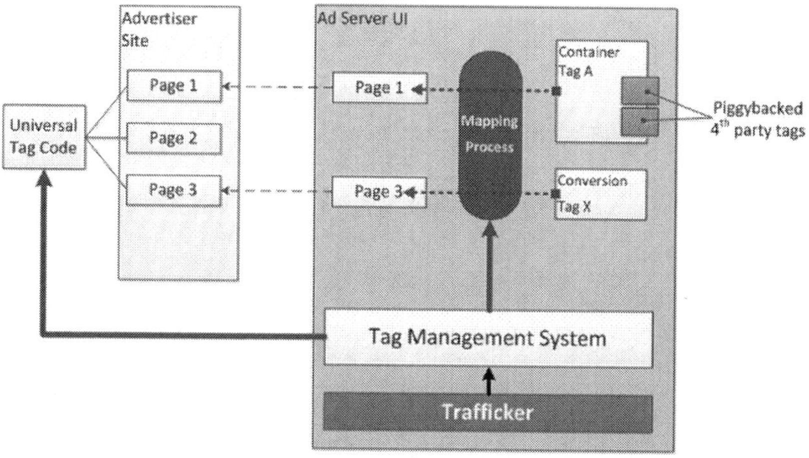

Figure 4.1.9 *Universal Tagging is enabled through a Tag Management system (which can either sit within the ad server or be supplied by a point solution). The trafficker accesses the tag management system in the first instance to deploy the universal tag code which the Advertiser site management team deploy across all pages of the site. Now via the Tag Management system, the trafficker can map existing conversion tags and container tags to pages or URLs on the Advertiser site without needing to bother the site management team to make changes.*

Universal Tagging Security

Universal tagging allows marketers a 'backdoor' into web pages on their own site without needing to wait for the website release cycle to come round. With such power comes the responsibility to ensure that any implemented tags and code are tested in full before deployment. Some such solutions also offer the ability to issue a proposal to the site management team for them to grant permission to implement tags via the ad server on a tag by tag basis. This is a security mechanism that prevents the trafficker from inundating the pages of the site with heavy tags or code that is outside the policies adopted by the site management team.

Tag Management Systems are sometimes packaged to include features that measure the speed at which the pages load, which can be an important factor in determining a user's interest in the Advertisers pages beyond simply firing a conversion tag.

Typically an Advertiser or Agency will deploy such a system long before campaigns are due to go live and then conversion tags will mapped to the relevant URLs closer to the ad campaign launch date or during the campaign lifetime.

Once again "point solutions" have cropped up in the industry to provide this service at an additional cost to the Advertiser, although Universal tagging solutions built into the ad server tend to be cheaper but with fewer features. Examples of such point solutions include *Tagman, Qubit* and the server-side tagging solution *BrightTag*, all of which can be somewhat integrated into the available third party ad servers using piggybacking. Beyond this Universal tagging is very useful to the world of first party data collection and the DMP (see Chapter 8).

Conversion tags provide much needed accountability in digital advertising. Advertising dollars can be attributed to events that provide a direct return on the investment in the ad campaign. Conversion tags allow marketers to learn more about their customers, transforming the behaviour of users into the definitions of audiences. Audience identification allows marketers to correctly target relevant ad campaigns to users and avoid wasting valuable media spend on showing ads to users that will not be interested in an Advertiser's goods or services. Conversion tags do this by allowing the marketers to correlate conversion data across all users that have been engaged in an ad campaign and check that target audiences are the same users making the purchases.

The next section looks in depth at audiences and targeting to transform the delivery of ads from mass reach to relevance in order to drive valuable conversions.

Chapter 4 - Section 2
Audiences and targeting

- Audiences and Targeting at a media/inventory level
- Audiences and Targeting at a creative level
- third party ad server targeting rules
- Layered Targeting
    - *Figure 4.2.1*
    - Geo-targeting
    - Behavioural targeting
    - *Figure 4.2.2*
    - Contextual targeting (page-scraping)
        - *Figure 4.2.3*
    - Search keyword targeting
    - Targeting based on Verification Data
    - Additional Data targeting
- A/B Testing
- *Figure 4.2.4*
- Tru lift
- *Figure 4.2.5*
- Audience Assignment
    - Channels which bend the rules

Setting up a campaign for any channel within the third party ad server can be a tricky undertaking for a trafficker new to the process, but practice makes perfect. Beyond assigning the ads to placements and sending tags to Publishers, the trafficker has the opportunity to take advantage of more advanced settings in the ad serving interface to ensure better performance (improved interaction, click and conversion rates) from ads in a campaign.

Audiences and targeting settings on a placement level, within the third party ad server interface is a different, more subtle approach to improving relevance than make such adaptions in the planning and buying phase of the creation of the media plan. These two distinctions can sometimes get confusing:

Audiences and Targeting at a media/inventory level
Part of the role of the media planner is to locate an Advertiser's target audience for an ad campaign among the available Publishers and channels in the online space. Choosing the right audience and procuring that inventory is the first step in ensuring that ads are seen by the relevant users.

When Publishers sell 'audiences' to planners, they are selling ad space which they believe attracts a certain demographic of individual. The methodology behind the demographics should be questioned in depth by the Advertiser before purchasing the ad space. To check that the audience being sold is marketer's target audience, planners can check independent audience verification tools like *Neilsen* or *Comscore* before the campaign goes live, or verification reporting during the campaign (see Chapter 5).

Sometimes Publishers define the audience traffic themselves by allowing a sample size of logged in users (with completed demographic information on the site) visiting those pages where the ads are shown to be scaled up based on the volume of impressions to those pages. Publishers package these audiences for sale in the premium space and label it up for sale directly to planners and buyers or by packaging it for sale on Ad Networks and Ad Exchanges. In programmatic buying the audience can be distinguished using additional audience data or with the help of SSP's (see Chapter 8).

Despite the importance, Audience labelling is not industry standardised so particularly in the Exchange space, it pays to ask questions to be able to verify the audience being purchased. Once the purchase of the inventory has gone ahead and the labelling of the purchased audience by the Publisher has been accepted, the trafficker can use the ad server as a safety net to ensure that more costly ad formats and creative messaging are shown to the right audience.

Audiences and Targeting at a creative level
An 'audience' in third party ad serving terms means a group of users labelled by trafficker as having a common set of properties (such as users in a particular geography). These groups can be ascertained by either capturing web-page level information in real time or looking back at a user's cookie history and IP data. This level of audience recognition and targeting does not usually omit the delivery of ads to certain users but rather ensures relevant and cost-effective creative is shown to specific audiences.

This section will look in-depth at the ability of the trafficker to apply rules to ad server targeting, to decide which ad to display to the user when the ad server receives a request from a Publisher to display an ad.

Third party ad server targeting rules
As a default setting, the ad server does not encounter any targeting rules on a placement level when displaying an ad other than to show the main ad where-ever possible and fall back to a backup image if the user's browser does not support flash (and falling back to HTML5 for the mobile channel). In Chapter 3 we also looked closely at the ability for the trafficker to set ad controls to rotate ads or shown them in a sequence.

Targeting rules add a new layer to a decision tree that the third party ad server will execute upon, to decide which creative to display to the user. Essentially a series of questions; the rules can be layered up to form complex queries, but there is always an 'other' bucket at the bottom of the decision tree which contains an ad that would be shown if the user did not fit into any of the targeting rule descriptions. Such an ad would be described as a non-targeted ad. As an example:

- The marketer purchases ad inventory from a Publisher to target only users with a Spanish IP address.
- The trafficker sets up a placement with the targeting criteria to target users with a specific ad for those users based in Spain and sets up a more generic ad in case a user sees the placement outside of Spain.
- The trafficker traffics the placement to the Publisher.
- The Publisher does not honour the targeting criteria for some of the purchased inventory because there are not enough Spanish IP addresses viewing the site to fulfil the agreed number of impressions on the IO. Perhaps even if the site is a Spanish site, Spanish speaking users are still expected to arrive to the site from other locations globally.
- A user from a German IP encounters the placement.
- The ad server receives a request from a user with a German IP for the placement.
- Since the user does not meet the criteria for the 'Spain IP targeted ad' the ad servers deliver the ad in the 'other' bucket setup by the trafficker.
- When the trafficker checks ad server reporting, the trafficker will know that the Publisher did not fulfil the requirement on the IO and may ask for the Publisher to remunerate the cost of the mislaid impression.

In this example it is clear that the third party ad server provides a safety net. Such a feature becomes more relevant if, for example, there are strict advertising guidelines for advertising medical products in Germany compared to those in Spain. The third party ad server can be used to ensure that the Advertiser does not breach such guidelines even if the Publisher fails to fulfil the targeting criteria on the IO.

Layered Targeting

Given the range of available targeting criteria, it is clear to distinguish how many targeting rules could be set up in the ad server but there needs to be corresponding creative for each defined audience. Complexity can easily become inefficient, if it takes more work to manage the decision tree than the revenue that the targeting generates. If there is no obvious uplift in ROI as a result of the targeting rules in place, it is important try to simplify the decision tree. Branches which attract larger numbers of impressions, conversions, clicks or interactions are worth keeping but those with just one or two conversions or limited engaging behaviours should be scrapped. Complex targeting requires a lot of creative which can be costly and even DCO (see Chapter 3).

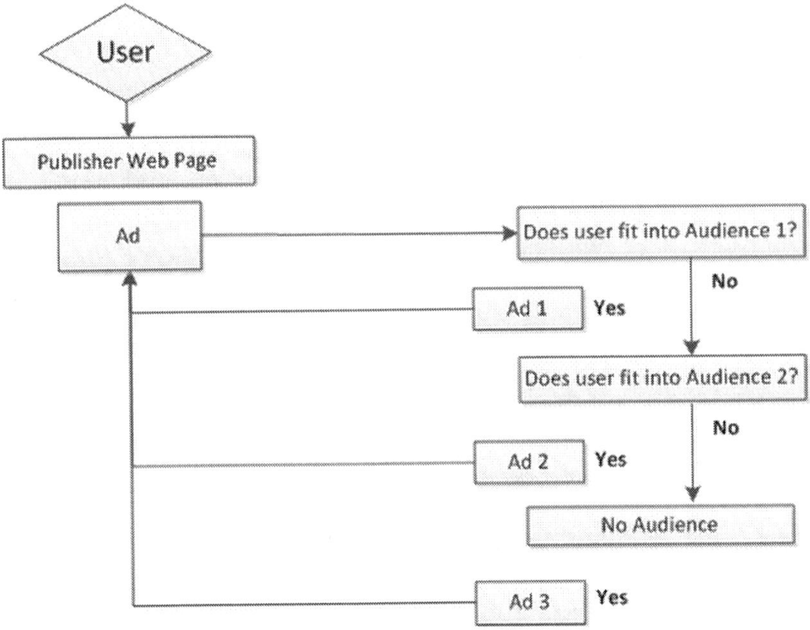

Figure 4.2.1 *A user encounters a placement on a Publisher page. The placement makes a call to the ad server to decide which ad to display based on targeting rules or criteria setup by the trafficker. Each rule corresponds to the definition of an Audience inside the ad server interface. In this example, if the user fits the criteria for Audience 1 - Ad 1 is shown. If not, the ad server checks to see if the user fits the criteria for Audience 2 in which case Ad 2 is shown. If the user fails to meet the criteria for either of these defined Audiences then the user is shown the 'other' non-targeted ad - Ad 3. If a user's browser cannot support Flash, then the user will not enter the decision tree and instead will be shown the fall-back backup image.*

The third party ad server interface allows the trafficker to setup various forms of targeting designed to match the marketer and planner's intended audience criteria. The trafficker can navigate to the placement level within the campaign setup to apply targeting rules to the ads which are assigned to the placements. These targeting forms are:

- Geo-targeting
- Behavioural targeting (also called retargeting)
- Contextual Targeting (also called Semantic targeting)
- Targeting based on Verification Data
- Additional Data targeting

In addition some ad servers offer the chance to implement an additional frequency cap at the audience level. This can act as an override to the rule in place, bringing the user down to the next section of the decision tree pre-maturely. This is useful so that the Advertiser can ensure that the targeted audience does not suffer creative fatigue. This differs from placement level frequency capping (which shows the user a different ad when the cap is met) here, when the cap is met at an Audience level, the user drops down the decision tree and might slot into another rule to be shown a different placement.

Geo-targeting
Before the ad server delivers the ad, it receives the cookieID and the IP address of the user. The IP address can be used to work what geography the user sits within, with a decent degree of accuracy. Upon receiving the IP data, the ad server runs this against a mapping database based on additionally purchased data from IP mapping providers such as *Digital Element*. This will return a geographical location primarily at a country level but then with a greater granularity in some markets when the internet is more heavily used. The US is one of such countries where breakdown to DMA and state level retains a decent accuracy.

The mapping data across the board is not one hundred per cent accurate because not all IP addresses are correctly mapped to the country the user is sitting within. It is sensible to suggest that IP mapping is closer to 80% accurate but this is still enough to perform geo-targeting, especially if this data is paired with other data sets for targeting. Beyond state or region levels IP data does not fare so well (such as falling to postal code or zip code level) in terms of accuracy so it is recommended to avoid this level of geographical granularity using geo-targeting alone.

To utilise geo-targeting, the trafficker needs to setup placements so that the ads assigned to them are geo-targeting by selecting the specific country or region from the ad server ad-assignment interface. Once the assignment is complete and the campaign goes live, users in the specified geographies will be shown a targeted piece of creative, if not then they are shown a non-targeted ad. Geo-targeting is useful to add relevance to the creative, so a user sitting in Chicago seeing a Rich Media ad from a flights provider such as American Airlines may see a data collection form inside the ad which can calculate the cost of a trip from Chicago to other destinations. Geo-targeting would ensure that the creative is used where Chicago is a pre-populated field in the form. This creative optimization may save the user time when engaging with the ad and prove to increase the total number of conversion events as users navigate to the site to purchase flights.

Although it is possible for the Publisher ad server to perform IP level targeting (thereby geo targeting ads) the control would then sit with the Publisher. The trafficker in the third party ad server interface would need to set up hundreds of tags to provide Publisher-independent granular reporting and would not be able to stop a Publisher serving a high cost rich media unit to the wrong geography.

Behavioural targeting

Behavioural Targeting or Retargeting is now so extensively utilised in digital advertising that it has been given its own Chapter in this book (Chapter 7). To summarise very briefly: users that have performed a particular action on a website, such as making a purchase of a particular product, are added to a retargeting audience or cookie pool, so that specific creative can be targeted to those users in the future. It is wise to add retargeting pixels to the Advertiser site pro-actively so that a corresponding audience and relevant ad can be set up inside the ad server on the placement level.

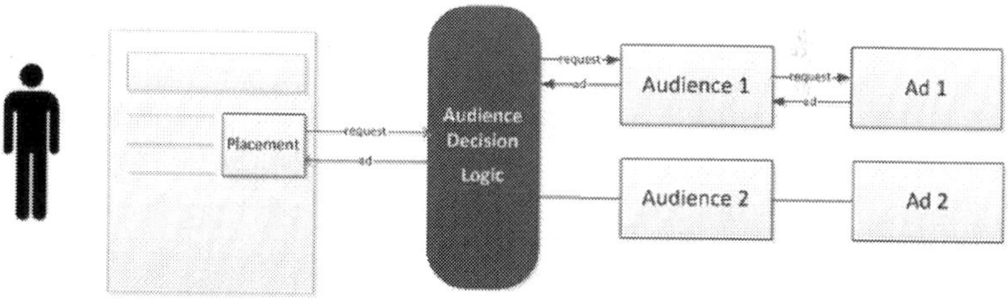

Figure 4.2.2 *Audiences have ads assigned to them. When the ad server receives a request from the Publisher page via the placement, the audience decision logic in the ad server selects the correct audience (such as the correct geography) and serves the corresponding ad.*

Contextual targeting (page-scraping)

The page that the ad is served onto provides great contextual information, since the user has navigated to the page for a reason and this is reflected in the content surrounding the ad. A placement can be setup therefore, to gather information about the page itself before choosing which ad to show. The keywords codes or variables present on the page can be used to inform the third party ad server targeting system; the trafficker only needs to setup an audience and therefore an ad to match with the corresponding keyword or variable.

To go about gathering the information on the page, the placement can either scrape the page automatically or the site management team can write a script to accompany the third party ad tag, passing contextual information into it. The former of these options is the kind of contextual targeting that *Flashtalking* offers, which is a page scraping mechanism which can lift keywords from the page to inform the targeted ad. The latter example is what is referred to in the *DG/Mediamind* ad server as Keyword targeting; here the Publisher passes a variable across such as 'female54years' which may not appear in the visible context of the page but is available as a variable because the user is signed into the Publisher site. Keyword targeting can be useful for demographic targeting where the audience data is being informed by the Publisher's own database.

Gathering semantic information is invaluable when considering the delivery of ads to pages in Belgium. Because Belgium is a tri-lingual society (French, German or Dutch), the semantic of the page informs the placement which language to display the ad in. In this example the trafficker needs to have set up three audiences with corresponding ads in each of the three languages along with a non-targeted ad. The page can pass a variable or keyword across when the placement requests the ad from the ad server to display the ad with the corresponding language.

Contextual targeting can also be utilised in combination with DCO so that the ad passes a value into a dynamic creative which appears to mirror the context of the page in real time.

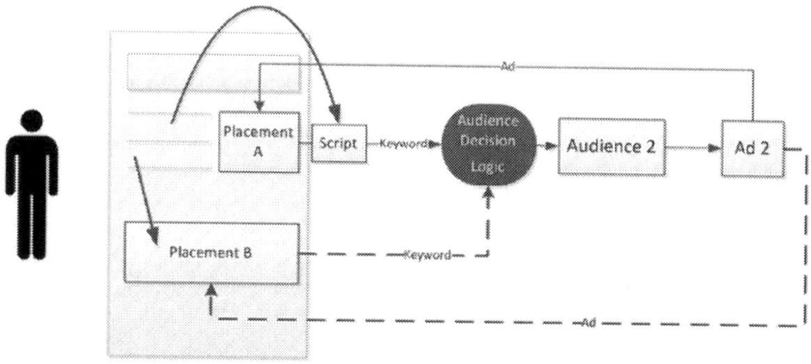

Figure 4.2.3 *Placement A is an ad supports by keyword targeting. A script is developed by the Publisher site management team to pass a specific keyword into the ad request. The keyword is processed by the ad server decision logic and requests an ad from the corresponding audience assignment. In placement B, the placement code contains a scraping mechanism which processes the semantic of the page, passing a value through to the Audience decision logic. Here the same action is taken as with Placement A and the ad request serves the ad for the corresponding audience.*

Search keyword targeting

Search Engine owners *Google* and *Microsoft* have the advantage of looking beyond the ad serving data to look at a user's full search history even if they did not click on the paid search ads tracked by the ad server. This search history can be tied to the user's local cookie data or signed in Windows Live or Google accounts on the local machine. The ad servers of these two companies (*DoubleClick* and *Atlas*) can then match the ad serving cookie with the activity of the first party network/search engine cookie offering a wealth of new targetable data to Advertisers using these technologies. Advertiser can setup their ad campaigns to target users based on specific search terms as keywords that they have actively searched on in the past.

As far as other ad servers go; the keyword data is captured in paid search campaigns which are tracked under the search channel by those ad servers and there is an association between those keywords and the cookie. In the future it is likely that these users could be targeted based on paid search click activity although this would probably constitute a form of retargeting rather than be considered true search keyword targeting (since the user has to perform the action of a click for the data to be collected).

Targeting based on Verification Data
Verification data (See Chapter 5) is already being catered for in the world of targeting on most levels:

- Geographical verification is catered for in Geo-targeting
- Brand Safety and Content Categorisation is catered for in Contextual targeting
- Device verification is partly catered for using the ad server fall back mechanism for HTML5

The outliers for Verification data include verification metrics beyond brand safety which determine the quality of the content on the page. Such metrics would include the presence of a large number of ads (called "ad clutter") or the presence of user generated content (UGC) or commenting. Today ad servers are not detecting these occurrences as part of the standard placement delivery (for premium direct inventory buys) but it is likely they will do so in the future. Within the DSP and Exchange spaces this is a different story completely (see Chapter 8).

With regards to targeting for viewability data, the placement upon loading would only be able to gather viewability data in real time, and as such the % surface area seen and the duration of time the user sees the ad for will be subject to constant change. Ad server targeting is not yet sophisticated enough to contend with targeting ads based on this information. Instead it may be possible for traffickers to use previous data collection regarding average viewability metrics for ads delivered to the same placement as a benchmark to determine the most suitable ad to serve. Once again this level of sophistication has not yet been introduced into targeting because (at time of publication) viewability is still in its infancy. Once again technology is available in the exchange space to buy inventory and target users based on a rudimentary viewability detection method; detecting for ads served above or below the fold of the user's browser.

Additional Data targeting
All of the targeting methods listed so far in this section are actually using additional data to make targeting decisions:

- Search targeting - Search Engine Data
- Verification targeting - Verification Data
- Contextual targeting - Page Level Data
- Keyword Targeting - Publisher-supplied Data
- Behavioural targeting - Retargeting Data in the ad server retargeting pool
- Geographic targeting - Addition Data set from IP mapping provider

There are a significant number of other data points that could mean that Advertisers are targeting users with more relevant creative messaging and more impactful ads. Unfortunately as yet many of these capabilities have not been built directly into the ad server and require a complex customisation of bolt-on or partner technologies such as DMPs or Data Providers (See Chapter 8). These data providers can sit halfway between the placement and the ad server to nourish the placement call to the ad server for the ad with more information about the audience. In this instance both Retargeting and Keyword targeting can be adjusted to build out audiences in the ad server from external sources of data. This more complex capability is explored in more detail in Chapter 8.

Beyond external sources of data, the ad server is collect high volumes of data which can be transformed into addition targeting options. These are standardised in some ad servers while others may need to set up custom scripts to perform them:

- Targeting by the age of the user's cookie
- Targeting by the date the cookie was dropped
- Targeting users based on their historical cookie level data
- Predictive Behavioural targeting (comparing the actions and engagement of converting users to non-converting users to make targeting decisions)
- Targeting users based on over-zealous frequency

Targeting methods in a decision tree-type workflow allows a trafficker to use trial and error to narrow down the audience left seeing the non-targeted ad. This methodology is highly useful for targeting users that perhaps are accessing the internet from a non-US IP address by customising the decision tree and making full use of the non-targeted ad. In this way, traffickers can calculate what impact certain creative messaging is having as well as creating various "experiments" to split out the users seeing ads to determine if one ad is better than another. Two examples of these are "A/B testing" and "Tru Lift" studies.

A/B Testing

A/B testing means splitting the users that see a placement out so that different users see different ads and then the results between the two groups are compared. This enables the segmenting of cookies into random test or control groups so that the control group always sees the same ad while the test group sees an ad that changes. The resulting increase in effectiveness of the new ads can be attributed to the creative displayed rather than unaccountable trends.

A/B testing can be conducted in two ways:

1. The first time the user encounters the placement, they are forced into a group (either the control or test group). If the user sees the placement again, they will see the ad for the group they were originally forced into.

   By creating a control group the trafficker can test various creative formats, creative messages and even post-impression windows against users that have been served the ad in the control group. With this method, if an offer is never shown to a user in the control group, yet they actively search for it and convert, that media in other channels (such as TV or word of mouth) may be attributed to the conversion.

2. Every time the user encounters the placement they encounter the logic from the top of the targeting decision tree.

   This way the control group changes so that the division between users is relevant only to that session in time. This way if users in the control group had a propensity not to convert any way, the control group would not always stay the same so those non-converters could be balanced between the control group and the test group.

   This is not a true A/B test as individual users commonly visit both experiments. However it controls creative exposure equally and more fairly at a specific point in time, to establish the value of creative messaging.

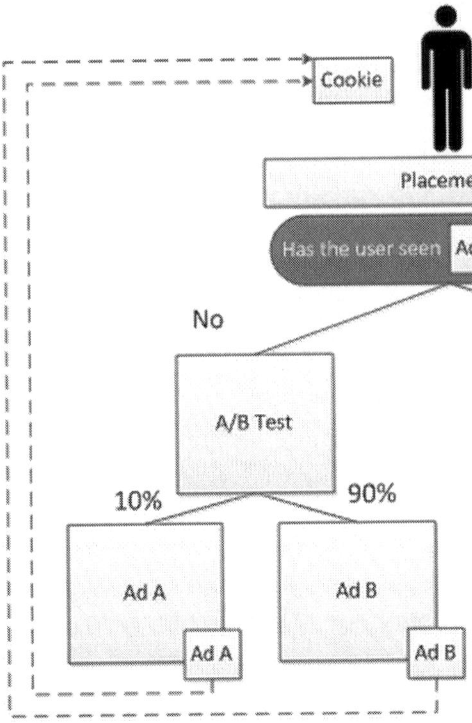

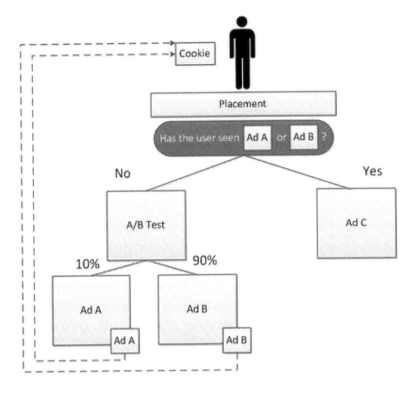

Figure 4.2.4 *An A/B test allows a trafficker to control the delivery of specific message to a sample of the total number of users. When the user first encounters the logic they enter the A/B test, 90% of the users will see the usual Ad B, while 10% will see the experimental message Ad A. When the user encounters another placement from the same campaign they are shown the next usual message in the sequence. Did the presence of Ad A instead of Ad B improve the campaign performance? A trafficker can check reporting to see. If the experiment failed to point to a performance increase or worse; if Ad A had a detrimental effect, at least only a small sample of the total users were ever exposed.*

A/B testing helps expose the strength of the creative message and its relationship with Advertiser KPIs such as conversion events. A "tru lift" study is the name given to an experiment using A/B testing that allows the Advertiser to demonstrate that any digital advertising is having an impact on conversions versus users that are not exposed to the campaign at all.

Tru lift

A tru lift study tries to prove that an exposure to an advertising campaign causes (at the most rudimentary level); an increase in the number of conversions for an Advertiser over a given period of time.

To conduct a tru lift study the trafficker needs to split the audience of the advertising campaign into those that have never seen an ad for the Advertiser and those that have ever been exposed to an ad. Given the limitation of the impression based cookie window it is actually very difficult to create such a clean break in the audience; some audience members may have seen Advertiser ads from previous campaigns and therefore be influenced to purchase with the Advertiser on that basis alone.

In an ideal world if the user has never been exposed to an ad from this campaign or Advertiser before, the trafficker should set up targeting to create a retargeting pool for users that have seen ads previously and allow the control group to see the non-targeted ad. This non-targeted ad would not be for the Advertiser but rather a public service a (such as an anti-smoking ad). If the ad server observes the same rule every time the user encounters one of the placements for the campaign they will never be shown the targeted ad and therefore the group remains controlled. The third party ad server allows audience to be split and weighted so that the first time, 50% of the users enter the control group and 50% are shown the Advertiser's ad. For a tru lift study to work, the rule which determines which ad the user sees, must permanently drop that user into a cookie pool.

One problem with this approach is that to be a water-tight control group, the Advertiser must begin delivering retargeting pixels (see Chapter 7) with their ads from day 1 of their first campaign otherwise some users will be influenced by previous campaigns.

The retargeting cookie window also needs to be left open long enough to allow the tru lift study to be undertaken. The other problem is cookie-deletion, which cannot be avoided where a user who was seeing advertiser ads could end up no longer seeing them as they are placed into a control group.

Across the board, tru lift studies are a poor indicator of the power of online advertising. The studies undertaken are commonly full of holes that cannot be plugged and the results the advertiser was expecting to see rarely come to fruition. This means that a lot of time and money can be wasted under taking such studies with little or no return.

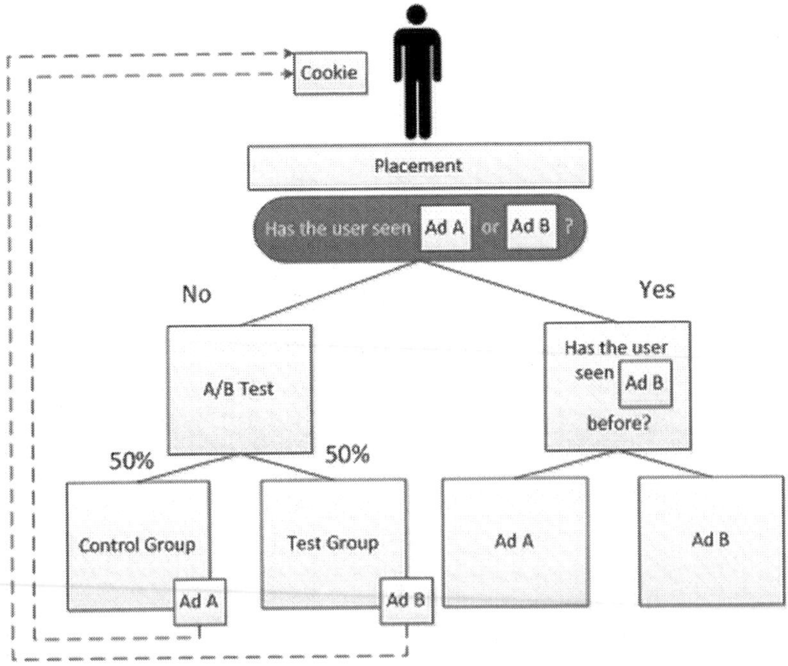

Figure 4.2.5 *A tru-lift study. The user arrives at a placement, never having encountered the campaign before. The audience criteria asks if the user is in the retargeting pool for Ad A or Ad B. If the user is in neither audience type then they enter the A/B test. Here the ad server randomly separates out the users equally so that*

50% of users are in the control group while 50% of users are in the test group. The corresponding ad includes a retargeting pixel so that the user is labelled as belonging to one of the audience groups. The next time they encounter a placement from the same campaign, the logic kicks in and recognises that the cookie is in a retargeting pool. It shows them the corresponding ad for their audience type. Now the control group can always be shown the same ad or even an ad for a public service while the test group are shown Advertiser ads for the purposes of creative testing. In reports the performance across the two ads for both clicks and conversions can show if the creative message in the test group is showing an improvement in performance over users that may have only seen a public service ad.

Audience Assignment

Targeting, experimentation and audience assignment differs between third party ad servers. At its heart the audience is defined by the trafficker and then that defined audience is paired with a particular ad or ad version.

A placement follows the list of audiences down the tree of targeting decision criteria to determine which ad to show. One would think that it makes sense to always try to target an ad to a user to increase the chances of the ad getting noticed and action being taken but a long list of targeting rules for each placement increases the work required to setup and optimize the campaign. High complexity in setup (such as setting up five or more different targeted audience combinations for each placement) causes the following issues:

1. Much heavier processing required at the ad server when delivering the ad, which could impact the user experience of the ad load time

2. Keeping tabs on the effectiveness of various audiences becomes very complex when only very small numbers of users convert on each targeted ad

3. Committing to so many audiences and granulating the setup so much means having to create many ads to support it (although DCO will do this well the setup and assignment can be lengthy and the optimization will not work if the audiences are so small because of the diminished effective sample size).

These can be avoided by using the same audiences for multiple campaigns. In addition, the recommendation is to reduce targeting and audience complexity with consistent optimization off of the back of well analysed reporting with the ultimate aim to use only a handful of very well targeted and effective audiences. In essence targeting is a science experiment that if pursued intelligently can yield great results.

Channels which bend the rules

Audience targeting within the ad server will not work for pure Paid Search Campaigns (since the ad server is not delivering a creative), this is also the case with Affiliate and Email campaigns. Within the Instream channel, targeting is available but since the video is part of a running stream (where a pre-roll is followed by video content), there is no need for a non-targeted ad. In this instance the ad server receives a request from the placement to serve an audience-specific ad. If the criteria is not fulfilled, the ad server returns no information, meaning that an ad never loads and there is no non-targeted ad and no fall back. In this sense the ad server (at least for Instream) has the power to affect the actual media delivery.

> In addition to this, Ad blocking (a feature of verification) could also be considered a feature of targeting, where, if the page does not meet the targeting criteria for verification, a non-targeted ad is displayed. However, in this instance the non-targeted ad is a public service image and its delivery is specially separated out in reporting for the purposes of remuneration (see Chapter 5 - Verification).

This concludes the work of the trafficker in the pre-campaign setup interface in the third party ad server.

The trafficker will return to this interface to set up subsequent campaigns for retargeting (see Chapter 7) as well as adjustments to the existing campaign for the purposes of optimization (see Chapter 6). The next step for the trafficker is to access the ad server reporting interface. This will allow the trafficker to check ad delivery, performance and verification.

Section C

Ad Server Analytics

Section C
Ad Server Analytics

The process of Researching the right Publishers for the media plan, followed by planning and buying the media for the campaigns is followed by the process of trafficking, all for the proof of delivery, verification and performance. Reporting and analytics are the ultimate a feedback mechanism for an Advertiser, that yields the results and insights to ensure bountiful effectiveness and future campaign optimization.

The next section looks in depth at reporting, analytics and metrics. Just knowing what data can be returned from ad serving systems, can be enough to find the great in any campaign or improve a failing one. Surprisingly, statistics are rarely difficult to digest in spread sheet form, where the uniform layout of the data in a standardised to read the data quickly, becomes a task easily achieved.

The stories of the data spring out of reports pulled in the right way and at the right time. The ad serving providers continually improving the look and feel of the interfaces and data outputs that make it easier to digest that data and find actionable insights. Even at time of publication, ad server analytics suites are undergoing transformations of this nature. The current state of play comes down to three core areas:
ad Verification, ad Delivery and ad Performance, this following chapter will dive deeply into each of these areas in depth but first it is important to understand What reporting is made up of, Where the reporting is generated, When the data is processed and how the data is outputted.

Chapter 5

Reporting Technology

Chapter 5
Reporting Technology

- What is ad server reporting?
- Aggregated Data
- *Figure 5.0.1*
- *Figure 5.0.2*
- Reporting API
    - *Figure 5.0.3*
- When is the Data Processed?
- Real time reporting
- Processing Clock
- Where is the data processed?
- How is the data filtered?
- Where is the data displayed?

This section is an introduction to reporting technology within the third party ad server. It explains what ad sever reporting is made up of. When and where the data is processed and what the outcome of the processing is.

What is ad server reporting?
Third party ad server reporting is an interface that sits on top of the data which has been collected during a live campaign. In the core databases of the ad server, the data is virtually incomprehensible, it needs to be collated and presented in a fashion that is easy to understand, the outcome are the available ad server reports. This section will explore the relationship between the collected data and the reporting interface. This relationship carries certain conditions which put the reports into a context which must be taken into account when analysing the reports themselves. These conditions include how the data is processed, where it is processed and when it is processed.

Conditions are commonly presented alongside fields inside ad server reporting and give clues as to why certain trends may exist in the data.

Third party ad server reporting is divided into two distinct types: Aggregated data and Cookie Level data.

Aggregated Data

Aggregated data describes data that is presented to summarise the count of certain metrics (such as impressions and clicks). Summaries of this data include time periods and ad server hierarchy entities (such as placements and Publishers). These summaries are commonly selectable as filters in the ad server reporting interface such that they control the amount of data that will appear in the generated report. The filtered list of entities will usually be presented in spread-sheet form down the far left column to describe the content of each row. The titles of the columns will be the metric names themselves and the cells will contain a count of the occurrence of each metric against each entity. The design of the spread-sheet is such that a human can analyse the data right across one or more campaigns.

									Impressions	Clicks
Campaign									0	0
	Network								0	0
		Publisher							0	0
			Site						0	0
				Package					0	0
					Placement				0	0
						Ad			0	0
							Creative		0	0
								Version	0	0

Figure 5.0.1 *An aggregated report from a third party ad server aggregates metrics across an entire campaign. The data will be available for each level of the ad server hierarchy. To 'pull' a report of this type required the trafficker to navigate to the analytics interface of the third party ad server and input several filters such as the Campaign name, the specific hierarchy entities and the date range.*

The ad server typically takes a few seconds to bring the data together before churning out a spread sheet or visual representation of the request (referred to as a dashboard). Commonly, the ad server has already processed the data it is returning and the delay accounts for the front end of the ad server communicating with the backend storage systems to retrieve the data in the requested view.

Cookie level data by comparison is not available in the ad server interface but is available via a feed mechanism, send very granular data on a given time period to a location outside of the ad server. This information is usually too granular for a human to process and would normally feed into an external reporting system or data warehouse. Cookie level data will be covered off in more detail later in this Chapter.

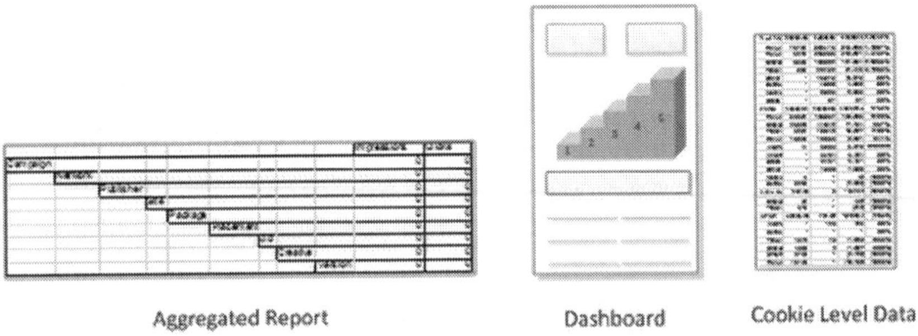

Figure 5.0.2 *Third party ad server reports are available in three main formats. Aggregated reports display high level data which can be pivoted across various hierarchy entities and metrics. A Dashboard will be a more visual representation of the aggregated reports (useful to lift out trends and to present the data. The cookie level data is a more raw output which tends to be a broad spread sheet, table or database in the most granular form available. Here each engagement with an ad or conversion tag is displayed row by row.*

Reporting API

In Chapter 3 - Display ad serving, we made reference to the capability of the third party ad server to supply access to reporting data via an API. Different ad servers are able to provide different levels of reporting granularity via their reporting APIs. Almost no ad servers today will allow a developer (with the right level of security access to the API from outside the ad server) to return cookie level data. Only aggregated data is supported by the API. In addition to this not all metrics and ad server entities can be retrieved, so to this extent the API is less detailed than the data that can be collected from pulling reports directly from the interface. Reporting APIs can be of used by developers in conjunction with other APIs provided by the ad server such as a Campaign Setup API or Planning API.

As an example an Agency could hire a developer to build a planning tool for Agency use only which sets up campaigns and placements in the ad server from a distance and colour co-ordinates the buys to correspond with levels of impressions at which ads are being delivered.

The difference between third party ad server analytics and Site Side Analytics

Chapter 2 explained how an Advertiser would install a site side analytics tool (such as *Google Analytics* or *Adobe's Omniture Suite*) onto their website to establish the sources of the traffic coming to the site and to determine how users navigate around the site. Although this data remains very useful, it is still just describing user behaviour on site and cannot explain how user engage with or see ads on the rest of the web. It is true that Site Side Analytics can track referral traffic into the site but attribution beyond the last engagement is challenging unless the third party ad server is integrated with the site side analytics tool.

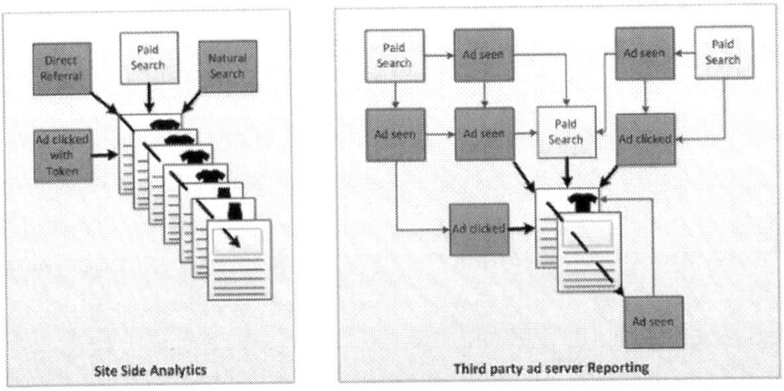

Figure 5.0.3 *Site-side analytics is useful for page-level marketing optimization. The data retrieved from Site Side analytics shows how users arrive to and depart from individual pages and the journeys that are taken when the user is on site. By comparison, third party ad servers will only detect the traffic to a handful of key pages where conversion tags are sitting but reporting will extend out to the plethora of served and tracked ads across channels and Publishers to represent the effectiveness of paid-for advertising.*

Having said this, the technologies cannot be perfectly synchronised because the methodologies are fundamentally different. One example is that the ad server definition of a unique user is different from site side analytics (which can adjust its methodology depending on the report time frame. Unique's per month and Unique's per year is not comparable with want the ad server tracks which is one unique user per lifetime of the cookieID.) Site side analytics can also not detect for post impression conversion events and does not offer Cookie level reporting. There are numerous other differences as well around the click methodologies and the position of the code on the

Advertiser page (site side analytics code versus the position of the conversion tag).

There is still value to be attained from Site Side analytics and integrations are possible through the use of token values passed through in the user click pathway. However the two systems cannot replace one another, they are doing two very different jobs.

When is the Data Processed?
The way an ad server collects data and processes it, differs according its core architecture. Ad servers are structured to try to bring data collection as close to reporting as possible in time. While impressions and clicks can be passed into reports soon after user events have occurred, it is not as easy for conversion data, where the ad server must compare conversion events across Publishers to establish the attribution. This means that the conversion information requires a longer processing time. At time of writing conversion metrics are still available after a window of around 6 hours for most ad servers (or 4 times a day). This figure is decreasing as ad server processing power improves year by year to try and reach "real time reporting".

Real time reporting
Real time data allows the Advertiser or Agency to make decisions immediately after users engage with ads. While retargeting makes real-time targeting possible already, if the data needed to be processing by human eyes before decisions were made then the process would slow down. For human eyes to see what is going on, reporting needs to present data, which in itself is subject to a minor delay. His human touch might also be called manual optimization (See Chapter 6) so to speed everything up, decision engines are being created and many already exist, to automatically optimize campaigns as they run to avoid the delay caused by human interaction. Such systems eradicate the need to pull reports for the purposes of optimization.

Having said this, real time reporting remains in demand for direct response Advertisers where a trafficker needs to react to adjust the purchase of media to reflect the data displayed in ad server delivery. For instance: over the course of a day, if a big event happens unexpectedly, the trafficker cannot react to a spike in search traffic for certain terms (so as to pay more or less for certain keywords) since the spike would appear in reporting which may not be available until a few hours later.

> If there is ever a fault with the ad serving technology, ad server reporting can usually expect to be delayed while the collected data is correctly presented. In such an instance Advertiser teams can often be waiting to make changes to a media plan; literally prevented from doing their jobs until the conversion data has become available.

Processing Clock

Conversion processing can take several hours, so often the ad server has a hard cut off time for data collection on a particular day or processing period: such as 11.59pm. Then the conversion data will be made available within a few hours, leading up the this cut-off point. The freshness of the data is therefore impacted not only by location of the processing servers but also for the amount of time it takes to process and return the data sets. When pulling reports and comparing data sets for discrepancies it is an important step to ask questions about when the cut-off point was for data processing, what time the reported data was available from. Sometimes an ad server report may be pulled in the CET time-zone but the data it displays was cut-off on an EST time-zone, owing to the location that the data was processed from. This calls into questions where the data is being processed exactly?

Where is the data processed?
Due to the global nature of third party ad serving, the backend systems have a very real and complex consideration to make with regards to what are called "server clocks" (i.e. the local time of the server where the data is being processed). Running all the conversion processing from a single location and then distributed worldwide means the data is available at different times in different countries and really all counties would like the data available as early as possible in the working day, so that Advertisers and Agencies are working to optimize against the freshest data sets.

Matching up data between time zones can be a big headache. Account settings will usually allow the account to be setup for data processing a certain time zone but this isn't always enough a reliable indicator to explain what time periods the report is truly presenting. It is work enquiring with the support team at the third party ad serving provider to see what clock settings are in place and how this impacts the reporting data. In some instances these questions can help to remedy many discrepancies between reports which appear to be for the same time period but were processed for different cut off points.

How is the data filtered?
Data processing does not just mean reporting, it means cleaning up the data. This can mean mapping different tables of data together into a single report, calculating metrics and of course filtering the data. Third party ad servers have their own blacklists for IP addresses that have been compromised and have ways of sweeping the data sets for bots and data deemed to be created by unauthorised machines creating fraudulent clicks or wasting impressions not seen by human eyeballs. Some ad servers allow this information to be presented in reporting. It is also worth asking the ad serving provider if test impressions, clicks and

conversions can be filtered from reporting. Some ad servers have the capability to do this by filtering out activity from certain IP addresses as a backend service. It is also not fair to expect an ad serving provider to divulge the methodology behind the filtering of the data for fraudulent activity since the availability of the methodology might compromise the filters. With this in mind ad servers will usually be industry accredited for methodologies which filter fraudulent traffic.

Where is the data displayed?

Processed data can be accessed via the third party ad server reporting interface. Aggregated reports will exist in templates so can quickly be run (such as a report containing all the standard delivery metrics). The interface will also allow the customisation of the aggregated reports to add specific metrics or filters to the report so that it can be generated by a particular time period or for specific ad server hierarchy entities. Run reports will usually output an excel spread-sheet or in a visual interface where the trafficker or analyst can analyse the data. Aggregated reports can also be shared once created or scheduled (delivery an updated copy of the report directly an inbox on a given time period).

With an overview of aggregated reporting now completed, the remainder of this Chapter will detail out the different kinds of reporting available within the aggregated category before covering off Cookie Level reporting. The sections within this chapter are structured in the order that the trafficker or analyst might retrieve the data from the reporting interface in the ad server once a campaign has been set live. The first stop over is Verification reporting, the first set of aggregated reports that the trafficker will encounter when analysing a live campaign.

Chapter 5 - Section 1
Basic Aggregated Reporting

- QA Reports
- Global reporting
    - *Figure 5.1.1*
- Delivery reports
- Verification Reports
- Performance Reports (Conversion and Attribution Reports)
- Cost and ROI reports
- 404 error reporting
- Expiring cost packages
- Channel Specific Reports
- The Standard Metrics
    - Impressions
        - A new impression?
        - *Figure 5.1.2*
    - Clicks and Click-through Rate (CTR)
    - Conversions & Conversion rate

There are a flurry of standardised aggregated reports that the trafficker can pull from the third party ad server reporting interface. The following section will detail these report types and then examine the most common metrics to be found in said reports.

The basic aggregated reporting types are:

- Global reports
- Delivery reports
- Verification reports

- QA reports
- Cost and ROI reports
- 404 error reports
- Expiring Cost packages
- Performance reports (Conversion and Attribution reports)

QA reports
QA reports are reports that can be pulled before a campaign is put live or from the very first few minutes of a campaign lifetime to monitor key metrics to ensure that the implementation of tags has been conducted correctly. Some ad servers bolster this offering by connecting it to a monitoring platform with a faster data refresh rate than the other data sets. Monitoring platforms such as this can be connected to specific email alerts that can be setup to warn a trafficker when a campaign is delivering or performing unexpectedly. This ensures a trafficker can quickly react to any sudden turns in data trends to perform the relevant optimization (see Chapter 6) or test the live tags for errors. QA reports are particularly useful to check that conversion tags are live and pulling in the correct extended data parameters. Without QA reports, the trafficker would have to wait until data has been refreshed in more complex reporting such as cookie level data, even in cases where extended data collection is just being tested.

Global reporting
Third party ad serving technology can support the needs of international Advertisers and advertising campaigns by offering the single co-ordinating team an access level in ad server reporting that gives a view across all countries. Within this structure, each local country team can only view their in-country reporting data and layers can be added to support regional data access as well while ensuring that only those with global access, see everything.

It is important to remember that when running global campaigns that it is challenging to compare cost data since each country might pay for media in local currency and as such costs need to be standardised to a single currency such as US dollars before being compared with each other.

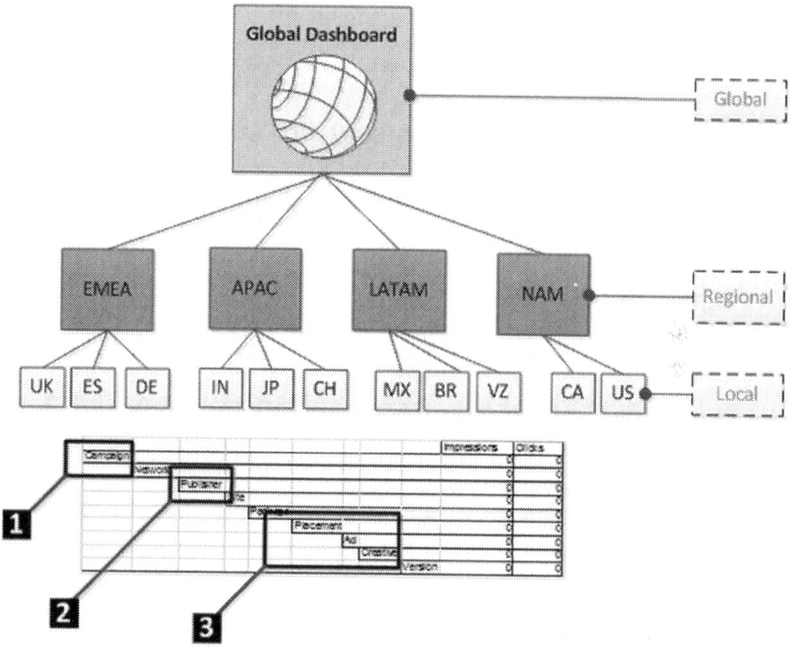

Figure 5.1.1 *Within global reports, there are various access levels to the ad server reporting interface, granted to the analyst or traffickers depending on what level of data they require access to. Centrally managed campaigns (campaigns managed for the whole world from a single location) benefit from this style of reporting, where the supporting teams in local markets see less information in their reports. Access can be granted at Global, Regional and Local levels. Consistent naming conventions are essential to producing "clean data" in global reporting. A consistent global Advertiser, campaign and media plan naming convention (1) allows the global Advertiser to compare performance and*

delivery across the regions at a brand and product level. A consistent Publisher name (2) allows for global benchmarking so that the delivery and performance of the same formats can be compared showing if Publishers and Placements are just as strong region to region. A consistent placement, ad and creative naming convention (3) identifies how the creative and execution compares between locales.

Delivery reports

Delivery reports aggregate data about the core ad serving responsibility: i.e. Serving the ads. Such reports can be very useful to Advertisers that have a strict delivery plan, to check that they are on course to deliver the paid-for impressions over the intended time period. Such reports are commonly shared with participating Publishers who can use the data to adjust the controls in a Publisher ad server for over or under delivery. It is best practice for Advertisers and Agencies to check delivery reports at least once per day during a campaign.

Verification reports

The trafficker would run and look at a verification report when a reasonable amount of impressions have been served to produce a large enough data set for the purposes of ad and campaign verification. It is recommended that at least one day passes on longer term campaigns before checking verification reporting. Verification reports are very extensive and a growing area for third party ad serving, as such there is a full section covering this area following this section within Chapter 5.

Performance reports (Conversion and Attribution reports)

Once the ads have begun delivering the trafficker can check in on how the ads are performing to drive certain marketer KPIs. Performance reporting displays the numbers of clicks and conversions broken down by Publisher, Site, Placement and Ad. For each of these ad server entities, the trafficker can view the total number of clicks on the ad, but then a breakdown or drop-off to each of the conversion tags on the Advertiser site. This shows which creative is driving the most effectiveness. In addition, the e-conversions attribution, explained in Chapter 4, can be displayed alongside the figure for total conversions to each entity. Where it is possible to do so, the metrics from performance reports should be combined with verification reporting so that post impression conversions that occurred on impressions that were not in view, are omitted from the conversion tally.

Cost and ROI reports

By inputting the media cost data into the campaign management interface, reporting can show the granular detail of actual expenditure over time, showing how much it has cost the Advertiser to advertise to different Publishers, Sites and Channels. Furthermore this style of aggregated reporting links performance (conversions, clicks and interactions) back to cost to show how much engagement, exposure and conversion is won from how much media spend. Some ad servers will go a step further and display the ad serving costs alongside the media costs so that the Advertiser can work out the total cost to serve and deliver an ad. When the metrics from cost and ROI reports are combined with the metrics from verification reporting, the Advertiser is informed how much media spend is being wasted on ineffective impressions.

404 error reports

Third party ad servers that do not have a close-to-real-time monitoring and alerting report functionality, offer weekly reports that show which ads are reporting which ads are clicking through to non-existent pages. This is a very useful report to check at the start of a campaign to ensure that ads are clicking through correctly. Those redirects that land users on non-existent pages through up an HTTP 404 error which can be reported by the ad server.

Expiring cost packages
Some ad servers offer a report which provides another alert-style system, showing when certain cost packages and placements are nearing their end date. Sometimes ad campaigns can last a year or more and although traffickers will insert the campaign end date at a point in the future, these end dates can quickly creep on and it the campaign hits the end date, start serving fall back creative such as backup gifs.

Channel Specific reports
Some third party ad servers group reports together (which are really channel specific reports) into categories like Engagement reports (for Rich Media interaction reporting). As there are an extensive number of channel specific reports, with metrics that need detailed explanation, there is an addition section dedicated to this topic within this chapter.

The Standard Metrics

Outside the channel-specific metrics almost all aggregated reporting comes back to a handful of core metrics. These metrics have already been referenced numerous times in this book, the following is a deep focus on exactly what each means:

Impressions
Most ad server reports, flooded with numbers, represent the increment of impressions for a particular metric. To be found inside the core aggregated reports within the ad server reporting interface is a column purely called "Impressions". Strictly speaking, impressions are a count of the number of ad requests coming from a user's browser for a single ad. The request is counted when it is received (see

Chapter 1) in accordance with the IAB industry approved standard definition of an "Impression". This is what is referred to as the standard industry "trading currency", since the majority of cost models are performed on a CPM (cost per thousand impressions). Ad serving in particular is charged to the Advertiser on this same cost model.

A new impression?

Impressions may have had their day. There are now a few potential candidates in the works that might push impressions off of its held spot as the "trading currency" for digital advertising but there is contention over what might happen. The first contender, which has cropped up a number of times over the short years that digital advertising has been around, is "Delivered Impressions", also referred to as "ad loads" and "ad starts". Rather than count on the ad request, the count is made when the first frame of the ad is loaded. The delay between the standard impression and the delivered impression can be significant enough for Advertiser to question the standard metric imposed by the IAB.

The second contender is the viewable impression (see the next section in this chapter) which only registers an impression when the ad is in view on the users screen. Again there can be a large difference in the number of counted impressions on the ad server versus the number of viewable impressions.

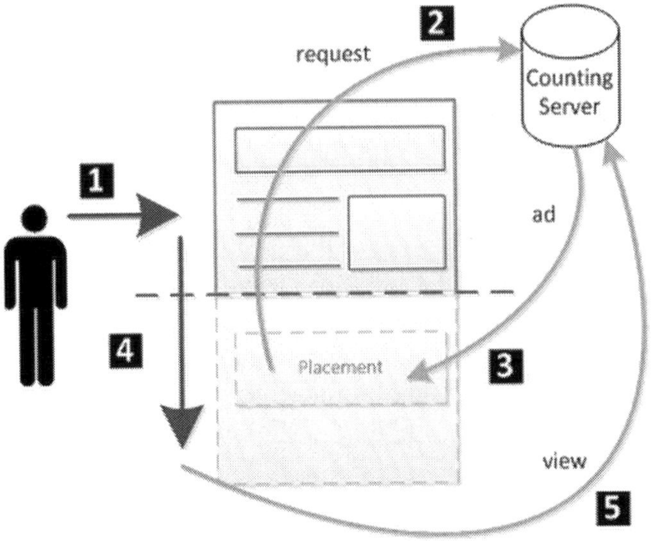

Figure 5.1.2 *As the user arrives on the Publisher page (1) a request for the ad is sent to the ad server. The counting server registers an impression as it deploys the impression tracker followed by the ad (2). Ads are usually loaded in this way, so those below the fold of the user's browser will also load up and an impression will be counted (3). If the user scrolls down, any ads which then are shown above the fold will trigger a "viewable impression" metric (5).*

Some argue that the industry factors in the difference between the cost of an impression and the cost of a delivered or viewable impression by keeping a low cost where a delivered impression or viewable impression may be provided at a higher charge, because of the delivery verification that surrounds it.

Clicks and Click-through Rate (CTR)

Clicks are a recorded increment in the ad server, counting a user clicking on an ad. As a component of the click redirect, the ad server is pinged and the master database of the ad server appends a row stating that a particular cookieID clicked on an ad at a particular time from a particular Publisher site.

For many years, the click was the only way a user could interact with an ad and show some intent to purchase. On the early web, Advertisers and Publishers were obsessed with the CPC model. With other methods of counting now available such as rich media interaction or view based conversions, the click has lost a lot of value in the display space. Having said this, a click is some indicator of interest and many Advertisers try to separate out their audiences by those that show some interest from those that don't.

Clicks remain integral to digital advertising owing to the support of them by the performance channels (Affiliate and Paid Search). Clickthrough-rate composes of the number of impressions divided by the number of clicks to determine how many viewers successfully became clickers. Usually this can be expected to be a very low number, certainly much lower than 1% of the total impressions. On a big enough scale this is still a considerable number of interested users, but it is difficult to determine what caused the click itself. Sometimes the creative may have been the most enticing part of the click action (creative optimization) and sometimes it may just been down to the correctly targeting audience (media optimization). As explained in Chapter 4, experimentation can help determine what is driving the user to click.

Conversions & Conversion rate

Just as with clicks, conversions are presented in aggregated reporting as a measure of campaign success, particularly where the user is driven to make a purchase online. Conversions are really; impressions for which a conversion was reported. Conversion reporting will typically displayed so that the total number of conversions is attributed to each ad server entity (channel, Publisher, site, package, placement, ad, creative and version). Conversions to a particular conversion tag will be labelled in reporting along with a conversion rate (conversions divided by impressions) to calculate how many of the users that were exposed to the ad, went through to convert.

As a reminder from Chapter 4, conversions can be broken out into post-impression and post-click conversion events, allowing the Advertiser to dismiss conversions based on impression only exposure to the user. Furthermore it is important when pulling basic aggregated reports (such as performance reports) to remember that conversions are calculated based on the settings shown on the conversion tag in the campaign management interface of the ad server. Both attribution settings and conversion windows will have an impact on the total number of conversions displayed in the conversions column.

With a good grasp of the basic reports, a trafficker can go into the ad server reporting interface and pull the report directly or setup a schedule so that it delivers to the trafficker's inbox frequently. Third party ad servers design these basic aggregated reports in the interest of time saving so that the trafficker does not have to assemble a report from scratch by collecting up and filtering by a wide range of metrics and hierarchy entities that may not fit together. An example would be trying to report a channel specific metric across a campaign running in a channel that does not support the same metric.

Further in this Chapter we explore Advanced aggregated reports, which the trafficker would attend to a week or so into the campaign, so that enough data has been collected to be able to action the results.

Leaving behind the campaign setup and having the Publisher set the ad tags live means that the work of the trafficker now moves to monitoring and reporting on the progress of the campaign. The first stage in this process of involves checking that the campaign has actually kicked off (i.e. are the ads delivering, clicking through and are the users converting). It is recommended therefore for the trafficker to check basic aggregated reporting within twenty four hours of the campaign going live. The initial data available in delivery reports would just be an indicator that things kick off well. The trafficker would then move onto looking at verification reports before taking a deeper dive into the available data via more advanced aggregated reports, fully customised reports or channel specific reports.

The next section looks at this second step: verification reporting.

Chapter 5 - Section 2
Ad Verification & Viewability

- Effective and Ineffective Impressions
- Reactive, Preventative and Pre-Emptive Verification
    - *Figure 5.2.1*
    - Publisher and Placement quality indicators
    - Contextual Verification Quality Indicators
        - Content Classification
        - Brand Safety
        - *Figure 5.2.2*
        - Demographic or Audience Verification
        - The panel-based Audience Verification Method
        - *Figure 5.2.3*
        - The social profile-based Audience Verification Method
        - *Figure 5.2.4*
    - Discoverability Verification Quality Indicators
        - Geo Reporting
        - Device Verification
        - Viewable impressions
        - *Figure 5.2.5*
        - Double Implementations and Fraudulent Serving techniques
        - *Figure 5.2.6*
    - Page Level Verification Quality Indicators
        - Domain URL Reporting
        - Other uses for Page Level information
        - White Lists and Black Lists
        - *Figure 5.2.7*
    - See through, View through and Recordability Rates
        - *Figure 5.2.8*
- Preventative - Ad blocking
- Pre-emptive - Verification in Programmatic
- The Verification landscape

After checking delivery reports briefly to see that the campaign started without a hitch, the next most important area for the trafficker to look into is Verification reporting.

Effective and Ineffective Impressions

Verification is a means of auditing the delivery of the ads. By consulting Verification and delivery reports early and often in campaign management, the wastage of ads can be minimised. Impressions which are not wasted are sometimes referred to as "effective impressions" while the wastage would be "ineffective impressions".

Verification tools have only just started to appear integrated into the third party ad server. Up until 2012 the role of the Verification toolset has been played by smaller independent technology companies but separate tools mean a bigger headache for the setup of the campaign and a larger room for reporting discrepancies. Ad servers with integrated Verification mean that enabling Verification can be as little work for the trafficker as flicking a single switch.

Verification asks a simple question "Is my campaign being delivered to the right audience?" Incredibly this is still a conundrum. It's up to the Publishers to ensure the advert gets to the right eyeballs but being a third party, the ad server allows the Advertiser to verify the delivery independently. Verification tools started life seeing if ads were delivered into a "Brand safe" environment i.e. no adult content, violence or disaster news stories and now offer something wholly more attractive to Advertisers.

Reactive, Preventative and Pre-Emptive Verification

At the time of this book's publication, Verification is one of the hottest topics on the lips of Advertisers, Agencies and Regulators.

Verification can spell trouble for Publishers who defy targeting and audience criteria and are out to make a fast buck by bending the truth about what they are selling to Advertisers. Verification is available to Advertisers and Agencies through three methods:

- Reactive:
  as in detecting that the ad was served into an unsuitable environment and then reporting the fact in ad server reporting. Such reporting would be used to leverage conversations with Publishers for better targeting in future or remuneration.

- Preventative:
  as in preserving the delivery of ads and creative messages from unsuitable Publisher pages by serving a public service ad instead. This is currently being called "Ad Blocking".

- Pre-Emptive:
  as in verifying that an ad will be served on a suitable page and in a suitable spot before the inventory is even purchased (currently only available in the programmatic and RTB spaces - see Chapter 8).

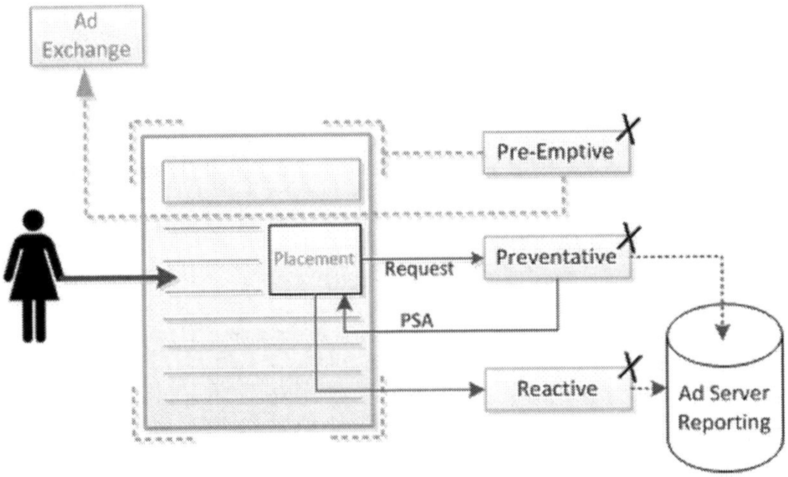

Figure 5.2.1 *When the user arrives on the Publisher site, it is possible to verify that both the page and the user are suited to the ad being displayed. An Advertiser has three options. Either the Advertiser buys the ad spot programmatically (see Chapter 8) or by buying directly from the site. In the first instance a pre-emptive tool can be triggered when the placement loads, checking the page content to verify if it is a good place to serve an ad. If the page does not appear to be brand safe, the pre-emptive tool will ensure that the ad spot is never purchased in the first place (sending the available impression back into the Ad exchange). If the Advertiser does not use a pre-emptive tool then Preventative technologies like Ad Blocking can be enabled on the ad server (so that if the page does not look brand safe, the ad server will serve a Public Service Ad (PSA) instead). If neither pre-emptive nor preventative methods are being used, the Advertiser can be reactive and detect the delivery of the ad on an unsafe page. This detection (occurring for both preventative and Reactive methods) feeds through into Verification reporting.*

The remainder of this section will look in-depth at these three classes of verification before looking at how the definition of verification is adapting and changing the way Advertisers look at their reporting.

Publisher and Placement Quality Indicators

Reactive verification works across a series of quality indicators. When these indicators mount up against an individual placement or Publisher they might paint that placement in a negative light (in which case the trafficker should consider having the Publisher target away from the page, domain, geography or device in question) or in a positive light, in which case more impressions should be purchased against such a placement in future. In this way, verification begins to eradicate wastage as Advertisers and Agencies use their collected verification data to map out and benchmark the safest and most valuable placements in the Publisher ecosystem to match the needs of their brands and campaigns.

Different brands and campaigns will have different creative messages and different target audiences. This means that what might be considered a negative quality indicator for one brand may not be true for others. For instance, an ad delivered to a news site featured against a disaster news story featuring a plane crash may be dangerous for an airline Advertiser but might be seen as good opportunity for a particularly risqué financial Advertiser selling life insurance. It is important for the Advertiser or Agency to make this consideration when analysing verification reporting.

These quality indicators are:

1. **Contextual:** which includes Content Classification, Audience verification and Brand Safety

2. **Discoverability:** which includes Geographic and Device reporting, Viewability and Fraudulent tag Implementation

3. **Page Level:** which includes Domain, subdomain and URL reporting and Whitelists and Blacklists

Contextual Verification Quality Indicators

Content Classification

Verification tools which specifically analyse the content of the page are also referred to as "CV tools". CV tools operate most effectively in real time. This means that when the third party ad is served to a page; the domain name, sub domain and URL are passed into the CV tool, where-upon the tool either looks the page up in its database of ready-scraped pages or it scrapes the page in real time. The scraping process captures information on the page including words, phrases, word combinations, multimedia; including video, and digests the relationship between these elements.

These elements are then categorised so that for instance, a page-level reference to a particular celebrity mean that the URL of the page is categorised in a celebrity category. Superior CV tools can analyse the semantics of the page in multiple languages and even calculate the cultural significance of certain phrases. The outcome is a statistical analysis which places an affinity of the page towards a particular categorisation. This means that if an Advertiser paid for ads to appear next to sport related content and the CV tool reported it was shown against music content, the Advertiser could take the third party report back to the Publisher in order to have future ads targeted away from the incorrect pages and onto more relevant, promised content. Publishers have access to the same level of reporting to assist them in managing their own inventory to avoid selling inventory that is not relevant to an Advertiser from the outset of the campaign.

CV tools are interesting pieces of kit because they do not utilise user cookie information in order to provide information about page classifications. This means that they do not fall subject to any limitations surrounding privacy constraints around cookie based targeting (see Chapter 7).

The trafficker would check verification reporting around content classification and compare it to the goals of the planner in agreement with the Publisher to appear on pages geared towards certain types of content. If there is a mismatch, the trafficker would alert the planner to speak with the Publisher about the targeting and delivery concerns.

Content tends to be classified into a finite number of categorisations which are defined by the CV tool. Until these are universally accepted categorisations by all parties around the table (Advertisers, Agencies and Publishers) and written in stone by regulators like the *IAB*, there will be disputes about the methodology because content classification.

To make negotiations more challenging, custom content categories are available for Advertisers to create and define so that reporting lays out where an Advertiser's ads have appeared next to content geared towards a certain sentiment or alongside praise about a competitor. In such situations Publishers may not have the available technology in their Publisher ad server to avoid delivering ads towards or away from such pages in the future.

Brand Safety
CV tools are predominantly marketed as protection against unsafe content rather than the interference of a content categorisation. If the ad serves to a page with content deemed to be categorised as adult in nature, display violence, have content about death or disaster news stories, the CV tool can clarify this in reporting and separate it out from standard content classification.

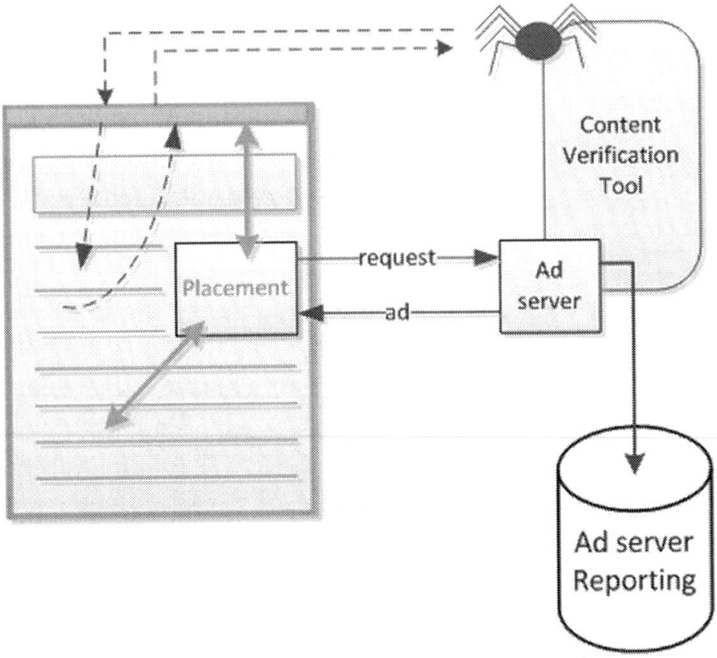

Figure 5.2.2 *The spider from the CV tool crawls sites across the internet and harvests page level keyword information and relates the information back to the page URL. The data is stored in the CV tool database. When a placement enabled for verification reporting loads it captures the page URL and passes this back to the ad server in the ad request. The ad server then matches this URL to the CV tool keyword*

database and presents the contextual information in Ad server verification reporting.

Such occurrences are serious problems for Advertisers since they cause unwanted media attention or bad press when they do happen. An Advertiser may not want the carefully positioned brand to appear alongside unsuitable content. Adhering to such brand guidelines, the CV tool allows the planner to gather the data about occurrences to inform a conversation with the Publisher. The planner would initially ask a Publisher to target ads away from such page when procuring the inventory. The CV tool will show if the Publisher has honoured this agreement.

Where occurrences of failed brand safety do occur, CV tools report the occurrence alongside the location of the problem in ad server reporting.

Demographic or Audience Verification

Publishers have long been plagued by the ability to label and sell their audiences to attract Advertising spend. The methods used by the Publishers today are not standardised by the industry but the more Publishers and Advertisers that use a system of audience measurement, the more accurate and verified the audience can be. There are two mainstream methods for conducting audience verification today:

> **The panel-based Audience Verification Method**
>
> *ComScore* and *Neilsen* with their large audience panel data can give an idea (using sampling) about what audiences are connected to which pages. As a reminder from Chapter 2 - Agency Planning; *ComScore* and *Neilsen* are providing top lists of high traffic sites but can also break these sites down into matching demographics based on their panel, a product Neilsen refers to as *Neilsen OCR*.

A Publisher may sell empty ad spaces on a page to an Advertiser with the claim that it matches the Advertiser's audience targeting requirements (say Males aged 18-25). To verify that the audience is indeed Males aged 18-25, users on the *ComScore* panel verified as belonging to this audience type, would need to be shown ads from the tracked ad campaign.

A *ComScore* pixel, embedded in the creative or as part of the placement code loads when the ad loads and can cross reference with the *ComScore* database to see if the user belongs to the panel, and if so, what demographic they fall into. Here the trafficker needs to ensure they piggyback a *ComScore* pixel on to the served placement code within the ad server.

For the trafficker to obtain such a pixel and to get access to *ComScore* reporting (which confirmed that the ad was delivered to the right audience on the panel) would involve the Advertiser having a separate relationship with *ComScore* and paying extra for their services.

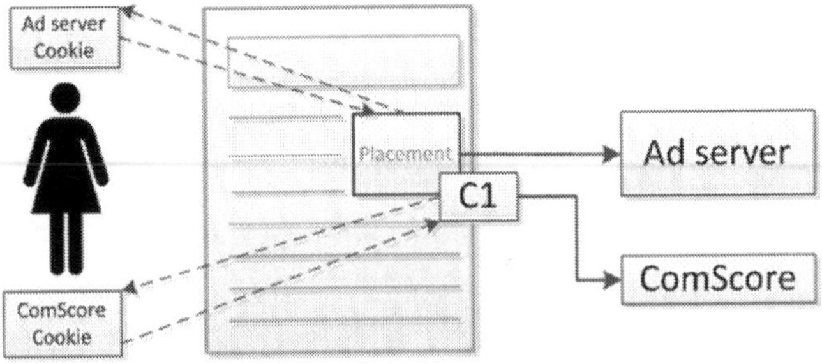

Figure 5.2.3 *When a user arrives on Publisher page, it is possible to verify the demographic of the user by piggybacking a ComScore pixel onto a served ad. When*

the ad loads, the ad detects for an ad server cookie in the usual way but in addition the ComScore pixel looks for a ComScore cookie. Relaying this information back to the comScore servers, the Advertiser can pull a report from ComScore to determine what demographic the ad was served to, providing the user made up part of the ComScore panel. Despite the sampling of the panel, across the scale of the whole ad campaign it is possible to determine an average demographic across the campaign and across each Publisher.

The social profile-based Audience Verification Method

Another methodology utilised by the verification provider *Adagoo* provides a demographic verification where page content can infer the demographic of the audience to that page. *Adagoo*'s spiders crawl public facing social profiles and mine age, gender and other audience data. In addition to these data points the spiders look at links posted on the walls of these profiles, crawl to those pages and mine the keywords and content available there. The content of those pages is then mapped to these demographic groups.

Such a system can then process the content of any page by being passed the URL of that page and report on the statistical likelihood of that page being viewed by a certain demographic group based on the already gathered data. The catch is that this is a cookie-free technology and it is not actually verifying the actual users that arriving to those pages but is rather reporting on the demographics of users that should be arriving at those pages according to the methodology.

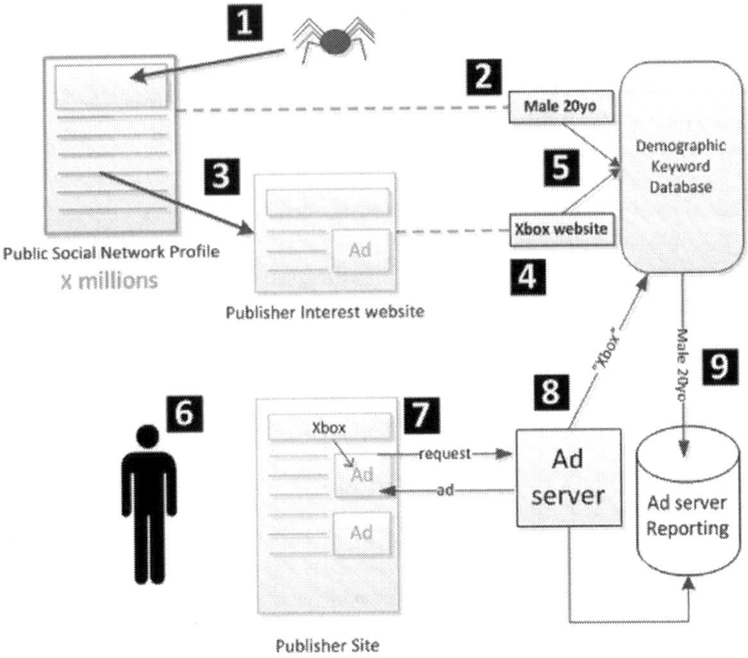

Figure 5.2.4 *The Adagoo method to deduce demographic is a little more complex. The Adagoo spider (1) crawls to a public social network profile page and extracts the Age and Gender information there (2). The spider then crawls to profile to a posted URL and goes to that URL. The spider than gathers keyword information from the page (4). The Age and Gender (2) are inferred to the keywords and stored in a demographic keyword database (5). This happens across millions of profiles and pages to build up the database. When a user (6) visits any Publisher page, the ad served placement on the page captures the semantic information on the page before serving an ad (7). The ad server passes the semantic keywords it finds, related to the ad, placement and site to the demographic keyword database (8). The database returns into ad server reporting, the inferred Age and Gender to match the keyword.*

In both situations, additional code (either from Adagoo or ComScore) needs to be added to the placements by the trafficker when they are setup. But there is no solution available today to wholly verify audience information at scale. The only methods currently available entail a complex process of trying to map delivery information with extra audience data (available from data providers) and match it at the cookie level inside a DMP (see Chapter 8).

Advertisers should liaise with Publishers before the campaign begins to set expectations about the usage of Audience verification tools. The classification of content and pages must be agreed and accepted by both parties before any negotiations are made regarding those ads that were effectively wasted. If both parties are in agreement in terms of content and audience classification, Advertisers may either be reimbursed by the Publisher for ad wastage or the Publisher can use the same reports in the ad server in order to avoid wastage altogether by identifying it early on and blacklisting the pages.

Discoverability Verification Quality Indicators

Geo Reporting

Probably the most well established verification technology is Geographical Reporting (also called "Geo-Performance"). Third party ad servers can detect the IP address of the cookied user. The IP address can then be run through a mapping database which maps IP addresses to their location, the same method used for geo-targeting.

Third party ad servers will keep an up to date list of IP mappings and so are able to provide reports that show where the ads were delivered to at the country and in some instances city, DMA and zip/postal code levels. Just as with geo targeting, region accuracy declines sharply the closer that the data tries to get to pinpoint user exact location.

Geo performance reports show the exact numbers of impressions and clicks delivered to these locations. Those campaigns intended for display purely to an audience based in the UK for instance and are shown in Geo reporting to be distribute worldwide create means for the Advertiser to approach the Publisher or network to demand the campaign be adjusted to match the right geographic audience.

> Geo performance can also be used in conjunction with conversion data, to identify which regions or countries are responsible for the majority of conversion events across the campaign. Those regions found to be more lucrative could then be geo targeted with a specific creative message.

Since the Publisher can control the IP delivery inside the Publisher ad server to correct the problem of incorrect geographical delivery, third party ad server reporting is directly actionable. For the trafficker it is usually just a case of enabling the collection of IP data at the Advertiser level within the account in the third party ad server interface before the campaign goes live or during delivery. To view reporting, the trafficker needs to only look into the reporting interface in the third party ad server.

Device Verification

Browsers make publicly available their version number (referred to as a "User Agent") which can be captured by a third party ad server via a JavaScript call. The version number reveals some indication about the device type. For instance the safari browser is only supported on IOS (Apple) devices and products, therefore the presence of Safari for any version verifies that the user is using an IOS device.

Owing to the vast number of devices in use and the flexibility to install different browser versions to different devices, this verification method is more of an indicator of device type rather than make and model of the device in question. The third party ad server needs to have a general mapping database to understand which version maps to which device in order to display the results in reporting.

Device collection is becoming more standardised as part of third party ad server verification reporting, the trafficker can simply look at verification reporting inside the ad server interface to see what device types ads were delivered to. If it is found that HTML5 ads for example, are being delivered to unsupported devices or non-targeted users, the Publisher may not have installed the ad onto an HTML5 specific entity, domain or application.

Viewable impressions
The most commonly discussed verification metric among Agencies and Advertisers is Viewability. Viewability describes how much of the ad is in view for the end user and viewability is measured on viewable impressions. Viewable impressions at a minimum are impressions served above "the fold" of page as it is viewed in the users the browser. The design of most web pages contains content which fills the active browser window and trails off below the bottom fold: hidden from view. Scrolling down the browser using the scroll bar, reveals the hidden content and content disappears at the top of the browser. Strictly speaking each of the sides of the browser window are 'folds' as the content can disappear behind any of them if the page is designed to scroll in those directions.

The viewable impression count is triggered by a JavaScript embedded in the ad code which checks how much of the ad is in view and for how long (the same technology can be used to reveal if the ad is served into the active window or tab). Some Publishers offer their inventory classified by whether the placement appears above or below the fold, and price the inventory accordingly. Increasingly in the digital marketing space, viewable impression complexity is causing advancement the capabilities of the verification measurement technologies.

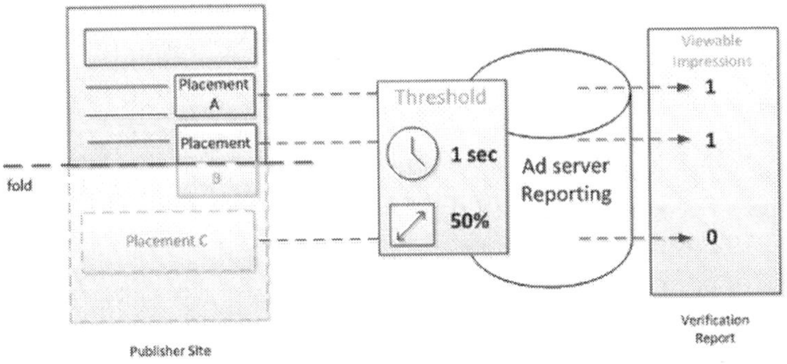

Figure 5.2.5 *Viewability as a form of verification. When the user loads the Publisher site some ads will be served above the fold of the user's browser while some may load beneath. The ad server delivers the ads and counts standard impressions. In the ad server interface the trafficker defines the threshold for a viewable impression (duration of exposure of a percentage surface area of the ad). Under the definition shown, Placement A would be reported as a viewable impression, as would Placement B, Placement C would not qualify as a viewable impression. If the user scrolls further down the page before closing it, Placement C may also count a viewable impression.*

As the *IAB* develop a fixed standard for viewable impressions; Advertisers are seeking the ability to have a flexible definition of "viewable impressions". These definitions consist of a percentage of the surface of the ad exposed to the user, for a set duration of time. User impressions that match a definition such as 90% of an ad seen for 5 seconds and above, fall into this categorisation of viewable impressions. This is called a "viewability threshold".

Ad server reporting reveals the total number of viewable impressions against each placement and when combined with media cost data, can show the Advertiser how much media spend they are wasting on ads not in view. Some Publishers will have contractual agreements with major Advertisers and big Agencies where the media cost for a viewable impression inventory reflects a standardised definition between the two parties or the definition set by the IAB. The third party ad server enables a customised threshold to be set by the trafficker at the Advertiser or Campaign levels and the data is collected and presented based on the definition.

Viewable impressions are under high demand from an industry that believes that this new metric will challenge the usual definition of standard impressions in the future. Some believe that since ads that are not being seen (according to the viewable definition) they should be dis-associated from post impression conversions and subsequent attribution. This presents interesting questions for rich media content where audio is automatically enabled; ads that are heard and not seen are still a grey area for digital measurement. In addition to the ad servers providing a record of viewable impressions, point solutions are also available for measuring viewable impressions such as *Alenty*; who bring to the table a more "dynamic threshold" methodology (where the threshold does not need to be set before the campaign begins, but the trafficker can choose the definition when the report is pulled).

Viewability is harder to measure than content categorisation because it requires JavaScript which means it is more complex to execute on Instream and Mobile ads. Viewability is also much harder for the Publisher to control and many Publishers are well aware that a fair amount of their inventory may never be seen but won't be aware of it until the ad is served. Such Publishers might argue that their pricing for the inventory is adjusted to reflect the possibility of wastage from viewability which is a conundrum for the Advertiser unless viewability can be guaranteed in the IO. To assist in eradicating this wastage some technologies are being developed that only make a request to the ad server once the placement is coming into view, rather than loading the ad tag when the whole page loads.

Double Implementations and Fraudulent Serving techniques

The publisher is not always aware that wastage may be occurring on their site, false implementations that result in poorly targeted ads (to the wrong geography for instance) do occur, especially when the operations team are working with thousands of ad tags every day. Pressing the wrong key can mean implementing the same ad tag twice in the same place and even removing a tiny piece of the ad tag code will affect the delivery of the ad which can result in a double implementation or no tracking at all (all common reasons for Publisher discrepancy).

Although these mistakes are accidental some Publishers (particularly in the long tail exchange space) fraudulently adapt ad tag implementation on purpose the serve the ad in their favour. For example if a Publisher only had a handful of pages they could double their available ad inventory by double serving ads. This way the inventory appears to be served at a rate which matches the Publishers promise (that there are twice as many pages to serve to). Lies and deceit never work in the Publishers favour and increasingly techniques such as these are captured by CV tools and third party ad servers resulting in Advertisers stopping spend with those Publishers.

Other techniques include layering ads on top of each other, hiding ads in spots on the page that are not seen (but where code has been used to manipulate the detection of a viewable impression) and loading ads into layers which are hidden to the user. Advertisers should pay particular attention to lucrative ad spots such as for Instream ads where the opportunity to manipulate the data for the purposes of generating higher earnings is a motivation for greed.

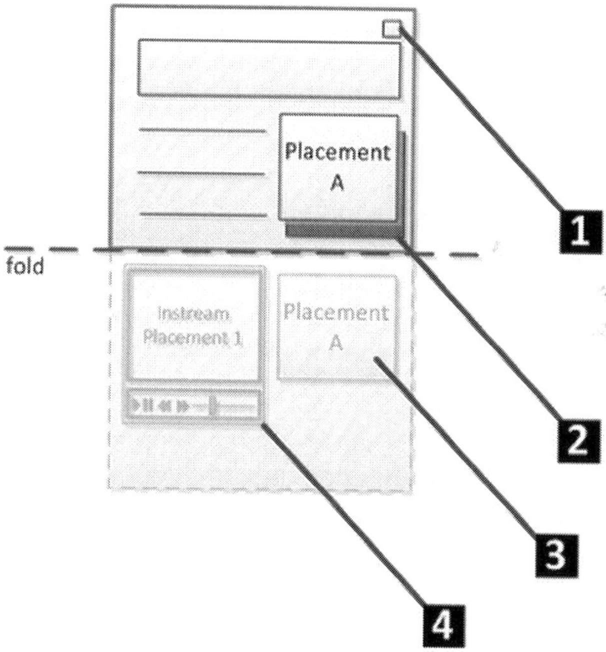

Figure 5.2.6 *Fraudulent serving techniques see the Publisher implementing the ad in such a way so as to perform less in*

favour of the Advertiser and more in favour of the Publisher. Some ads are served into tiny iframes so that the ad cannot be seen but still registers an impression (1). Some ads are cleverly layered behind other ads, ensuring the impression is counted as a viewable impression even though the ad cannot be seen (2). The same placement is loaded up onto the same site at the same time as a copy of itself so as to serve more impressions on fewer pages (3). Instream video players set to auto-play, running below the fold, the video metrics all fire off but the ad is never seen so the Publisher still gets paid once the video has completed playing (4).

Page Level Verification Quality Indicators

Domain URL Reporting

As the ad server is able to capture the URL of the page on ad delivery, this information can be sent back into ad server reporting. By returning a full list of these URLs or even just the top ranking sub domains, the Advertiser has peace of mind that the specific ad spots that were purchased in agreement with the Publisher are the ones the ads are appearing on. Despite the fact that some buys may be across "blind networks" (networks where inventory is cheaper because the buyer buys the Audience and does not know the end page the ad appears on), ad severs can still capture and report on the page URL.

Contractually the Advertiser should ensure (via the signing of the IO when the media buyer buys the ad space) that there is no room for the Publisher to intentionally waste the delivery of ad impressions for their own gain. This is particularly prevalent in the DSP and exchange space where long-tail Publishers have a very disjointed relationship from the Advertiser and "ad brokering" is common place.

Other uses for Page Level information

Page URLs which appear in Cookie Level reporting (see Chapter 5) allow the Advertisers more insight into the CookieID itself and therefore the user. This is because a browsing history allows an inference to be made about interest categories for that very specific user (no two browsing habits are entirely the same). Aside from being useful for verification this can be utilised for targeting and even establishes itself as a unique pathway which can be transformed into part of a unique identifier for a user. This methodology is being tested for cookie-free technology in the privacy space (see Chapter 7).

White Lists and Black Lists

Across the internet Whitelists and Blacklists are enforced to certain rules. Websites can end up on Google's blacklist because of SEO violations and the rules which determine Google's indexing of websites consult the blacklist before displaying results. Verification technology can be viewed in the same way: those keywords and terms on a page that violate brand safety are considered blacklist terms and those keywords that are well matched and even contextually improve the performance of the ad on the page can be considered white list terms. Advertisers can keep record of those pages, subdomains and domains which violate brand safety and issue these to the Publisher in the IO process as a blacklist. A Publisher network may also categorise certain pages on their own networks as belonging to a blacklist, such that these pages are never sold to Advertisers for their ad space.

The URL, domain or subdomain is essentially the marker by which verification can be established. At scale, smart Advertisers and Agencies will begin to use this data to build up a picture of the quality of the whole of the premium inventory available on the web and use this data to benchmark sites and placements against each other. This will help determine buying and planning strategies for future campaigns.

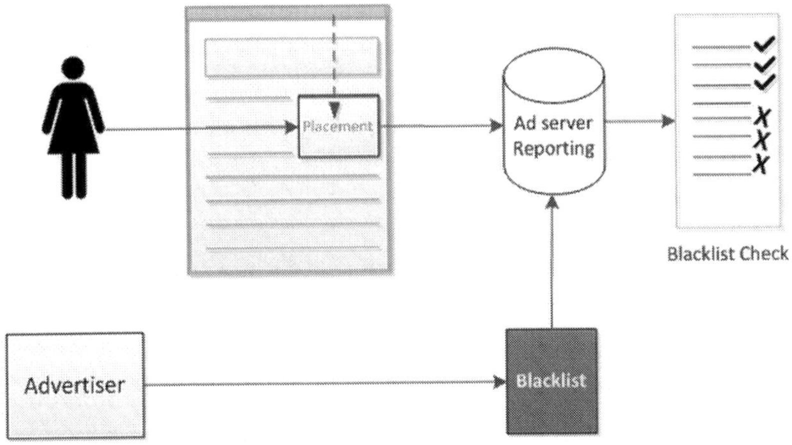

Figure 5.2.7 *Placements checking for semantic and content verification can pull in the domain and URL of the page the ad is being served on. This information is fed through to Ad server reporting where Advertisers can cross reference the delivery against any existing blacklist they may have.*

The combination of these quality indicators summarises the most popular methods of verification, allowing the Advertiser to check they are getting what they paid for. But in some instances the Advertiser wants to go a step further than reporting to actually screenshot the ad failing the verification quality indicators. Although not a standardised feature, some third party ad servers have crawlers technologies which can screenshot these pages and save them for the trafficker to view in the third party ad server interface. Such technologies do not always catch the ad in the act (such as with geography or device) so in the future we may see adaptions that move from a screenshot to a short movie clip of the ad served into the Publisher page failing Verification.

See through, View through and Recordability Rates

Despite the availability of such a range of indicators, many of these will fail to report if the ad tag is loaded up in an environment which does not support the capturing of this data. Some Publishers (particularly in the exchange space - See Chapter 8) will serve ads from within an HTML iframe. Although verification works from within an iframe in most instances, iframes can be nested within other iframes. The effect is that the user sees the ad still but the tag is actually sitting in an invisible set of frames. Bursting out of multiple frames is crucial to reading the viewability of the ad and the context it is placed into. A failing to read viewability is a failure in the "recordability rate" of the ad, while a failure to read contextual verification is a failure in the "see through rate" or "view through rate" of the ad. In ad server reporting these numbers are presented against the verification data. If the rates are less than one hundred per cent then only a sample of the impressions have verification data against them. Although this transforms reporting from a full-picture into a sampling, it is still possible to determine the verification quality of placements and sites.

The Publisher has the control in most instances to prevent the nesting of iframes and in the interest of Advertiser transparency can do their best to remove such nesting in response to an Advertiser or Agency query based on the ad server reporting. Publishers which retain iframe nesting from the Advertiser perspective look like they have something to hide without such transparency in place.

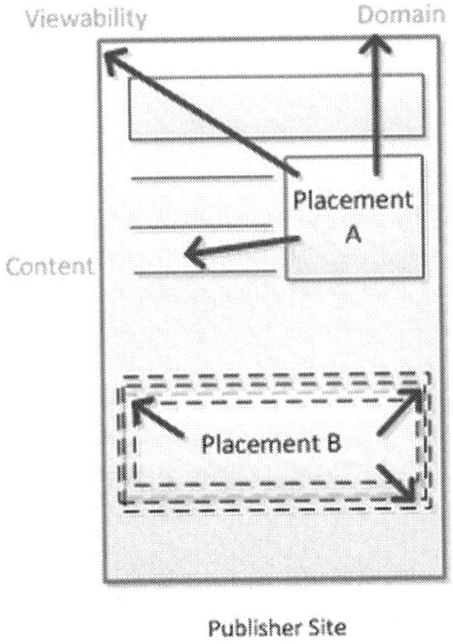

Figure 5.2.8 *Deep nested iframes affects both the recordability rate and the see-through rate for ads. If an ad is served onto the Publisher page within too many iframes (produced as a result of overly guarded security or excess technology on the page) the code within the placement cannot look into the rest of the page. This affects verification quality indicators such as content verification, domain reporting and viewability.*

So far this section has put a lot of focus on Reactive verification which is detecting ad verification after the ad has been served. The data generated in ad server reporting is then used to help the Publisher to eradicate the wastage on future ad delivery. However, this method does not stop the ad from appearing altogether. This is where ad blocking plays a role, preventing the ad from being served based on the quality indicators.

Preventative - Ad blocking

In Ad blocking when the placement loads up on the page, if the content is found to be unsafe or if any of the other quality indicators are breached, then a Public Service ad is displayed instead, using up the impression. Ad impressions which are ad blocked by the ad server enter an ad blocking report which the Advertiser or Agency can view and download in ad server reporting to share with the Publisher. The Publisher can then either reimburse the Advertiser for the wasted ad or commit to avoid delivering the Advertisers ads to such pages or domains in the future.

As with reactive verification, in preventative verification, the domains, subdomains and even URLs can be extracted from most third party ad server reporting and given or fed to the Publisher. The Publisher ad ops team can then add this list to a campaign or Advertiser level blacklist management facility in the Publisher ad server to prevent the delivery of the Advertiser's third party ad tags to such locations moving forwards. This process is not usually undertaken by the trafficker on the Agency or Advertiser side but may sit with an additional service team setup to engage the Publishers in a remuneration discussion: pulling the data and having such conversations. Unfortunately such negotiations can take time and the campaign in question may end before a Publisher's new billing cycle which means that recovered media costs cannot be injected back into the same campaign.

The most effective method for eradicating ad wastage in digital advertising is to use Pre-emptive verification.

Pre-emptive - Verification in Programmatic

At the time this book is being published, Pre-emptive verification technologies only work in the DSP space (see Chapter 8) and involves *not* buying or bidding on inventory because the page the impression does not meet the quality indicators for verification defined by the Advertiser. Pre-emptive verification collects page level information about the placement, site and domain, informing the bidding process before the ad is ever served. This is much more difficult for viewability but works well for almost all other quality indicators.

Before the development of bidding technologies, the networks and Publishers were held on the promise to deliver ads into a safe environment and commit to a legal agreement with the Advertiser through contracts like the IAB supported *iASH* initiative. As a formal agreement, those Publishers that failed to comply and ended up delivering the ads into an environment that fell outside the agreement were told could lead to fines and physical auditing. In the UK, *iASH* has been disbanded in favour of new initiatives currently being developed by the *IAB* and supporting bodies, of which CV tools are a recommendation but as yet are not a formalised standard.

The Verification landscape

There are more point-solutions available to the Advertiser for reactive verification than both preventative and pre-emptive technologies. Reactive verification point solutions include *Double-Verify* and the technology formerly called *Adsafe* (now named *Integral*) such tools include an ad blocking feature as well. Just as with survey and research technologies, verification point solutions required an extended campaign setup as an additional line of code needs to be added to all placements in the third party ad server pointing at the technology in the point solution. Increasingly research panel data suppliers such as *Neilsen* and *ComScore* are investing in verification technologies to improve the validity of the demographic and audience data they supply. For pre-emptive verification tools are available separate from the ad server which plug directly into the popular DSPs such as *Peer39*.

The line between verification, delivery and performance can be difficult to distinguish, particularly with around the definition of impressions and certain interaction metrics like video completion rates for Instream (which some ad servers label up as verification metrics).

Delivery and Verification reports are useful in ensuring that things kicked off okay. Once the data begins to gather in volume, the opportunity arises to conduct a more thorough analysis of that data. Beyond the most basic standard reporting templates, there are a series of more advanced aggregated reports that allow the most insightful and cost-saving trends to surface. In the next section we examine a series of these advanced aggregated reports, ensuring that live campaigns are meeting the success criteria defined by the marketers.

Chapter 5 - Section 3
Advanced Aggregated Reporting

- Cross Channel analysis
    - Day Part Analysis
    - Cross Channel Reports
        - *Figure 5.3.1*
- Advanced Conversion Analysis
    - Time to Convert
        - *Figure 5.3.2*
    - Engagement Mapping Factors report
- Reach and Frequency Reporting
    - Unique Reach
    - Average Frequency
        - *Figure 5.1.3*
    - Effective Frequency
        - *Figure 5.1.4*
    - Reach and Frequency Report
        - *Figure 5.1.5*
    - Adjusted Unique
        - *Figure 5.1.6*
- Advanced Site and Creative Analysis
    - Unique Site Overlap
        - *Figure 5.1.7*
    - Ad format reporting
    - Global Benchmarks
    - Advertiser Specific Benchmarks
        - *Figure 5.1.8*

Ad server reporting is a gold mine of data. Based on the foundation metrics of impressions and conversions, comes a whole series of answers about how to calculate effectiveness and pinpoint which impression and engagement are offering the most value in an Advertiser's digital campaign.

The following section looks at the more advanced reports available from a third party ad server reporting interface and explains their uses to the Advertiser, beginning with reports related to cross-channel analysis, before moving onto advanced conversion-focussed reporting, followed by reach and frequency reports before concluding with site and creative-focussed reporting.

Cross Channel Analysis

Day Part Analysis

Distribution of impressions, clicks and conversions can be viewed on a timeline and used to expose trends in user activity for segmented audiences at different times. These reports will expose spikes in activity that may fall in line with internet usage expectations (such as increased performance for the commuting city worker demographic, in both the lunch hour and after the evening rush hour. Day part analysis can therefore be used by the trafficker to update the time based rotation of creative messaging for that particular audience (when combined with a form of targeting such as Publisher-keyword targeting to expose the demographic of the user). In addition, day part analysis can be used to see if impression delivery at a particular time is more effective at driving conversions across certain audiences than others. This will inform the way the planner and buyer purchases ad space, since some ad spots may be more valuable to accessing their target audience at different times. Since impression volumes will be shown in day-part analysis to fluctuate throughout the day, it might be an idea to use this evidence to justify paying more for a time based delivery, cemented into the IO from the Publisher as a commitment to that delivery.

Cross Channel Reports

Third party ad serving collects data across each channel for the purposes of de-duplicating the users (unique users seeing ads across many channels and Publishers will produce a complete pathway to conversion). In addition to this benefit is the benefit of being able to compare the performance of channels as a whole. Cross Channel reporting allows the trafficker to identify which channel is adding more value compared to others and if one channel is causing an improvement in the performance of other channels.

Cross channel reporting allows the Advertiser to recognise the value of a channel that might not directly be causing conversions, but the presence of which in a user's pathway to conversion may statistically be causing uplift on the last-click conversions of a more dominant channel.

The more commonly used "search display synergy report" demonstrates that although paid search appears to drive the most conversions under the last ad model; the display channel when paired with the search channel, creates more of an uplift in conversions than the search channel does on its own. As more channels get added to the digital marketing mix and get de-duplicated by the third party ad server; more of this style of reporting will be in demand, to ensure that there aren't channels inadvertently acting as a counter weight to the performance of their sibling channels.

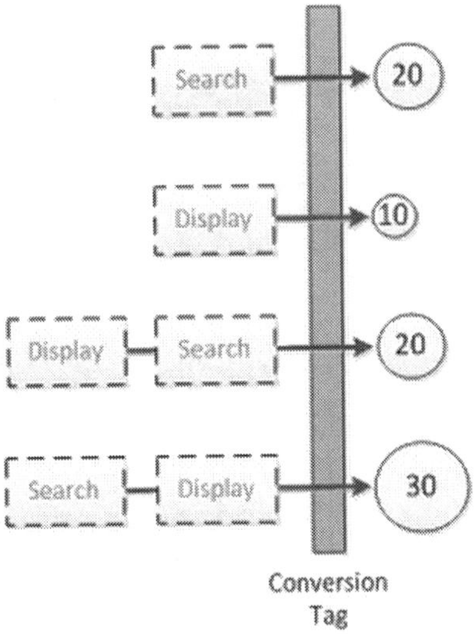

Figure 5.1.1 *An example of how a channel by channel uplift report adds value. If a channel is considered on its own, by just looking at a basic aggregated conversions-by-channel report, it will appear to be driving a limited number of conversions on its own. Here, where the Search channel is the last touch point by users before conversion, the Search channel is just as effective without a user encountering a Display channel ad beforehand. There are still 20 conversions, so display is not having uplift on the Search channel. However look at users converting from the Display channel as the last touch point and the analysis shows that if users encounter search ads before seeing a Display ad, there is a significant uplift. Here, the Search channel is causing a three hundred per cent uplift on the Display channel.*

Channel by channel uplifting reporting allows the trafficker to clearly see how much assistance one channel is providing to another and the planners and buyers can use this data to plan when to run channel-specific activity. The same report can be used to get more granular, calculating precisely which Publishers and placements within these supporting channels are deemed responsible for the up-weight.

Advanced Conversion Analysis

Time to Convert

Setting the correct conversion window for a conversion tag is not an easy task since it is prone to fluctuations in terms of what the optimum conversion window settings should be in order to the get maximum number of conversions. A Time to convert report is an advanced aggregated report that plots the conversions on a graph according to temporal increments such as days or hours. At a point, for a particular conversion tag and corresponding campaign, the conversions drop to a level where they trail off in a long tail fashion. Chasing this long tail by cranking up the conversion window may mean leaving that window open too long and allowing ads in a campaign to become responsible for conversions where the conversion window length exceeded a reasonable consideration period. In particular this style of report can be useful to show where additional conversions would have been reported, had windows been increased. Frequently pulling this report keeps the conversion window settings in check.

Time to convert reporting, should also consider advanced attribution modelling. In addition to showing the average time taken for a user to convert via impression or click based conversion, the report can be adjusted to show how long such a conversion would take under different models. For example, with a custom attribution model that awards a greater share of conversion to clicks on rich media ads , the time to convert report would show the amount of time it takes for a user to click on a rich media ad in the conversion pathway, to finally converting. Although there may be other clicks later in the pathway, the report would only take into account, the click-to-rich-media attribution model, to advise the optimum conversion window to exploit the maximum increment of conversions for this type of attribution.

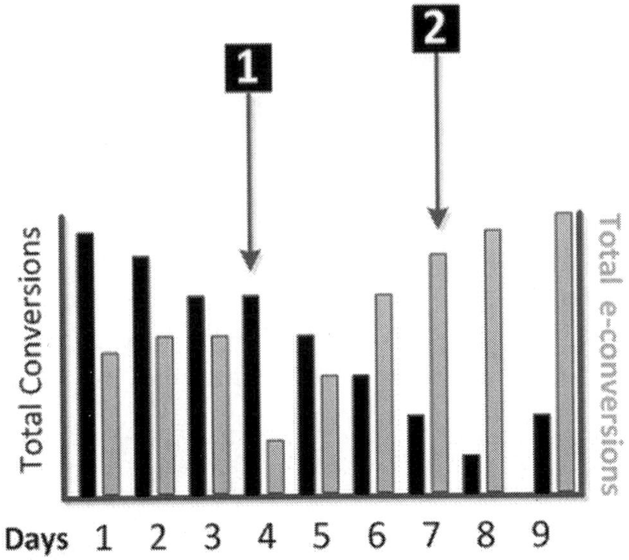

Figure 5.1.2 *A time to convert report shows how long it takes users to convert after being exposed to or click on an ad. The diagram shows that at point (1) the tipping point for the total number of conversions occurs at the 4 day mark. The trafficker could choose to set the conversion window at this point or extend it out further to catch more conversions. This chart also maps on a consideration for e-conversions, showing how long it takes users to convert under an alternative attribution model. At point (2) is the conversion tipping point. To satisfy both models on the same conversion tag, the trafficker might choose to set the conversion tag to sit between these two markers.*

This advanced aggregated report includes data from all touch points that occurred within the click or view window for each converting user so as to make a consideration for the optimum conversion window for e-conversions alongside standard conversions. The report will allow the trafficker to ensure that the windows are kept wide or narrow enough to correctly report on conversions under this alternative attribution model.

Engagement Mapping Factors report

Basic aggregated reporting can be used to show the total number of conversions and e-conversions that each placement and site might increment under the selected attribution model. *Atlas* specifically offers an advanced aggregated report which looks back at old data and applies a new attribution model to it, to calculate what the e-conversions of placements and sites would have been, had they been run under that new model. In addition to this, new attribution models can be invented and tested against existing data to see which model, provides the best results. Although this kind of reporting may seem to be manipulating the output conversion data, the models created might be a better real-world representation of how conversions are accurately attributed.

An engagement mapping factors report is useful in deciding what kind of attribution model to apply to future campaigns, providing a trial and error report output from the third party ad serving interface without affecting the originally processed core conversion data.

Reach and Frequency Reporting

Unique Reach

The concept of 'uniqueness' is an important consideration in ad server reporting. Impressions reported in the basic aggregated reporting "impressions" column are really gross impressions (to steal a term from the financial world) where as some Advertisers are interested in actual impressions or to be more specific: Unique Impressions. The number of unique impressions will be significantly lower than the number of total impressions, since it will only count the number of unique users or cookieID's that are exposed to an ad. In third party ad serving this is called "Reach"; the total number of unique impressions. Unique reach can be controlled by the media buying process (requesting from the Publisher to only purchase space based on its unique viewing) and the creative targeting process. Creative targeting is used to ensure that either the previously encountered users are not shown any ad by the Advertiser, or are shown a different creative from the creative that they have already seen. This can easily be setup by the trafficker using ad server retargeting (see Chapter 7).

Unique reach reporting can also be setup to see if the campaign is being delivered to a growing new audience over a set period of time. The report can extend beyond the insight of new unique users being delivered ads to also see if existing users are becoming new clickers, engagers or converters as a result of adjustments to the media plan to obtain new reach.

Average Frequency

Another of the most common metrics is the "frequency" or the number of impressions that saw an ad more than once, more than twice and so on. At an ad level inside reporting the trafficker can include the column "average frequency" for an ad or creative. This will show how often unique cookieIDs are being bombarded with the same ad or creative. This is an important metric since a high frequency can have a negative impact in campaign performance and truly tarnish a brand image, while a low frequency can cause the campaign to have a lower impact. The frequency can be controlled by the frequency cap setting at the ad and audience levels (as well as on the Publisher ad server by the

Publisher ad ops team) and keeping an eye on this metric avoids creative fatigue for the user.

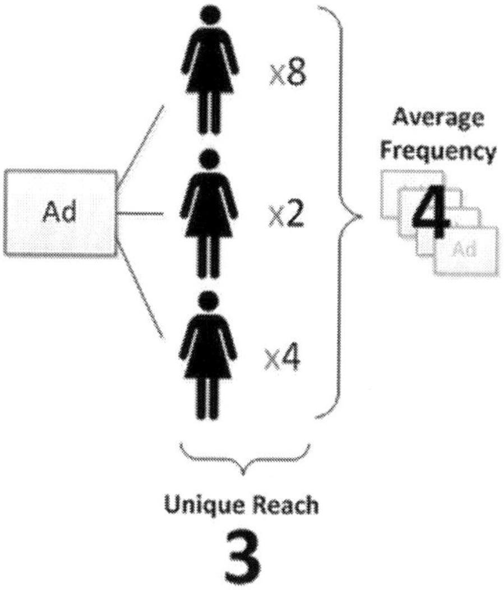

Figure 5.1.3 *In this example an ad is served by the ad server across multiple Publishers for a total of fourteen impressions. By utilise the metrics of Unique reach and average frequency at the ad level within ad server reporting, the same ad is seen by three separate users (identified in the ad server by having separate cookieIDs). Each user is shown the same ad a different number of times but across all unique users, the ad is shown at an average frequency of four times. A simple aggregated delivery report what not show this insight, without it, the marketer could infer that the ad was shown to fourteen different people.*

Effective Frequency

Effective or optimal frequency checks at which frequency level the frequency cap should be set to optimize the number of conversions, engagements or clicks for a specific ad, placement, site or campaign (and similar to the time to convert report). Just as with the time to convert report, the Optimal Frequency report will present an optimum point followed by a drop off. However it is not advised to set the frequency cap at the point of drop-off but instead to consider setting the cap a little earlier or later depending on the goal. This consideration should be made at both a creative and site level to determine which sites or creative might require a lower frequency to maintain the target goal. The following goals can be mapped onto optimal frequency reports so that it is clear what the optimum frequency level should be:

- Maximum number of total conversions
- Highest ROI output or CPA - determined by the extended data revenue output or the cost input data on the package level (bearing in mind that an Advertiser would achieve the lowest CPA on the first impression/frequency because any subsequent exposure per user increases the cost per acquisition).
- Maximum CTR
- Maximum engagement rate or dwell
- Maximum number of specific interactions
- Optimum uplift in conversions in a separate channel (by combining with channel by channel uplift reporting)
- Optimum unique reach

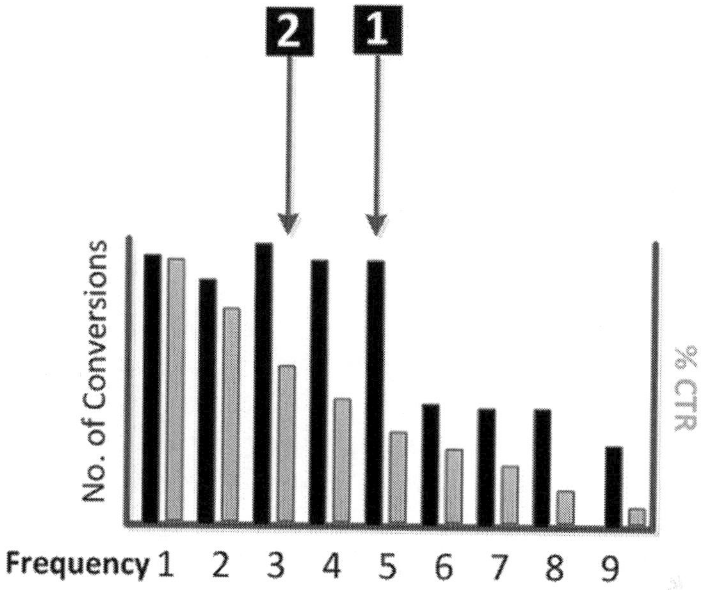

Figure 5.1.4 *What is the most effective frequency to hit both maximum conversions and the highest click-through rate? At a frequency of five (1) a high number of conversions are attained, after this there is a drop off. But rather than set the optimum frequency at five, the click-through rate drops off before that with the average optimum click through rate for the total number of impressions at around a frequency of three (2). To reach a balance between the two goals, the trafficker may use this report to suggest the Publishers set the frequency cap at four.*

This last goal consideration is the most common pairing for optimal frequency. When the two metrics of reach and frequency are combined, an advanced aggregated report emerges: the Reach and Frequency report.

Reach and Frequency Report

The two metrics together are inversely related controls for ad spend because with a limited advertising budget only a limited number of impressions can be shown. This means either showing the same ad to total users just once or showing the same ad many times to a smaller group. This report is aggregated to show the number of new users reached at a given level of frequency.

Reach and Frequency reports need a larger data sample than a single day in order to perform the right calculations. Typically reach and frequency reports cannot be pulled daily from the ad server but rather can be pulled weekly. With a full week's worth of data across the campaign, better optimization decisions can be made by the trafficker since it will typically take several days to establish a baseline from which to diminish frequency or improve reach. If new goals are set to increase unique reach, the report can be used to see if at the same or lower frequencies, the campaign goals are being affected.

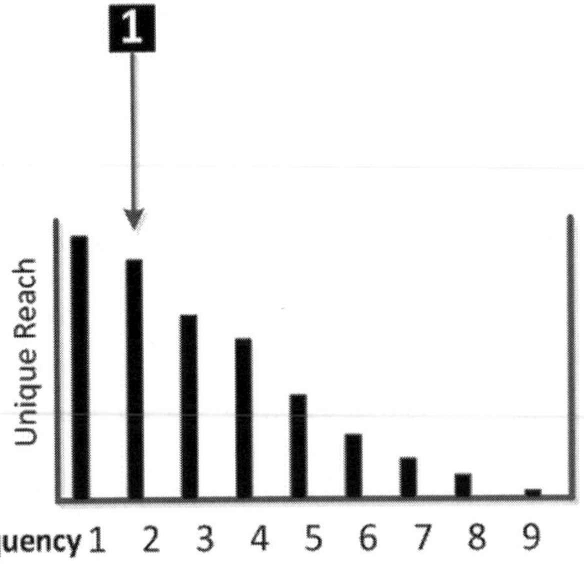

Figure 5.1.5 *Since Reach and Frequency have an inverse relationship the first frequency offers the highest unique reach and additional frequency hits the initial diminishing*

unique audience. If the frequency cap was set at two (1), the impressions spent on hitting the same audience at greater frequency, could be used to establish greater unique reach on the first and second frequency.

Adjusted Unique

In Chapter 1, the problem of cookie uniqueness and cookie deletion was explored. Since cookie deletion cannot be avoided, the *IAB* has approved the use of a metric called "Adjusted Unique" which counts the number of unique impressions to calculate unique reach while accounting for a percentage of users that delete their cookies. In particular, the *DG/Mediamind* ad server allows analysts to pull this metric where-ever unique reach is used, such as in combination with frequency or determine a more realistic view on total unique conversions.

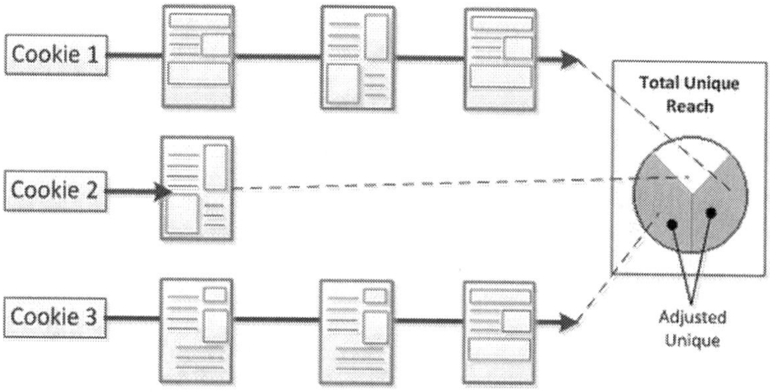

Figure 5.1.6 *Adjusted unique, is a metric that takes into account cookie deletion. Here, ad serving reporting analyses all cookie to find those cookieIDs that have a longer shelf life, spanning several campaigns. This activity is then taken as a sample and the results scaled up, based on the limited pathway details available for such cookies as Cookie 2 shown in this diagram. The data from Cookies 1 and 3 is used as a*

yardstick within the Adjusted Unique algorithm to predict results beyond cookie deletion and multiple device usage. The metric is adjusted for changes in cookie deletion activity over time and by user geography.

Advanced Site and Creative Analysis

Unique Site Overlap

The strategy of the Agency planner buyer is to optimize the display of ads to users in such a fashion so as to get the best response. Reach and frequency reporting gives the Advertiser insights into the relationship between the overall campaign reach and the frequency at which users are exposed to ads and creative. The site overlap report informs the planner buyer about which audiences overlap for particular sites. Since the aim of buying on multiple Publishers and Networks might be to extend the unique reach of the campaign to encounter new users, having sites which heavily overlap one another is useful to boost frequency but can damage reach. Site overlap shows how many users belong to more than one site or are unique to a site and is calculated by the ad server based on the movement of unique cookieIDs cross site and channel.

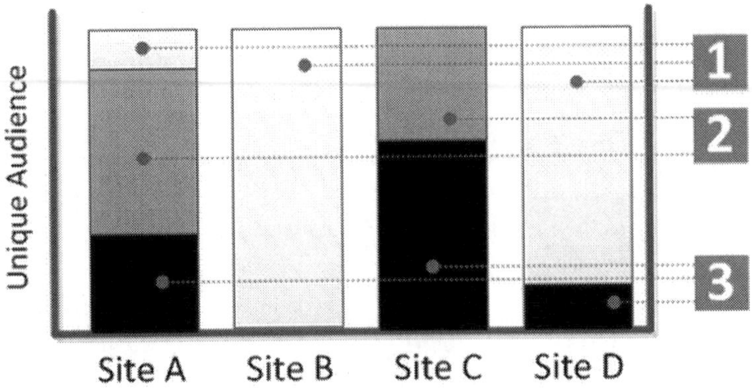

Figure 5.1.7 *Unique Site Overlap reports take the insights attained from a cross-Publisher de-duplicated third party cookie and allow planners and buyers to determine if they can reach the same eyeballs with fewer sites. The three unique audiences are shown (1, 2 & 3) revealing a clear overlap. The report indicates that Site D can be omitted from the plan, if the plan is to reach a unique audience but utilising the impressions delivered from Site A and Site B.*

An additional consideration is whether spend to reach users on a previous campaign are affecting this one. Although the Advertiser may be advertising a different product, the old messaging may still have had some impact, potentially adding to user exposure in the form of frequency. In this way, the spend on those placements may be contributing to the performance of the new campaign. Pulling a report which layers unique reach and frequency, cross campaign, channel and site, allows the planner and buyer to consider reducing spend after a high spend campaign, owing to the marginal impact it may have on the upcoming campaign.

Ad Format reporting

Although it is possible to pull basic aggregated reports for delivery on a campaign level by Publisher and to show the best performing ad format, it is more challenging to just see if one format outperforms the others in every situation. Some ad servers make this easier for the analyst in the third party ad server reporting interface by aggregating click through rates, effective frequency, effective improvements in unique reach, total impression delivery, conversion rates and effective ROI lead by ad format. Such reporting is useful to justify spend for Rich Media for example and is most useful for Creative Agencies and planners in deciding what dimensions of ads to buy and develop.

Global Benchmarks

The urge to look over a friends shoulder in an exam is not always to cheat but rather to check that your answers look right. Third party ad server benchmark reporting takes campaigns results from all Advertisers that are opted in, to aggregate those results. Results are broken by country to make them more relevant to analysts. This mass aggregation allows Advertisers to see which sites, placements and formats are the most effective before running such activity themselves. The aggregation is fully anonymous so that it is not possible to determine the source of the data by analysing the results. This would normally be possible if an Advertiser from a particular vertical was the only Advertiser in that vertical to either be utilising a particular Publisher or be saturating digital advertising in a particular market.

To make the data more relevant, ad serving providers compartmentalise the results by Advertiser marketing vertical so that Advertisers in the Financial vertical can see how well 300x250 expandable ads may perform as a CTR on specific section of a specific Publisher site based on the benchmarking results from the previous year. Conversion rate data is also available, but since conversion tags can be used on all manner of Advertiser pages, the ad server will group together all conversion tags labelled as "sales tags" to determine aggregate conversion rates.

Typically ad serving providers will offer benchmark data at a very high level to all Advertisers and Agencies using its interface while offering deeper insights to a different set of benchmark data aggregated by specialist opt-in Advertisers and Agencies, who only get deeper insights by offering up more of their own data to the pool. These deeper levels of collaboration are tricky to operate, they require a blanket level of consensus among all participants which in practice is complicated to maintain. Some participants to the data set may feel that they are giving away more than they are getting back and convincing contributors that there is universal fair access is challenging to prove, especially if Advertisers differ in size. To provide a fair balance, there is usually a minimum contribution requirement for reporting. This can mean that despite the huge amount of data available in ad server reporting, the benchmark report may display blank results where only one Advertiser in a country has any ad serving data for a 300x250 expandable ad on a specific Publisher site.

Advertiser Specific Benchmarks

Large Advertisers and Agencies also generate such benchmark reporting outside of the ad server, by feeding their ad serving data into a separate reporting system where they can layer in cost data and more specific performance data. The cost data would also be a record of what was paid previously to determine which sites, placements and formats that are the most cost effective for their expected performance. Such benchmarking information would likely feed directly into an Agency or Advertiser planning tool or Agency trading desk to better inform the planning and buying process.

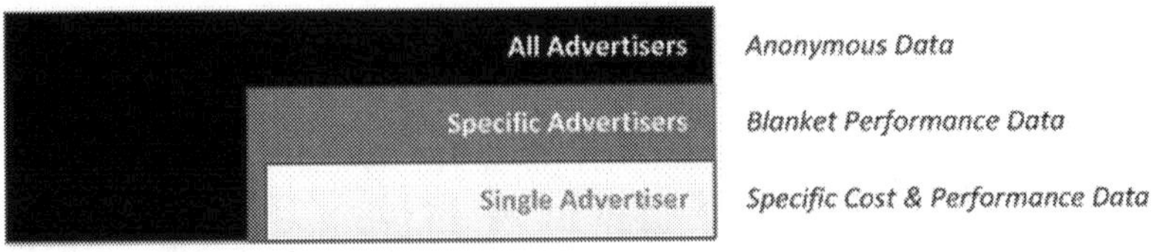

Figure 5.1.8 *Benchmarking data is universally available from ad servers, fully anonymous showing a breakdown of performance benchmarks per vertical and ad format. Specific Advertisers could also opt in to a pool where more of their data contributes to a better indication about performance data down to a site or Publisher level. Beyond this large Advertiser run enough activity across Publishers to allow their planners to view specific cost and performance data by format and placement. This informs the decision to buy those ad spots again in the future but typically this is not information that is shared with the Publisher.*

This data is not just useful for future planning but also to compare with existing performance to check that the campaign is on track. Numbers reported to be an improvement on the benchmark are a positive story for the Agency analyst who can use the benchmark to set expectations with the Advertiser or marketer for the reported results.

Advanced aggregated reporting is a method to pivot and adjust the way that data is viewed, building on top of basic aggregated reports. Advanced reports are useful because they provide a way to make more sense of the data without diving deeply into the cookie level reporting, also available from the ad server. The next section looks at more niche channel-specific reporting, which is useful in silo, allowing marketers heavily focussed on Search or on Video, to just look at the delivery, engagement and performance of those channels in isolation rather than looking at the bigger picture.

Chapter 5 - Section 4
Channel Specific Reports

- Display Channel Reporting
- Rich Media Channel Reporting
- DCO Channel Reporting
  - Multi variant testing
  - Dangers in Version Overwriting
  - Version reporting
    - *Figure 5.4.1*
- Instream Channel Reporting and Metrics
  - Video Started and unique video starts
  - Ad duration
  - Increment ad play-through (25, 50, 75, 100%)
  - Average % video completion
  - VPAID custom interactions
- Mobile Channel Reporting
  - Cookie Duplication
  - Cookie Absence
  - Device Finger Printing
  - Cookies in applications
  - Device and Carrier reporting
- Paid Search Channel Reporting
  - Search Overview
  - Keyword Pathway Analysis
- Natural Search Reporting
  - Double counting and Single Counting
    - *Figure 5.4.2*
- Affiliate Channel Reporting

The third party ad server reporting interface offers traffickers and analysts reports that contain metrics relevant only to specific channels. These channel specific reports match well to the same major channels described in Chapter 3 - Campaign Management by Channel. The following section will outline the proprietary metrics, methodologies and analytical considerations within channel-specific reporting.

Display Channel Reporting

Reports specific to the display channel (omitting rich media, DCO and video from the definition of the display channel) are the most basic kind of reporting available and would be the same basic aggregated reports described as delivery and performance reports. Here reports predominantly relate to impression information and click information for the Publisher sites, packages, placements and ads. The additional considerations, more unique to the display channel are those where the naming convention can be adapted to give more information about the creative. These fields in reporting would be "creative name", "ad name" and ad and placement classifications. Creative name and ad name, as described in Chapter 2 - should match a description of the imagery used in the creative or relate to the product advertised within the ad. Within reporting these names can be aggregated so that if they are used. The ad and placement classification fields are also useful for this purpose but serve to provide additional meta information. Ad classification one might be populated by the trafficker to contain the date that the creative was swapped out for another with the same name. Rows within reporting could then be aggregated to show the different in performance based on this information.

Also relevant to Display reporting is the ability for the ad server to reporting on backup image delivery. Sometimes a basic aggregated delivery report will hide the number of impressions where users saw a backup image instead of the flash creative, channel specific reporting should provide the analyst with the ability to see this information as well. An indication to the delivery of a large number of backup images may mean that unsupported devices are being targeted at the Publisher level; a control which can be adjusted by having the trafficker feed this reporting information to the Publisher to target away from non-flash supported results before a high delivery of backup images equates to wastage.

Rich Media Channel Reporting

The primary difference from a reporting perspective between Standard Display and Rich Media, is Rich Media's ability to track interactions and subsequently pass them back into reporting. Interactions can be divided into two groups; default and custom interactions. Default interactions apply to the counting of the trigger of certain Rich Media specific functions such as Expansions. Total number of expansions, for instance is a standardised metric in Rich Media reports. Custom interaction tracking for Rich Media allows the creative developer to place a trigger inside the creative anywhere, so that an action within the creative will count that custom interaction occurrence. Creative developers are encouraged to work with marketers and Agency teams to put useful custom interactions within the creative, tracking anything from a user hovering over an object to clicking, pressing a button or even sitting idle.

In reporting, interactions can be tied back to unique impressions and conversion events. The overall time spent interacting within the ad (such as a mouse pointer hovering over the creative for an extended period of time) is reported in metrics such as "interaction time" or "dwell". The measure of such metrics is protected from accidental trigger by putting such safeguards in as waiting for one second to pass with the mouse pointer operating within the confines of the ad before counting begins. The key here is that Rich Media creative can also support a timer such that an analyst can pull from reporting a "total brand exposure duration" metric which is a total count of interaction across all users. Such metrics could be used to compare with TV ad campaigns that are measured by minutes of exposure to the total audience base.

Some ad servers offer a heat mapping tool, which layers hotspots over the creative to show analysts where users were predominantly engaging or interacting with the ad. Although such reporting is aesthetically rewarding the analyst, the interpretation of such reporting can be subjective and difficult to optimize from creatively speaking.

DCO Channel and Audience Reporting

DCO reporting can be viewed at a high level; such as to view the effectiveness of versions based on the version name, but deeper insights are available by ensuring such reports display the detail of the dynamic elements of that version so that results can be tied back to the correct recipe of those elements. Multi-variant testing specifically allows for the analysis and identification of best performing versions or variants based on those best performing elements.

Multi variant testing

With the dynamic elements of the ad exposed in the creative the reporting may expose trends such as that a particular price point across lots of different types of creative always seems to pull a high number of clicks or conversions. The same could be said of a background image, colour or font type used although clearly some co-incidental trends may surface which fall to the best judgement of the campaign manager to dismiss or de-prioritise in favour of optimizing to elements which logically make attract a better performance (such as price point or offer type). In reporting for multi variant testing, the usual column for the version name is replaced with the name of the varying asset and reporting such as impressions, clicks, conversions and interactions can be layered up by site and placement so as to find out if a combination of assets equates to a better performing version when they are combined together. Such reporting is of particular interest to the creative developer.

Dangers in Version Overwriting

Updating a price point or any other dynamic element for a specific version in the setup of a DCO campaign is a bad practice in the ad server without changing the name of the version entirely. Some ad servers do not place restrictions on version updating simply because restrictions would add extra steps for Advertisers and make the setup more challenging. However; the amendment of a dynamic element in an existing version is not a recorded event so inside DCO reporting, a top performing version which was changed at some point in the day could not attribute its success to the amendment.

Even at the cookie data level the DCO version amendment is not time stamped so the trafficker would need to make a full record of changes made to existing versions. The solution is to always create new versions when any dynamic element is updated and ensure there is some relationship between the new version and the old version to understand the version evolution (this can be done with a good version naming convention).

Version Reporting

DCO reporting within the ad server reporting interface costs of reports that shows version delivery, performance and engagement at the version level instead of at the ad level. Detailed reporting of this type will also show which audience or placement the version was assigned to, to allow the trafficker to optimize the delivery, targeting and rotation of best performing versions. Version level reporting can become complex to analyse if only the version number was displayed for each row in the report since the number or ID does not give away an accurate description of how versions differ from one another.

For this reason, larger version reports that include a list of the content of the dynamic assets is useful although the reporting quickly begins to replicate the spread-sheet based mass version interface within ad server campaign management. To reduce report size, some ad server reports for DCO will omit rows or versions which recorded no delivery or poor performance, reducing a potential pool of thousands of versions at a by day, week or month granularity, down to just a few rows. This makes life much easier for the analyst and trafficker.

Version	Audience	Clickthrough	Impressions	Clicks
901	UK	uk.msn.com	80000	170
902	DE	de.msn.com	67000	511
903	ES	es.msn.com	87000	601

Version	Background	Logo
901	red	logo.gif
902	red	logo2.gif
903	black	logo2.gif

Figure 5.4.1 *Version level reporting (shown left in this diagram) reveals the delivery and performance of the various versions. Each of the versions is seen to be running against a different defined audience type, here by geography and clicking through to a different part of the MSN.com website. Beyond this the differences between the versions are not revealed in the report. Navigating the ad server campaign setup interface reveals more information about each version by how they vary from one another. The analyst would need both these data sets to adequately analyse each version and explain whether the aspects of each version or the targeting are responsible for the performance.*

Instream Channel Reporting and Metrics

The metrics that can be tracked in the Instream channel have growing synergy with TV measurement. Historically big Advertisers, advertising through the medium of television have been able to track a sample of ad delivery and exposure. This allowed Advertisers to pay for TV ads in new ways: such as only paying if the video of the ad was played in full. Apart from the Display channel and Search channel, the Instream channel is the only other channel where Advertisers are paying Publishers not on ad delivery, but on channel-specific metrics: video plays and vide completions. The following is a list of notable metrics available only in Instream specific reports.

Video Started and unique video starts

At the creative level, the analyst can determine how many times the video was watched and how many unique users watched in (some users will play a video through more than once). Video started is useful to compare with the number of impressions for the same ad. Since the video started playing after the impression delivery, some Advertiser may prefer to pay Publishers based on the video started metric.

Ad duration

Ad servers can provide meta data about the video creative itself such as the quality of the video stream (in bits per minute) and the total length of the video. This information can help analysts perform side by side comparisons between different video ads which may be of differing lengths and quality.

Increment ad play-through (25, 50, 75, 100%)
The amount of time that the user views the video ad for, is another Instream metric (but one that is also recommended to track in rich media video units). These metrics will show user drop off as the video nears its completed play. A video which is too long to hold user interest would show high drop off of the total number of unique impressions as time goes by. As an action the trafficker would request a shorter video length from the creative developer and to buy shorter video ad space from the planner and buyer.

Average % video completion
At the ad level the analyst can see which percentage of users watched the video to completion. This can act as a marker for delivery, performance or verification depending on how the analyst interprets the data.

VPAID custom interactions
Just as with Rich Media, Instream video supports custom interactions. These are inputted by the creative developer before the campaign launches and can be positioned anywhere in the video creative. Buttons which allow the user to share the video on a social network or open an Instream video gallery from within the VPAID creative can have such actions tracked and incremented within Instream specific reporting.

Mobile Channel Reporting
Mobile specific channel reporting, although very similar to standard Display delivery reporting, has some considerations to make which relate the identification of a unique user. In standard Display reporting, knowing a cookieID is unique or not unique allows the user pathway to conversion to be

mapped cross Publisher for the same device. Once a second device or a mobile application is introduced into the mix, the cookie dependent technology related to establishing unique users and conversions, is lost.

Cookie Duplication

The human race now accesses the internet more frequently through a mobile device than a PC but the environments from a browsing experience across devices is unbalanced. In the PC environment, the ad server drops a cookie, labelling the user and tracking them. So long as the user only uses that same PC and browser to access the web, the Advertiser only needs to worry about cookie deletion, but Mobile presents a problem of cookie duplication.

A single user that switches between devices means that the ad server sees multiple users in its data collection at the cookie level, than the true single user. If there are multiple cookies in existence at the same time for the same user these need to be tied together to establish the true reach of the campaign and for pathway to conversion data (see the final section in this chapter). To overcome this problem a single technology needs to be used on both devices so that in reporting there is a common link between the two cookies. An additional data set can be applied to the mobile cookie level reporting to perform what is known as "Cookie Matching" to filter the report to establish the unique users.

Such datasets are available for Advertisers to buy; the marketers would then pull this data into the ad server cookie level data inside a DMP environment to cookie match. Data sets that could be used are ones where the user has logged in to the same place on several devices (an example of which would be signing into a browser as is possible with *Google's Chrome* or logging into a cloud-based account such as an email provider). This is all well and good while there are cookies to match; but the stinger is that third party cookies are not ubiquitous across mobile devices.

Cookie Absence

Apple made a decision to have the *Safari* browser not allow third party cookies as a default setting. This has damning consequences for tracking activity on *Apple* devices. If a cookie cannot be dropped there is no way to knowing if an individual browsing user has seen an ad and if they have seen it more than once. Inside the third party ad server database, the cookie is simply given no ID. As apple grows in adoption, so the number of traceable users decreases using the cookie level method.

To try to get clever, technology providers realised that they did not need a cookie per say, but rather just needed a common identifier for the device. The identifier would need to be unique so that the user on the device could be detected as a single individual and be measured as a separate "cookie" from the others being tracked by the technology. This identifier is referred to as "Device Finger Printing".

Device Finger Printing

At the core of the Apple device sat the "UDID". A Unique Device Identification label which technically speaking could be accessed by browser based technology and then a matching "cookie" could be built remotely in the server environment. The effect is that the ad server would "see" a single user. But the UDID was not to be the saviour for the cookie problem that many had hoped. Apple scrubbed the label from all devices, well aware of the workaround, and at time of Publication had begun presenting access to a new identifier to ad developers, specifically for the purposes of Advertising.

The purpose-built identifier has the possibility of user control so that they can opt out of cookie-based targeting by switching it off. This exposed the control *Apple* has over third party ad delivery and tracking, by blocking or controlling access to a unique identifier it is not possible to make an independent audit of the true number of unique cookies on such devices which is a problem if *Apple* decides to enter the world of Advertising Technology and supply of their own media space.

Workarounds do exist to try and circumvent the problems of identifying and counting unique mobile users such as creating a unique "session ID" on the fly, or using the IP address to establish a single cookie but these techniques remain flawed and the problem of a lack of common cross-device cookie remains in place.

Cookies in applications

Cookies are enabled through browser usage and are unique to browsers so in-app advertising presents a challenge for data collection since there is no standardised in-app cookie to speak of. The apple device identifier for advertising could be used in this instance (captured by the app using a specific line of code and then passing up to the ad server when the ad is delivered) but this still means there is a need for cookie matching.

Some SDKs force the mobile device to momentarily load up the browser on first use of the app so that the ad server can look into the browser to detect the browser cookie ID before sending the information onto the ad server. From that point forward the device can be associated with a traditional third party cookie. This is not a technique recommended to the development community by the leading app stores but again another workaround that helps demonstrate the jerry-rigging required to data collect in a yet-to-be standardised channel.

With the knowledge that cookies remain elusive in the Mobile channel, ad server reporting for Mobile restricts the universal metrics available for the analyst to look at. Impressions, and clicks are available at a Publisher, Site, Package, Placement and Ad level but reach, frequency, cross-channel and conversion reporting are as yet unavailable or unreliable across the board. Rich Media ads within mobile will support interaction reporting for HTML5 ads and flash where it is supported. IP delivery can also be complex due to the portable nature of the device, so geographical reporting is ill advised. In addition verification has limitations for devices that do not support JavaScript meaning that at time of Publication it is very challenging to measure viewability in mobile.

Device and Carrier reporting

Some ad servers have the technology in place to allow the Publisher to return values on mobile placements which may provide more information about delivery. These include fields such as Device and Carrier information which a Publisher could pass back to ad server reporting when the ad delivers. Having said this, few Publishers will not go that step further to providing this extra information since there is very little that can be done on their part to control this form of delivery for the purposes of media optimization later on (See Chapter 6).

Paid Search Channel Reporting

Although paid search reporting is available from inside the Search Engine marketing (SEM) interface, the ad server reporting interface presents the analyst with the opportunity to see this same data alongside the data from other channels all within the same interface as well as conducting keyword path analysis.

Search Overview

Standard Search channel reporting allows the trafficker and analyst to look at the delivery and performance of keywords, ad-groups and search ads alongside the CPC cost data retrieved by the ad server from the search engines via the search engine's own reporting API. The difference is the ad server can establish conversion reporting (to ad server conversion tags) as well as look at the uplift in conversions and clicks from the search channel to other channels like display (as explained in Channel by Channel uplift reporting).

Keyword Pathway Analysis

A keyword path analysis report aggregates the most commonly searched for and clicked on search terms in their lead up to the conversion. These combinations of search terms and the time stamps between them help the analyst understand where various keywords sit in the user's pathway to conversion and allow the trafficker to subsequently up-weight or optimize the bidding on certain keywords back in the engine. This can be done by analysing the reporting or by connecting pathway to conversion feed data (see next section in this chapter) back up to the bid management tool. In addition, some keywords may not be driving conversions at all, as such the trafficker can effectively eliminate them from the bidding process for the rest of the campaign or subsequent campaigns.

Natural Search Reporting

Natural search tracking allows the trafficker to track natural search as though it was another channel in the paid-for marketing mix. However, the key to making the most of the collected data, is setting up reporting correctly. The risk is that if user pathways to conversion were analysed, most pathways would end with the click of a natural search keyword in an engine. Under a basic attribution model like "last click", natural search would appear to be driving all conversions. In standard conversion reporting it would then appear as though all other paid-for channels could be removed from plan without any affect. In fact conversions would drop off or disappear completely, so for the Natural search channel, the trafficker must ensure that full attribution is not awarded to Natural search. This can be done using an advanced method in ad server reporting to separate out the activity completely from all other channels and then rebuild the user pathway to conversion later on.

Double counting and Single Counting

To still provide visibility on the natural search impact, while not diminishing the value of other channels under the last ad model (see Chapter 4), natural search should sit completely separately from other campaign activity by having it live in another Advertiser account entirely separate in the ad server to avoid de-duplication. There is an option in the Atlas ad server, called Single Counting Vs. Double Counting, which allows for this same affect.

If the user sees a display ad, and then search on a search engine for the featured product and clicks a natural search result on the search engine results page the following happens:

- The display ad, trafficked under the Advertiser's main Advertiser account records an impression followed by an impression based conversion from the display ad to the conversion tag on the landing page. The impression and conversion are recorded against cookieID 001 in cookie level data.

- On the landing page, the natural search script fires a click tracker, originally setup as a tracking placement under the Advertisers natural search Advertiser account. A click is recorded in this account against this separate Advertiser but also against cookieID 001.

- The same script then fires a conversion tag, setup under the natural search advertiser account, recording a click-based conversion against cookieID 001 in cookie level data.

If the analyst looked in the pathway to conversion data (see next section in this chapter) for the main Advertiser account the attribution for the conversion, under the last ad model would go to the display event, with no natural search activity recorded in sight. The analyst could then log out and log into the natural search Advertiser account. The pathway to conversion data report here would show attribution to the natural search click activity. These two reports would need to be combined at the cookie level with timestamps matched, to see the user's true pathway. What this work-around does, it that it preserves the attribution of the conversion to the display ad in the main Advertiser account without needing to create a custom attribution model or undermining the impact of the paid for activity.

Some ad servers offer SEO specific attribution considerations automatically along with a JavaScript embedded into full-site distributed conversion tags such as with a universal tagging solution (see Chapter 4) so that there is little or no effort on the part of the Advertiser but predominantly ad servers require the style of workaround described to support natural search tracking in ad server reporting.

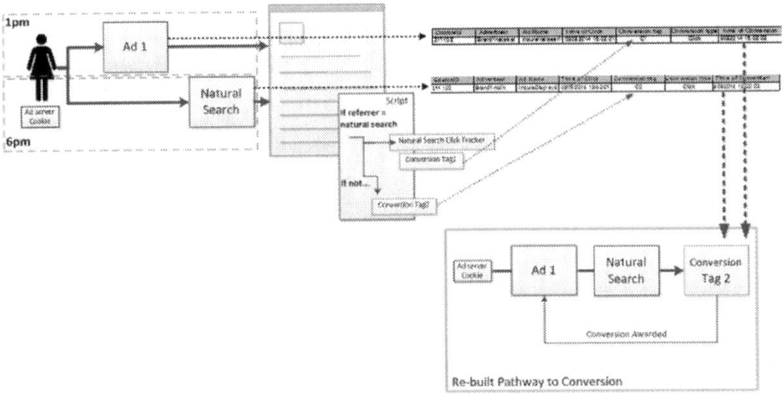

Figure 5.4.2 *To calculate where Natural Search sits in the pathway to conversion, the setup requires a workaround which feed reporting data into two separate Advertisers. A report can then be built from the cookie level data to see the pathway to conversion while still awarding the final conversion to paid media channels in aggregated reports. This diagram shows how a single sees an ad at 1pm. Later in the same day the user searches a keyword and navigates through to the same landing page as was designed for the paid-for ad (Ad 1). The script on the page registers conversions in separate Advertiser as the tracking is setup in the campaign management section of the ad server interface. At the cookie level, the cookie history can be used to re build the pathway to conversion across the single user.*

This setup style for natural search means that within aggregated reporting, natural search behaves the same as any reporting related to click counting. This means that total clicks and click based conversions can be recorded against this channel within the specific natural search Advertiser.

Affiliate Channel Reporting

The idea of affiliate based reporting within the ad server is to determine which affiliate in the affiliate network, given the use of a single ad, is responsible for the click and conversion activity.

To calculate which affiliate site was responsible for each sale, the affiliate network generates a unique reference number for each affiliate when they generate the Advertiser campaign code before placing it on their website. When the user clicks the activity and goes on to purchase, the affiliate ID is carried all the way to the purchase page in the click pathway where the data is collected and a feed of information is returned to the affiliate network about affiliate so that they can distribute the payment to the affiliate sites. To achieve this the click through URL consists of separate parts which each report back to their various tracking technology. The combination of these parts is referred to as "Daisy Chaining".

The output from ad server reporting on affiliate activity, lists the affiliate site name or unique identifier on each row along with the total number of attributed conversions and the aggregated ROI. This is based on the extended data revenue passed through at the point of conversion on the conversion tag extended data parameter.

The vast range of reporting options means that the number of metrics possible to pull down from the third party ad server will be in excess of one hundred different values. Reporting templates which can be customized will usually allow users to bring metrics into reports which may have no place being there: such as Rich Media metrics in customized Paid Search reports. It is for this reason that traffickers and analysts using the reporting interface are urged to play around inside the interface, before pulling reports for a more urgent purpose. Without thorough practice, the act of report pulling can quickly become frustrating unless it is clear which report will report the required stats.

This section concludes the summary of aggregated reporting options. The last section in this chapter covers off the reports that are usually found outside of the ad serving interface, although the data still originates from the core ad serving database. An example of such data is cookie level data which is usually so detailed and granular that it requires much greater processing power to output and present. As such this style of reporting will usually be delivered manually to the Advertiser or Agencies FTP (File Transfer Protocol) site.

Chapter 5 - Section 5
Cookie Level data

Aggregated reporting brings together various metrics to give a high level view about the total number of those metrics counted for a given ad server hierarchy entity over a given period of time.

This means that the trafficker or analyst can log into the third party ad server reporting interface and download a report by a given date range to show total impressions, clicks, conversions, interactions by Advertiser, Brand, Publisher, Site, Section, Domain, Package, Placement, Ad, Creative and Version. To really learn exactly how users came across ads and the story behind the pathway to the conversion, it is essential to dive much deeper. In cookie level data, instead of each row of the report being a summary or activity by entity, each row is a summary of activity by cookieID or at the maximum granularity can be a summary of a single recorded action or event for a cookieID.

Reporting at the Cookie Level

Cookie level data exposes every recorded event in the third party ad server for an Advertiser as it is related to each user (or each unique cookieID) and places time stamps against various activities. In just a few rows or columns of this level of raw data, it is clear to see how and where a user saw or clicked an ad in a campaign over an extended period of time if or before they reached a conversion tag and converted. This is enormously useful for analysts and for support teams troubleshooting misbehaving ads as it demystifies the aggregated data. The simplicity of the aggregated data fails to explain how or when the aggregated data was collected and without this context, the reports can be misunderstood.

This is particularly true when asking the analyst to answer more complex questions with the data such as: What products did my most effective ads, drive users to purchase? Or is there a relationship between the final cost of the purchased product and the Search keyword? Only cookie level data can glean these answers without specialist build aggregated reports to pivot the data in ways that may be more specific to a particular Advertiser. Cookie Level data is typically available to the Advertiser or Media Agency filtered in the following ways:

- Cookies to all Impressions only (with the option of adding interactions and IP)
- Cookies to all Clicks only

- Cookies to all Impressions and Clicks only
- Cookies to all Conversions only
- Cookies to all Impressions, Clicks and Conversions (with the option of adding interactions and IP)
- Pathway to Conversion

Each filter method provides a different output to the Advertiser although all will be in a view that looks like a spread-sheet or CSV format; make it easier to conduct analysis across the data. The benefit of choosing one filter over another is the amount of data that the file will contain.

Cookie ID	Action Type	Time of Action	Advertiser ID	Ad ID	Placement ID	Site ID
00001	Impression	3.45pm 01/01/2015	8192	9675748	49495993	4994

Figure 5.5.1 *an example of a single row of cookie level data filtered by impressions. Here a unique cookieID was seen for a specific ad to generate an impression, within a specific placement on a specific site at single point in time. A cookie level data report will typically contain many thousands of such rows.*

Cookie level data can be vast. For each passing second, millions of users are encountering ads and then taking actions or converting which creates hundreds of millions of rows in an enormous database behind the scenes at the ad server. Cookie level data is commonly misconstrued as the raw third party ad server counting database (which is built in the moments that ads are served and metrics tracked). This is rarely the case; cookie level data is constructed from the raw data later on. The raw counting database is produced and stored separately in a much more garbled format, that cannot be read by the analyst without assistance or decryption (this dataset is often referred to as the server "log files").

Cookie level data is typically provided to the Advertiser or Agency by the third party ad serving provider at additional cost, since it takes a lot of processing power to churn through and build the data set, before using up a lot of bandwidth to deliver it.

How is the data supplied?
Cookie level data can be supplied in two types.

1. A look-back of cookie activity over a period of time (depending on how long the third party ad server stores or has been collecting the data for)
2. A feed which supplies data from the previous day or week.

Look-back Data Dump
Third party ad serving providers do not usually collect cookie level data as a default. The collection of the data (in a format that can immediately be presented in a cookie level report) needs to be switched on by the trafficker or the ad server support team. From the point at which it is enabled is the earliest date on which cookie level data will be available as a report. A look-back data dump can provide to the Advertiser or Agency at a point in the future, a massive file containing some or all of the cookie level data. These files are usually very large and are difficult to open and read. It is recommended for analysts working with data of this size to instead opt for receiving a trickle of the data every day as a feed. This will allow them to build up a larger database of the data on the Advertiser or Agency site later on.

Cookie Level Feed
Requesting a feed of cookie level data from an ad serving provider allows Agencies and Advertiser to store the most granular data available with the freedom to run complex formulae across it at a later date (or in parallel to running aggregated reporting from the third party ad server analytics interface). Larger Agencies invest in technologies that pick up the cookie level data delivered by the ad server, process

it, and present it in customized ways. Some of these in-house technologies then automatically take actions as a result of the data such as buying media programmatically for search via a bid management solution or for Display inventory (see Chapter 8).

Report delivery, size estimation and storage considerations

Cookie Level datasets can be monstrously large in the look back form and even as a feed; the amount of data quickly begins to add up. Therefore the biggest cost is not the retrieval of the data but the long term storage of it. Despite the global cost of data storage still shrinking, these data files are too large for even the best ad servers in the world to afford to store data for all Advertisers for a lifetime. Furthermore as ad servers release more sophisticated technology and features, the amount of data that can be collected quickly and quietly grows, creating further storage demands.

Usually an ad server will supply cookie level data to a secure FTP site where the Agency or Advertiser will retrieve the data set on a rolling cadence. The ad server is therefore expected to deliver such data at the same time each day or week so that subsequent analysis from that data set can be planned for effectively. The trafficker could calculate how large the cookie level data files will be by looking at aggregated reports. The total number of impressions will indicate the total number of rows in the cookie level data report.

Metrics in Cookie Level Data

Cookie level data typically matches four key metrics of data to the ad server hierarchy entities; impressions, clicks, conversions and rich media interactions. On occasion cookie level data is enhanced with geographical information or verification data. Analysts and marketers that plan ahead would think getting all of the available data is the wisest decision but of course this means much larger file sizes for storage. Some ad serving providers get around this issue by offering mapping files (where names in a particular column or group of columns is just repeated over and over). In such an instance a mapping file is supplied to allow the analyst to transform the repeated data, this method shrinks the file size of the larger data set and makes the data more portable. An important consideration for cookie level data is user cookie deletion. A user can be expected to delete cookies within 90 days or receiving them, so the data is not useful long term for the purposes of retargeting the same users again (see Chapter 7). Rather the data is used to surmount trends and predict behaviours for the purposes of optimization (see Chapter 6).

Tracking impulse conversions

Since basic aggregated reporting predominantly reports at a day by day level, those campaigns requiring a faster response, targeting and buying by the hour instead of by the day, require timestamps to optimize accurately. Although day part analysis can be revealing to an extent, it fails to answer questions about user actions undertaken such as "impulse conversions" which may only happen moments after user exposer to an ad. Cookie level data can reveal this information where aggregated reporting cannot.

Pathway to Conversion Reporting

The most common reason Advertisers and Agencies use cookie level data, is to understand more about the cookie-level Pathway to Conversion (P2C) also called "Exposure to Conversion" or "E2C". This granular report shows how each converting cookieID encountered any tracked or served Advertiser activity before going on to trigger a conversion tag. The record of the total number of touch-points shown in this report for each cookieID, on its pathway to conversion before the conversion activity is typically limited, so that the file size is not too large. Smaller Advertisers are usually comfortable with a touch-point look-back of ten "events in the pathway" but the larger Advertisers, with bigger marketing teams, more budget for data analysis and complex, wider reaching campaigns may require a pathway length of more than one hundred touch-points or events.

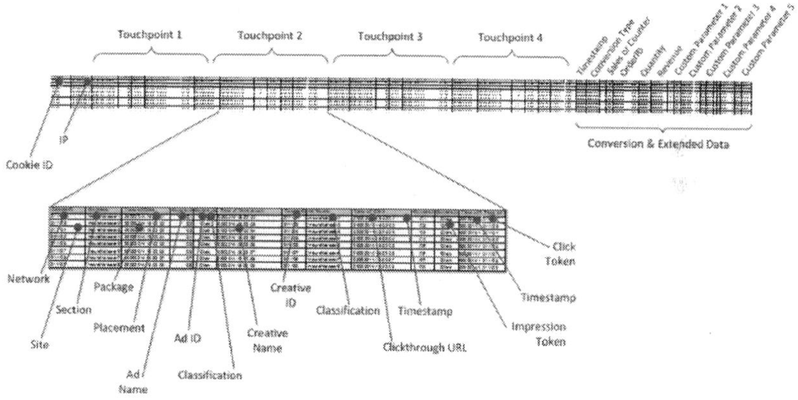

Figure 5.5.2 *Full P2C (pathway to conversion) reporting at the cookie level. Such reports are granular and very extensive. Diagram depicts just four touch points on the user pathway to conversion which in actual fact could contain many more touch points. Each touch point or event is made up of data about the Publisher page and the ad. This includes the timestamps for seeing or clicking those ads as well as ad and placement classification information. The final touch point is followed in each row by the conversion information and extended data so that for each CookieID it is clear to the analyst all the data points that were captured that in some way could be attributed to the conversion event.*

Having ten events in the pathway means that any events that occurred before the last ten are removed from the dataset, since these were so far away from the actual point of conversion that they can safely be disregarded. On the other hand, if some of these events logged the user encountering particularly impactful executions, then it may make more sense to look back further or to have a more intelligent way to filter the events. This is where attribution modelling is useful, since it can filter out or play down pathway events and provide an indication as to the contributors to the conversion from within aggregated reporting (see Chapter 4).

Advertisers that run a lot of activity, saturating the online space with ads will want to look at more events in the pathway to determine what impact all their ads are having across multiple campaigns for all converting cookies. Such situations are highly complex and require analysts to write additional programs to process the cookie level data, assigning statistical value not just to attribution that a single pathway event would had to a conversion tag, but to all conversion tags across all campaigns.

Point Solutions for Advanced Cookie Level Attribution
Beyond the conversion, some Advertisers want to analyse what impact pathway events have when such events lead to non-conversion performance events such as clicks, interactions or improvements in verification and viewability. Many technologies in the space are ill equipped to deal with this level of complexity but some point solutions have emerged to address such analytical demands. These solutions include *ClearSaleing*, *Encore Metrics* and *Visual IQ*. All can be setup to re-process cookie level data out of the ad server at the maximum granularity or have their own pixels placed in ads, click pathways and

conversion tags in order to replicate the data set in these separate systems. The issue with implementing additional tracking for this purpose is that they can come at a high additional cost to serve and track the campaign for insights which may not provide the best ROI. In addition, the additional tracking technology will be counting the impressions, clicks, conversions, actions and interactions at a very slightly different time from the ad server so there will be a minor data discrepancy which must be taken into account when conducting an analysis. For these reasons it is recommended that advanced attribution point solutions take and process the existing cookie level data, returning the insights to the Advertiser or Agency directly.

Reporting on Conversion tag Actions

Granular reporting beyond aggregated reports are referred to by some ad serving providers as "Raw Data Reports" or "Data Pass Back" reports, and offer a granularity such as an aggregated by conversion tag extended data custom parameters (see Chapter 4) or a list of conversion tag "Actions"; showing the number of times that a conversion tag has fired in addition to conversions. A report of this nature can be crucial to troubleshooting the behaviour of conversion tags as it shows the number of times a conversion tag is loading and not just the total sales or counts attributed to traffic to the conversion tag, coming from an ad.

Advertisers that look at this data are able to make a better inference about the impact of online tracked activity because of how many non-conversion Actions are taking place on the conversion tag. If the number is very small then the Advertiser-side analyst can be assured that the majority of sales are being tracked and attributed to paid-for activity online. If the number of Actions is very high then it becomes tougher to identify the sale attribution for untracked channels and may indicate a need to extend tracking to other channels or marketing activity.

Conversion-based extended data at the Cookie Level
Cookie level reporting is also one of the few places where extended data parameters from the conversion tags can be captured. This would include the OrderID, Quantity of items purchased, and revenue generated, as well as customised parameters such as the names of the products purchased or their properties. These properties are presented on each row of the cookie-level data within additional columns featured after the conversion tag name and type, where a cookieID has performed a conversion activity.

Extended Parameter Mapping Table

Custom 1	Custom 2	Custom 3	Custom 4
(Location)	(Destination)	(Mode of Transport)	(Seats)

Cookie Level Conversion Data Report

CookieiD

Conversion or Action

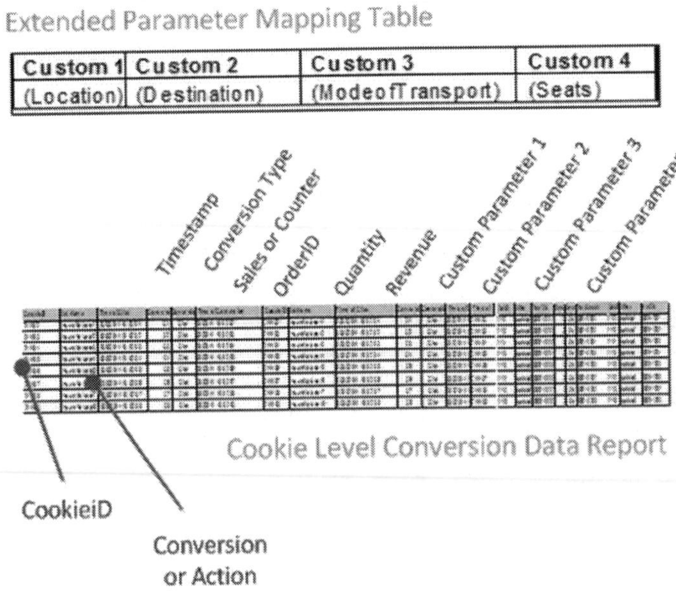

Figure 5.5.3 The Conversion Cookie Level data contains the extended data parameters passed through by the Advertiser script. Apart from the default parameters such as OrderID and Revenue, this includes the custom parameters. It is

worth the analyst consulting the trafficker to obtain the campaign setup information regarding the conversion tags so that a mapping table can be created to interpret the extended data. In this example a travel Advertiser collects data about flight bookings. Each custom parameter contains more information about the booking.

To enrich the cookie level data further, an Analyst at the Advertiser or Agency side can marry the OrderID field between the third party ad serving data and the Advertiser POS or CRM. This is best achieved bringing the two data sets together in a Data Management Platform (a DMP - see Chapter 8). Bringing these data sets together allows an Advertiser to build a full map of specific customer behaviour, since the cookieID becomes enriched with data that might offer the chance for the analyst to perform a method of profiling.

For example, the OrderID could indicate from the data in the CRM that the Order belongs to an account ID which had undertaken purchase actions over the last few years to indicate a compact buying pattern in the lead up the Christmas holiday with the same Advertiser. Using the ad serving data, the cookieID may have undertaken a certain pattern of site visits displaying the Advertisers ads before purchase. The analyst could see if there was a trend between users of look-a-like profiles and decide whether or not to inform the planners and buyers to consider buying more inventory on such sites closer to the end of the year to attract the buying behaviour from these users and similar users. Alternatively creative messaging could be adapted using DCO to perform a targeting function across inventory that had already been purchased on such sites.

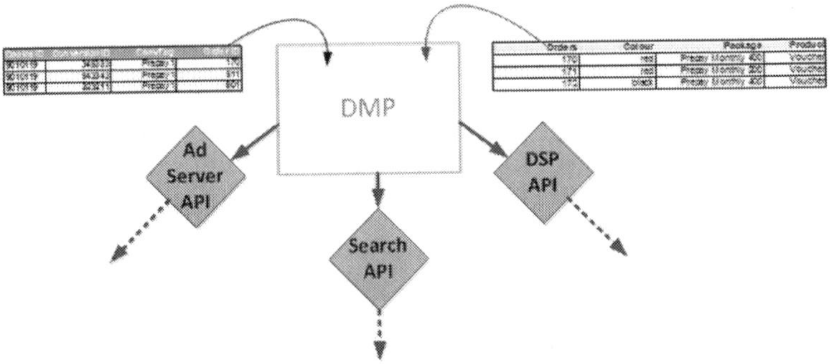

Figure 5.5.4 *the extended data from the Cookie level on the conversion tag can be married with the CRM information from the Advertiser side inside a Data Management Platform (DMP). Such systems enable the data to be connected with a programmatic optimization (see Chapter 8) in order to either adjust creative messaging or targeting for channels like DCO, adjust bid prices on keywords for paid search or auctions and bids in the programmatic space through a DSP (see Chapter 8). Of course the married data is also hugely insightful for the marketer.*

Impression and Click based token data at the Cookie Level
Publishers can pass information into the impression call or the click pathway of the ad by populating a token field in the ad tag code when the ad tag code is fired. This is executed by a Publisher created script that sits on the Publisher page. Any extra information passed through in either of these dynamic token fields can be used to populate additional columns in cookie level data. Both of these fields are highly favoured by marketers that want to get a better idea about exactly where the ad appeared on the page. Since the Publisher ad ops team is the one implementing the ad, even page scraping the domain or page level URL where the ad was displayed is not enough information to convey where about on the page the ad sat. These fields can be populated

by placement position information such as 'position 4' so that when analysing the cookie-level data, the analyst can determine if ad performance or verification are affected by the position of the ad spot.

These advanced strategies take careful planning analysis. Some Agencies or marketing teams hire Data Analysts who process such data sets full time, for the purposes of campaign optimization. Analytics come with an important cost consideration when purchasing the media in the first place, so the full budget should not be blown on ad space but also on interpreting and presenting the results. Even bolting on other technologies like third party data providers (see Chapter 8) instead of physical analysts to get this data insight, can add significant cost and therefore affect the bottom line.

What is missing from ad server reporting?

Ad server reporting is absent one key component in both aggregated and granular forms. The efforts and the controls that the trafficker implements do not always have those setting fed down to reporting. This can mean that if the trafficker changes a conversion window, a rotation setting or the definition of an audience to omit a certain geography, these "optimizations" are not recorded in reporting. If the report displays a sudden spike in activity, the cause may be down to the optimization but only the campaign management section of the ad server interface will retain a record of the existing settings and may not event have kept an accurate log of changes to those settings.

It falls to the trafficker to maintain an accurate log of both campaign setup and any subsequent changes to the settings, so that reporting can be coloured with those optimizations that were responsible for the analytics output.

The next section focusses on optimization, a responsibility for the trafficker to undertake, in response to the ad server reporting information in order to improve existing campaigns, utilising ad server settings to do so.

Chapter 6

Optimization

Chapter 6
Optimization

- Questioning reporting data
    1. Where did the report come from?
    2. What kind of report is it?
    3. Do the numbers look right? Does the data add up?
    4. What time was the report pulled, what time zone is the account in and are these the correct date ranges?
    5. Are these the correct metrics, conversion tags and hierarchy entities?
    6. Do the names of the entities in the report (including the account name) match those in the campaign management interface?
    7. What is the methodology behind these metrics?
    8. Is the shown granularity providing enough or too much information?
    9. Is there enough data in the report or were the traffic volumes large enough to gauge decent statistical accuracy?
    10. Is there a chance that the data in the report be adjusted again later on?
    11. Are all the rows and columns displaying?
    12. Was the campaign setup in way that might affect a governed outcome?
    13. Did the ad server encounter any kind of counting fault?
- What is Optimization?
- Optimizing to Campaign Objectives
    - Optimizing towards Delivery Goals (ideal for Brand Advertisers)
        - Unique Reach
        - Target Audience

        - Verification (quality safety) goals and impact
    - Optimizations towards Performance Goals (ideal for Direct Response Advertisers)
        - Engagement and Interaction
        - Total Clicks
        - Total Conversions or E-Conversions
        - ROI (& extended data) goals
- Optimization Sample
- Recording changes in Optimization strategy

An analysis of the ad serving data early and often in a campaign provides an invaluable feedback mechanism to the Advertiser or Agency. By either making changes at a creative level or making changes to the planning and buying strategies, the outcome of the overall campaign can be influenced before its final impression has been delivered. Reporting therefore can act as the safety net to ensuring a campaign ends meeting the campaign goals or it can be used to take lessons from one campaign to apply to the next. The application of this learning to a live campaign is referred to as either a Media or a Creative optimization, depending on whether the media planner/buyer or the trafficker takes action.

The following section explains how to query the reporting data, before explaining how to understand it, to take positive action on it.

Questioning Reporting Data

Once the relevant report has been run and exported from the third party ad serving reporting interface. The analyst needs to make sense of the data. The following questions add much needed context to the data and ensure that it is of sufficient quality to make optimization decisions from. The analyst should know the answer to these questions before proceeding. If the answers are not available from the report or the help section within the interface itself, the analyst can usually contact the support team at the third party ad serving provider.

1. **Where did the report come from?**
   Having a colleague supply the data is not enough of a safeguard to ensure the numbers have not been tampered with by human hands. This is why third party ad server reporting interfaces grant access to a very wide range of users including the Publishers and the Creative Agencies, so that they can ensure the data is genuine.

   Pulling a campaign directly from the third party ad serving reporting interface or securely receiving the data from the third party ad serving provider's delivery system (email or FTP) is the only way to ensure the validity of the source of the data.

2. **What kind of report is it?**
   The report being pulled from the interface may not contain the right metrics to answer questions about the delivery or performance of the campaign. Pulling a report and running it, only to find it contains the wrong data can be frustrating and very time consuming.

   Check the report description and title before running or downloading it. If it is not clear if it is the right report, ad servers will have supporting documentation or hep sections to define the metrics it contains. In addition it is possible to display a preview of the report template without any data in it to see if it looks like it might be the right one.

3. **Do the numbers look right? Does the data add up?**
   It pays to start with a hypothesis before looking at a report. This sets the analysts' expectations about the data that will

be revealed in the report. In addition it is worth tallying up the numbers manually to check that the total columns add up. If the numbers are wildly off, something might be wrong with the report, the data or the campaign.

If the data does not look right, pull the report again to see if the data looks any better. A single glitch or bug in the reporting interface for a temporary period of time could be affecting the way the numbers are outputted. If the data does not appear as expected, the trafficker can go back and test the ads, retargeting tags and conversion tags with *Fiddler*, checking that they right calls are being made to the server. These same pieces of code can also be tested in the live environment of the campaign to see if the code is implemented correctly or if the tags are being affected by other code on the page. If everything is performing correctly, read the rest of the questions in section and perform those checks before consulting the support team at the third party ad serving provider.
For reports that contain conversion data, check the conversion window settings and attribution settings for conversions. These may be causing the total numbers of conversions to be higher or lower than expected.

4. **What time was the report pulled, what time zone is the account in and are these the correct date ranges?**
   Data processing occurs at different times and in different time zones. Processing can also be affected by the time zone that the Advertiser, Agency or Publisher account is set to. Pulling a report in a different time zone to the time zone on the account can mean that the latest data may not be available yet. In addition to this, it is common to pull a report with a date range that did not match the dates that the campaign was live.

To resolve this the trafficker can check the account settings in the campaign management interface. In addition the analyst can check that the date ranges in the report, match the ones required. It may sound obvious but a sizeable amount of queries about data are down to incorrectly matching date ranges.

5. **Are these the correct metrics, conversion tags and hierarchy entities?**

   In haste it is possible to pull reports with the wrong metrics inside or looking at conversions for conversion tags that are not on the pages the analyst is looking to analyse.

   When creating any naming conventions these should be shared with all parties so that it is clear which names match with what. Also analysts should be sure to understand ad server hierarchy levels, for new beginners it can be common to confuse a placement with a package for instance.

6. **Do the names of the entities in the report (including the account name) match those in the campaign management interface?**

   The analyst may be working from information which is not true, being asked to pull conversion tag results for completely the wrong conversion tag.

   The analyst can flip between the campaign management interface and the reporting interface to ensure that the right entities are being selected. The analyst should be wary that if the Advertiser does not use an integrated tag management system it is not possible to confirm which page conversion tags are implemented on. Analysts that suspect faults in conversion data should ask traffickers to check that conversion tags have been implemented correctly.

7. **What is the methodology behind these metrics?**
   The definition of a metric may provide an insight into why it is low, high or zero. For instance the definition of an impression according to IAB is to count when the server receives the ad request. An impression elsewhere might count when the ad is displayed on the page. Comparing reports of the same activity but different methodologies is not recommended, the data will never be the same.
   Also, not all counting systems can count things at exactly the same point in time. Usually one system is counting things before another which at ad serving scale can result in different figures when systems are compared.

   To resolve this, the analyst should check to see if a known and accepted discrepancy exists between a comparative report. The *IAB* confirm that an accepted level of industry discrepancy for reports that track the same things in different systems (using the same methodology) should not be over or below ten per cent. There are three types of possible reporting discrepancy.
   a. Between data from the same source (reports pulled from the same ad server)
   b. Between data comparing third party ad server with Publisher ad server
   c. Between data comparing the third party ad server with another technology provider such as a 4th party or third party ad server

   Although an ad serving provider can commit to investigating reporting discrepancies, type b. is much more challenging to resolve, since the two types of system report in very different ways and it is in the best interest of the Publisher to report inflated figures. Instead Publishers can be granted access to the third party ad server reporting interface.

8. **Is the shown granularity providing enough or too much information?**

   The most granular kinds of reporting are difficult to action without spending more time or resource on trying to extract the right insights. On the flip side, if a single ad tag had been provided to a Publisher to run on all page types of their website, reports could not give an indication of performance by site section for instance.

   Getting to know which reports will display what level of data granularity will make the process of analysing and pulling reports less frustrating. Displaying a preview of the report template before running it will give a good indication of the level of granularity that will be available. It also helps to have a strong understanding of the definitions of the various levels of reporting granularity. If reporting does not seem to yield granular enough data, analyse the cookie level data instead. By comparing the domain URL captured from the page level where the ad was delivered and amalgamate up the results by subdomain, the analyst can get section summaries without having to traffic more ad tags. To save costs on analytics however, the trafficker should create more tags, replicating the same ad assignment to placement setup with section names, for the Publisher ad ops team to implement.

9. **Is there enough data in the report or were the traffic volumes large enough to gauge decent statistical accuracy?**

   When dealing with very big numbers, very small numbers in reporting become close to insignificant. If a campaign was delivering one hundred million impressions, a placement or a single ad version that had incremented a thousand impressions alongside versions that had incremented millions of impression, is a version that may just as well had incremented none at all.

The trafficker and campaign planning team should have accounted for distribution of data across the setup. This is relevant to the creation of audience segments and versions for DCO. On such a scale, wait for ad server entities to increment larger amounts of data before conducting an analysis. This is why it is recommended for the analyst to wait a day or two before pulling reports for the first time when a campaign goes live, ensuring that the data displayed are more than just the Publisher running a few tests on the ads while implementing them. If the data continues to be too small the trafficker can take the execution of the campaign setup altogether or simplify the experiment.

10. **Is there a chance that the data in the report be adjusted again later on?**
The analyst will want to conduct an analysis across the final results rather than have to undergo two rounds of analysis on almost the same data set because the numbers change. In particular, numbers in ad server reporting sometimes change for conversions and for Search channel cost data. Conversions can change when the ad server conducts several rounds of data processing owing to complex attribution modelling and de-duplication. The *Atlas* ad server used to run one round of conversion processing, delivery a near-accurate conversion figure to get early results available in reporting, before conducting a more thorough sweep and delivery within twenty four hours. Also *Google Adwords* sometimes recalculates search engine cost data over the course of a week, which is presented in ad server reporting.

In all instances check with the support team at the ad serving provider that the reporting numbers displayed will not change and get confirmation about timings and conditions on which the data can change. For conversion data, the analyst can wait until conversion processing is complete before pulling reports for the more accurate numbers. For search cost data, the analyst can pull reports daily for the previous week look back and compare those numbers to ensure cost data has remained fixed and is not changing.

11. **Are all the rows and columns displaying?**
    Sometimes, particularly with large Advertisers, old campaigns can get archived by the ad server to speed up the time it takes to run big reports. This is also sometimes true of rows or entities that display no data or zeroes. This is useful to speeding up the performance of the reporting interface, but is an incomplete view for an analyst that may want to take old or low figures into account when analysing the data.

    If a report is pulled and rows or columns expected seem to be missing, the analyst can run the report again, ensuring that the filters included are not filtering out certain metrics, entities or forms of data. Also it is worth the trafficker checking the account settings to see if and when the ad server is archiving any of the data. Where reports cannot be retrieved back to a certain date, the analyst can check to see how long the ad server keeps data stored for by asking the support team at the ad serving provider. In addition there is merit in asking the same support team to check that none of the old data is being archived.

12. **Was the campaign setup in way that might affect a governed outcome?**

Careful planning is essential in the campaign setup process. If the trafficker and the creative developer are less experienced, they may not have thought about the report outcome as a result of the setup. Creating too few tags for instance won't give enough granularity to provide the most insightful results. In addition there might be high numbers associated with more negative metrics such as incomplete video plays for Instream or no click data on a high reach Display execution.

Before starting any Rich Media campaign, the trafficker should have a kick off call with the creative developer and Publisher, making sure interactions are in the right place. Following this, the ad implementation should be thoroughly checked during the ad QA process. Once the campaign is live, verification reporting will report errors in targeting on the Publisher side such as ineffective brand safety. By checking delivery reports early and often, the analyst can avoid results that demonstrate an incorrect implementation by having the trafficker work with Publishers fix incorrect implementations. To reach certain goals, a campaign should be correctly optimized; this is covered in full detail at the end of the section.

13. **Did the ad server encounter any kind of counting fault?**

If the data reports significantly lower or higher volumes for delivery and performance there is a possibility there could be a counting fault in the ad server itself. This is a very rare occurrence and should only be considered as a concern as a last resort.

After all tags have been double checked and there still appears to be bad data in the report, the analyst can contact the support team at the third party ad serving provider. This team will be able to conduct an investigation. In the rare occurrence of a fault, data can usually be re-processed and re-published to the correct time periods in ad server reporting. Depending on the severity of the issue depends on how long this fix will take. When considering using an ad server for the first time, the provider can supply information about data security and data integrity. The Advertiser or Agency can expect certificates of accreditation from well-known internet and hardware security institutions who vet the ad server to ensure that data faults and server downtime are virtually zero.

Once the analyst has established that the data is an accurate reflection of the live or completed campaign, the process of optimization can begin.

What is Optimization?

Optimization is utilising ad serving data to make an improved change in the campaign setup. This change can either occur in the ad serving campaign management screen or adjustments can be undertaken by the planners and buyers, changing which Publishers and audiences the ads still to run would run against. These are referred to as Creative Optimizations (in the ad server interface) or Media Optimizations (adjustments to the media plan outside the ad server).

Chapter 3 - DCO explained how the ad server can make use of the ad serving data without anyone needing to pull reports. The ad server would make use of the data in real time to adjust the creative optimization of the ads using "auto-optimization". The remainder of this section will look instead at the alternative, manual optimization. This means exporting reports from the reporting interface and having an analyst look at the data and instruct the trafficker or the media planner to make changes to the campaign to improve performance or delivery. In this sense optimization might allow an Advertiser to reach a campaign goal faster or exceed it, ideally without increasing costs, but reducing them in order to do so.

The most stringent of Advertisers will insist that optimizations occur as often as possible. This means implementing an optimization strategy and then waiting for the adjustments to take effect before optimizing again. It is for this reason that having real-time time available data is not so useful for real-time optimization on small-scale campaigns. Optimizations will usually need a minimum of a day or twos worth of data to clarify if the adjustments have worked and daily aggregated reporting from the ad server is usually sufficient for this need.

Optimizing to Campaign Objectives

Optimization means making the media budget go further. First, the analyst can pull cost reporting from the reporting interface to see where the majority of the media spend is going, then look more deeply at the data to see if those Publishers or the Creative is driving ad spend to those goals effectively or having a strong contribution to it. If goals are not effectively being met (or to improve things further) the analyst can consider having traffickers and planners make some the following adjustments as optimizations, depending on the campaign goal.

Optimizing towards Delivery Goals (ideal for Brand Advertisers)

If an ad can be seen by the most relevant audience it can have the most impact, even if the Advertiser has not set any performance goals. By ensuring ads are delivered to the most quality, relevant pages, at the right reach and frequency and to the target audience, there is a better chance to create awareness with those users that encounter the ads.

Unique Reach

The optimization of Unique reach is a goal to find an untouched audience or recognising how much exposure a unique audience requires to cement the impact the ad can have on those users. It is advised to first set a baseline to establish how many unique eyeballs or users the campaign is reaching. To do this, pull a reach report by Publisher and by Channel. Some channels and Publishers may be more effective than others at reaching the intended audience. This data can then be combined with frequency information to show the levels of frequency that each Publisher and Channel is incrementing on each unique user. Combining this with cost reporting will show what it is costing to deliver at the baseline.

The next step is to consider the importance of reaching a unique audience. Usually the goal is harbouring a goal of performance to reach a certain number of sales. If this is a goal that can be reached online then the analyst can consider optimizing the campaign to conversions as a primary goal over unique reach. By analysing the attribution funnel in cookie level data, the analyst might reveal that might show that frequency is more effective than unique reach at driving that conversion goal, so frequency can be adjusted to match this need either on the third party ad server or with the Publisher ad ops team directly. Sometimes the goal for unique reach does not tie back to online conversions but instead might be designed to his an effective "GRP" goal. Here an Advertiser will combine the online reach data with reach data for other media channels such as TV to calculate, project and forecast sales offline.

Unique Reach - Creative Optimization

- To perform a creative optimization on unique reach (show a different message to new eyeballs) requires the use of retargeting (See Chapter 7) such that old users are labelled and fall into a defined audience where new users are a separate audience.

- If retargeting is combined with DCO it will not cost the Advertiser much more to create personalised messaging for the retargeting audience, improving the campaign ROI.

Unique Reach - Media Optimization

- The unique site overlap report will show which sites are offering the best unique reach, an analyst running this report can have planners and buyers adjust their buying strategy accordingly.

- A reach and frequency report will reveal the effective frequency for sites, placements and ads so that the frequency cap can be adjusted at the Publisher ad server. Less budget could effectively be transitioned away from frequency to hit a higher unique reach goal.

- If a reach goal needs to be very high, it may be more effective to pay Publishers based on alternative payment models such as sponsorship or to utilise a channel like Affiliate.

- A device report will show high delivery to mobile devices that do not support third party cookies. These devices will hinder a unique reach goal since it would not be possible to determine if the same users are receiving ads cross-device.

- Analysts can also conduct an analysis on conversion tags for total "actions" and compare this data to site side analytics reports on referral information. If high volumes of traffic are reaching the Advertiser site without being tracked by the third party ad server and these users are arriving to the website from Publisher sites directly, there is a gap of user traffic that the ad server is not capturing. The analyst can report these gaps to the planners and buyers to reach out to these Publishers to implement third party tracking and delivery. Without this in place, true optimization to unique reach goals becomes much more challenging.

Target audience

Use content classification verification reporting to establish the baseline and distribution of the audience on a non-specific audience buy across multiple publishers. The affinity between audiences and content or audience verification reporting specifically will reveal what audience groups are seeing ads. Once it is clear which geographies and inferred demographics the users belong to, the optimization can begin.

Target Audience - Creative Optimization

- Where higher cost ad formats such as Rich Media are delivering to an ineffective audience, the trafficker can add audience targeting to the campaign setup in the third party ad server interface.

- Fluctuations of user traffic for various demographics are known to map to times of the day. Rather than pay for additional audience targeting data, the trafficker can utilise ad controls to show different creative messages at different times of the day.

- To lower creative costs, the Advertiser can utilise DCO and retargeting for personalisation as well as creative message sequencing.

Target Audience - Media Optimization

- Since Verification reporting for content and audience verification, will reveal the audience types that Publishers provide, planners and buyers can use this data to spend less with Publishers that do not attract the target audience. This saves money by circumventing the need to increase spend on a guaranteed audience targeting with that Publisher.

- If planners and buyers invest in inventory with a price based guarantee against a target audience goal, such as geography, there is an optimization opportunity. When the activity goes live, the analyst can run a verification geo report to catch Publishers that fail to setup the geo targeting. The remuneration of the failure can be spent on audience targeting with a Publisher that does not breach the audience targeting conditions.

Verification (quality safety) goals and impact
To deliver more quality impressions and user viewability, the analyst begins by comparing campaign verification and viewability results with the benchmark report for the same Advertiser vertical as the Advertiser in question. Alternatively it makes sense to look at verification reporting from previous campaigns with the same Advertiser across the same Publishers. This will set a baseline from which the Publishers and Creative in use must meet.

Verification - Creative Optimization

- Viewability reporting or Rich Media reporting can be used to reveal the average view duration that users look at ads for. The trafficker can use this information to remove ads from rotation that have low view duration. The same optimization can be made with Instream reporting.

Verification - Media Optimization

- An analyst can use the brand safety and domain URL features of verification reporting to produce a blacklist of sites that breach the brand safety requirements. By issuing this blacklist to the Publishers, optimizes the inventory by ensuring ads are not shown again the blacklist in future. This proactively negates the risk of a high cost associated to bad PR around a failure of brand safety. This cost can add hindrance to the cost of running the campaign in the first place.

- Pre-emptive verification utilises a similar strategy. The unseen benefit is that inventory which adheres to verification requirements is considered a higher quality and lower quality inventory could be bought at a lower cost to satisfy a secondary reach goal.

- A buyer could introduce a new cost model to pay on viewable impressions only. This penalises poor viewability in the marketplace and means Publishers may make more of an effort to optimize media to appear in view. The in-view guarantee may inflate media costs which the buyer must consider worthy of the in-view goal before proposing the cost model adaption.

Optimizations towards Performance Goals (ideal for Direct Response Advertisers)

Determining the performance of the ads is seen by most Advertisers as the most important consideration when running digital campaigns. Any trends in reporting which can be shown to boost performance are worth carefully monitoring and applying to a wider audience reach. It is important also for the analyst to consider not just optimizing to one performance goal. High levels of engagement might diminish clicks or conversions for instance, so gathering a wide set of data before presenting the argument for the optimization to the trafficker and marketing team is a best practice. As with Delivery goals, storing old performance information or looking at publicly available data for the purposes of benchmarking allows expectations about performance to be set from the beginning of the campaign. Performance goals exist for engagement, clicks, number of conversions and value of conversions as an ROI.

Engagement and Interaction

Interaction and engagement is only going to be available on Rich Media and video ads. Although the cost to serve formats in these 'channels' will be higher, engagement can be a valuable indication of performance if creative and media fail to instigate users to click, convert and buy from ads.

Brand Advertisers that rarely look at performance would do well to monitor engagement levels in reporting. At the least, they can provide an indication of awareness.

To establish a baseline for engagement and interaction as a success criteria, the analyst can begin by checking the benchmark and performance reporting for engagement on previous campaigns. At a minimum, format performance for engagement by country and Advertiser vertical will set an expectation before optimization begins. The goal is then to beat the benchmark or improve on the previous campaign.

Engagement - Creative Optimization

- Sometimes creative developers and designers recycle old creative templates to save time but user engagement has an affinity towards novelty and difference. The Creative Agency can make the ad more appealing to the user by using the latest available components in the ad serving provider supplied component pack for Flash. Inspiration for new executions can be attained from ad serving provider showcases. Some providers also offer in-person support to inspire innovation based on the available technology. More innovative executions will boost engagement levels.

- Creative designers can now utilise HTML5 to deliver executions with better opportunity for engagement through motion, touch and device-specific features. The Advertiser may wish to consider paying the Creative Agency to deliver a new execution, if the campaign is already running, if the campaign is not performing well on engagement across the board.

- Instream Video, runs at a higher media cost and cost to serve but is shown to provide significant opportunity for user engagement. In particular the analyst may have to consider switching from VAST formats to VPAID or DCO for Instream. These formats are emerging and will attract higher levels of engagement due to their novelty.

- The analyst can look at ad server reporting by format cross-Publisher. The reports may indicate that some formats attract better engagement than others. The analyst can instruct the trafficker to drop low engagement formats from the placements or up-weight those with higher levels of engagement. It is possible that if the frequency and reach levels of badly performing formats were adjusted that they might improve to even higher levels that those ads that appear to have high engagement at low frequency rates.

- The analyst should also consider looking at cookie level data to extract information about what ads and formats may have influenced levels of engagement in events on the pathway to a specific custom interaction.

- In addition optimizing to a refined audience targeting may reveal an affinity between audience types and engagement levels to present the rich media ads to those audiences that are more inclined to engage and display ads to the rest.

Engagement - Media Optimization

- Analysts may wish to look closely at engagement reports and interaction metrics to see which Networks, Publishers, Sites, Site sections, Placements and whole channels are driving the optimum interactions. The analyst can advise the media planners and buyers to adjust the media plan according the results to improve the campaign performance.

- Traffickers can place retargeting tags (see Chapter 7) on the custom interactions within the creative and then programmatic buying (see Chapter 8) could be used to seek out those same users again by buying media that they are actively on. By extending further media cost to those users above all others, the optimization is being undertaken on engagement.

- By introducing a cost model based on engagement, such as cost per engagement or pay out on a video duration metric, the campaign will self-optimize towards this goal.

Total Clicks

The analyst could begin optimizing to clicks by establishing a baseline: checking the benchmark and performance reporting for clicks on previous campaigns. At a minimum, format performance for clicks by country and Advertiser vertical will set an expectation before optimization begins. Previous effective click cost data (based on a CPM) will also provide an indication as to the expected number of clicks based on the spend alone.

Total Clicks - Creative Optimization

- Standard reporting will indicate which ads and creative drove the most clicks from within the placements. The trafficker can adjust the ad controls such as weighting on placements so that ads and creative attracting more clicks are shown more often. If different creative is being shown to different Publisher sites, consider swapping the creative over if creative of the same dimensions with different messaging is performing better elsewhere as long as the Publisher can be ruled out as a reason for the improvement. Collating all historical reporting together can help form a benchmark to be clear if the Publisher is responsible for the improvement. Since the adjustment to the creative happens in the ad server, the live campaign will not be affected by the change.

- If creative messaging is not standardised across all ad sizes and one message is found to be responsible for improved performance, consider having the Creative Agency build addition ads with the optimum message. The trafficker can then put these into rotation. To cut creative costs, consider using DCO from the outset to take advantage of dynamic text fields.

- In this process the analyst can analyse the user pathway to the click events. A pathway to conversion report may indicate that clicks are influenced by other ads and creative messages.

- Some ad servers filter multiple clicks on the same ad. If multiple clicks by a single user can still be classed as a contribution to the goal, consider converting the display ad to rich media and counting additional clicks using custom interactions.

Total Clicks - Media Optimization

- Pulling campaign reports will indicate which sites, sections, Publishers, Networks, channels and formats provided the most clicks. Planners and buyers can consider revising the proposed media spend, distributing the remaining budget to better performers where possible. This may include excluding some Publishers from the remainder of the campaign.

- Before removing anything from the plan, the analyst can look at pathway to conversion and cross channel reporting to ensure that any changes to the media plan will not inadvertently affect click performance elsewhere.

- Pathway to conversion may also provide stronger case to demonstrate that some Publishers are adding no value across the board.

- For search specifically planners and buyers could pay more for the keywords that drive the most clicks. Keyword path analysis can play a role in showing which keywords and combinations of keywords are driving clicks across all tracked channels.

- The analyst can use cost data to determine how much it is costing to get a click, even if none of the activity is running on a CPC model by calculating based on the impression to click ratio (CTR). Use this to calculate an effective CPC. Propose paying Publishers on a CPC is an unlikely ask but it will ensure that the media is totally geared towards click performance. Use the effective CPC to convince the Publisher to lower the cost of the media so that the impression costs will yield the click costs based on the performance to date. A CPC model might be possible across affiliate activity.

- Channel reporting may reveal that some channels have a greater impression to click ratio such as email. So long as the reach volumes are high enough to reach the click goal with the available inventory, use the ad serving data to demonstrate that planners can spend more across those channels.

Total Conversions or E-Conversions

The analyst can begin optimizing to conversions by running conversion reports by format as well as by Publisher. This will indicate where and when conversions are occurring. Establishing a baseline for conversions as a success criteria, can be more challenging for conversions, as the amalgamated conversion data in the benchmark might include conversion events that are not comparable to an Advertisers goal. For this reason, previous campaign data is more valuable to set expectations.

Audience quality plays an important role in conversion optimization. This does not always mean making an adjustment to planned delivery by Publisher. It can mean acquiring more data to provide better audience intelligence. For instance, those users with insurance policies up for renewal may have made this information available to a data collection company. Marketers could use the marketing budget to borrow the data to establish which cookieIDs are more valuable to the conversion goal. An advanced data management strategy could achieve this using a DMP and be followed by a creative or media optimization. In addition it is important to decide what conversions are the established goal. Selecting view based conversions or click based conversions come with their own considerations. Also, with conversion optimization, where click-to-land is priority for the Advertiser, click based conversions would take priority and the attribution settings on the conversion tag can be setup to meet this need.

Total Conversions - Creative Optimization

- Just as with clicks, standard ad server reporting will show which ads and creative drove the most conversions. The trafficker can adjust the ad controls accordingly so that these ads are shown more frequently. As with clicks and engagements, the analyst can consider how other ads and creative in the same campaign contributed to the conversion before making any changes.

- Conversions are also affected by the Advertiser site, so analysts can also focus on the clickthrough URL to establish if conversions were more likely if the user arrived on a particular landing page.

- Advanced Time to convert reporting will reveal if the conversion window has been set too liberally or not. Having the trafficker make the adjustment to the windows on the conversion tag based on the analysis will ensure conversions are not being missed.

- The trafficker could also carve off some of the audience to see if A/B testing exposes that one audience performs better on conversion events that another. The traffickers can then work with the analyst to optimize to this audience.

Total Conversions - Media Optimization

- Once again, the analyst can look at which sites, sections, Publishers, Networks and channels provided the most conversions and consider removing those that are not driving as many conversions or any at all from the media plan.

- For e-conversions, it will be essential for the analyst to look further up the conversion funnel in cookie level data at the pathway to conversion. Although engagement mapping will take into consideration the conversion influence by other factors, the analyst should keep checking reporting to ensure the most effective attribution model is in place for the optimum representation of e-conversions.

- With regards to cost model in display, the media planners and buyers could agreement to pay Publishers based on an agreed attribution model as a CPA. This will ensure the Advertiser's unique conditions for conversion optimization are being met in the buying cycle.

- For the search channel, the media could be optimized by the trafficker by paying more for the keywords that drive the most conversions and bringing in P2C data to enhance the decision.

ROI (& extended data) goals

The ROI is revealed in the conversion tag extended data, so the analyst will want to look at cookie level data on the conversion tag. Where the extended parameters have been populated the cookie and the pathway to conversion are the key to ROI. Comparing costs for media and technology with the revenue figure (real costs for the purchased item) will reveal the ROI.

ROI Creative Optimization

- The analyst can determine if there is a link between creative, format and the final revenue.

- The trafficker could implement a DCO campaign to lower creative costs across the board, improving ROI whatever the final revenue figure turns out to be.

ROI Media Optimization

- The analyst could build profiling around those cookies that spend more money and target users which have similar behaviours with a media and creative strategy that worked to get the profiled users to buy.

- The analyst could establish a baseline for the audience based on content verification reporting and by Publisher to ensure that planners and buyers adjust the media plan to buy across more affluent audiences.

- As with other forms of media optimization, the planners and buyers could choose to pay Publishers based on an ROI model. This would be articular effective across performance channels such as affiliates.

Optimization Sample

The audience size for any optimization (both manual and automatic) will also dictate the success for the optimization strategy. A very small audience size does not provide enough data to give a true indication of performance when scaled up (because in a smaller group some users do not behave according to the general population but can swing favour if the consideration set is low).

Recording changes in Optimization strategy

Successful strategies can be kept on record and potentially reapplied to campaigns under the same or similar conditions later on. Traffickers can record where and when changes to a setup are made, what data drove the choice to make the optimization, and the outcome of those optimizations so that those that yield positive results can be re-applied later on or in a future campaign.

We have looked generally at how reporting data can be applied to campaigns for the purposes of optimization but one form of optimization has proven to be consistently effective at reaching some goals. In particular, it is cyclical nature of auto optimization that has driven high adoption for behavioural targeting, the retargeting to users that have encountered the Advertiser before.

Chapter 7

Retargeting and Privacy

Chapter 7 – Retargeting and Privacy

- Retargeting Tags
- *Figure 7.1*
- Cookie Pools
- Retargeting Windows
- Retargeting for Creative Optimization
    - *Figure 7.2*
    - Dynamic Retargeting
    - *Figure 7.3*
    - Carousel Ads
    - *Figure 7.4*
- Privacy and Behavioural targeting
    - The Ad Choices Program
    - *Figure 7.5*
    - Do Not Track
- Retargeting for Media Optimization

Retargeting is a way to reach leads and former customers over the noise of other ads online and is considered to be the most evolved and effective optimization strategy. Using retargeting tags allows the trafficker to plan how creative messaging and media buying will automatically be adjusted if the ad server has encountered or not encountered a user before. This Chapter will explain the workings of retargeting and how it adds an extra dimension to DCO enabling a programmatic media buying strategy. In this sense, retargeting can be classed as an automatic optimization as oppose to a manual optimization.

Retargeting Tags

For retargeting to work, the trafficker needs to generate a retargeting tag from the campaign management interface of the third party ad server. Retargeting tags behave in a very similar fashion to conversion tags. These are small pieces of code that, like the conversion tags, are sent to the site management team at the Advertiser site to implement the tags into places on the site which would benefit from capturing user behaviour. Such locations include product pages, landing pages, pages in the booking or payment process and the "thank you" or confirmation page. Strategically placed, these tags can be set to trigger when the user behaviour is performed. Examples include when a user prematurely closes their browser window before completing a transaction, or demonstrating some interest in a product of a particular size and colour. The flexibility of these tags means that the strategy for the Advertiser or Agency can be complex; building groups of users that have exhibited a particular on-site behaviour.

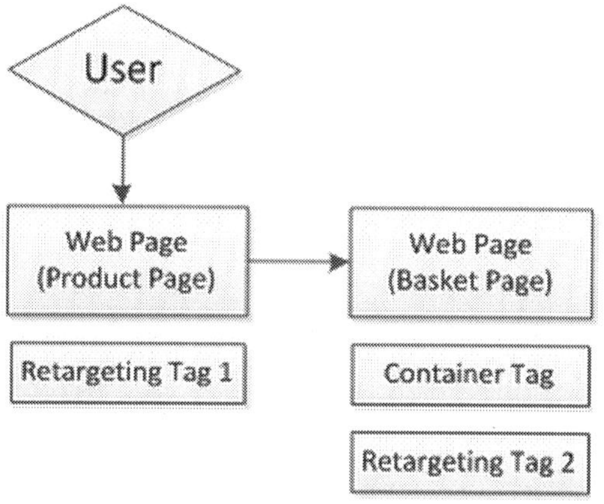

Figure 7.1 *Retargeting tags are flexible and can be added to multiple locations to build up groups of users that have performed similar actions or have arrived on similar pages.*

Since retargeting tags can also be piggybacked on conversion tags they can capture some of the same extended data parameters that a sales conversion tag can capture. This allows for retargeting strategies that only show certain ads to users that, for instance, spent a certain amount of money on a purchase. Retargeting tags can also be placed inside ads themselves during the development and setup stages of the campaign. Such retargeting tags can load when the ad loads or when the user triggers a certain interaction or behaviour inside the ad. Some Advertisers adopt a policy of ensuring that users should never be allowed to encounter an Advertiser without being labelled using retargeting. This method would ensure that future efforts to message this user would become more personalised. This is based on knowing that a strategy used in the past to target this user had failed to incite a conversion and that a different strategy should be adopted.

It is not uncommon for Publishers to restrict the use of retargeting tags inside ads on their sites and networks. Building such retargeting groups effectively diminishes the value of the audiences that the Publishers are attracting and trying to sell against. This was referenced in Chapter 2 as "Publisher Leakage". Having the creative developer and trafficker, checking Publisher specifications before implementing a retargeting strategy into ads directly, will ensure that no expectations are being breached once the ad tag code is trafficked.

Cookie Pools

Retargeting Tags can be implemented during a campaign for the purposes of optimization, but work best if placed before the campaign begins, to ensure that users can be targeted based on this information from the outset of the campaign. When a user encounters a retargeting tag their cookieID is placed into retargeting group or "cookie pool". This pool is a way of categorising that user so that they can be messaged later on.

Some ad servers allow Advertisers to see how many users are in a specific cookie pool. This allows the Advertiser to know if it is worth setting up a campaign or ad specifically targeting the group. Very small pools are not always worth considering because on a big scale the effort to target these users later on can cost more in man-hours to set up and manage, than the potential increase in earning by targeting those users again.

Retargeting Windows

The aim of retargeting is to show an ad to that same user at a later date with the hope that by seeing the ad, they will be contributing to the campaign goal. The opportunity to build up a pool of cookies and show that pool targeted ads at a later date is attractive to marketers but is limited by a time frame which is rarely adjustable. Most ad servers offer a 90 day window in which those users in the pool can be retargeted. After that point, the cookies are removed from the pool (but as long as cookies are always being added to the pool, it will not diminish entirely).

Retargeting for Creative Optimization

Retargeting strategies for large Advertisers are rarely simple affairs. If a user can perform a number of actions on an Advertiser site or if a web-based product catalogue is particularly large, then re-targeting rules in the ad server need to be structured and prioritised. Users that go to a product page and then purchase and pay via a gift voucher, present some interesting possibilities for the Advertiser later on. Should a user encounter an ad from the Advertiser later, the ad can be designed to use the retargeting information so that the creative does not contain a reference to that product again.

Within the ad server interface, a retargeting audience is treated as any other audience type. In Chapter 4 we explored how the ad server can be setup to consider if each user is a suitable match for an audience type before moving on to the next 'rule'. The trafficker has the option to setup ads on the placement level so that when a user encounters an ad, the corresponding creative can be shown. This option works most effectively with DCO. The trafficker can ensure that a corresponding version matches with the user behaviour that triggered the retargeting tag.

For instance if a user visits the basket page but never reaches the confirmation page, two retargeting tags can be setup, one on each page. The trafficker can setup a target audience in the on the placement level that declares that if a user is not in the cookie pool for the confirmation page retargeting tag (but is in the one for the basket page) then the version displayed should have a message related to the user abandoning to shopping process. To make the creative message more relevant to the user, it could be adjusted to specifically reference the items that were not purchased. This requires a more complex form of retargeting called "Dynamic Retargeting".

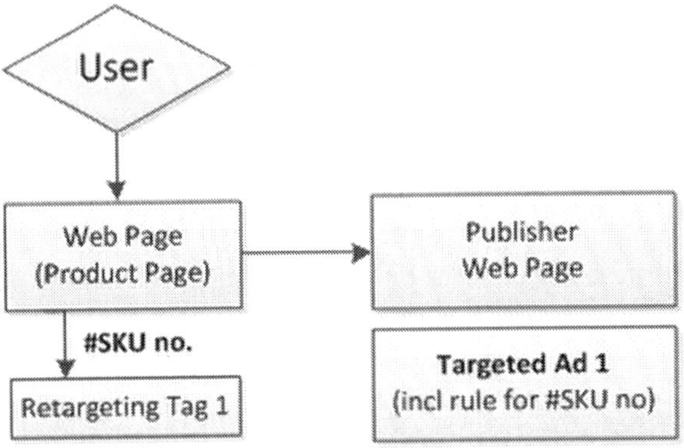

Figure 7.2 *Dynamic retargeting tags allow Advertiser to pass dynamic variables into the retargeting tag so that the variables can be used in the version or ad later on. In this example the SKU number (a unique product identifier) is passed in the retargeting tag as the user cookieID is placed into the retargeting pool. When the same user navigates to the Publisher page, the displayed ad or version is targeted based on the SKU number, featuring the same product again or displays an ad which corresponds to the product. The decision is made based on the rules setup for targeting by the trafficker.*

Dynamic Retargeting

Retargeting tags have the ability to capture a unique identifier, an example of which would be a product ID. A script can be implemented by the Advertiser site management team, allowing the page that the retargeting tag is sitting on, to pass a value into the tag. As a user arrives on the Advertisers page (such as an e-commerce page featuring a jacket) the retargeting tag on that page receives the product ID passed in via the script. The retargeting tag then it sends a call back to ad server to add the user to the retargeting pool specific to the dynamic retargeting tag while writing the specific variable to the user's cookie. This way, the user becomes linked to that variable and the ID can be recovered when the Advertiser comes to show that user an ad later on.

The user is now associated with all other users that encounter this same tag but the difference with a dynamic retargeting tag is the deployment of the tag. A dynamic retargeting tag can be deployed to all product pages on the Advertiser ecommerce site as a single piece of code. The unique identifier passed into the tag is stored against the user's third party cookie.

When an Advertiser comes to run DCO activity the ad serving interface allows the trafficker to request that the version of the ad to be displayed depends on the product ID fed into the selected dynamic retargeting tag. Having connected the versions to a product feed for mass versioning, where all the product IDs are displayed, the result is that the user is per shown a version displaying the same product again. When the user encounters a placement, the code checks the user's cookie, passing the dynamic variable through to the ad server. At the placement level, the rules setup by the trafficker check to see if the user is within the cookie pool for the dynamic retargeting tag. If they are, the ad server matches the dynamic variable from the user's cookie with a corresponding ad version and displays this version to the user.

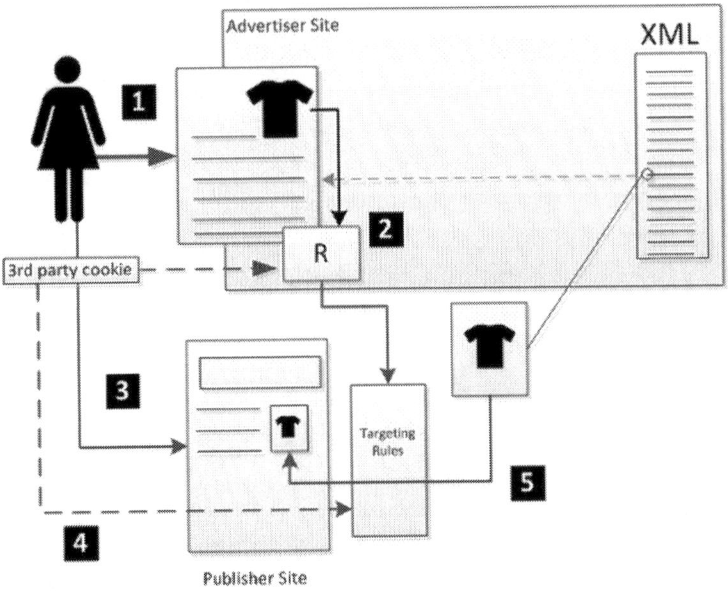

Figure 7.3 *Dynamic retargeting connected with DCO. The versions of the ads for the campaign are built out based on the Advertiser product XML. This same XML is used to populate the product pages of the Advertiser site. The same SKU identifier is used to match the page with the version. The user enters at Advertiser site at (1). The product SKU number is passed into the dynamic retargeting tag (R). The dynamic retargeting associates this value with the user's cookieID and passes the information into the ad server (2). The user then navigates to the Publisher page (3) the placement carries the users cookieID to the ad server (4) where the targeting rules see that the user's cookieID is associated with an SKU number in the retargeting pool. The version with the corresponding SKU number is displayed on the page (5).*

To make things more interesting, the trafficker and planning team can plan ahead and choose for the dynamic text field in the version to display a cheaper offer than the price shown on the site for the product. The dynamic click through URL within the DCO version can be used to carry a token to the Advertiser page that could be used to dynamically change the physical price of the jacket. Another strategy is not to display the same product, but to display a complimentary product as a version of the ad.

Carousel Ads

Dynamic creative can be taken a step further by not just capturing the last item a user was exposed to, but to store several items or variables in the user's cookie. This can correspond to a historical record of the user's journey on the Advertiser site, capturing all of the product ID's encountered on the way.

When setting up Carousel or Catalogue ads, the trafficker has the option to utilise this data to display all previous products seen, or only certain products inside the delivered ad version. These could just be the most expensive products or those with the highest available stock.

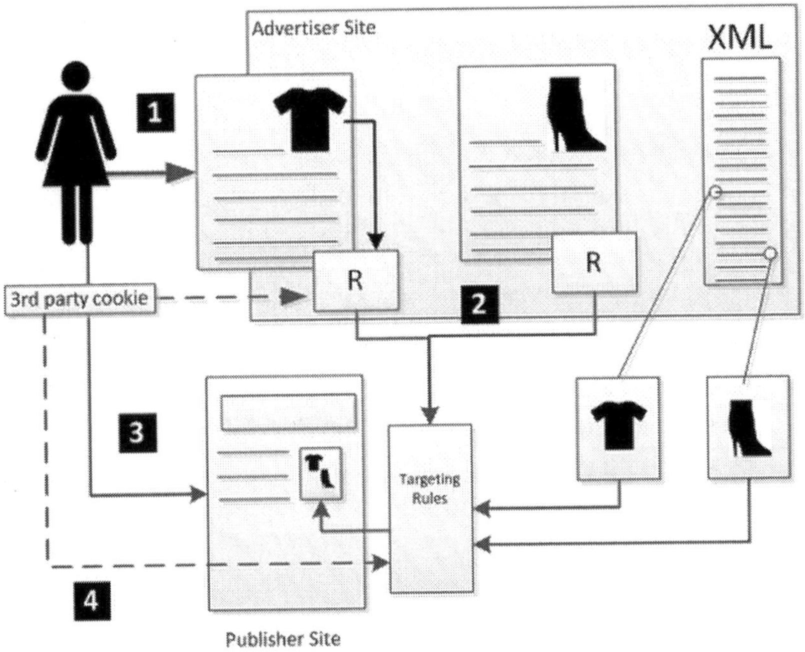

Figure 7.4 *Carousel ads keep a record of the users dynamic variable engagements on the user cookieID. The user navigates the advertiser site (1) where the dynamic retargeting tag captures the SKU number for the product in question. The user then navigates to the second page where the same thing happens. The cookieID records against both variables (2). When the user navigates to the Publisher site (3) the ad server serves an ad which displays both previously seen products by looking at the variables on the matching cookieID (4) and bringing versions together as a new ad version displaying the carousel of products in the placement on the Publisher site.*

Privacy and Behavioural targeting

Governmental and legal bodies the world over are in support of internet users having a right to control the information that is collected about them. Strictly speaking the third party ad server is collecting information only about the cookie and not about the user themselves (the information is not personally identifiable "PII"). It is the identifiable data that users are keen to eradicate and the cookie is not storing any of that information. Despite this fact, legislation is emerging to protect users, so that any behavioural targeting information collected about them can be made anonymous (or pseudonymous) or removed from databases completely. This relates directly to the topic of retargeting, since opting out of retargeting will mean that ads no longer to appear to 'chase' users across to different pages, Publishers and channels.

The Ad Choices Program

The ad choices program is a system that allows users to opt out of behavioural targeting via a small icon in the corner of the ad. The icon can be implemented by the trafficker inside the third party ad server even during a campaign, and the icon and its functionality will be added to a visual layer on top of the creative. When clicked the user is taken to a page where they can choose to opt out of retargeting altogether or by each technology provider or network collecting user data.

Point solutions by *Evidon* and *Trustee* have emerged to provide more complex management facilitates of the user opt-out including statistics for Advertisers specifically. These services come at an additional cost.

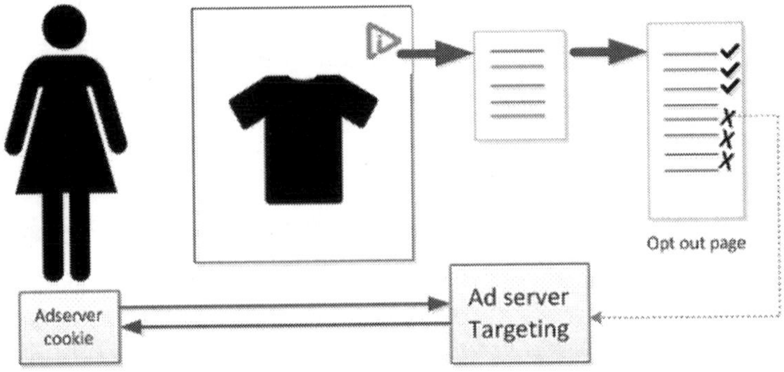

Figure 7.5 *The ad choices program requires that all behaviourally targeted ads carry an ad choices icon. When clicked, the icon provides the user with information about retargeting and allows the user to navigate to the ad choices cookie opt out page. On this page the user can select or deselect cookie level technologies such as third party ad servers to opt out of. If an opt out is chosen, the ad server is informed. In future when the same user navigates to a Publisher site, the ad server will check the cookieID first to see if the user has opted out of behavioural targeting before deciding which ad to display. Those users that have opted out will no longer see targeted ads.*

Incidentally, opting out of these pools using the opt out methods provided by such programs, requires the dropping of another cookie on that users machine to remember their settings. Deleting of these cookies, removes the memory of their choice to opt out and so users must opt out again after the cookie is expired or deleted.

Do Not Track

To get round this browsers are attempting to implement a cookie-free catch-all for the opt-out or opt-in of cookies which is called the DNT functionality ("Do Not Track"). Discussions between legal parties, browser operators, governmental bodies, regulatory bodies and politicians continue to wage, as consensus around opting in and opting out at different levels of informed consent is mismatched. What is important to note is that opting out of behavioural targeting via a cookie opt out, will not stop ads altogether, but rather stop the occurrence of targeted (and some would say relevant) advertising which seems counter-intuitive to the best interests of all advertising stakeholders including consumers.

DNT is a privacy standard that is sends through a flag to the ad server on the http call and if it is turned on; servers shouldn't set up tracking cookies for the specific http session. This means that no cookie is dropped on the device. If a user disables the setting, the publisher ad server calls the third party ad server to add a parameter to allow cookie dropping. If the user enables the setting, the third party is called to disable cookie dropping. This will also disable piggybacked technologies from placing tags.

More concerning for Agencies and Advertiser is that disabling cookies will eliminate ability to do attribution reporting and count unique audiences for the purposes of de-duplication. While giving the users a choice to opt out of behavioral targeting and cookies may seem alarming to some marketers, when given a choice, few users choose to disable cookies altogether, according to *IAB* research. However, some browsers are choosing to ignore consumer choice and are instead force the disabling of some cookies, in particular third party cookies that would allow for retargeting. This directly damages the ability for third party systems to operate effectively and fairly and should be addressed with concern by governmental bodies against the browser's ability to over-ride consumer choice.

Retargeting for Media Optimization

Retargeting technology can also be used for media optimization, literally buying audiences based on retargeting tag encounters. This is enabled using DSP and programmatic technology in the ad exchange space covered in full detail in the Chapter 8 - Programmatic. At a high level, the DSP technology providers offer their own retargeting tag technology. This tag can be piggybacked alongside any other retargeting tag such as inside an ad server container tag. The user encounters the retargeting tag from both providers and as such is added to the retargeting pool. Within the DSP, the retargeting pool can be used to identify potential impressions as they become available on the ad exchange. If there is a match, then the Advertiser or Agency can bid on the impression through the DSP. Once the impression is won, the ad server is called, whereupon the trafficker setup of the ad checks to see if the user is in a retargeting pool from a creative perspective. They will appear to be so as the user triggered both of the retargeting tags and the user will be shown the corresponding creative. Tech providers such as *Criteo* have made a very lucrative business out of this offering but tying together the creative and media optimization capability of retargeting to buy and optimize against retargeted users at enormous scale.

This chapter has quietly offered a sneak peek into the topic of the next Chapter - Programmatic. Which, largely due to the success of retargeting campaigns, is seeing phenomenal growth and represents a true evolution in display advertising. Here, smart decision engines begin to replace the manual work of optimization and buying strategies. This replaces long operational man hours by agency and marketing teams to date so is being welcomed as game-changing by industry stakeholders.

Chapter 8

Programmatic

Chapter 8 – Programmatic

- Advertising Exchanges
- Supply Side Platforms (SSPs) for the Publishers
- Demand Side Platforms (DSPs) for the Advertiser
- *Figure 8.1*
- Connecting the ad server to the DSP
- *Figure 8.2*
- Quality Inventory Sources
- The Second Highest Bid Auction
- Real Time Bidding (RTB)
- Cost Reporting in the ad server
- DSP Strategies
    - DSP Retargeting with DCO
    - *Figure 8.3*
    - DSP Keyword Targeting
    - Negative Retargeting
    - DSP delivery controls
    - Building Private Exchanges
    - *Figure 8.4*
    - Strategies based on Publisher Audience Descriptors
    - Cookie Level Data Providers
    - Data Management Platforms (DMP)
    - *Figure 8.5*
    - Page Level Data Providers
- Channel-Specific Complications in RTB
- DSP - ad server of the Future?

Programmatic describes a fleet of technologies with the vision to automate the planning and buying processes of digital campaign setup using the power of reporting and audience data. These technologies are still in their relative infancy and are evolving but the infrastructure they create is very real and rigid, founded on the principles of the financial exchanges. This Chapter will provide an overview to the different technology types that exist within this space and explain how ad serving 'plugs in' to the programmatic stack.

Advertising Exchanges

In the traditional model of buying ad space, the Advertiser or Media Agency would contact the Publisher directly and make a deal to purchase inventory for the proceeding ad campaign. This was followed by the emergence of sales houses or Networks that worked on behalf of some Publishers, to sell the space to Advertisers. Networks aggregated the inventory together so that they could benefit from a wider pool of available ad space for the purposes of delivery fulfilment. On the relationship front, Advertisers and Agencies had relationships with both Networks and the Publishers that sat outside of them.

Network and Publisher negotiations person to person are a slow, time intensive processes relying heavily on relationships and to an extent; industry politics. By having machines make the negotiations, the process of buying and selling inventory becomes much faster, more efficient and more cost effective. It is now possible for Publishers to load their available inventory into a marketplace called an "Advertising Exchange" and Advertisers and Agencies come into the marketplace to buy and bid on the available space.

There is not one major exchange, rather a few that have been setup and some exchanges are channel-specific so that exchanges for video inventory exist such as *Tubemogul* separate to exchanges for mobile inventory. There are also broader exchanges that exist, attempting to be established as the main marketplace. Major Networks have transformed their businesses from Network into an Exchange. This has given rise to the *Microsoft Exchange*, *Google's DoubleClick Exchange*, *Right Media* (Yahoo's offering) and marketplaces from more traditional Networks such as *HiMedia*.

Supply Side Platforms (SSPs) for the Publishers

Supply Side Platforms (SSPs) have been developed to bring Publisher inventory into the marketplace as soon as it becomes available. SSPs take the available inventory from the Publisher and classify or label it in order to sell it. Since Advertisers are looking to buy media space based on a target audience, the SSP gathers this information from the Publisher as a database that maps pages and placements on the Publisher side to audience types and demographics. Major SSPs include *Google's AdMeld* and the *Rubicon Project*.

Demand Side Platforms (DSPs) for the Advertiser

Advertisers and Agencies also have a gateway into the marketplace. This gateway is another technology called a DSP (Demand Side Platform). Heavyweight players in the DSP environment include *Turn*, *Mediamath*, *Appnexus* and *Google's Invite Media* and there are more emerging offerings to Advertisers such as *DataXu* and *X+1*. These systems are operated by what are referred to in the industry as "trading specialists" and the environment of buying and selling in the ad exchanges is termed "trading". Trading specialists will typically work either directly on the Advertiser marketing team; at the Media Agency or for an independent outsource company. As explained in Chapter 2, these teams are referred to as "trading desks" and each trading desk may work to access the inventory in the exchange via one or more DSPs. Those that sit within the Agency are referred to as ATD's (Agency Trading Desks) and those that are outsourced are called ITD's (Independent Trading Desks). By working continuously in the programmatic environment, trading teams can maintain a history of programmatic buying activity and cost information, much like the planners and buyers would do when buying digital media non-programmatically with the assistance of a planning tool.

Using a DSP is the overhead cost of accessing what is referred to as the Open Exchange. In other words, the DSP is the Advertiser's ticket into the marketplace from where they are free to browse and buy all the inventory on offer.

The DSP technology is very similar in its working to a Search Engine Marketing platform (SEM) such as *Google's Adwords*. The DSP operator has a record of the available media budget for the campaign and sets goals to buy target audiences within a certain period of time. The combination of these variables is called a "strategy" and the trader will setup a strategy and put it live to allow the DSP to enter the marketplace to seek out inventory that matches the variables. To set a strategy live requires the trading team to connect the variables to an ad so that if the correct conditions are met; 1) the Advertiser pays the Publisher through the marketplace 2) the ad is released from the DSP to the SSP, where 3) it is presented to the user on the Publisher page via the Publisher ad server.

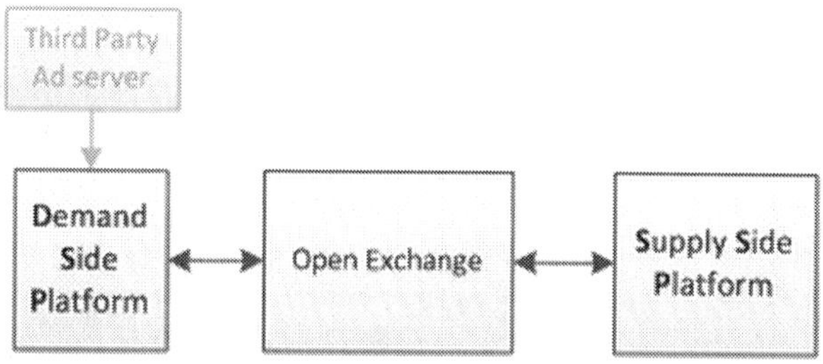

Figure 8.1 *Programmatic simplified. The open exchange is a marketplace where sellers present the available ad space via the Supply Side Platform and buyers examine and pay for the space via the Demand Side Platform. When the deal is met, the DSP*

provides the ad to the SSP from the ad tag provided by the third party ad server.

Connecting the ad server to the DSP

To have this work requires that the trafficker, working in the third party ad server campaign management interface, set up a placement against a site entity which has the same name as the DSP or the trading desk. For example, if the media plan received by the trafficker from the Media Agency stated on one of the rows that an ad tag needed to be trafficked for the *GroupM* trading desk – *Xaxis*; the trafficker would setup the campaign within the ad server interface such that the site was *Xaxis*. The trafficker would then assign the right placement and ad to that site and traffic the ad tags to the *Xaxis* team. The *Xaxis* trading team would then load the ad tag into the DSP interface and the DSP would connect to the open exchange to find a suitable ad spot.

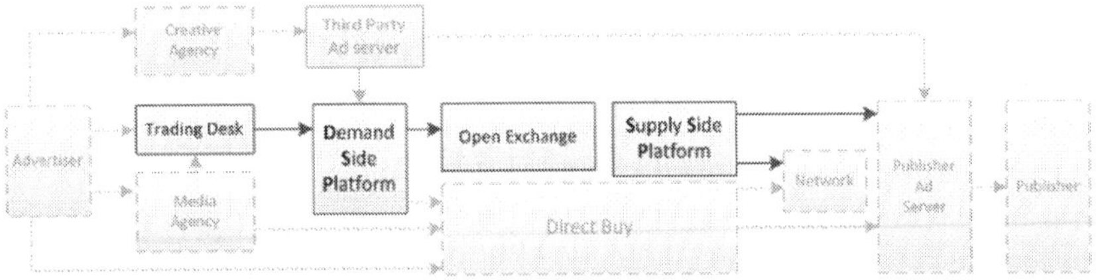

Figure 8.2 *The programmatic space fits into the buying and selling process between the Advertiser and the Publisher. The direction of the arrows in this image represents the direction of the ad and of the media budget. Greyed out is the traditional buying model: Media Agency or Advertiser buys the space directly from the Network or Publisher and reserves the inventory. The creative agency then loads the creative into the ad server, the tags are passed to the network and the ad is served at the right time. With programmatic in the picture the ad is only passed to the Publisher when the agreement or strategy is fulfilled and the process is managed by the trading desk.*

Quality Inventory Sources

DSPs will typically connect to multiple exchanges in order to fulfil a strategy but this is not a default setting and something an Advertiser should check when using a trading team or DSP for the first time. The various marketplaces carry inventory of differing quality.

The idea of the advertising exchange emerged to try and sell off all of the available ad space. Advertisers and Agencies would traditionally use the Publisher sales teams to find quality or premium inventory to display their ad within. They would be willing to pay a higher cost for the space. In such an environment, bottom-of-the-barrel or "remnant" ad inventory went unsold.

The ad exchange provides an environment to sell ad space based on the price that Advertisers are willing to buy it for to reach their goals. This has led to some exchanges carrying more valuable ad spots while some are happy to carry the remnant. The major debate of contention arises in this space where the definition of available quality inventory must be very concise and clear so that the goals are met and the right price is paid without giving either the Publisher or the Advertiser a bad deal.

The Second Highest Bid Auction

Programmatic can work by having an SSP present ad space, available in the future in the exchange. This inventory can be presented in multiple exchanges so as to increase the number of DSPs that can see it. Once the inventory is presented, the DSP strategy will identify the inventory as applicable to the defined variables and will make an offer for the ad space. Other DSPs are invited to do the same on behalf of other Advertisers whose strategy might also be a good fit for the available inventory. An auction then begins for a set period of time in which DSPs make higher proposals for the ad space. When the auction ends, the second-highest bidder will be awarded the space and be asked to pay around a cent more than the bidding price agreed. This model is used so that a single Trading Desk cannot control the auction by buying all of the inventory that matches their strategy. If the highest bidder was allowed to win the auction, the biggest spending Advertisers would be able to pick off the best quality inventory.

The final agreed price pays the trading desk team, the use of the DSP, the access to the exchange and the Publisher fee for the ad space which would include cost of the use of the technology on the Publisher side such as the SSP and the Publisher ad server. On top of this, the Advertiser needs to also consider the cost of ad-serving.

Real Time Bidding (RTB)

The Publisher does not have to load volumes of available inventory via the SSP at a given time, but rather an available ad spot can be presented into the exchange **as soon as it becomes available**. This is completely transformative in digital advertising because it means that when a user arrives on a Publisher page, the available ad spot can load a tag belonging to the SSP, which channels the availability down to the exchange in real time. This opportunity is literally to present one ad, to one user, on one placement, on one Publisher in real time.

Essentially this is a yet un-fulfilled impression and as it loads in the exchange, the DSPs leap on it like fresh meat in a hungry piranha tank. The auction begins and ends in microseconds, the spot is paid for and the DSP connects the ad server ad tag to the SSP so that the ad arrives on the page as it loads. The user notices no difference between this method and any other method of ad delivery. This is referred to as Real Time Bidding or RTB.

To work most effectively the DSP strategy must already be set live and the SSP tags must be sitting on the dormant pages on the Publisher website. These SSP tags can be designed to carry extra information about both the user and the page down to the exchange for real time bidding. If a user is logged in to the Publisher page, these details could be funnelled down along with page-level contextual information or the URL of the page. If the user information is funnelled down, it needs to have had the users consent before the ad space is offered out to a third party to adhere to privacy compliance. Such compliance however, may have been granted when the user signs up to get access to the Publisher site.

Cost reporting in the ad server

Apart from the delivery of ads from the ad server to the page, the DSP can facilitate the flow of reporting data from the exchange back into ad server reporting. This ensures that cost, delivery, verification and performance information is all still captured in a single system of record at the ad server. Since the ad server is counting based on a succinct definition of impressions, the connected cost information must be based on this methodology for the sake of data accuracy. This information can be channelled using data and API integrations between the ad server and the DSP. Advertisers and Media Agencies should connect with ad serving providers to understand more about this data flow.

DSP Strategies

When compared to buying ad space directly from Publishers and Networks, DSPs offer a greater access to available inventory ad strategies based on algorithmic optimization. A DSP will ensure it is not making bids on the same inventory twice. It will also make bids for inventory based on different cost models and calculate if the goals can be met with the available media budget, adjusting the strategy as it works its way through the budget so as to meet the goal.

Those bids which are lost to competitors contain insights which assist in winning bids for inventory with the same competitors in the future. This is referred to as "win and loss level data" and is a proprietary data offering available to Advertisers from the DSP technology provider.

DSP Retargeting with DCO

As described in Chapter 7, the DSP strategy can incorporate retargeting information. For this to work the trading team can generate a retargeting tag within the DSP interface and send this to the trafficker working in the ad serving interface. The trafficker can piggyback the DSP retargeting tag onto a container tag or ad server retargeting tag sitting on the Advertiser site. When the user triggers the retargeting tags their ad server, the cookieID is added to the ad server retargeting pool but the DSP retargeting tag also drops a cookie on their browser. When the user arrives on a programmatic-enabled Publisher page, the SSP placement can be used to capture the cookieID for the DSP and pass it down into the consideration for the yet un-purchased impression in real time bidding. As the DSP recognises the cookieID, the corresponding strategy can activate a bid on the impression. If the DSP wins the auction, the ad server ad tag is delivered, first checking the ad server cookieID on the user's machine. Since there will be a record of this cookieID in the retargeting pool the ad server will serve the ad or version that corresponds to the user.

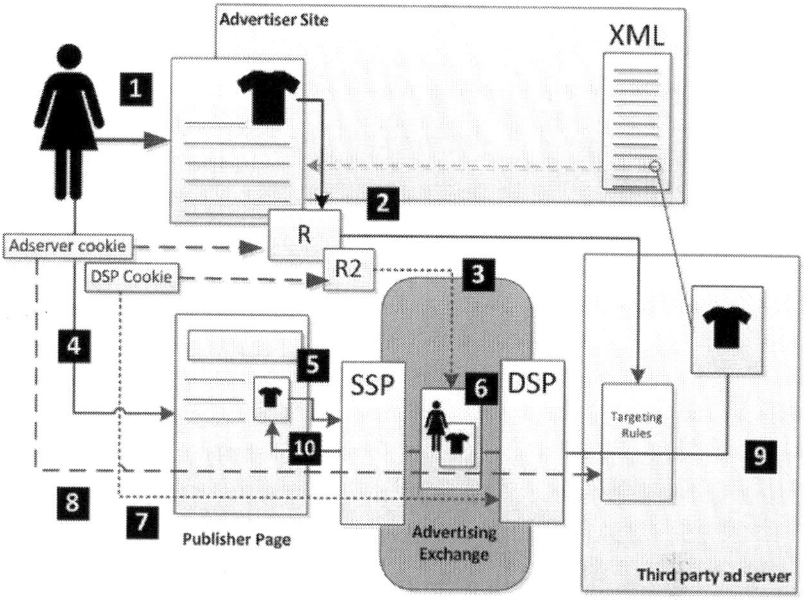

Figure 8.3 *Dynamic retargeting with DCO purchased with programmatic. The user arrives on the Advertiser site, the versions in the ad server as built out on mass versioning from the Advertiser product XML. The same XML updates the Advertiser product page. The unique identifier for the product as an SKU number is passed into the retargeting tag for the ad server (R) as is associated with the cookieID on the ad server (2). The retargeting pixel for the DSP is piggybacked on the ad server retargeting pixel. This information at the cookie level for the DSP cookie is passed onto the DSP (3). The user then navigates to a Publisher page programmatically connected to an Advertising Exchange via an SSP (4). The placement loads into the ad exchange via the SSP (5) and (6). The DSP sees that the cookieID meets the retargeting strategy (7) and bids on the as yet un-served impression. Winning the auction, the DSP passes the ad tag onto the Publisher page. The ad tag reads the users ad server cookieID (8) and sees that it is matched to a dynamic variable as an SKU number. The ad server selects the corresponding ad version (9) and serves it into the Publisher placement (10).*

Such strategies are employed by technology providers like *Criteo* and *Struq* who specialise in this specific kind of audience chasing. Unfortunately, with saturated audience chasing, such technologies will always win the conversion under the traditional last ad attribution model. Even if the user may have had every intention of buying the item without clicking such an ad, the convenience of the placement acts as a shortcut to Advertiser site. Marketers should think carefully about awarding full conversion attribution to such Publisher inventory.

DSP Keyword Targeting

An alternative strategy to retargeting would be that when the bid is won that the SSP passes a keyword value from the page, through to the ad server via the DSP. As with keyword targeting the ad server can use this value to display a corresponding ad or ad version.

Negative Retargeting

The DSP gives the option to offer greater audience reach by ensuring users are targeted that have never seen an ad or landed on an Advertiser site before. The strategy setup in the DSP can state that if the user is not in a retargeting pool, that they should be the target of the strategy. This is enabled via the presence of a specialist retargeting technology called an "exclusion pixel". Exclusion pixels can be generated from any of the DSPs and work using the opposite methodology to retargeting pixels.

DSP delivery controls

Popular features formerly reserved for use in Publisher ad servers are available in the DSP such as geo-targeting, strategy prioritisation and frequency capping. The settings get quite granular so that the DSP can effectively distribute the marketing budget.

Building Private Exchanges

Advertisers and Agencies that have more money to spend and like the idea of real time bidding but would prefer access to more premium Inventory, can work with the DSPs to setup restricted or "Private Exchanges". These are invitation-only marketplaces designed to give Advertisers with more money to spend, a "first look" at the available premium inventory before it is offered out on a public exchange. Alternatively a set amount of inventory can be procured at an agreed price between the Advertiser and the Publisher first, and the marketplace can act as management system to decide which ads to show to audiences based on decisions about the state of the inventory. If an Advertiser has multiple brands, there is no commitment to supply specific creative to the inventory until the very last moment before impression delivery. This makes for a more efficient use of first access to a private arsenal of inventory.

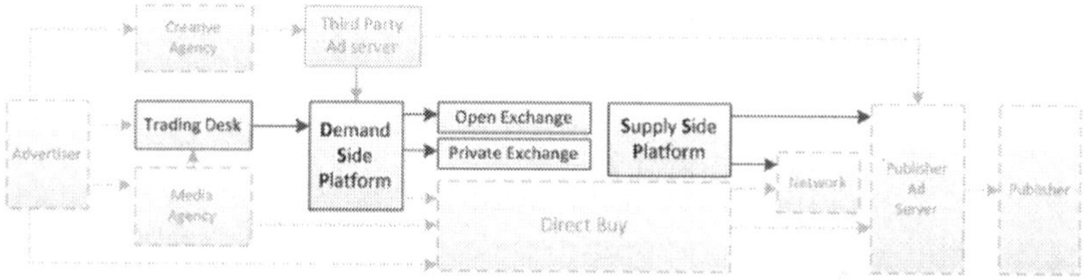

Figure 8.4 *Private Exchanges sit alongside open exchanges as options for Advertisers and trading teams with enough budget to support the availability of the private marketplace.*

Strategies based on Publisher Audience Descriptors

Since Publishers, Networks and SSPs bring the inventory to the marketplace and label it when it arrives; the Advertiser-side trading teams are not making decisions about the media space based on an independent system of audience classification. A Publisher may well have dressed up the inventory to make it more attractive to sell and the Advertiser can end up displaying an ad on a page which has little or no match to the user seeing the ad. Trading experience and historical reporting on ad performance will demonstrate which of these Publishers are classifying their audience ineffectively. But the demand for a good match every time has seen the emergence of systems that bring more information to the trade. The collection and presentation of this information can be facilitated by a third party, which can establish more value to the inventory in the marketplace.

Cookie Level Data Providers

Trading teams can buy audience data from specialist third party data providers such as *VisualDNA*, and *BlueKai.* Alternatively data is available from collectors of traditional digital data points such as email addresses from providers such as *Axiom*. These providers have datasets about audience types based on cookie level information. The Advertiser can use this dataset to look up more information about the user of an un-purchased impression before the decision to bid on the impression is made.

In addition to using third party data, the Advertiser can use their own datasets from systems like their CRM to get a better understanding about the un-purchased impression. This is referred to as first party data and is considered by many to be the most valuable data that an Advertiser can collect and activate for use in the programmatic space. Providing there is a cookieID attached to the dataset, the data can be used. To do this, the dataset is synchronised with the available cookies on a user's machine in a complex process called "cookie matching" and is facilitated by an intelligent data warehouse system called a DMP or Data Management Platform.

Data Management Platforms (DMP)

DMPs are easily plugged into the DSPs to inform the bidding strategy and some DSPs come with their own DMP facilitates. Players include platforms such as *Audience Science* and *eXelate*. These platforms are growing in popularity as they provide more effective decision making on the buying of inventory in programmatic by improving the ROI. Data activated via a DMP might show that a user is on the cusp of making a purchase. With the DMP activated, programmatic facilitates the opportunity for an Advertiser to pay a relatively high price (once data costs are factored in) to get the ad in front of the user. If the purchase that this triggers offsets costs then the DMP data enablement strategy becomes a particularly lucrative one and the data can acts as a competitive advantage over other bidding Advertisers in the marketplace. Examples include providers that specialise in optimization such as *RocketFuel*.

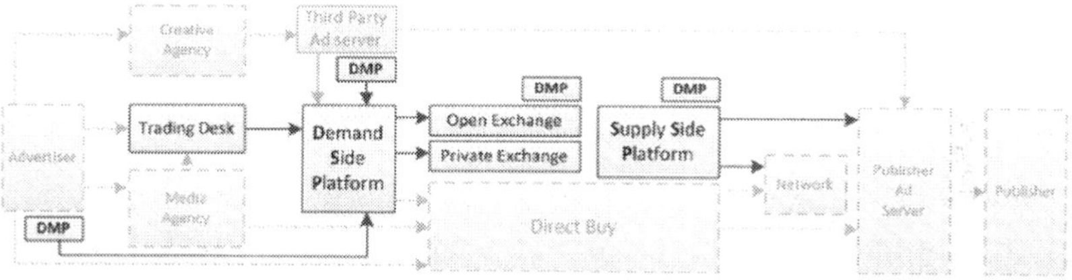

Figure 8.5 *DMPs can offer value in multiple positions in the buying and planning cycle within programmatic. Data that can be matched to existing cookieIDs at the user level add more information about the user to the Advertiser buying decision and will allow the trading team to adjust the buying strategy accordingly. Without additional data plugged in via the DMP, the Advertiser is almost buying blind, taking the existing audience classification as truth without independent verification.*

DMPs are data storage and activation facilities for data that Publishers can also utilise. In buying or hiring third party data, the Publisher can independently verify the quality of their inventory as it is loaded into the marketplace to make it more attractive to Advertisers. The cost for doing so can be set in the minimum bid price that the Publisher is willing to set as the auction begins.

Page Level Data Providers

Outside of the cookie space, data can also be plugged into the DSP that does not depend on user based information but instead on page level information. Examples include *GroupM's Crystal Semantics* or *Peer39*.

As explained in Chapter 5 - these technologies can be used to pre-emptively verify that the page in question is a suitable environment in which to display an ad. The DSP can incorporate this information into the buying strategy to target towards or away from the defined variables. DSPs will also typically enable traders to load blacklists of sites as part of their strategies to ensure that banned sites or pages are never considered within the marketplace.

Regulatory bodies encourage DSPs, exchanges and companies in programmatic to facilitate the safe purchase of inventory such that universally recognised banned sites and blacklists are adhered to as part of a crackdown against fraud and cybercrime.

Channel-Specific Complications in RTB

In the current landscape, inventory can be bought for almost every media channel through the exchanges. There are specific issues related to RTB for Video and Mobile. Mobile suffers because an impression loaded into an exchange in real time may not necessarily be able to deliver the ad before the mobile signal drops out. Video inventory suffers from a problem of supply where there is high demand for Instream video ads but limited sources of quality content. This is why ad server verification and fraud reporting is in high demand within programmatic.
The allure of high pricing on Instream inventory has led to some long tail Publishers engaging in fraudulent activity to bury Advertiser inventory among poor content or into spots that were misrepresented.

DSP - ad server of the Future?

DSPs and ad server have not merged as technology providers due to the impartiality offered by the ad server in its total separation from the interests of the Publisher. Since the ad server independently declares how many ads were tracked or delivered, the ad server reporting shows the Advertiser how much to pay the Publishers and it is of paramount importance to keep these technologies separated.

Third party ad servers can continue to offer de-duplication at the cookie level and provide rich channel ad serving for DCO while encumbering Search, Mobile, Instream, Affiliate and Display. The reporting alone in pathway to conversion, cookie level data, adjustments for cookie deletion, post-delivery verification and viewable impressions means additional first party data for the Advertiser to activate inside the DSP. However, the third party ad server remains the hub of creative optimization where the DSP is emerging as the hub of the media optimization in the future of digital advertising.

Chapter 9

The Big Picture

Chapter 9
The Big Picture

- *Figure 9.1 - Display and Programmatic*
- *Figure 9.2 - Layering in Paid Search*
- *Figure 9.3 - Layering in Affiliates*
- *Figure 9.4 - Layering in Users, Advertiser Properties, Ads and Trafficking*
- *Figure 9.5 - Layering in Retargeting*
- *Figure 9.6 - Third Party Ad Serving - the Diagram*

Having covered the aspects of ad serving at a high level, it is possible to piece the management of the channels together to get a third party ad server perspective of digital advertising. The first diagram picks up from Chapter 8 by incorporating Display and Programmatic.

Figure 9.1 - Display and Programmatic

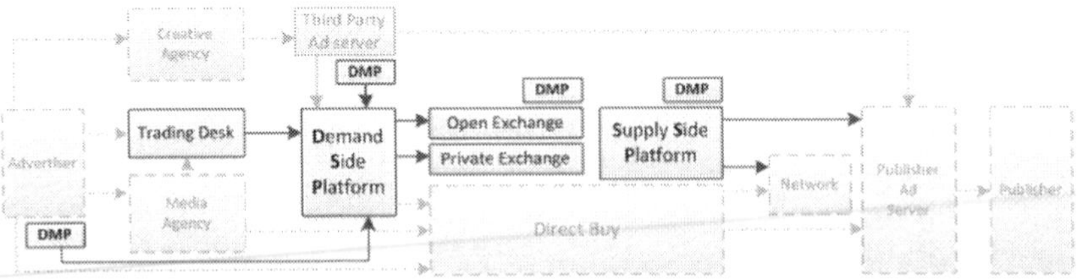

The Media Agency or Advertiser can procure media inventory either through the direct buy channel; speaking to Publishers and networks directly to make a deal on the ad space or rules can be set up in the DSP along with a budget to bid on inventory in the exchange environment. The DMPs ad context to the impressions and ad spaces being purchased with the option to trade in real time. This same method can be applied to all Display channels

(Standard Display, Rich Media, DCO, Instream video and mobile). The third party ad server plays a role in supplying the creative as an ad tag to the DSP or direct to Publisher to be implemented into the Publisher ad server.

Figure 9.2 - Layering in Paid Search

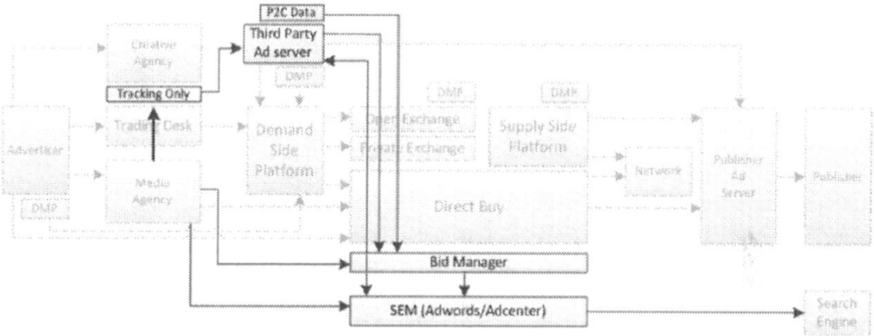

Search has matured programmatically faster than Display. The established technologies sit with the Search engines as SEM systems like *Adwords* and as bid management solutions. The third party ad server offers tracking integration to each to have eyes on these channels, while offering cross channel data through a pathway to conversion feed to add intelligence to the bids on keywords.

Figure 9.3 - Layering in Affiliates

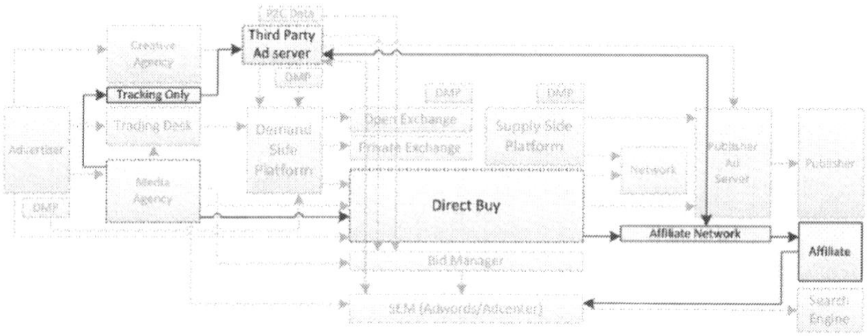

Since affiliates also utilise search there is a line in to the same SEM tools. The third party ad server also offers click based tracking to the affiliate. Affiliate reporting is fed back into the ad server.

Figure 9.4 - Layering in Users, Advertiser Properties, Ads and Trafficking

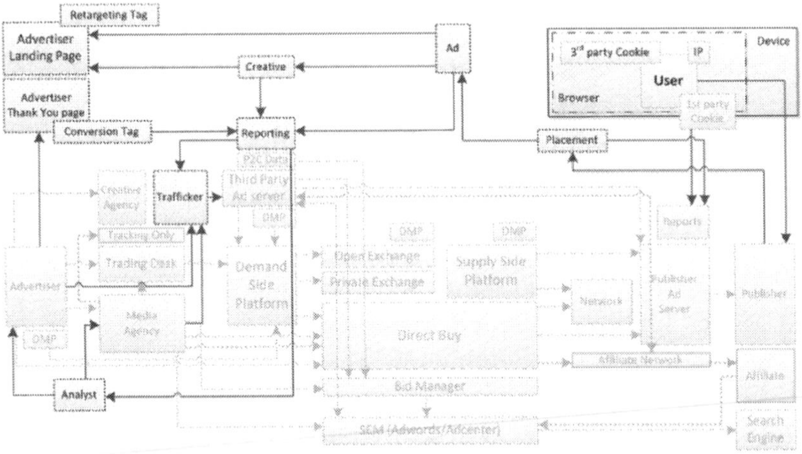

Introducing basic views on the user perspective and Advertiser perspective; The user visits Publisher pages, properties, Search Engines or affiliates to utilise content via the browser and device, carrying a publicised IP address and, providing they have not opted out of third party advertising, a third party cookie. The user is delivered an ad via a placement on the Publisher site. The ad server counts the delivery and the creative is displayed. Should the user interact or click, the ad server counts the actions and redirects the user via the clickthrough URL. The user arrives at the destination page such as a landing page. The landing page and subsequent pages can carry retargeting tags and conversion or container tags. The conversion tag feeds the user conversion event into ad server reporting. The analyst can read the reports and provide insights based on behalf of the Media Agency or the Advertiser

Figure 9.5 - Layering in Retargeting

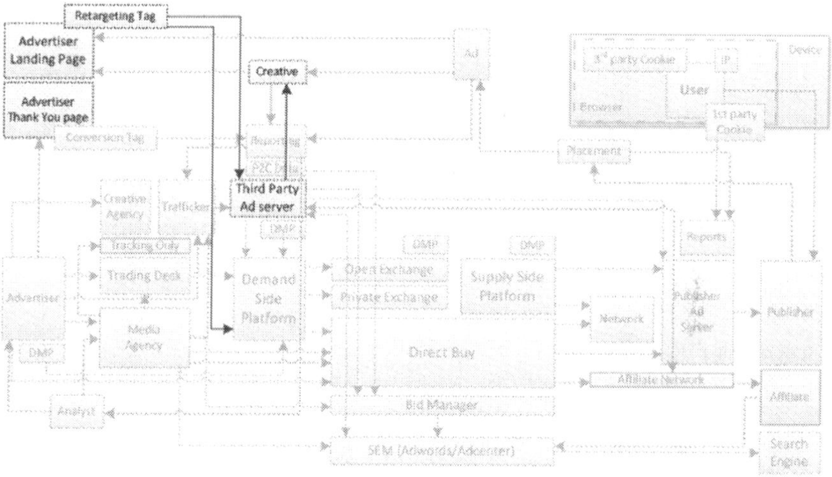

The retargeting tag can be used to segment an audience or cookie pool. The data can be used for creative optimization in the ad server or pushed to the Demand Side Platform as a data set to target audiences for media optimization.

Figure 9.6 - Third Party Ad Serving - the Diagram

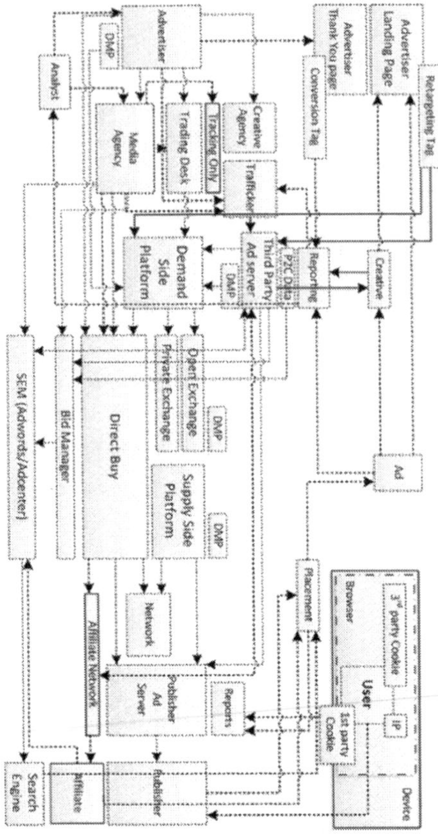

The full picture is significantly simplified but the established channels (bar social) are captured in ad serving data, allowing for de-duplication, attributing the value of paid for media to the buys. Diagrams of this nature do not represent the true click path, the flow of cost, value, and data or spend. They also do not represent the complexity of an industry that supports hundreds of thousands of businesses. Each entity depicted can be multiplied and entities intertwine where data adds value to all nodes. The image depicted on the cover of this book is an abstraction of this view, a model I have struggled to present visually in more simplified terms.

Closing Chapter

Third party ad serving technology is a marketing revelation.

Far from being a tracking and serving technology, the data that the third party ad server produces is an industry backed independent record for Advertisers to establish a security around the purchase of digital media space.

It is relevant to draw attention to the apparent parallel which exists between banking and ad serving. The attitude is one of trust. Housing the data which tells the Advertisers what to pay the pay Publishers; this highlights the value of account-keeping across a single methodology with global scaling, a level of commercialisation required to support the global communications system we call the Internet.

Taking a step back from the technicalities and evolving features, the foundation laid by the third party ad server brings economical wealth to the digital stakeholder groups: Creative Agencies, Media Agencies, Advertisers and Publishers. And as this technology diversifies and changes, it becomes ever more important that as an industry, we remain educated and informed; challenging the foundations of Advertising so that it's benefits always nourish the end user above all else. Advertising as a whole is not always embraced by consumers but its value in providing a free internet for all must mean that users and Advertisers can reach a mutual partnership.

This book is designed to make the technology side of digital advertising more accessible to everyone. The concepts covered here may seem fresh and new but digital evolves by the day. To extend the value of advertising technology further involves reaching forward towards the goal of better advertising effectiveness. And Advertising rightfully must lay its claim in a meaningful and scientific way on the outcome of a purchase as a direct influence over the behaviour of the consumer.

Business efficiency demands that the general art of indirectly influencing a purchase be made fully accountable to prove that general advertising is not a waste of money. As we have seen, ad serving technologies and new additions to the scene like DSPs and other point solutions are gradually filling in the data gaps. However if advertising were truly effective there would be no doubt as to its capabilities and all profits would be diverted to the cause, to generate ever more sales until brands and their products and services saturate the consumer space.

Saturation is a genuine problem, far reaching campaigns that overlap one another have a maze of data to process to realise effectiveness and cement true attribution. The race to track all channels reaches out into the TV and video space as mediums converge and the user consumption of advertising evolves in new ways. And where TV and Online teams both meet, the goal remains the same. The technology, it is perceived, if used correctly, can do what advertising has attempted to do since its advent: correctly predict and drive user action to purchase indefinitely.

Today's third party ad servers are gathering the data that marketers need to realise this dream but the information remains in silos. In the economic competition of advertising, the data sits with the Advertiser; their successes are their secrets and the best stories told in the best performing data, feed cleverly into the sales algorithms of marketers. Ad serving technology is the enabler to this end and is the metal detector revealing the hidden treasure of this success.

For it is the long labour, cost and learning of the marketer, that bring the fruits of such efforts to the possibility of such a future. But we are only at the start of the journey. Hopefully this book invites greater opportunity to those eager to shape the bright future that lies ahead for digital advertising.

Thank you for taking the time to read this book. Once again I welcome any feedback from you, and I will endeavour to assist in any way I can to improving the industry for everyone through my work.

Further Reading and Study

This book has been carefully compiled of ad serving and advertising technology fundamentals. The detail contained within these pages could be classed at an 'intermediate' level of knowledge. Including the whole swath of upcoming trends, custom technologies and start-ups would have made this book too extensive to focus on those fundamentals. This is the framework from which to build new platforms, concepts and see how to find evolving opportunities in these technologies. As I was writing this book I was still learning new things and I have actively omitted some concepts which are more advanced. Truly I could have been writing forever and never published if I had included everything I know about Digital Advertising.

To help your learning beyond the fundamentals or to be trained on any of the concepts in this book in person please visit my website: http://cristalconsultancygroup.com here you will be able to attend training courses, receive private tuition and sign up for consultations for your business. Advertised training courses tend to be based out of London, UK but I do travel frequently so get in contact if you would like me to arrange training overseas.

..and to stay on top of the very cutting edge in Online Advertising Technology, beyond the fundamentals, please subscribe to my blog, published on the same website: http://cristalconsultancygroup.com

Acknowledgements

This book took me a long time to write, I was not aware of the enormous amount of time I would have to dedicate to finally get it out 'into the wild'. Although there are very few references to outside academic material (mostly due to the infancy of the industry and technology) I want to very sincerely thank those that have helped educate me up to this level of knowledge. The list of names exceeds a hundred people, but at risk of missing off any names I just want to send a huge thank you.

In addition there have been whole rafters of proof readers, editors, minor contributors and supporters that have my unrelenting thanks. The efforts we undertake every day assures the free, public availability of the information technology we call the internet. For this there can be no greater reward than to keep our industry knowledge up to date and spend the days of our lives giving birth to inspiring new ideas, building new intelligent technologies and contributing directly to the evolution of our civilisation for generations of *mad men* and *women* to come. I wish you all eternal prosperity in heart and mind.

Finally I would like to thank my family, who have always believed in my capabilities and have supported my passion for writing and technology at every turn.

Ruby Hirsh, Ashley Cristal, James Cristal, Nick Cristal, Michelle Miller

Glossary

Term	*Definition*
302	An HTTP code to tell the browser that the page in question had been moved. This is called a server side redirect and is used by ad servers as a method to count and track ad activity.
third party code	Code belonging to an external system to the one being used. Third party code is typically used in a first party system. Such as example is where a Publisher uses a Publisher ad server and brings third party ad server tags into the system. The tags contain third party code.
404	An HTTP code to tell the browser that the requested page had not been found. 404 errors typically come up in ad serving when a click through URL lands the user on a page that doesn't exist.
4th party code	Code belongs to another technology provider from the third party provider. An example is where code is generated from a survey vendor and provided to the trafficker to implement on an ad such that when the ad closes the survey is launched from the fourth party survey vendor system.
Action tag	Another name for a conversion tag from the Atlas ad server. Action tag might be a more accurate description since conversion tags do not just measure

	conversions but can also measure non-conversion events: also called "actions".
Actions	A conversion tag loads whenever the code is rendered by a browser. If the user did not encounter an ad previous to the conversion the ad server does not register a conversion but makes a log of the code load. This is called an Action and an Action is not tied to a unique cookieID.
Ad assignment	The process undertaken by the trafficker inside the third party ad serving interface to assign ads to placements.
Ad brokering	A Publisher, network or exchange may be selling inventory with the claim that it falls under their ownership but in fact they are acting as a middleman to another Publisher network or exchange to procure the inventory at a certain cost. Be wary of ad brokering. More middlemen mean more technologies, greater discrepancies, larger margin for delivery error and hidden costs. Verification can provide some level of control but the industry is rife with the practice given the ease of passing ad tags onto an additional party.
Ad clutter	A Publisher that swamps web pages in ads clutters the page and reduces the value of the content and subsequently the ad space. Get a commitment from the Publisher that ads will be delivered to clutter-free pages and utilize advanced verification technology to detect for ineffective impressions under the guise of

	ad fraud.
Ad controls	The name given the settings on the placement which allow ads to be rotated, sequenced, targeted and delivered at a given frequency governed by a set of rules setup by the trafficker. If there is only one ad assigned to the placement then ad controls are limited.
Ad location	Once implemented on a Publisher site the ad appears to live in a fixed location on the web page when it loads into the browser. Although intrinsic to standard display ads, Rich Media ads can stretch away from the original ad location into an expanded state or not have a fixed location at all (such as with a Floating ad). The ad is essential anchored in the ad location which from a Publisher's perspective is sometimes what is referred to as the "placement".
Ad server macro	Macros are small tokens or tiny pieces of code usually a single word long surrounded by symbols. The macro is an instruction to the ad server to load addition data into the position of the macro. This will typically be an identifier such as a Placement ID.
Ad serving Hierarchy	The tree-like folder system within an ad server in which campaigns are set up.
Ad spot	(see ad location)
Ad Tags	Once ads have been assigned to placements inside the ad server campaign

	management interface by the trafficker, the code can be sent to the Publishers. The code for each specific placement is called an Ad Tag.
Ad blocking	There are two types of ad blocking. One is performed locally on a client device usually within the browser to block an ad loading. The other is within a verification tool to prevent an ad delivery based on the ineffectiveness of the site or environment in which it is being requested to load.
Affiliate Auditing	Affiliates within a network or subscribed to a program are checked regularly by the team managing the program to ensure that the Affiliate site is still suitable to be included.
Affiliate program	An ad campaign extended across multiple Affiliate sites usually managed by an Affiliate network. The campaign creative and click-through for the affiliate program are available from the affiliate network or the program manager working at the Agency or Advertiser.
Affiliate Screening	A process undertaken by the Affiliate program manager or the Affiliate network to check that an Affiliate is suitable to join an Affiliate program.
Aggregated reports	Reporting templates constructed from ad server analytics and counting data, amalgamated across ad server entities so that reporting is a summary of activity and can be analyzed and understood easily

	without the specialist skill of an analyst.
API	Application Programming Interface
ATD	Agency Trading Desk
Behavioral Targeting	Another name given to Retargeting.
Black Box Technology	Not disclosing the workings of a technology owing to the complexity or implication of doing so. An example would be revealing Google's search algorithm. Google as a search engine is a black box technology. The workings remain a mystery but it is agreed that it does the job. Revealing the workings would allow others to defraud the system.
Blind Networks	To reduce the cost of inventory, planners and buyers can purchase inventory based purely on audience information and not on the name of the site where the final ad will be delivered. This gives Publishers and Networks more flexibility to optimize delivery of ads across Networks based on inventory availability, rather than having to commit to the final location earlier on. To ensure the audience matches the Advertiser requirement, verification reporting and ad blocking can ensure the page is brand safe on ad delivery.
Blind Networks	A blind network is Publisher network where inventory is labeled only by the audience type such that the final location of the delivered ad is not known to the Advertiser. Blind Networks typically sell

	inventory at a lower cost so as not to have to commit to the exact page location of the ad before it is known if that spot will be available.
Booking pathway (on an Advertiser site)	The design of the site to drive users from the point of arrival (the landing page) to the point of conversion (the thank you page).
Brand Advertisers	Advertisers whose main goal is deliver a creative message. This might be to create awareness rather that to direct traffic for the precise goal of making a sale. The sale event may happen a long time after the brand activity of the ad campaign. This Advertiser is focused on delivery goals and GRP. Common Brand Advertiser verticals are FMCG and Autos.
Cache	A machine will store copies of files and information to make the retrieval of that information faster if it is requested again. A cache should be refreshed often so that the user does not get out of date information. This applies to ads and websites and a cache can occur locally on a user's device or in the cloud.
Call-to-action	A part of an ad or web page designed to be engaged with by the user. This could be a submit button or trigger.
CDN	Content Delivery Network
Channel	A channel within the context of digital marketing consists of any sub-channel within Digital. This also spreads itself to

	format complexity such that the most popularly referenced channels are: Standard Display, Rich Media, Search (SEM), Natural Search (SEO), Dynamic Creative (DCO), Mobile, Instream Video, Affiliate, Social and Email.
CLD	Cookie Level Data
Clean Data	A consistent naming methodology produces large sets of data that can easily be sorted, concatenated or normalised. This is clean data and is used in reference to utilises consistent naming conventions as ad, campaign or conversion tag names.
CMS	Content Management System
Code Wrapper	Code which sits either side of the main subject to effectively wrap the subject up.
Companion Ads	An ad that sits within visible range of an Instream video ad to accompany it.
Container Tags	Conversion tags which are capable of having other third or 4th party tags or pixels piggybacked on top. The conversion tag therefore acts as container to the other tags. In the DoubleClick ad server these are referred to as Floodlight tags.
Contextual targeting	Also called Semantic targeting. The placement code extracts phrases and words on a page to understand the subject matter of the page in question before deciding to deliver an ad based on the interpretation of that information.
Contracted State	An expandable ad that is dormant or has

	already completed its expansion effect.
Conversion Event	A conversion event is just another way of describing the event that is the conversion. Conversion event is a more universal term than "conversion" which has a connotation that the event in question was a completed sale.
Conversion tag	Generated within the ad serving interface, the conversion tag is a piece of code that can be placed in an ad or on Advertiser site. If a user has previously been encountered by the ad server they will trigger a conversion event in ad server reporting.
Conversions	A record of an event performed by the user, such as the loading of a specific page or ad which signifies the satisfactory completion of a marketing goal. This is most commonly a sale.
Cookie Matching	If two separate datasets both use cookies as the unique identifier for the user, the cookies can be matched together to see where a user is common to both databases. For instance an Advertiser could produce a script to site on the Advertiser page that can read the users first party cookie ID for the website. The same script could take the cookieID and pass it into the extended data of an ad server conversion tag. The cookie level data would reveal a match between the two cookieID's.
CPA	Cost Per Acquisition. A common model to

	pay Publishers based on their effectiveness at driving users to convert or purchase based on the subject of the ad.
CPC	Cost Per Click. A common model to pay Publishers based on the user clicking on the ad. CPC is most effectively used in the Paid Search channel.
CPL	Cost per Lead. Another name for CPA. The conversion event in question is the collection of user data.
CPM	Cost per "mille". Cost per thousand impressions measured. The most common cost model in digital advertising.
CPQ	Cost per quote. Another name for CPA.
Crawlers (Search engine Crawlers)	See "Spiders"
Creative Agency	An external provider of design and development services to build code and deliver the creative which eventually becomes the ad.
Creative Fatigue	Most commonly a failure to implement frequency capping so that the creative message is shown so often that the user sighs in disappointment upon seeing the ad again and again with no control to stop its repeat appearance around the web.
Creative shop	An umbrella term to mean Creative Workshop and will mean a Creative Agency or an internal creative team at a Media Agency. The Creative Shop is home to the creative designer and developer

	roles.
Creative team	A reference to the creative developer and designer roles that can sit within a Media Agency or at a Creative Agency. The creative team is responsible for the design, development, build and delivery of the ad creative and may also be involved in the design and maintenance of the Advertiser website.
CRM	Client Relationship Management system. An example would be *Salesforce* or *Microsoft Dynamics*.
CTR	Click-Through Rate. A percentage of the number of user that saw (incremented an impression) and then clicked on the ad.
CV Tools	Content Verification Tools.
Data Leakage	Publisher audiences can be harvested using retargeting tags. The harvesting of these details for further use later on is considered a leak of that Publishers audience. The claim may be that the audience is the property of the Publisher.
DCO	Dynamic Creative Optimization.
De-duplication	Always making sure that the entire audience for all ads belonging to an Advertiser is tracked in a single system such that users can be recognized as unique and their unique pathways to events such as conversions can be described in the ad server without any question that some data belongs to the

	same user more than once.
Delivery	A reference to ads being delivered by the ad server. A delivery is measured in impressions so delivery relates to impression based goals and data. Delivery of ads online can be compared to TV ads being delivered to TV viewers. The ad is simply sent to the end recipient with no confirmation that it was ever seen.
Desktop Device	A desktop device is a name given to a computer that remains in a fixed position such as a PC. A tablet is not classed as a desktop device but a laptop may fall into this category.
Device Fingerprinting	For mobile advertising, devices do not carry a universal unique identifier such as a third party cookie in every case. A device fingerprint is an identifier used in place of a cookie for the purposes of attribution and the measure of unique reach and frequency.
Direct Response Advertisers	Advertisers more focused on driving conversion events or sales. This Advertiser is focused on performance channels like Search and Affiliate as well as performance goals like clicks and ROI. Common direct response verticals are online retail and travel.
Display Ads	Also called Standard Display ads. These are the most predominant visual ads as flash seen across the web.
Domain	The main folder in which a website

	resides. The domain sits at the top level and subdomains sit within it.
DPB	Data pass back - the *Atlas* ad server version of Cookie Level Data.
Drop off rate:	The diminishing percentage of users arriving to pages. Those that arrive on the landing page but fail to convert on the thank you page are said to have dropped out of the booking pathway.
DSP	Demand Side Platform
E2C	Exposure to conversion reporting - the DoubleClick equivalent of P2C. See P2C reporting.
E-conversion	Dividing the attributed conversion among touch-points on the pathway to conversion allows each touch-point to be valued. This assigned value is rarely a whole number and is referred in the *Atlas* ad server as an e-conversion.
Effective Impressions	Impressions that met the Advertiser criteria for quality verification.
Entities	Ad server entities are named parts of the ad server hierarchy that will typically have a corresponding entity ID such as Advertiser, Placement, Site, Channel, Ad, Creative and Version.
Events in the pathway (to conversion)	Also called "touch points". User see, click and interact with ads for an Advertiser before finally converting. These ad engagements are referred to as non-conversion events on the pathway to

	conversion.
Exclusion Pixel	A retargeting pixel specifically used to negatively retarget against the cookie pool it collects. Predominantly used by the DSP.
Execution	The Creative is sometimes referred to as a "creative execution" or just an "execution". Another way of saying the final delivered ad.
Expanded state	A Rich media expandable ad, at its most full dimensions maintained for a period of time or until a user engages to reduce the size, changing the state of the ad to the contracted state.
Experiment	(for user targeting testing like AB testing);
Factors Report	A report that can recalculate attributed conversions based on different attribution models from the one used to calculate the conversions in the first instance.
File weight	The size of the file. For ads this is measured in kilobytes (kb) and megabytes (mb).
Flash Cookies	A storage facility within Flash to remember information about the user and their relationship with the ad for the information to be used later on. Flash cookies are not favored in Digital advertising because flash cookies are hidden from the user as a default and are more difficult to remove from a user's de vice.

Floodlight tags	*DoubleClick's* name for a container tag. See container tags.
FLV	Flash Video. A reference to the file type that creative developers supply to play video within an ad.
Frequency	The number of times that a unique user is exposed to an ad. Can be capped by frequency caps.
FTP	File transfer protocol. Referenced with regards to large data sets that can be posted to an Advertiser's FTP site for the purposes of large file delivery and storage from an external system such as the third party ad server reporting system.
GDN	The *Google Display Network*
Geo Performance	Also called Geo Reporting. The name given to a report that shows user IP address mapped to a location from country level down to postal and zip codes in some regions with varying accuracy. Geo performance is used to ensure Publishers are correctly targeting ads to users in the agreed geography.
GRP	Gross Rating Point. A measure from TV advertising to extrapolate effective reach and frequency. A GRP number can be so refined and calculated so as to accurately point at a given number of in-store sales if the goal is reached.
Hierarchy	The tree like folder structure housing the ads in the ad server interface. Advertisers,

	campaigns/media plans, networks, Publishers, sites, sections, packages,
HTML5	The latest edition of the mark-up language HTML with improvements to support video and JavaScript.
IAB	Internet Advertising Bureau
Impulse conversions	A user conversion which occurs within a single ad exposure and within a short time frame.
In-App	Ads that appear within mobile applications.
Ineffective impressions	Impressions that failed to meet the Advertiser criteria for quality verification.
Inventory	The amount of advertising space available.
ISP	Internet Service Provider
ITD	Independent Trading Desk
Jump Tag	A *DFA* click command that can be used to carry the user to an over-ride page URL.
KPI	Key Point Indicator. A marketing term used to describe a goal set by the marketing team seen as a priority for success.
Media Buy	The purchased ad space.
Media Plan (ad-server hierarchy entity)	Within the third party ad serving interface, the media plan is the name given the campaign level.
Media Plan	The documentation that lists all of the

(Agency document)	media buys.
Negative Retargeting	See Exclusion Pixel.
Optimization	Using the reporting data to make decisions to improve campaign performance, delivery and verification.
Order ID	The unique identifier for the conversion event generated by the Advertiser and passed into a conversion tag on the Advertiser page.
P2C reporting.	A pathway to conversion report. Typically a cookie level data feed showing how each cookieID encounters events or touch-points as ads before reaching a conversion tag with timestamps. A P2C report allows the Advertiser to construct attribution models. P2C is the acronym given to the *DG/Mediamind* cookie level pathway to conversion report.
Parallax	A creative effect common to eastern cartoon where background and foreground move at different speeds. The effect requires a high capacity of user RAM and so is only being adopted recently.
Pathway to Conversion	See "P2C Reporting".
Payload	The payload is the content of a token which could be an ad server macro. For example: "?rtu=payload".

PCP	A Publisher custom parameter. A token which can be populated in the ad call or click on the Publisher side to populate ad server reporting with more information such as a player ID.
Performance	A reference to non-delivery data about the relationship between ads and users received and processed by the ad server. Performance is measured in clicks, conversions and engagements/interactions so performance relates to goals and data based on these metrics. Performance is a feedback mechanism, allowing the analyst to determine if ads effectively met goals related clicks, conversions or engagement.
PII	Personally Identifiable Information
Placement	Just like with the word "tag", the word "placement" has dual meanings. From the perspective of an Advertiser and third party ad server, placement means the code package that is sent to the Publisher and from which the ads or creative called to serve from within it, are played. Placement in this context is the portable housing in which the ads in rotation or sequence reside. From a Publisher perspective "placement" refers to the fixed ad spot on a page which never moves. Traffickers supply to the Publisher ad operations team code as an "ad tag" which when inputted into the Publisher ad server are eventually served into the Publisher's 'placements' all around the

	Publisher site.
Point solutions	Specialist technology solutions typically with advanced features in the field of their expertise. Utilizing a point solution in addition to an ad server will incur higher costs and integrations between point solutions and the ad server are paramount to ensuring clean data. Many such technologies are start-ups. Question the ability to scale to multiple markets, and the extent of the available support.
POS	Point of Sale system.
Post Click Conversion	A conversion where the attribution model in place awards this conversion to the user clicking.
Post Impression Conversion	A conversion where the attribution model in place awards this conversion to the user being exposed to an ad.
PPC	Pay Per Click. Another name for CPC
Pre-emptive Verification	Technology which checks the yet-un-purchased user impression at the page level to determine if the environment is suitable for the Advertiser using the DSP to proceed with the auction.
Premium Inventory	Ad space which is in high demand and comes at a high cost relative to remnant inventory.
Publisher Audiences	Publishers will sell their ad space based on the marketers request for a matching audience. The ad space is labelled up and sold by describing the audience that will

	be exposed to the ads that will eventually occupy the space.
Publisher Property	A Publisher website is part of the Publisher's property as is a Publisher's app. This phrase is most commonly used as an alternative to describing a single part of the Publishers
Publisher Specs	Publisher requirements and limitations for the development of ads that will be permitted to be delivered on their site or properties.
QA	Quality Assurance. The period of testing and ad to check that it fits with ad server or Publisher specifications.
Query String	A token appended to ad tag on either the click or impression portion to carry out an additional function. Query relates to a request for information from a database.
R&F	A shortened form in reference to Reach and Frequency
Reach	The total number of unique impressions.
Recency	This describes the order by which things happened with the most recent in the primary position. The term is mostly used when describing custom attribution modeling in order to place a value on events that occurred more recently.
Recordability rate	See VTR.
Referral URL	The URL of the page before the page the user is on. The referral URL is counted as

	the URL responsible for driving the user to the present URL. The referral URL can be the page the ad was shown on.
Re-messaging	Another name given to Retargeting.
Remnant Inventory	Ad space which is not popular with buyers and is available at high volume for low cost from a Publisher.
Rich media specs	A common term used by creative agencies and developers to ask what coding requirements and restrictions the ad server will enforce to ensure ads pass QA.
ROI	Return on Investment. A marketing/business term to establish what the Advertiser gets in return for the marketing spend. Intelligent marketers can use ad serving technology to establish ROI goals and see if advertising efforts are generating incremental sales or reach.
RTB	Real time bidding. In reference to programmatic buying.
SDK	Software Development Kit. In reference to mobile application development.
Second Screen	The user may be using one device to consume media at the same time as another. The primary screen attracts most of the user attention, the second has less. User trends suggest users consume social media on the second screen while consuming premium video content on the primary screen.
See through rate	The percentage of user impressions that

(STR)	could be checked for Verification.
SEM	Search Engine Marketing or Paid Search. Also used interchangeable to describe the keyword creation and buying toolsets (such as *Google Adwords*) or used to describe a bid management tool (such as *Marin*)
SEO	Search Engine Optimization or Natural Search. A non-paid for advertising channel where a website is optimized by the site developer to attract more search engine user traffic.
Single-counting Vs. Double-counting	A setting at an account level which allows conversions to be de-de-duplicated (single counting) or duplicated (double counting). Predominantly used to control attribution reporting for Natural Search.
SKU number	Also called a Product ID. Used in reference to DCO.
Spiders (Search Engine Spiders)	Spiders are programs that crawl the web, simulating a user, loading pages, digesting the information those pages and passing the information back to the source database for cataloguing. In Search Engine Optimization these technologies are called Spiders.
Spotlight tag	A term from the *DoubleClick* ad server to mean a conversion tag that does not have container functionality.
SSP	Supply Side Platform. In reference to programmatic.

Staging environment	A test page or series of pages on the Publisher or Advertiser side which tends to receive traffic by invitation to test ads and content before putting the live on the main website. The staging environment is controlled by the CMS and is a term common to tag management and ad QA.
Subdomain	The prefix before the domain or directly after it. The subdomain is designed to depict an area of a site or domain that might indicate a site section. Subdomain is referenced in ad serving as part of domainURL verification, reporting subdomains where page level transparency is unavailable to call out ineffective impressions that may impede verification such as brand safety.
SWF	The file type of flash animations. Most non-mobile display ads are SWF files.
TMS	Tag Management System or Universal Tagging System.
The Cross Domain File	A security feature of websites such that the implementation of the file allows for the reading and writing to remote domains. In reference to DCO.
The Fold	The fold of the user's browser is the horizontal or vertical cutoff where the remainder of the ad or web page is not visible. Scrolling the page reveals content or ads previously hidden by the fold. A term commonly used to describe the functionality of Viewability.

Token	An addition to an ad tag to perform a function such as carry additional information to another system. See "Payload".
Trafficker	The role which manages the campaign setup inside the third party ad serving interface. Traffickers are usually employed at a Media Agency or on-site at the ad serving provider. Traffickers can also be hired to work remotely via a trafficking outsource company.
Universal Tagging	See Tag Management System
URL	A web address for HTTP
User Agent	The technical term for a user's browser on any device. The user agent is a code passed to the ad server to identify the browser type.
Version	A reference to a variant of an ad for DCO. Each version is essentially an ad in its own right but would have been generated by a machine rather than created by a creative developer.
View through rate (VTR)	The percentage of impressions for which Viewability could be measured.
VOD	An overused incorrect industry reference to the Instream Video channel.
Wastage	A reference to impressions delivered ineffectively such that the delivery of the ads will be irrelevant to the user and could not possibly be used to attribute the ad to a marketing goal. The marketing

	budget is wasted.
White Labeling	Disguising technology ownership such that a technology appears to be owned by one party but in fact is licensed from another vendor.
XML file	In reference to DCO. An additional file to accompany an ad to allow the ad to be updated without requiring a flash developer to do so.

FIN